ME̲ AMERICAN MOJO

REFIGURING AMERICAN MUSIC

a series edited by

RONALD RADANO AND JOSH KUN

Charles McGovern, contributing editor

MEXICAN
AMERICAN
MOJO

popular music, dance, and

urban culture in los angeles,

1935–1968

Anthony Macías

Duke University Press

Durham and London

2008

© 2008 Duke University Press. All rights reserved.
Printed in the United States of America on acid-free paper ∞
Designed by Amy Ruth Buchanan.
Typeset in Scala and Matrix by Keystone Typesetting, Inc.
Library of Congress Cataloging-in-Publication Data appear on
the last printed page of this book.

To Tony, Sherri, and
Denise Macias

&

To Connie, Paloma,
and Anand

I have made theories, sought histories,
    tried to explain.
But the music itself is not about any of
    those things.
    –LeRoi Jones, 1967

We need our *marae* [spiritual/ceremonial
    community grounds
with traditional meeting houses] for a
    host of reasons . . .
That we may sing,
That we may dance,
That we may learn our history,
And then know the richness of life,
And the proud heritage which is truly ours.
    –John Te Rangiāniwaniwa Rangihau,
New Zealand scholar and Māori leader, 1973

CONTENTS

ILLUSTRATIONS

ACKNOWLEDGMENTS

This research project has come a long way since its inception as a dissertation for the Program in American Culture at the University of Michigan, Ann Arbor. Accordingly, I would like to thank my longtime mentor, George Sánchez, who recruited me, helped me mature intellectually, pushed me to push myself, and unfailingly encouraged my research. George taught me much about U.S. and Chicano history and historiography. More important, he has shown me not only how to survive in the profession, but also how to succeed in it. Frances Aparicio taught me much about Latin American and U.S. Latino popular music and culture, and she helped me build my intellectual and professional confidence by giving me perceptive comments on my work, early conference and publishing opportunities, and friendly advice. David Scobey improved my writing and expanded my knowledge of, and critical thinking about, cultural history and the culture industries. He also taught me to apply myself to the serious intellectual work of academia. Charles McGovern helped me to better understand the social history of popular music and consumer culture in postwar America and, at a critical early juncture, to steel my resolve. María Cotera graciously gave me eleventh-hour assistance, including fruitful feedback.

I was inspired and encouraged by Cherríe Moraga, Lawrence Levine, and Cornelia Sears at UC Berkeley; Brenda Stevenson at UCLA; George Lipsitz during a directed reading; Robin Kelley, Kristin Hass, and Eric Porter at the University of Michigan; and Michael Roth and Roger Keil at a Getty Research Institute for the History of Art and the Humanities dissertation workshop. My educational achievements have consistently been made possible by affirmative action funding, from the Project 88 Fellowship at UCLA to the Rackham Merit Fellowship in the Horace H. Rackham Recruitment and Retention Office, as well as the travel grants in the Office of Academic Multicultural Initiatives at the University of Michigan.

At the César E. Chávez Center for Interdisciplinary Instruction in Chicana and Chicano Studies at UCLA, thanks to Reynaldo Macías, Abel Valenzuela, and especially Eric Avila, who recommended me for a lecturer position at UCLA, and then for an assistant professor position at UC Riverside. For a postdoctoral fellowship, as well as an ethnic studies research grant, thanks to the UCLA Institute of American Cultures, to Los Tigres del Norte, and to the UCLA Chicano Studies Research Center, particularly Chon Noriega and Carlos Haro. For crucial assistance at UC Riverside, thanks to Carlos Vélez-Ibañez and Patricia O'Brien, both former deans of the College of Humanities and Social Sciences; to the faculty and staff of the Department of Ethnic Studies; and to Jacqueline Shea Murphy, Juan Felipe Herrera, Carolyn Murray, Emory Elliot, Tiffany Ana López, and Devra Weber. At UCR I also received the Faculty Development Award, the UC Regents' Faculty Fellowship, Academic Senate Omnibus Research Grants, and the Ernesto Galarza Applied Research Center's Faculty Research Grant. For a quarter-long resident fellowship, thanks to the UC Humanities Research Institute, particularly David Theo Goldberg, and for financing a summer research trip to Mexico City, thanks to the UC Institute for Mexico and the United States (UC MEXUS).

A heartfelt thanks goes out to the friends/colleagues who read my book manuscript work in progress and gave me invaluable constructive criticism: Daniel Widener, Raúl Villa, Eric Porter, Catherine Ramírez, and Raúl Fernández. Thanks also to the following people for helping out a fellow human being along the way: Richard Kim, Patrick Hill, Wilson Valentín Escobar, Nancy Mirabal, George Sánchez, Robert Perez, Tharon Weighill, Sherrie Tucker, Lisa Lowe, Herman Gray, Rosa Linda Fregoso, George Lipsitz, Joseph Jordan, Michelle Habell-Pallán, Jaime Cárdenas, Sergio de la Mora, Keta Miranda, Luis Alvarez, Sara Johnson, Dylan Rodríguez, the members of the Los Angeles History Research Group at the Huntington Library (2002), Cristina Frias, David Torres, Raul Rico Jr., Margo Sesma, Xiuy Velo, Audrey Logan, Reynaldo Rivera, Michele Kotler, Brenda Cárdenas, Aaron Luc Levy, Sabena Toor, Madison Richardson, Ratziel Bander, David Hawthorne, Ken Waterstreet, Don Mathis, and Jack Pelletier. From UCLA, I am indebted to research assistants Wendy Sánchez, Luis Reyes, and Milo Alvarez, and to reader Ralph de Unamuno; from UC Riverside, to research assistants Daisy Aguilar and Edgar Nájera, and to teaching assistants Manuel Barajas, José López, Juan Pitones, and Mike Chavez. Thanks to former students Manuel González, Reyna Diaz, Vanessa Tico, and Mike Amezcua.

Reference librarians Norma Corral and Richard Chabrán at UCLA's Young/University Research Library were very helpful, as were Octavio Olvera at UCLA's Department of Special Collections; Dacy Taube at USC's Regional History Collection; Salvador Guereña, director of the California Ethnic and Multicultural Archives at UC Santa Barbara's Department of Special Collections; Carolyn Kozo Cole, curator of photographs at the Los Angeles Public Library; the staff at the Huntington Library, Dr. J. Fred MacDonald, president of MacDonald and Associates; and Don Larson and Mary Swab at Mapping Specialists. Kudos to the editorial staff and outside manuscript readers at the *American Quarterly* and at *Aztlán* for helping me refine my arguments, tighten my writing, and publish my work. Some material in chapters 1, 3, 4, and the conclusion appeared in my article "Bringing Music to the People" in *American Quarterly* 56:3 (2004), 693–717, © the Johns Hopkins University Press, and is reprinted with permission of The Johns Hopkins University Press. An earlier version of chapter 5 appeared as "Latin Holidays: Mexican Americans, Latin Music, and Cultural Identity in Postwar Los Angeles" in *Aztlán: A Journal of Chicano Studies* 30:2 (2005) and is reprinted with permission of the UCLA Chicano Studies Research Center Press. I have nothing but the highest praise for Ken Wissoker, editorial director at Duke University Press, for his overall vision and specific suggestions, not to mention his professionalism, creativity, wit, and savoir faire. Ken has made the entire publication process a smooth, efficient, and rewarding experience. Thanks also to the Duke University Press editorial and production staff for their assistance, and to the outside manuscript readers for their thorough, timely reports.

I would like to extend a special thanks to all of the generous people who passed along interview referrals, contacts, and phone numbers, and to those who gave me some of their time, even welcoming me into their homes to share oral histories, personal photographs (originals, scans, and reproductions), concert fliers, compact discs, cassette tapes, LPs, 45s, meals, and games of chess (Chico). I feel a great responsibility to tell these elders' stories accurately and respectfully, in recognition of them as important historical actors, and so this book is also dedicated to them. In particular, the musicians I interviewed taught me much about music and life. Our meetings, discussions, and impromptu lessons were in the finest tradition of informal music education that the book itself chronicles. Paul Lopez, Anthony Ortega, Tommy Saito, Jim Baiz, and Chico Sesma deserve additional praise for their close readings of articles and manuscript chapters.

Of course, I must conclude this section by thanking my parents, Tony and Sherri Macias, for nurturing my talents in drawing, painting, and athletics, for instilling in me a love of reading, watching movies, and listening and dancing to all kinds of music, for inspiring me to attain ambitious goals, for encouraging me to succeed through education, for showing me the value of long, hard hours, perseverance, and workers' rights, and for selflessly providing me with decades of loving support and guidance. Thanks also to my big sister, Denise Macias, for broadening my knowledge of popular music and dance, for sparking my interest in creative writing, and for being someone I could always look up to and confide in. My finest poetry and prose cannot convey my gratitude for everything each of them have done for me.

Finally, thanks to my wife, muse, and sounding board, Connie Rivera, the magician in my corner, for keeping me joyous with her big *corazón* and hearty laugh, and for helping me try new things, visit new places, and live life. Ever since we met, she has brightened my days, calmed my nerves, and balanced my mind, body, and spirit. Thanks to my daughter, Paloma, and my son, Anand, for keeping me active, for teaching me patience, for letting me see the world anew, and for lightening my load by putting a smile on my face and a song on my lips. All three of them bring out the best in me, and their love kept me going through the lonely journey of the writer. May this book justify their collective faith in me and somehow compensate for all of the hours together we have sacrificed.

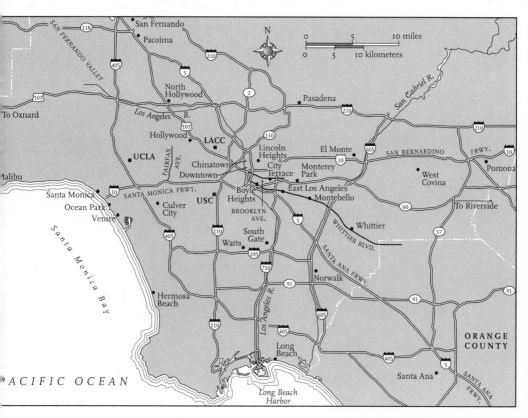

1. Metropolitan Los Angeles.

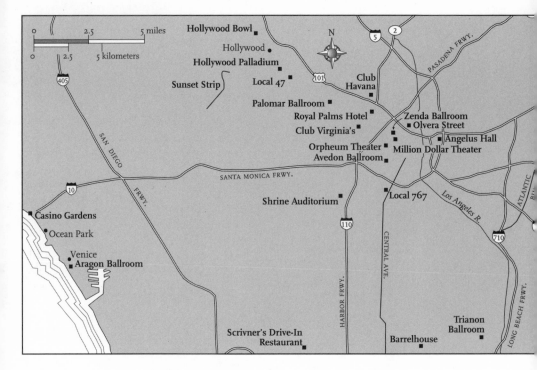

2. Los Angeles Music, Dance Sites.

the mexican american generation, music, and los angeles

[Like jazz], History is also everybody talking at once, multiple rhythms being played simultaneously. The events and people we write about did not occur in isolation but in dialogue with a myriad of other people and events.
—*Elsa Barkley Brown, "Polyrhythms and Improvization"*

I don't want to be put in a label, in a category. It's the same with my music.
—*Gil Bernal, interview by author*

Mexican American Mojo documents the culture, consciousness, pride, and prejudice of a generation of Mexican Americans who worked hard, served their country, composed music, studied theory, wrote lyrics, and pushed ahead. As an urban cultural history, it analyzes mixed-race neighborhoods, dance spaces, and music scenes that challenged the attempted containment of Mexican Americans and African Americans in a segregated city marked by racial discrimination. As a Chicano cultural history, it shows how, from the Great Depression to the Vietnam War, Mexican Americans created prototypically Chicano and Chicana cultural expressions, refusing to remain marginalized as they both contributed to and struggled against the larger society. Particularly in Southern California, they represented a "hep" wartime, and "cool" postwar counterculture with a street edge and a tough, working-class masculinity and femininity. They produced, consumed, and customized mass culture, yet as members of a "racialized" group they never completely melted into the pot, maintaining Spanish and interlingual usage and exhibiting a distinctive sensibility.[1] As workers, they ran the gamut, hustling in underground economies, toiling in anonymous jobs, joining labor unions, acquiring skilled trades, and even achieving fame, both fleeting and long-lasting. During this period, Mexican Americans rejected second-class citizenship, transformed Los Angeles, and enriched American culture.

Chicano historians have employed a political generation paradigm to describe the successive cohorts of urbanized, educated Mexican Americans who came of political age during the 1930s, 1940s, and 1950s. As illustrated by existing social, political, intellectual, and musical histories, members of the "Mexican American generation" were neither passive nor monolithic.[2] This book sheds new light on their creations, aspirations, acculturations, and associations, brushing layered details into a historiographic portrait of a generation, while arguing for an alternative geography of Chicano Los Angeles that ranges far beyond East L.A., and an alternative genealogy of Chicano music that incorporates jazz, and even classical, family tree branches. In addition, by proceeding from the assumption that Mexican American and African American cultures were mutually constitutive in wartime and postwar Los Angeles, the book also brings Chicano studies into dialogue with African American studies. Connecting these two fields opens a third path of interpretation, beyond a limiting binary pitting an assimilationist Mexican American generation against a nationalist Chicano generation. Based on the evidence presented in this study, both assimilationist and nationalist arguments could be seen as flights from blackness that raise problematic issues regarding Chicanos and whiteness. Even though some Mexicans and Mexican Americans have distanced themselves from black people over the years, scholars need not unnecessarily distance Chicano history from African Americans. With this in mind, the book traces the ways that African Americans and Mexican Americans informed each other and the English language, particularly in the realm of popular music, as illustrated by the West African–derived word *mojo* in the title.

Mojo is a small flannel bag, worn on one's person, containing powerful amulets and charms intended to conjure spells for winning luck in gambling, attaining or preventing love, and starting or stopping a hex or jinx.

Mojo is linked with New Orleans, the birthplace of jazz, where Afro-Caribbean folk medicine took root in the United States. As it evolved, the term *mojo* went hand-in-hand with African American popular music, from 1920s New Orleans jazz parlance to 1930s rural blues lyrics. In 1957, gospel singer-turned-secular shouter Ann Cole recorded "Got My Mo-Jo Working (But It Just Won't Work On You)," a saxophone rocker in which the lovelorn narrator follows a gypsy woman's advice by using, among other things, cured, dried "black cat bones," and "hoodoo ashes." That same year, urban blues guitarist Muddy Water's version became one of his signature songs, influencing countless British and American rock bands of the 1960s and ensuring that the term entered into the mainstream completely.[3]

As the Afro-diasporic word *mojo* crossed over into common usage, it lost much of its original association with magical talismans and supernatural luck. Hence, the *American Heritage Dictionary* also defines *mojo* as "personal magnetism" or "charm."[4] *Mojo* is used herein to signify good fortune, but also personal character, strength, and inner ability. In particular, it describes the ability of Mexican Americans to control their lives, fight for their civil rights, pursue higher economic standards of living, and influence popular culture with their innovative styles. Just as Clarence Major's *Dictionary of African American Slang* defines having one's "mojo working" as experiencing "good luck or success," the members of the Los Angeles Mexican American generation had their "mojo working."[5]

In other words, "Mexican American mojo" refers to the power of Mexican Americans as everyday historical actors to exert agency, choice, and free will in the face of multiple structural constraints.[6] At the same time, it also refers to their modern urban expressive culture. Chicanos and Chicanas are a multifaceted group of people whose culture cannot be reduced to a static set of essentialized, stereotypical traits; however, they have developed a cumulative, collective way of expressing their relation to the world. Specifically, their suave, laid-back style, which includes a visual aesthetic favoring clean lines and stylized silhouettes, is reflected in their attitude, body language, walk, talk, dance, fashion, automobiles, and even bicycles. As heard in certain musical genres more than others, there is also something unique in their phrasing, intonation, and accent. Over centuries, the Spanish language in Mexico borrowed many translated Indian expressions, as well as many indigenous words, pronunciations, and spellings. The special lilt of Mexican Spanish has been called the *canto mexicano*, or

Mexican song, and it shaped the Mexican American generation, as did the gypsy-borderlands-barrio youth dialect *caló*, as well as the rhyming jive of Harlem and Central Avenue "hep cats."

Culturally, rather than identifying pure Mexican features, hidden Indian strains, or latent Chicano aspects, the book indicates how people used popular music, dance, and style to articulate a point of view—an identity— both Mexican and American. Artistically, across the period the recurrent theme remained eclecticism, as Mexican American musicians consistently selected what they considered the best elements and methods from diverse sources. Not every one of their many compositions in the popular styles of each era must be labeled "Mexican American music." Nevertheless, taken together, their songbook should be considered the music of the Mexican American generation, even when based on black forms, or when conveyed entirely in English. In general, Mexican Americans produced their own soulful, cool Chicano aesthetic, whether they were *pachucos* and *pachucas* in all-black zoot suit fashions dancing to black big bands; low-riding *cholos* in tinted sunglasses cruising their customized classic cars to rhythm and blues; or dapper mambo dancers stepping and twirling to interlocking Afro-Cuban polyrhythms. These vibrant creative expressions embodied a deep spirit of ceremony, revisioned in urban musical environments. I therefore use the African American term *mojo* to evoke a kindred Mexican American oral culture that tells stories to the next generations, a folk healing that utilizes an ancient knowledge of curing roots and herbs, a paganish spirituality that maintains relationships with one's ancestors, and a ritualistic music and dance that raises the spirits of both performer and audience.[7] Ethnic Mexican peoples have their own histories of transculturation and canny adaptation; their own relationship to percussion instruments and the rhythm of the drum, to what is deemed not sacred but superstitious or savage by white European Enlightenment societies. They have their own tradition of "trickeration"—of struttin' their stuff and stoppin' the show.[8]

Like the black "race rebel" zoot suiter, "El Pachuco" is a "bad man" in the Stackolee, or Staggerlee mold, while the "Black Widow" pachucas from the Eastside paralleled the African American "slick chicks" from Central Avenue.[9] Mexican Americans and African Americans in Los Angeles shared strong bonds, from the zoot suit and the jitterbug to neighborhood jazz instructors and high schools, from boogie woogie and jump blues to doo wop, Motown, and Afro-Latin music. Although they began the 1940s as despised racial groups, their respective social, racial, and class statuses seemed to diverge, as Mexican Americans managed to benefit from the wartime and postwar booms by exploiting the slight but significant advantages they enjoyed over African Americans. Still, while some Mexican Americans secured higher positions, the majority of them suffered through regional economic contractions, and their realization of the American dream was often thwarted by Anglos and white ethnics who still perceived them not only as dark, dangerous, exotic "others," but also as expendable manual laborers. Thus, visible gains during the period notwithstanding, Mexican American Angelenos still experienced class insecurity and instability.

Yet this story is not one of victimization in which Mexican Americans were entirely constrained by what the larger society would allow. For example, Mexican Americans were not trapped in Eastside barrios. Instead, they insisted on having a run of the city—a contested run, but one in which they asserted their freedom of movement, their freedom of assembly, and their social mobility. Since they refused to be held back physically or artistically, the city's music and dance scenes enabled them to occupy different spaces in various neighborhoods, providing them room to maneuver further. As a result, Mexican American Angelenos not only claimed public space across the city and the region, but also infused American culture with a sardonic, satirical, and improvisational Chicano style. At a time when European Americans protected segregated social gains, Mexican Americans merged black music, dance, and fashion idioms with their own, entered the popular culture industries, and succeeded, as I will show, at the intersections between the margins and the mainstream, between the minority and the majority. I therefore examine their cultural practices and creative productions in order to reveal the political possibilities and outward ambitions, as well as the social imagination and interior life, of a people.

In 1970, Chicano studies scholar Fernando Peñalosa outlined a continuum of Mexican American identity, arguing that rather than make sweeping generalizations about such a heterogeneous group, we should try to establish a "range of variation."[10] In that spirit, the following account attempts to render the Mexican American generation in its full diversity and complexity, especially its thematic, stylistic, and conceptual orientation, open-minded enough to draw from Mexican, Latin American, African American, Anglo, Jewish, and even British cultures. The book illuminates a historical moment in which Mexican Americans connected and engaged with other racial, ethnic, and class groups, in which they interacted with, and even entertained the dominant society. Mexican Americans adopted mass culture to satisfy their need for music and dance, tailoring both mainstream and antiestablishment forms to speak to their specific situations.[11] Meanwhile, their own modern, versatile styles covered the full spectrum of moves, sounds, rhythms, harmonies, and melodies, while continuing certain Mexican and Latin American forms. Mexican Americans were included in some arenas yet excluded from others, and their bicultural, hybrid sensibility produced a kind of "double consciousness."[12] Moreover, during a period when many Mexican American Angelenos were frustrated with their socioeconomic position yet hopeful about the benefits of assimilation, African American music and style proved to be an ideal model of both participation in and resistance to Anglo American society.[13] Conversely, the detached attitude, or "studied indifference" of the pachucos, and later, the cholos, resonated with disaffected blacks, as it eventually would with many white youths.[14]

Politically, Southern California's climate of racial retrenchment created a cultural landscape in which civic institutions and grass-roots collectives mirrored competing discourses of morality. This postwar drama played out in a regional context of federal defense contracts, population explosion, rapid decentralization, and a growing disparity between an affluent white suburbia and a poor "colored" inner city. In particular, nightlife entertainment venues became sites of contestation over public policy and civic values, as city politics met cultural politics. Viewing Los Angeles through the prism of popular music therefore produces a fresh take on a city open to multiple readings. Mapping the multicultural terrain of popular music, in other words, reimagines the racial geography, and scholarly biography, of Los Angeles.[15] Similarly, inscribing Chicanos and other Latinos into the literature on jazz, rhythm and blues, and rock and roll reorients popular music studies from black/white binaries and New Deal/ postwar divides, while grafting Los Angeles to the body of scholarship on Latin music mitigates any East Coast exceptionalism. Finally, my Los Angeles "case study" can help illuminate the ways that other people navigate the public spaces of, and construct democratic civil societies in, other multicultural cities.

on organization and themes

The book is composed of five research chapters, framed by an introduction and a conclusion. The first four chapters proceed in chronological order, although the second focuses on the war years, while the fifth chapter doubles back and spans the entire period again. Chapter 1 begins to sketch the contours of the Mexican American generation in Los Angeles by presenting everyday music lovers who danced the jitterbug to nationally famous and local big bands, and by introducing a cohort of professional modern jazz musicians who also grew up during the Great Depression, came of age during the Second World War, and took part in the cultural life of the swing era. Chapter 2 traces the evolution of the early 1940s African American zoot suit style, situating pachucas and pachucos in the local urban music and dance scenes, comparing them to black hep cats, and even contrasting them with Mexican American "squares." Chapter 3 follows not only the continuing black-brown cultural cross-pollination as postwar Mexican American Angelenos produced and consumed jazz, jump blues, and "pachuco boogie," but also several of the swing-era musicians' careers, as well as the broader Mexican American stylistic aesthetic, and socioeconomic struggle, into the rhythm and blues era.

Chapter 4 examines Mexican Americans' intensive involvement in doo wop and rock and roll, placing the familiar histories of white disc jockeys, Mexican American car cruisers, Ritchie Valens, El Monte American Legion Stadium, and the Eastside rock music scene in the book's analytical and theoretical framework. In addition, this chapter continues tracking our straight-ahead jazz, and all-around entertainer protagonists, as well as Mexican American style, upward mobility, and political praxis, into the rock and roll era. Chapter 5 completes the study, re-creating the city's Latin music scene of rumbas, boleros, Latin jazz, mambos, and cha cha chás, while adding the final texture to the overall generational portrait. Specifically, this last chapter argues that Mexican Americans repudiated segregation and an Anglo-imposed cultural identity as labor commodities by participating in a sophisticated, Spanish-language Latino cosmopolitanism, through which they demanded dignity.

In sum, the book details the development of a distinct Mexican American expressive culture, and of a "multicultural urban civility," while profiling key neighborhoods, high schools, and musical venues. As Mexican

Americans responded to injustice, and opportunity, chapter 1 shows how they began to push out beyond the downtown and Eastside areas, while in chapter 2 the clash between antagonistic forces, each with its own vision of civil society, intensifies, as the Anglo powers that be, and everyday whites, push back. Chapters 3 and 4 can be read as dispatches from the many postwar flashpoints in what had become a cultural cold war, even as more Mexican Americans moved from the central and eastern city to surrounding suburbs. Another line of inquiry, threaded throughout, is the extent of interracial ties and tensions, principally Mexican Americans' complicated relationships with whites, blacks, Mexicanos, and other Latinos. The voices of unsung artists and unknown fans can be heard, while certain Chicano icons, from El Pachuco to well-known musicians and bands, are analyzed anew within the wider context of their contemporaries, the city, and the nation.

Gender is used as a category of analysis by highlighting the gendered innovations of Mexican American expressive culture, and the gendered limitations of urban civility. For example, pompadoured pachucas sported ensembles of exaggerated jackets, short, tight skirts, or, for those daring enough, the full zoot suit with the men's baggy slacks. The carefully coiffed, impeccably pressed pachucos, on the other hand, epitomized both classy pride and tough-guy stoicism, yet compared to typical business suits, the length and narrow waist of the zoot coat also evoked contemporary female fashions. Similar gender ambiguities arose in the 1960s, as Beatlemania invaded the Eastside, where some Mexican American women adopted British mods' straight bangs and international miniskirts, and where some male musicians wore long bangs and tight, skinny suits. By that time, Mexican American performers like Lalo Guerrero, Ritchie Valens, and Eddie Cano had introduced a stocky, *mestizo* masculinity into the culture industries; Gil Bernal, Don Tosti, and others had succeeded in the age of handsome Latin singers and bandleaders; and Mexican American women and other Latinas had increased their visibility in the urban public sphere as callers on rock and roll dedication shows, as members of all-girl car clubs, and as mambo dancers. Finally, a gendered power differential all too often reasserted male privilege, from limited job opportunities for female musicians to macho song lyrics, thereby lessening the egalitarianism of the music and dance scenes.

on terminology

The politicized term *Chicano*, which had long connoted lower-class status, was appropriated in the 1940s by some pachucos to signify defiant difference, and, in the 1960s, by militant activists to signify political self-determination, anti-assimilationist consciousness, indigenous racial heritage, and socioeconomic community empowerment. Even though the Mexican American generation originated many antecedent examples of contemporary Chicano culture, *Chicano* is, for the most part, used as a referent for the 1960s generation, rather than as a synonym for *Mexican American*, although both terms are employed to describe people of Mexican descent born and raised in the United States. The book uses *Mexican* or *Mexicano* for Mexican-born migrants and immigrants, and *ethnic Mexican* for both Mexicanos and Mexican Americans together. To acknowledge commonalitites with other mestizos from former Spanish colonies, the term *Latino* is used to include ethnic Mexicans, but also to specify Puerto Ricans, Cubans, and non-Mexican Latin Americans. *Anglo, white,* and, to a lesser extent, *European American,* are used for the descendants of English, Scottish, Irish, French, Dutch, German, and northern European immigrants, as well as for the many Midwesterners and "Dust Bowl" refugees from Oklahoma, Arkansas, and Texas who relocated to Los Angeles. *White ethnic* is also specified for the *Caucasian* children and grandchildren of Eastern, Central, and Southern European immigrants. *African American, black,* and, in its historical context, the period term *Negro,* are used for the ethnically diverse African descendats in the United States.

The term *assimilation* means something different in Southern California, where Spanish newcomers tried to convert Indians, who were forced to become nominally "Hispanicized," and where nineteenth- and twentieth-century migrants from various backgrounds acclimated to a foreign environment with a Native American and ethnic Mexican presence. To assimilate typically means for a minority population to become similar to the majority society, into which it is absorbed. Yet assimilation is a matter of degrees, and it is a two-way process. Mexican Americans, who were never fully absorbed, have selectively assimilated cultural elements from whites, and also from blacks, both of whom have themselves appropriated elements of Chicano culture. For most Mexican Americans, therefore, assimilation never meant the complete adoption of middle-class white values, or the complete rejection of working-class Mexican values.

Genre names are ideological terms that market lifestyles and sell commodities for the corporate profit of an Anglo-dominant, historically racist American music industry.[16] As this introduction's epigraphs attest, musicians did not exist in isolation, and many did not want to be pigeonholed by any one label, just as many music lovers and social dancers did not listen solely to one type of music or socialize solely with one group of people. Nonetheless, genre labels help theoretically conceptualize and chronologically organize my research findings, as demonstrated by the book's internal periodizations of different musical "eras." Geographically, the term *Eastside* is used broadly to denote the area east of the Los Angeles River, including Lincoln Heights, the neighborhood just northeast of downtown; Boyle Heights, the neighborhood just east of downtown; and of course, East Los Angeles proper, the unincorporated territory bounded by Boyle Heights to the west, City Terrace and Monterey Park to the north, Montebello to the east, and the City of Commerce to the south. The terms *Westside* and *West Los Angeles* are used broadly to denote the area west of Western Avenue, south of Hollywood Boulevard, and north of Venice Boulevard, although there is a "West Los Angeles" neighborhood just west of the 405 freeway, between Santa Monica and Olympic boulevards. For African Americans in South Los Angeles, the imaginary line dividing their version of the Eastside/Westside split has shifted westward through the years, from Central Avenue to Figueroa Street to Vermont Avenue to Western Avenue. The term *South Central Los Angeles* is used to denote the area south of downtown along Central Avenue and along Alameda Street. Finally, throughout the book, people's nicknames, stage names, maiden names, and married surnames are used as biographically appropriate, and when chronologically accurate.

take a little trip

As the "objective" historian, I will be your "omniscient" narrator, your tour guide on a trip that will examine ethnic identity, unpack essentialistic authenticity, and uncover cross-cultural connections—and disconnections. Along the way, we will meet Mexican American swing bandleaders with Japanese American drummers and Jewish American arrangers; young whites who became Mexican Americanized after growing up around ethnic Mexican families; Jewish American composers who wrote rhythm and blues songs for African American musicians; and Mexican Americans who played Afro-Cuban music. In the pages that follow, the cultural networks that facilitated these exchanges will be analyzed across the city's many classrooms, workplaces, leisure spaces, record stores, and dance floors. Furthermore, we will see how African American, Mexican American, and Latino styles migrated across class and racial lines, via radios, record players, jukeboxes, television sets, and movie theaters.

For Mexican Americans, the period was one of emerging middle-class formations and burgeoning civil rights expectations, yet despite their increased mobility and visibility, many of them were still beset by police brutality, vigilante violence, racial discrimination, underfunded schools, Anglo stereotyping, and a combination of real estate redlining, electoral redistricting, urban renewal, and freeway construction that isolated, destabilized, and dissected ethnic Mexican barrios. Whites tried to put uppity minorities back in their place, but in the end, Mexican Americans rose up and commanded respect for their cultural creations and social achievements. Beginning with "Rosita the Riveter" war workers and returning servicemen, an untold number of Southern California Mexican Americans purchased homes, jump-started small businesses, and acquired technical skills, higher education, and white- or pink-collar jobs. Determined not to be treated economically like cheap labor, or socially like blacks, those members of the Mexican American generation who were veterans utilized the G.I. Bill to obtain college or vocational diplomas, and those who were musicians joined the all-white musicians union local.

Taken as a whole, although they seized every opportunity, maximized any advantage, and exhibited some antiblack prejudice, they never fully embraced whiteness, nor fully benefited from it. All the while, their multiracial dance hall congregations defied the ruling social order, and their unique expressive culture blended various influences into a new mixture, as they found their voice, forged an identity, and made history. In short, in a context of bitter racism, über-patriotism, and anticommunism, Mexican Americans sang the pachuco blues and paid their dues—in labor unions and in life—while working their magic under circumstances, to paraphrase Karl Marx, not always of their own choosing.[17]

mojo in motion: the swing era

I grew up with the radio, with Jack Armstrong, the All-American Boy, the Jack Benny Program, the First Nighter Program with Les Tremaine and Barbara Luddy, the Lux Radio Theater, Ma Perkins, and Burns and Allen. That's my childhood.
—Paul Lopez, interview by author, September 2, 1998

For nearly a decade the Lindy—more widely known as the Jitterbug—remained the sole possession of a small group . . . of amateur dancers in a few big cities. As far as the general public was concerned, the dance arrived out of nowhere around 1936 to go with a new music called swing that was played by a man named Benny Goodman.
—Marshall Stearns and Jean Stearns, Jazz Dance

Later in the [1930s], dance halls became popular. There was the Bowery Ballroom downtown at Ninth and Grand, where Sal's Deluxe Big Band, probably the first Chicano dance band, used to play. It was a horn band playing swing, jitterbug, and traditional Mexican music—sort of like Bob Wills from the other side of the Rio Grande. Two of the other popular house bands at the Bowery, the George Brown Band and the Irwin Brothers, were black. But since there were still very few blacks in L.A., the crowd was mostly Chicanos.
—Billy Cardenas, music producer, quoted in Rubén Guevara,
"View from the Sixth Street Bridge"

In the summer of 1935 the Music Corporation of America booked "a barnstorming tour" from New York to Los Angeles for the Benny Goodman Orchestra.[1] After receiving cold receptions across the hinterlands, Goodman and his big band musicians were "certain they'd be a flop on the [West] Coast."[2] On August 21, 1935, the disappointing tour ended in Los Angeles with a scheduled three-week engagement at the Palomar Ballroom, "the most famous of all West Coast ballrooms."[3] Located on Vermont Avenue at Third Street, between Beverly and Wilshire boulevards, the Palomar was a huge building with Moorish architecture, exotic Moorish interior décor, a mezzanine, a balcony, a patio, a palm-lined terrace restaurant, and a dance floor that could accommodate four thousand couples. After a disheartening audience response on the first evening, "about an hour before closing time" Goodman's band played several "hot" swing arrangements by African American bandleader Fletcher Henderson, whose charts Goodman had been using since 1934. Suddenly the dancers "began to break out their fanciest steps. . . . People whooped, stamped, whistled, and shouted for more." As "Benny Goodman's music became fashionable and attracted the Hollywood people," mostly from the grand hotel and apartments near the neighboring Bimini Baths and Hot Springs, "the combination drew unprecedented crowds to the Palomar." According to one "explanation for the sudden success in Los Angeles," Goodman's earlier hit recordings on RCA Victor "were widely played on small radio stations, especially in California," so that when he arrived "he already had a following."[4] Earlier that year, young, hip Angelenos had been listening to live broadcasts of late-night Benny Goodman performances from New York City, on NBC's radio program, *Let's Dance*, and local fans turned out to hear the band in person.

After nearly two months at the Palomar, which included coast-to-coast remote broadcasts, Goodman, swing, and the jitterbug made the headlines of national newspapers, and by the time his orchestra played in Chicago and returned to New York, journalists dubbed Goodman "the King of Swing."[5] According to traditional jazz history periodization, the Palomar Ballroom engagement helped usher in the swing era and its youthful dance craze. The year of these historic performances also marks the beginning of the book's periodization, even though swinging jazz existed well before "white fans, journalists, and historians" crowned Goodman "the 'King' of something new called 'Swing.'" Regarding "conventional swing narration," Sherrie Tucker argues that "origin stories tend to mark white

production and consumption of black musical forms," while "periodization reflects episodes of successful commodification of jazz products to
white consumers."[6]

Yet the jazz histories that discuss Goodman at the Palomar do not
place the ballroom itself in the context of Los Angeles as a city, thereby
ignoring the probable presence of Mexican Americans. Although African
Americans were barred, Mexican Americans "were welcome" at the Palomar Ballroom, and in all likelihood they were there, dancing to Benny
Goodman, the Chicago-born Jewish American clarinetist, whose hard-
driving orchestra was powered by Gene Krupa, his Chicago-born Czecho-
slovakian American drummer.[7] Vicente "Vince" Ramírez, a resident of
East Los Angeles, believed that his older brother, Randolph Leon "Ron"
Ramírez, who loved jazz, "may have been there the night Benny Goodman
came in."[8]

By beginning at this moment, the book inserts Mexican Americans into
the history of big band swing music, and therefore into the cultural history
of the United States more broadly. As the chapter epigraphs suggest, the
members of the Mexican American generation were raised on the radio,
including adventure, theatrical drama, soap opera, and vaudevillesque
comedy series. They also grew up on Hollywood cinema, and of course, on
jazz music and dance. By the late 1930s Mexican Americans were avid
swing fans and jitterbug dancers, but they still wanted a little "traditional"
Mexican music thrown into the live mix, as well as Latin music.[9] This
chapter will follow a cohort of Angeleno jazz musicians, music lovers, and
social dancers who helped to create a distinct Mexican American expressive culture while contributing to the consumption, and production, of
American culture. They also exposed the cracks in, and thereby chipped
away at, the city's segregation, from which they suffered, and at times,
relative to blacks, benefited.

David Stowe argues that swing music proved "the possibility of tolerance, mutual respect, even affection" between whites and blacks, that it
"inaugurated a new chapter in race relations," and that the dance-centered
youth culture of the late 1930s represented a "swing ideology" of "ethnic pluralism and democratic equality" which became part of a national
"cultural mobilization" against fascism during World War II.[10] As Lewis
Erenberg contends, swing represented an unprecedented "creolization of
American youth culture," and it "offered a new model of social democracy
and group life" based on the pluralistic potentials of the jazz world.[11]

Indeed, Benny Goodman hired black musicians like pianist Teddy Wilson (1935), vibraphonist Lionel Hampton (1936), guitarist Charlie Christian (1939), and pianist Fletcher Henderson (1939). Goodman insisted that his band play for mixed-race audiences and that all of his musicians receive the same hotel accommodations. He refused to tour the South entirely. Similarly, Duke Ellington's "classic elegance" and "deep-seated sense of dignity" showed "that he was beyond the humiliations of segregation."[12] As Eric Porter notes, swing could be a means toward dignity and self-respect, as well as a commodity capable of bringing monetary reward and "respectability through popularity."[13]

But before big band swing music and jitterbug dancing burst into the general public's imagination in the mid-1930s, these two African American art forms had been evolving together at Harlem's Savoy Ballroom, where the nation's best black orchestras and its finest black dancers pushed each other to perfection. *Swing* as a verb refers to a propulsive rhythmic quality emphasizing the second and fourth beats in the 4/4 time signature, or meter. *Swing* as a musical style refers to large orchestras playing artful arrangements that showcased riding rhythms, catchy melodies, call-and-response between brass and reed sections, and standout improvisatory solos. For all of Duke Ellington's classy compositions and melodic masterpieces, his famed orchestra, with its star soloists, could swing and improvise with the best of them; yet perhaps the driving beats of the big band era were best represented by the drummer Chick Webb's Savoy Ballroom house band and by the pianist Count Basie's Kansas City orchestra.[14]

In other words, swing music meant dancing, and that meant the jitterbug. The basic jitterbug move is "a syncopated two-step or box-step accenting the offbeat," but the dance cannot be reduced to "an isolated step." Rather, it "is a fundamental approach," and like the music, it flows "horizontally" with "rhythmic continuity." Furthermore, as one dancer explained, "You have to sway, forwards and backwards, with a controlled hip movement, while your shoulders stay level and your feet glide along the floor." The man's right hand was held low on the woman's back, while his left hand enclosed hers at his side. Then, whenever the arrangement led into a solo, the dance partners would slip into the breakaway, separating from one another to "improvise individual steps" before returning to the original synchronized footwork.[15] During the breakaway, dancers could incorporate existing moves or create new ones like the truck, a move that mirrored the loose strut of urban "hep cats" and hustlers, head bobbing, arms swaying, and fingers snapping to the beat. Thus, just as jazz arrangements serve as "frameworks in time" that allow for a band's communal and individual improvisations, the basic jitterbug steps served as a framework, with the breakaway allowing for flights of fancy and creative "cutting."[16] As Marshall Stearns and Jean Stearns explain, "the breakaway is a time-honored method of eliminating the European custom of dancing in couples, and returning to solo dancing—the universal way of dancing, for example, in Africa."

The dancers at the Savoy Ballroom had long been performing the earliest version of what would be named the jitterbug, but they called it the lindy hop.[17] When Count Basie's visiting Kansas City band played Harlem, its high-hat cymbal-riding, twelve-bar bluesy riff romps created a "lifting momentum," which inspired new flash dance—or acrobatic—moves like the hip-to-hip, side flip, and over-the-back, as the male Savoy dancers flung their female partners above and across the floor. The "nervous energy" generated by the "constant pressure" of city life was reflected in the lindy hop's "tireless vigor and daring invention."[18] Even more so than earlier two-step dances, the lindy hop's smooth flow, complicated routines, and swinging rhythms enchanted young people.[19] Gaining ardent adherents throughout the country, the jitterbug revolutionized popular dancing, carrying people away with its free physical expression. Along the way, bandleader Jimmie Lunceford's bouncy 1939 swing song "Rock It for Me" reassured Americans, "Ain't no shame to keep your body swaying."[20] As a youth culture, swing crossed racial and class boundaries, and in most cities uninhibited working-class white youths were the first to pick up the jitterbug from blacks, introducing the energetic, athletic moves to middle-class whites. After high society dance studios began teaching a mild, genteel version of the lindy hop along with the standard fox trot and Charleston lessons, the general public discovered some variation of it for their social dancing.

The Detroit dancer George Wendler recalled that the jitterbug "did eventually open up dancing for white people. The sophisticated mask was discarded, you were permitted to get with it and be carried away."[21] The swing "beat made you come out of yourself, out of your seat; it made you want to dance." As dance music, swing offered entertainment and escape, yet still "moved one to elegance and refinement." At the same time, it "unleashed primal forces" and "released pent-up excitement and physicality."[22] According to Lewis Erenberg, swing evoked "the promise of the city" and "the aura of urban freedom," it encouraged improvisatory moves, and it enabled both individual and collective freedom via the body.[23] Indeed, Gena Dagel Caponi argues that black dance contains intellectual properties, preserves an improvisatory aesthetic, and transmits a communal worldview.[24] As Jacqui Malone claims, African American vernacular dance affirms and celebrates life, "even in the face of tremendous adversity." It is "a source of energy, joy, and inspiration; a spiritual antidote to oppression" that "teaches the unity of mind and body and regenerates mental and physical power." Black dance is marked by, among other things, "a certain ecstasy of motion," coupled with a "concern for elegance" and for the originality of one's ideas.[25]

Dance as theory and practice will be highlighted in spots throughout this book, but dance as an integral part of the city's music scenes remains constant. In particular, Mexican Americans' spirited expressive culture included a tradition of vernacular dance and bodily style, as well as a knack for adaptation and improvisation, for revitalizing the ethnic group in the face of hard times, segregation, and discrimination. In short, Mexican Americans had their mojo working. They demanded respect, publicly asserted themselves throughout the city, imprinted their mark on American popular culture, and made big band swing music and jitterbug dancing their own. Often they did so in the face of opposition. For example, in May 1940, the Los Angeles Police Department (LAPD) refused to issue La Fiesta Club a permit to host a concert featuring the Benny Goodman Orchestra at the Shrine Auditorium, a Moorish-style building across from the University of Southern California (USC), just southwest of downtown Los Angeles.[26] La Fiesta Club was probably one of the many Mexican American social organizations, common at the time, whose members sponsored local dances. As reported by the *California Eagle*, the city's oldest African American newspaper, the police commission told the club "that the permit was denied because white, Filipino, Mexicans and Negroes were permitted to dance together." South Central Los Angeles community leaders responded with "widespread indignation," branding the action "unfair."[27] Also in May 1940, Mayor Fletcher Bowron prohibited public entertainment establishments from serving alcohol after two in the morning, in an attempt to curtail what a *California Eagle* reporter called the "swarms of white visitors making the rounds" on Central Avenue, the heart of the city's African American jazz district.[28]

As these instances illustrate, popular music and dance performances provoked reactionary regulation by the authorities. This antagonistic relationship suggested a broader social dynamic in which two contrasting models of civil society—one of multiracial musicians, dancers, and entrepreneurs, the other of white urban elites and law enforcement—played out in multiple music venues, with the public freedom and cultural values of Los Angeles at stake, as I will discuss further in later chapters. Beginning in the 1930s, when Mexican deportation drives, restrictive housing covenants, and antimiscegenation laws were the order of the day, successive generations of Angelenos defied the city's rule of racial separation and white domination, creating a multicultural urban civility as they intermingled in dance halls, ballrooms, and auditoriums.[29] Mexican Americans, along with African Americans, maintained their own expressive culture and spearheaded a liberating public sphere in which bodies in motion both combined and circulated throughout the region. This civility was far from utopian, given the existence of sporadic racial prejudice within and between different groups. Nevertheless, dance music facilitated intercultural affinities that went beyond mere politeness or courtesy to include respect and tolerance. Although black, Mexican American, and Latino popular music and dancing could not completely erase all sterotypical preconceptions, cross-cultural contact and understanding flourished for many years in Los Angeles. In diverse music scenes, people sustained egalitarian social relations in the face of blatant attacks on their civil liberties. As part of a cultural corollary to ongoing political struggles for dignity and equality, jitterbugs and, in the next two chapters, zoot suiters and low riders, exercised their right to freedom of assembly in public spaces.

In the social, economic, and cultural context of the swing era, which included a racist music industry and segregated musicians unions, several professional musicians emerged whose successful careers and significant life stories we will follow throughout the book. Most prominent among these are three high school classmates from Boyle Heights, Lionel "Chico" Sesma, Paul Lopez, and Edmundo "Don Tosti" Martínez Tostado, as well as Anthony Ortega and Eduardo "Lalo" Guerrero. Since local musicians, jazz fans, and social dancers traversed the city's politicized popular cultural terrain, they provide pointillistic detail for the book's generational sketch in aggregate. Finally, we will survey several ethnic Mexican barrios, from the Westside to the Eastside, as well as the diverse neighborhoods of Watts and Boyle Heights, from the mid-1930s to the mid-1940s.

For example, Boyle Heights is located in the Hollenbeck district, just east of downtown and Little Tokyo, across the Los Angeles River. During the 1920s Boyle Heights was the Los Angeles entry point for foreign immigrants, and its heterogeneous population of 70,000 was predominantly Jewish.[30] In 1939, Federal Housing Authority appraisers designated Boyle Heights a "'melting pot' area literally honeycombed with diverse and subversive racial elements."[31] In 1940, ten of Hollenbeck's fifteen census tracts listed Mexicans as the predominant foreign-born group, five tracts listed Russians, and the entire district was solidly working class, with the overwhelming number of residents working in industrial occupations.[32] By 1940 the Jewish population of Boyle Heights totaled about thirty-five thousand, the Mexican population about fifteen thousand, and the Japanese population approximately five thousand.[33] The heart of Boyle Heights, at Brooklyn Avenue and Soto Street, was unmistakably Jewish, and traveling east along Brooklyn Avenue, "everything was commercial Jewish. The Jews used to live north of Brooklyn Avenue," and nearby City Terrace to the east was "all Jewish," with the exception of a few Mexican American families.[34]

Many Syrians and Armenians lived along Soto near Third and Fourth streets, with the Armenians eventually cornering the garbage collection business.[35] In 1940, the fifteen census tracts in Hollenbeck contained an average of 15 percent foreign-born population, but the proportion spiked up to 45 percent in Russian neighborhoods.[36] Most of the "White Russian" Molokans, a persecuted sect of the Russian Orthodox Church, were concentrated down the hill from Boyle Heights, along Mission Road between First and Fourth streets, just east of the Los Angeles River. A 1937 report noted that this "Russian Flats" section contained "thirteen foreign racial groups and practically a total absence of the white native element."[37] In 1940 the Flats neighborhood contained the area's two census tracts with the largest percentages of African Americans: 4 and 2.5 percent, respectively.[38] In Chico Sesma's words, in Boyle Heights "there weren't too many blacks, though there were a few."[39] Filipinos, Chinese, and Italians also rounded out the polyglot populace.[40] East of Indiana Street in East Los Angeles, especially in the Maravilla and Belvedere sections, there were large, concentrated ethnic Mexican populations, but in Boyle Heights, "the Mexican Americans were kind of interspersed—a few clusters of us here and there, as were Japanese Americans."[41]

Born in Boyle Heights in 1924, Chico Sesma was raised there by his Mexican American father, from Arizona, and his Mexicana mother, from

Sonora. His father, Samuel, was primarily a manual laborer, and his mother, Salomé, a housewife until her thirties, when she began working in the garment industry. Paul Lopez also grew up in Boyle Heights at the same time. Born in 1923 to Timothy and Adele Lopez, both second-generation Mexican Americans, Paul spent seven years, from age two to age nine, in a hospital bed, stricken with polio and undergoing a series of unsuccessful experimental operations. After that he lived with his grandparents, who had come to Los Angeles from Mexico, and he would henceforth get around on crutches and leg braces. Chico Sesma used to walk from his house to Hollenbeck Junior High School, which had a student body that was 38 percent Mexican, 35 percent Jewish, 9 percent Russian, and 7 percent Japanese in 1936. In addition to a symphony orchestra, the school had a marching/concert band, which Chico Sesma joined as a trombonist. Music instructor Wilfred J. Abbot served as conductor for the thirty-piece band, whose student musicians reflected the ethnically diverse area (see figure 1).[42]

The student body of nearby Robert Louis Stevenson Junior High was 50 percent Anglo and 31 percent Mexican, while that of Theodore Roosevelt Senior High School was 28 percent Anglo, 26 percent Jewish, 24 percent Mexican, 7 percent Russian, 6 percent Japanese, 1.5 percent each Armenian, Italian, and German, and 0.5 percent African American in 1936. Just two years later, in 1938, Roosevelt High's student body had become 4.5 percent Anglo, 40 percent Jewish, 27 percent Mexican, 5.5 percent Russian, and 9 percent Japanese.[43] During the early 1940s, Roosevelt students organized over thirty ethnic societies.[44] There was, Chico Sesma recalled, "an equal number of everything at Roosevelt High School." Despite the area's ethnic multiplicity, Sesma did not remember any "heavy racial attitudes."[45] As Don Tosti said, "It was amazing, and we all got along together. Oh yeah, we had our fights, but if somebody jumped a Jewish kid that was friendly and nice, we would protect him." People would socialize on the weekends—and even date—outside of their group, but "when you married, you married your own in those days, mostly; there were exceptions."[46]

Roosevelt High School "had an ROTC [Reserve Officer Training Corps] band, a symphony orchestra, and a dance orchestra. There were three music theory classes taught by three different music teachers who also ran the bands." For instance, music teacher Harry Grappengeter was the conductor, or musical director, of the concert orchestra, which played symphonic classical music. When Chico Sesma attended Roosevelt High

1. Hollenbeck Junior High School marching/concert band, ca. 1936–37.
COURTESY CHICO SESMA.

School, he took every theory class and played trombone in the ROTC, concert, and dance bands.[47] Although Paul Lopez taught himself to play the cornet, as a teen he attended, in his words, a "handicapped school" with poor facilities that had neither music courses nor a school band. After demanding to be transferred to Roosevelt High, Lopez eagerly joined the school concert band on trumpet and, in the absence of "personal instruction on an instrument," took harmony classes.[48]

Another important member of this generational cohort, Don Tosti, was born in 1923 in El Paso, Texas. Tosti did not meet his father, who was originally from New Mexico, until his mid-twenties. When he was very young, his Mexican American mother, Carolina, moved to Los Angeles, where she "married well." Tosti stayed in the Segundo Barrio of El Paso, where he was raised in "humble surroundings" by his Mexican grandparents and his mother's two sisters. At their insistence, for two hours every day he studied seven musical instruments and practiced solfeggio vocal exercises with "several teachers—Mexican Indians who . . . were very schooled." A child prodigy, Tosti began playing violin in the El Paso

Symphony at the age of ten. The Anglo ladies in El Paso's wealthy social clubs "saw this little boy play with the symphony," so they would invite Tosti "for a recital to entertain them" at their women's meetings, then buy him clothes or a bicycle, or give him money. In 1939, after one year of Catholic high school in El Paso, Tosti moved to Boyle Heights, where he lived "in a very fine home" with his mother, stepbrother, and stepfather. His mother's new Mexicano husband owned a beautiful home and "a lot of property."[49] By this time, at the age of sixteen, Tosti also played bass, piano, clarinet, and soprano, alto, and baritone saxophones. Chico Sesma recalled that Don Tosti made quite a musical impact when he arrived at Roosevelt High, as he immediately began leading the school's concert orchestra.[50]

A major feature of the musical landscape Tosti entered was the Neighborhood Music School, which had been founded in 1932 by a Boyle Heights philanthropist, Pearl O'Dell. Supported entirely by voluntary subscriptions and annual memberships, this nonprofit enterprise provided "the finest of training at little to no cost" to a monthly average of 120 pupils of all races and ages. In an old two-story house on Boyle Avenue near Third Street, a staff of instructors taught a different instrument in each room, including piano, voice, violin, viola, cello, trumpet, trombone, and guitar, as well as music theory. The school's "civic-minded" board of directors only charged the children of the local working families fifty cents a lesson, those students who were unable to pay the fee received free lessons, and those who showed exceptional talent received scholarships.[51] The board's Progressive-era goal was to achieve "solid-Americanization in teaching of music to the underprivileged." Originally modeled after the settlement schools of Midwestern and Eastern cities, the Neighborhood Music School was considered "one of the finest of its kind in the country."[52]

According to the Los Angeles County Music Commission, the school was not only "indirectly helping in the fight against juvenile delinquency," but also developing "a new generation of musical talent" by preparing its students for the music profession and a chance for a better life.[53] Chico Sesma had been receiving private lessons at the school since he was twelve, and both he and Lopez learned classical music technique there. When their skills had developed sufficiently, their instructor, Mr. Bunton, sent them for further training to his teacher, Dr. Heiner, in Highland Park (see figures 2–4). Don Tosti also studied at the Neighborhood Music School while in high school, but he soon began giving twenty-five-cent violin lessons to

2. Fourteen-year-old Paul Lopez and Mr. Bunton, Neighborhood Music School instructor, 1937. COURTESY PAUL LOPEZ.

other youths. Sesma also eventually instructed local residents, including Ray Vasquez and Ray Baxter, two young men who would later sing professionally.[54] Such neighborhood lessons illustrate the importance of music education in nurturing creative talent, acquiring technical expertise, and instilling discipline for serious study, practice, and professionalization.

From a young age and throughout their lives, Sesma, Lopez, and Tosti used music to pursue knowledge, self-improvement, and career opportunities, such as jazz touring, that broadened their horizons. Sesma credited "music for having influenced our way of life. Culturally, it really developed us into very special individuals. . . . when one invests time in any of the arts, there is only one way for you to go, and that is upwards, in terms of personal development."[55] When their high school classes were out they practiced at home for three or four hours, in the evening they rehearsed with a band, and on the weekends they performed on the Eastside.

3. Fifteen-year-old Chico Sesma with trombone, 1939. COURTESY CHICO SESMA.
4. Seventeen-year-old Paul Lopez with trumpet, 1941. COURTESY PAUL LOPEZ.

Consequently, they had time for little else. As Sesma explained, "Music was my life in high school and I loved the big bands."[56]

The Second World War triggered many social disruptions and demographic shifts that changed the face of the neighborhood, especially the relocation and incarceration of 110,000 ethnic Japanese, two-thirds of them U.S. citizens, beginning in February 1942. Indeed, some four thousand Japanese and Japanese Americans from Boyle Heights alone were "transferred" to what was euphemistically called an "assembly center" in Parker, Arizona, and eventually more than thirty-four thousand from Los Angeles County were driven from their homes, farms, and businesses, then herded off to overcrowded camps.[57] After the Japanese internment, African American migrant war workers tried to escape a severe housing shortage in Watts and South Central Los Angeles by pouring into the suddenly vacated Little Tokyo, which promptly became known as "Bronzeville."[58] That same year, in 1942, the entire Flats section of Boyle Heights was destroyed with municipal and federal funds, and the huge Aliso Village–Pico Gardens public housing complex was built in its place.[59] Many African American renters moved into the Aliso Village units, on ground that had previously been an established black niche in the Russian Flats, and many also moved into the recently constructed Estrada Courts public housing projects in East Los Angeles.

Despite this historical black presence, compared to South Central Los Angeles or Watts, "there were hardly any blacks in East Los Angeles."[60] Still, one georacial study, based on the 1940 U.S. Census data, noted that 13 percent of Mexicans in the Los Angeles area lived in the twenty-nine census tracts where the "Negro" concentration was greatest.[61] Accordingly, further insight into the Mexican American generation and the racial geography of Los Angeles can be gained by comparing and contrasting Boyle Heights with Watts. Located seven miles south of downtown Los Angeles between Central Avenue and Alameda Street, Watts, originally a railroad town and a sugar beet farming community, was by World War II a blue-collar neighborhood. The war initiated major population migrations that would transform Watts into a segregated black ghetto, but in the 1920s it was a diverse neighborhood of Germans, Scots, Mexicans, African Americans, Italians, Greeks, Jews, and Japanese.[62] As the African American jazz drummer Minor Robinson observed, "In Watts during the 1930s most people were either civil service employees or domestic workers" or common laborers. People who worked at the post office and those who worked for the City of Los Angeles enjoyed a higher standard of living than their neighbors. Robinson added that "the Mexicans and whites were mostly working-class, but [the whites] could get jobs at Firestone, GM Corporation, whatever. If a black person wanted a job at Firestone he'd have to get the broom and sweep up the place."[63]

Out of this segmented labor market and multicultural milieu emerged the jazz saxophonist, clarinetist, and flautist Anthony Ortega, who was born in Watts in 1928, four to five years later than the Roosevelt High School musicians Sesma, Lopez, and Tosti. Ortega's personal story and professional career reveal examples of the Mexican American generation's expressive cultural output and energetic mojo spirit, while providing evidence of the period's urban civility. For instance, Anthony Ortega's mother, Amparo, born in El Paso, used to take the Red Car streetcar from Watts to downtown Los Angeles. Anthony's father, Genaro, born in La Paz, Baja California, met young Amparo in a downtown dance hall in 1923.[64] Thus, well before the swing era, the city's music scene brought people together in real, meaningful ways.

Anthony was born in his parents' Watts home, just like his older brother James, called "Jimmie," and his older sister Katherine. After Genaro and Amparo divorced, his older brother lived with their father, and seven-year-old Anthony and his sister stayed with their mother. Amparo later married

Refugio "Cuco" Araugo, who had picked oranges in Orange County. When Anthony was nine, his father, Genaro, died from complications during an operation at Los Angeles County Hospital. Ortega grew up blocks away from La Colonia, the Mexican barrio in Watts, but his elementary school was "pretty well integrated," with Mexicans, blacks, and whites, and he did not remember any residential segregation. In fact, he recalled that "everybody got along fine."[65] Minor Robinson noted that due to segregated hiring practices, although he "grew up in Los Angeles" he "never had a black teacher," from kindergarten through high school.[66] On the other hand, Anthony Ortega said, "about all the teachers I had were pretty congenial people. They didn't seem to have like [a] racial prejudice thing. . . . they were all pretty fair." Regarding his elementary school, Ortega stated that "if it was a combination of different kids . . . you felt more at home . . . with the different nationalities," and that "as time went, it really developed into a nice thing where you had a much more open view of everything." In other words, students gained "more of a broader scope."[67]

By 1940 Watts was evenly divided among Anglos, ethnic Mexicans, and African Americans. The 1940 U.S. Census listed six out of the eleven total tracts having approximately 8 to 19 percent Mexicans, and approximately 11 to 28 percent "Negroes," with industrial work the predominant occupation in every tract.[68] At this time many nearby white neighborhoods in South Central Los Angeles, such as Compton and Willowbrook, used restrictive housing covenants to systematically keep out African Americans. As Minor Robinson recalled, at all-white John C. Fremont High School, north of Watts and just east of Central Avenue, "they even hung a black effigy when the first black person went." In contrast, the Watts area's racial heterogeneity was reflected in its David Starr Jordan Senior High School, which included a junior high school on campus for the seventh, eighth, and ninth grades. During the late 1930s, by Robinson's account, Jordan High was approximately one-third white, one-third black, and one-third Mexican, with a few Japanese; but despite occasional fights, "we got along as well as you could possibly think. . . . We just all got along."[69]

Jordan had a brass marching band and also a symphonic concert orchestra for both the junior and senior high schools. The instrument classes were for beginners, but if seventh graders displayed the ability to play at a higher level, they would go straight to the senior band and orchestra. The school also offered a harmony class, a glee club, and an a capella choir.[70] The choir class was led by Martha Abbot, the harmony class by Mrs. Parsley, and the junior orchestra, senior band, senior orchestra, and instrument class by Joseph Louis Lippi. An elderly Italian American, Lippi knew enough about each instrument to get his pupils started, and he encouraged them to develop themselves as professional musicians. Toward that end, he gave them practical business advice, urging his saxophone players to learn a second instrument like the clarinet or the flute in order to "double" with the big bands.[71] Minor Robinson recalled that Lippi "was a good motivator. He made you feel that being a musician was an important thing and you'd gain a certain status in life if you were a musician. He wanted us to take it seriously."[72]

Around 1938, a new music teacher, Vern Martin, a jazz reed player, "shocked" people by introducing a few swing arrangements into the repertoire of the senior band. Meanwhile, at predominantly black Thomas Jefferson High School, the legendary music instructor Samuel Browne had started a student big band, which at that time included the saxophonist Dexter Gordon and the drummer Chico Hamilton. By 1939 Buddy Collette and other Jordan High student musicians started a separate student swing band, calling themselves the Jordan Hep Cats.[73] In African American slang, "hep" meant to be wise, sophisticated, or in the know, and "cat" meant a musician in a swing band. Eventually two Jordan swing bands emerged, the Senior Hep Cats, upperclassmen who played in Lippi's class, and the Junior Hep Cats, seventh, eighth, and ninth graders who played sophisticated Count Basie arrangements in Martin's class.

In 1943, fifteen-year-old Anthony Ortega joined the Junior Hep Cats, which was then composed of twelve African American musicians, along with the trumpeter Albert "Kiki" Ybarra, the bassist Reyes Gaglio, a next-door neighbor of Ortega's who had an Italian father and a Mexican mother, and the drummer Jesús "Chuy" Ruiz, a friend of Ortega's who abandoned the pachuco lifestyle for that of the jazz musician (see figure 5).[74] For these young men, having the option to join a swing band in high school made a profound difference in their lives. For example, Ruiz would say later that if he "hadn't started playing music," he "probably would have ended up in the penitentiary or shot" like all of his friends in the neighborhood gang.[75] Instead, when Ruiz "started playing the drums, that's all he wanted to do, which . . . kept him out of trouble."[76] Another Mexican American youth, Rudy Loara, hung out with the pachucos in Watts until he "started taking up trumpet in the band there with Mr. Lippi."[77]

In addition to Jordan High's music curriculum, marching band, con-

5. Jordan High School Junior Hep Cats, 1943. COURTESY ANTHONY ORTEGA.

cert orchestra, choir, and two swing bands, special talent show assemblies were held twice a year, open to any pupil who wished to perform in front of the student body. After only one year of musical experience, Anthony Ortega performed at the assembly with the Junior Hep Cats, but when he stepped up to the microphone for a saxophone solo on a Glenn Miller arrangement of a blues song called "It Must Be Jelly 'Cause Jam Don't Shake Like That," he "tightened up." Rather than "playing a bunch of really like hip stuff, or a lot of notes," Ortega started "ridin' a note, like the old black cats used to play," and the audience of his peers clapped and cheered approvingly. The effect on Ortega was instantaneous. On campus, everyone suddenly knew and respected him (see figure 6). "Those talent shows [gave] a guy confidence." After that day, "there was one thing . . . in this world I felt confident in. . . . therefore, I had more self-esteem with anything I tried to do, whether it was a failure or not."[78]

Ortega's creative endeavors at Jordan High were typical of this period, when, as a 1940 essay on music in the Los Angeles public schools noted, "every junior high has its orchestra. Many have bands studying as regular classes and contributing greatly to the life of the schools through

6. Fifteen-year-old Anthony Ortega with saxophone, 1943.
COURTESY ANTHONY ORTEGA.

programs and various public gatherings." In a positive but veiled reference
to the jazz and swing introduced at Jefferson, Jordan, and other inner city
schools, the essayist noted that in "the senior high schools, a still more
colorful array of instrumental music is found, which contributes educational and cultural opportunities to participating students and enrichment
to the lives of all students." Certainly this aptly describes the impact of
grass-roots jazz music curricula, swing bands, and talent assemblies, all of
which provided "the opportunities for self-expression that come through
musical participation."[79]

While many youngsters performed "the more popular types of instrumental music," a select group of the most talented public school students
were chosen to partake in the All City Junior High School Orchestra,
which gave them the opportunity to rehearse every week in a classical

symphony setting, and "to interpret standard orchestral works." Promising instrumentalists were culled from the area's senior high schools to form the All City High School Orchestra, which performed "not only in many school and public concerts but also on local and national broadcasts, demonstrating a quality of work approaching professional standards."[80] Apparently this city-sponsored institution represented a model meritocracy, for the violin virtuoso from Roosevelt High School, Don Tosti, held the concert chair as concertmaster of the All City High School Orchestra from 1939 to 1941.[81] Five years later, Anthony Ortega joined the orchestra, which performed "concert music," or what he called "light-weight classical." As Ortega noted, "They had musicians from all over the city, from the schools. . . . we went out for auditions, and they picked you out." In addition to Ortega, his friend "Chuy Ruiz and a few others were chosen from Jordan, and Eric Dolphy was chosen from [Susan Miller] Dorsey [Senior High School]." To showcase the orchestra, the city put on an All City Band Festival at the Shrine Auditorium.[82]

This symphonic concert orchestra gave Ortega experience and exposure, but jazz remained his true love, and, like his counterparts at Roosevelt High School, he spent many hours practicing and studying. For instance, Paul Lopez remembered going to visit the teenage Ortega's house in Watts, where "his mother would be cooking beans, and he'd be practicing his scales right in the kitchen."[83] Like many black Angeleno jazz instrumentalists, one of the biggest influences on Ortega's life was the African American music instructor Lloyd Reese. Ironically, it was not one of Ortega's black Watts neighbors like Charles Mingus who put him in touch with Reese, but his Mexican American cousin, Ray Vasquez, who grew up in Boyle Heights but was then living in Watts and attending Jordan High School, where he sang in the choir and played trombone. Vasquez, who was a few years older, told Ortega to see "a private teacher" for lessons, "because you can only learn so much in the class at school."[84] Vasquez gave Reese's phone number to Ortega, who began taking the streetcar downtown to receive lessons for three dollars an hour.

Reese, an excellent trumpeter and saxophonist who played in both a swing orchestra and, occasionally, in the Hollywood movie studio orchestras, "had a way of communicating" with the youngsters under his tutelage, who looked up to him as "a perfect, well-respected man."[85] Studying with Reese from the age of fifteen until the age of twenty, Ortega practiced exercises out of Paul de Ville's 1908 tome, *Universal Method for Saxophone*, learned "facility . . . reading, and all the different keys," and gained "a good foundational background." Ortega called Reese "a good influence, a mentor, a role model. Everyone respected him."[86] Although Reese specialized in a system for mastering harmony and transposition, in essence, he ran a one-man conservatory out of his home, teaching mechanics and fundamentals, but also "musical philosophy." Moreover, he organized a Sunday rehearsal at the black musicians union local, where his students would work out their ideas alongside professional musicians, and where, as Minor Robinson recalled, "he'd have charts there for you to play, and he'd explain to you how it's done."[87] Reese also held band rehearsals one night a week at the playground of the Ross Snyder Recreation Center, where Compton Avenue meets 41st Street, a few blocks east of Jefferson High School. Young Mexican American and African American musicians from throughout the city would converge there for swinging rehearsal sessions and informal networking. Through these weekly practices Ortega met two Lincoln Heights Mexican American musicians his age—Ray Lugo, who was also studying with Reese, and Maurice Vendrell—as well as Eric Dolphy, then a student of Reese's.[88]

These practices and rehearsals were part of a foundation of formal and informal music education undergirding the jazz scene. Private music teachers like Bill Green also flourished in South Central Los Angeles, as did private institutions like the Gray Conservatory of Music and the Western School of Music. In 1933, Samuel Browne became the first African American high school teacher in the entire Los Angeles Unified School District when he was hired at his alma mater, Jefferson High School, as a music instructor. An accomplished pianist, Browne earned master's degrees in music and education from the University of Southern California. In addition to classical music and opera, he taught music reading, theory, harmony, counterpoint, arranging, and composing, and he encouraged his African American and Mexican American students to find private teachers for intensive study of their respective instruments. Browne conducted the school marching band and symphony orchestra, he organized student jam sessions, and he created a student swing band, for which he arranged concerts at predominantly white schools like Fairfax High on the Westside and Taft High in the San Fernando Valley. He also scheduled field trips to the Hollywood rehearsals of jazz stars, and invited professional musicians, visiting artists and former students alike, to play school assemblies, and to talk to, sit in with, and try out new arrangements on his young music students.

One of Samuel Browne's earlier protégés, a Mexican American swing pianist named Charles Caballero, would often come back to Jefferson High and talk to the students in the big band. Browne's guidance led Caballero to attend USC and eventually become a principal of nearby Thomas Edison Middle School. Browne was a visionary educator, mentor, and role model who gave his pupils the opportunity to study, compose, arrange, and perform jazz music. Devoted, respected, and inspirational, he would recruit budding musicians from junior high schools in the area and visit his students' homes to check up on them and meet their families. In short, Browne created the best music program in the city, and one of the best in the nation, on a par with those at Sidney Miller High School and Cass Technical High School in Detroit, Wendell Phillips High School in Chicago, and the historically black public high schools Douglass, Manassas, and Booker T. Washington in Memphis. Each of these school music programs treated jazz music as a serious discipline, emphasizing its theory and its practice, and were thus at least thirty years ahead of the rest of the country.[89]

Moreover, as seen in Los Angeles, the music instructors understood that many of their young students were already working evening and weekend jobs throughout the city.[90] For example, while Don Tosti was in high school he led a swing orchestra that included the Jewish American singer Nancy Norman, the drummer Al Rothberg, and the trumpeter Bernie Menecker, as well as the Mexican American singer Ray Vasquez, the female pianist Nelly Gonzalez, the trumpeter Paul Lopez, and the trombonist Chico Sesma. The Don Tosti Orchestra performed at Boyle Heights neighborhood weddings, at Betty's Barn, east of downtown, and at Diana's Ballroom on Pico Boulevard, west of downtown, as well as at more upscale spots like the Paramount Ballroom downtown, and the Avedon Ballroom, where Spring Street meets Main Street at Olympic Boulevard.

As early as 1937, the Roosevelt High School musicians Paul Lopez, Chico Sesma, and Don Tosti used to watch local Mexican American big bands rehearse in Boyle Heights in the back of Phillips Music Store, where the Jewish American owner, William Phillips, had converted a small room into a rehearsal area.[91] Phillips himself had played drums in a Navy band, and he worked as a recording studio fill-in percussionist for jazz bandleaders, played swing dance music in downtown Los Angeles, Hollywood, and Long Beach clubs, and occasionally played drums, timpani, and vibraphone in the Hollywood studio orchestras. Phillips started his music store in 1935, selling big band instruments and giving neighborhood musicians fifty-cent lessons. One of his students was a young Mexican American named Andrés Rábago Pérez, who took drum lessons as a youth and went on to become a famous singer under the stage name Andy Russell. Phillips Music Store, with its rare records, private listening booths, and designated practice area, served as a neighborhood resource for Mexican Americans like Sesma, whose parents bought him his first trombone there when he was in junior high school, and for Jewish Americans like Jules Titlebaum, a local trumpeter who later became a superior court judge.[92] Like the Neighborhood Music School, William Phillips helped train and sustain a pool of talented local musicians.

By the late 1930s, and continuing through the war years, Boyle Heights and East Los Angeles boasted fifteen- to twenty-piece jazz bands composed predominantly of Mexican American musicians. While still in high school, Paul Lopez joined the largest and most popular of them, the Sal Cervantes Orchestra, which also included the trombonists Fernando Venetia, Chico Sesma, and Wendy Torres, the saxophonists Antonio "Tony" Alonso, Manuel Ybarra, and George Rosen, the Lincoln Heights jazz singer Lily Ramírez, the drummer Hideo Kawano (who used the stage name "Joe Young" to avoid anti-Japanese hostility), the pianist Bobby Gil, the guitarist Luis Arvizo, and the band manager Raul Chavez (see figures 7 and 8).[93] Other Eastside bandleaders included Freddy Rubio, Eddie Castillo, Frank Delgado, the Armenta Brothers, and Phil Carreon, whose swing band featured the Jewish American songwriter, arranger, and Roosevelt High alumnus Lennie Niehaus, as well as the Mexican American saxophonist Ray Ramos, and the Mexicano singer Johnny Rico.[94] The De La Torre Brothers and Tilly Lopez orchestras were society bands in the nonswinging hotel style.

The Eastside swing bands playeds "carbon copy" cover versions of the popular tunes of Glenn Miller, Jimmie Lunceford, Duke Ellington, Harry James, and Benny Goodman from seventy-five-cent stock arrangements. However, they also played a bolero, ranchera, conga, or rumba "every now and then" to "identify" themselves, to distinguish themselves from local Anglo swing bands, and to please their audience of young Mexican Americans. Moreover, Sal Cervantes hired an arranger who would write some

7. Sal Cervantes Orchestra, on stage, Royal Palms Hotel, 1941. COURTESY PAUL LOPEZ.
8. Sal Cervantes Orchestra, in lobby, Royal Palms Hotel, 1941. COURTESY PAUL LOPEZ.

special arrangements of original tunes. As this chapter's final epigraph illustrates, downtown dance halls drew Mexican American dancers by hiring Mexican American bands like the Sal Cervantes Orchestra, as well as African American bands like the George Brown and the Irwin Brothers orchestras. In fact, the Sal Cervantes Orchestra used to compete against the George Brown Orchestra in "battle of the bands" several times a year in Boyle Heights at the Angelus Hall on First and State streets, and at the Paramount Ballroom on Brooklyn Avenue and Mott Street, as well as at Diana's Ballroom.[95] In 1943 Don Tosti disbanded his orchestra and began playing tenor saxophone with the Cervantes Orchestra. In downtown Los Angeles, Mexican American musicians performed all along Main Street, playing straight-ahead jazz at the Waldorf Cellar, Harold's Club, and the Burbank Theater, and even backing up burlesque dancers at the Follies Theater.[96]

In addition, Mexican American music lovers attended the All Nations Club at First and Main streets, and the New Mexico–Arizona Club at Second and Spring streets.[97] Downtown, Arthur Arenas stated, "there were a lot of blacks, a lot of Mexicans. . . . if you liked big band music . . . you had your choice, because it was packed. Everybody would go downtown. You'd see every color and creed downtown."[98] In the sensual nocturnal world of the dance hall, "there were lights, exciting lights," Gloria Rios remembered. "They had a huge mirrored ball and they shone different colors on it. And there was a lot of romantic music and they would dim the lights when you would dance to 'Embraceable You.'" In addition to "very romantic ballads . . . there was a lot of exciting dancing and songs pertaining to jitterbugging."[99] Clearly, Mexican Americans contributed considerably to the swing era's "democratization of dance hall culture," and they also produced their own tradition of social club dances.[100]

For example, the Zenda Ballroom, at Seventh and Figueroa streets, across from the downtown Los Angeles Hilton Hotel, attracted young Mexican American couples dancing the jitterbug. A Mexican American named Joe Garcia leased the Zenda, hiring Don Tosti's high school swing band to play for his weekly Club Juvenil Social dances.[101] In addition, Garcia copied a Mexico City tradition by hosting an annual "black and white ball" at the Royal Palms Hotel, located near MacArthur Park on South Westlake Avenue, and also at the Los Angeles Breakfast Club, off Los Feliz Boulevard near Griffith Park.[102] Joe Garcia founded this grand, classy black-tie affair "as the President of 'El Club Alegria,' and it became a bit of a money maker for him." It "was something to look forward to" and "a big deal for all the young men and ladies," who would wear rented tuxedos and white gowns. Out of several candidates, a black and white ball queen was crowned, and a handsome Italian American couple, Bertha and Tony Russi, were often "the main attraction." Joe Garcia also held Saturday night dances at the Royal Palms Hotel that were very popular among Mexican Americans.[103] As Paul Lopez revealed, in addition to the "black and white" balls at "Mexican social clubs" on the Eastside, and the various nightclubs downtown, there were ballrooms throughout the metropolitan area that would book big bands, and "Mexicans would go" dancing "among the Americans."[104]

Carey McWilliams has observed that during the war years many young Mexican Americans were lured beyond their neighborhoods "into the downtown shopping districts, to the beaches, and above all, to the 'glamor' of Hollywood."[105] Indeed, driving their automobiles, borrowing the car of an older friend, relative, or priest, taking the streetcar, or else sharing a taxi with friends, young Mexican Americans crisscrossed Los Angeles to hear the popular orchestras of the day. For instance, in July 1941 Duke Ellington's musical revue *Jump for Joy* premiered downtown at the Mayan Theater, which catered to African Americans and Mexican Americans, and seventeen-year-old Vince Ramírez took a cab from East Los Angeles to see the show during its run.[106] In 1943, nineteen-year-old Mary Gonzalez was living with her father in Watts and working at the Firestone tire factory in the Southeast Los Angeles city of Florence. Mary labored at her "monotonous" nonunion job cutting patterns out of rubber next to other young Mexican American Angelenas, and whites from Oklahoma, Arkansas, and Tennessee. Like other single, working-class Mexican Americans, Mary spent much of her pay on nice clothes, and many of her evenings out dancing. While her suitor, Gene Hernandez, was waiting to be sent to the Pacific theater, they danced the jitterbug in nearby South Gate, across town in Venice beach, and, frequently, in Hollywood at the Palladium. It was Gene who introduced Mary to "Duke Ellington, and Count Basie, and all the black jazz bands." The couple saw Lionel Hampton perform downtown at the Million Dollar Theater on Broadway at Third Street, where the crowd consisted primarily of well-dressed African Americans. When Duke Ellington played at the Orpheum Theater on Broadway at Ninth Street, the "good-looking blacks" that rolled up in their fancy cars impressed Mary, particularly "the upper crust" women, "slick looking" in their silver and gold trim dresses, and their fur capes.[107]

Edward Martinez Rodriguez, who was fifteen years old in 1941, saw black artists like Duke Ellington, Count Basie, Cab Calloway, and Lionel Hampton, but also white artists like Harry James, Les Brown, Tommy Dorsey, and Jimmy Dorsey. Rodriguez went downtown to the Million Dollar Theater, the Orpheum Theater, and, on Grand Avenue at Sixth Street, the Paramount Theater, but also to the Hollywood Palladium.[108] Similarly, Gloria Vargas, a working-class "Zoot Suit girl" from Lincoln Heights who often won playground dance contests at her high school, would attend various ballrooms and theaters around town with her friends whenever their favorite bands were playing. She loved the challenge and recognition of the dance contests, and "the high that [she] would get hearing the band playing."[109] Arthur Arenas "followed the big bands" to "nice" places like "the Casino Gardens" in Ocean Park or "the Palladium."[110]

The fact that these working-class Mexican American youths patronized the tony Hollywood Palladium illustrates their deepening assimilation into, as well as their curious racial position in, mainstream American culture. On Sunset Boulevard between Gower Street and El Centro Avenue, the Hollywood Palladium was the premiere venue for visiting name swing bands in wartime Los Angeles, six nights a week. The famous house of big bands was originally opened in 1940 "to provide a dancing spot with the atmosphere of a 'class' Hollywood supper club, but at prices within the means of the general public."[111] However, as we will see in the next chapter, this "better-class dance palace," which accommodated several thousand people with its two long balconies overlooking its spacious, solid white ash dance floor, would often deny entrance to potential paying customers based on their appearance, especially if they were Mexican American or black zoot suiters.[112] Nevertheless, fifteen-year-old Chico Sesma's mother took him to the Palladium to see "his idol" Tommy Dorsey.[113] Vince Ramírez "used to go [from East Los Angeles] to the Palladium a lot." As he said, "I never had any problem getting in. None of my friends did."[114] Don Tosti noted that "the audience at the Palladium was Anglo, although a lot of us Latins went."[115] Hortencia Esquivel and her Mexican American friends "would get a ride" to the Palladium from West Los Angeles "once in a while."[116] The Lincoln Heights pachuca Soledad "Chole" Camarena stated that although the establishment catered to a higher class of people, and was prejudiced against pachucos and black zoot suiters, she went there on two occasions to see Jimmy Dorsey and Tex Beneke.[117]

Yet Mexican Americans' excursions to Hollywood were to dance at the Palladium, not to dally or mingle after the show. As Mary Hernandez explained, "It wasn't like we walked the streets or went into restaurants."[118] Although people may have mixed in particular dance venues, this contact did not necessarily continue outside of the music scene, or back in their respective neighborhoods. However, clearly people kept mixing in high schools, record stores, and other sites. Moreover, the fact that people of color were unwelcome in certain sectors only highlights the power of their presence in nonsegregated spaces, as the city's urban civility changed over time across musical genres, and manifested itself differently across neighborhoods.

For example, a small but adventurous number of Mexican Americans were drawn to Central Avenue by the siren song of African American music in the early 1940s.[119] Eloisa "Loi" Vigil and Magdalena "Nany" Vigil, two jazz fan sisters from South Central Los Angeles who grew up in close proximity to African Americans, often hung out on the Avenue, where they would see Count Basie and Duke Ellington without incident.[120] Other Mexican Americans who strolled Central Avenue included Henry "Hank" Leyvas, the lead defendant in the infamous Sleepy Lagoon trial, and his sister Lupe Leyvas, both from Vernon, an industrial district just south and east of downtown. Vince Ramírez once went to the Plantation Club, on Central Avenue at 108th Street in Watts, when he took "a white girl" to see Dizzy Gillespie.[121] The Plantation Club was like a barn with "sawdust all over the floor," where all the best out-of-town black big bands stopped.[122] Chole Camarena "loved to dance to . . . black music."[123] Her pachuco friend Emil and her pachuca friend Josie also dug black music, and the three of them would dance to the bands of Count Basie and Jimmie Lunceford at the Plantation Club, then, after two in the morning, share a cab back to Lincoln Heights.

They would also rub elbows with African Americans during weekend matinee dances at the Elks Hall on Central Avenue at 40th Street.[124] The three-story Elks Hall held from five to six hundred people, and the Woodman Brothers Orchestra played afternoon dances on the smaller second floor auditorium, whereas the big bands played on Saturday nights in the first floor auditorium, which had a beautiful stage and balcony.[125] According to Chole Camarena, they never experienced any interracial animosity on Central Avenue, and "the blacks were friendly as long as the Mexicans talked to them."[126] One male Mexican American zoot suiter from the Echo Park neighborhood used to listen to jam sessions at "the Chicken Basket" on Central Avenue. A zoot suiter named Maria recalled that "Mexicans, blacks, Filipinos, and even the white kids" danced to the big bands on Central Avenue, and that "the black guys always looked so sharp and were the best dancers. We used to love to dance with them."[127] Unlike the Hollywood Anglos who went "slumming" at the Club Alabam, these young Mexican Americans engaged in real cross-cultural exchanges and forged a mutual acknowledgment based on respect.

In addition to the Eastside, downtown, and South Central musical outlets, there were also several big band venues frequented by Mexican Americans from the city's four historical Westside Mexican barrios: Culver City, Venice, Santa Monica, and Sawtelle/West Los Angeles.[128] Hortencia Esquivel, whose Mexican parents owned and operated a *tienda* (store), spent her early childhood in Santa Ana, Orange County, and her adolescence in the Sawtelle and West Los Angeles neighborhoods, just west of Sepulveda Boulevard, above and below Santa Monica Boulevard, respectively. This area contained a mix of Anglos and Mexican Americans. Hortencia, her best friend Suzy Villa, and Suzy's Mexican American friends from University High School in Westwood "loved dancing all the time." Hortencia, who was fifteen years old in 1944, started dancing very early, like many of her peers. They were underage, but they "dressed like [they] were nineteen." They would take the streetcar to the Casino Gardens ballroom in Ocean Park, the small beach community sandwiched between Santa Monica and Venice, then catch a ride back home. Owned by Jimmy and Tommy Dorsey, who "always played there," and located on the amusement pier in Ocean Park, the Casino Gardens was "the place to be." The clientele was predominantly Mexican American and Anglo, but the two groups did not dance or socialize together. In fact, even the Mexican Americans from the four different Westside barrios largely kept to themselves in different corners of the Casino Gardens dance floor. Depending on which band was playing, Hortencia and her friends would also occasionally go to the Casa Mañana in Culver City and to the Aragon Ballroom in Venice.[129]

Given the Jim Crow geography of Los Angeles, there were no African Americans at these Westside venues. Likewise, there were no blacks present when Vince Ramírez went dancing to big bands at the Pasadena Civic

Auditorium, or when he saw Louis Armstrong at the Trianon Ballroom.[130] Mexican Americans therefore patronized whites-only establishments like the Palladium in Hollywood, which barred blacks in the early 1940s, the Aragon in Venice, "another ballroom that blacks couldn't even go into," and the Trianon Ballroom in South Gate, where local ordinances prohibited the "mixing of races in nightclubs, ballrooms, and restaurants."[131] Dora Rico, whose oldest brother was a ballet dancer and owned every Glenn Miller record, and whose sister and brother-in-law were "jitterbug champions," put it this way: "As Chicanos, we never had to go in no back door."[132] The Mexican American Angelenos of the swing era thus used their slim but significant racial advantage vis-à-vis African Americans, from the Eastside to the beach, from Hollywood to South Central. While members of the Mexican American generation were constrained by restrictive housing covenants and other forms of real estate discrimination, they refused to be sidelined by social segregation.

Rather than illustrating an inherent downside to this refusal, the evidence underscores the contradictions of the racial order itself. Just as the development of urban civility was not uniform, the system of segregation was breaking down unevenly, as the ideology of the white racial state adapted to challenges to its legitimacy. For generations, segregation meant the separation of all people of color from whites, but it was beginning to mean the separation of blacks from whites, white ethnics, and some Mexican Americans. In California, where the Anglo social, economic, and legislative systems historically discriminated against Indians, Mexicans, and Asians, the increased spatial mobility and greater dance hall access insisted on by Mexican Americans defied their own general segregation, but it did not tacitly support that of African Americans. Instead, by demanding a full run of the city and insisting on equal access and fair treatment, male and female Mexican American dancers, singers, and musicians, often still in high school, contributed to a multicultural swing scene, a democratic civil society, and an ethnic expressive culture.

As part of these politicized dynamics, and in the context of the larger social, economic, and racial processes of the swing era, some Mexican American musicians played gigs and jammed in South Central Los Angeles. For example, Paul Lopez worked an engagement at the Club Alabam once with Johnny Otis's swing band, and he sometimes went down to Central Avenue to play in jazz jam sessions.[133] At one point, Don Tosti worked after hours in the house band at the Flamingo Club, on Central

Avenue and San Pedro Boulevard.[134] While black bands on the Avenue would hire an occasional white musician like the pianist Joe Albany, as well as Mexican American musicians like the trombonist Chico Sesma and the trumpeter Ruben McFall, black musicians did not yet play in East Los Angeles, nor did they play in all of the same venues as Mexican Americans. In essence, as Art Farmer argued, "the white people could come and work on Central Avenue, but the blacks had trouble coming to work in Hollywood."[135]

Sesma, Lopez, Tosti, and Ortega enjoyed one key advantage over their black peers: their membership in the segregated Anglo "Musicians Mutual Protective Association" union local. The whites-only Los Angeles Local 47 of the American Federation of Musicians was founded in 1897 "to organize musicians," and to "offer material rewards for protection, higher wages, [and] better working conditions."[136] Located downtown on Georgia Street, just east of Figueroa Street between Olympic and Pico boulevards, by the late 1930s the jurisdiction of Local 47 embraced "all the territory within a radius of 25 miles of the Los Angeles City Hall," an area that "includes the most varied classifications of musicians in the world, symphonic groups, ensembles, brass bands, dance bands, radio orchestras, motion picture orchestras, and virtually all other types of music and musicians." As of 1940,

> The person who would be adopted by the association of musicians . . . must make application to the A.F. of M. Next he must deposit $52.50 with the treasurer of the local. . . . Then and only then is he permitted to prove his merits. This he does by examination before a committee appointed for the purpose. Should he prove himself musically fit, in the eyes of the committee, he is subject to final approval by the board of directors.[137]

Union funds were "raised by admission fees, quarterly dues, fines" and "assessments," and members benefited from "the impressive treasury of the association," from a "revolving unemployment fund," and from the "employment division" at the union headquarters, charged with "seeking out engagements and recommending worthy members for employment. . . . In the case of motion picture studios, the local association holds no autonomy . . . insisting on nothing except that only members of Local 47 be employed." As a result of these and other "advantages . . . of holding a card in a union," "the musician of 1940 maintain[ed]" such a high standard of living that "his personal rung on the social ladder [was] nearer the top than the bottom."[138]

Membership certainly had its privileges, but these financial rewards rested on an apartheid architecture of locals that was common in every American city except Detroit and New York.[139] Excluded from membership in the white local, African American musicians in Los Angeles chartered the black union Local 767 in 1920. Originally located on Jefferson Boulevard near Jefferson High School, by the 1940s Local 767 had moved north toward downtown to Central Avenue and 18th Street. Buddy Collette recalled "a case where some of the white musicians tried to join our Local and weren't allowed."[140] However, the Jewish American saxophonist Rene Bloch, who played with Johnny Otis's all-black band, claimed that "Local 767 would accept musicians who were not black."[141] The Mexican American pianist Frank Ortega, who, like Bloch, was a former Jefferson High School bandmember and a student of Samuel Browne, also joined the black local. Bloch remembered that Frank Ortega "played his own style of piano, like Count Basie style," and that he later "had his own band at one of the big hotels" in an age when a black musician would never be allowed to play in, much less lead, the house orchestra at any of the city's white hotels.[142]

During the 1940s, some Mexican American Angelenos did not want to be associated too closely with African Americans, against whom they were often pitted in the workforce. For instance, in 1943 Don Tosti joined the white Local 47 of the musicians union because, as he said, "I had nothing to do with the blacks, man."[143] Although Tosti claimed that the decisive factors in getting work were simply one's technical ability and flair for self-promotion, membership in the white local also gave Mexican American musicians access to better jobs. African American Angeleno jazz musicians like Buddy Collette understood all too well the relationship between race and remuneration, for "the fact remained that Local 767 was treated as a subsidiary. All the work came into the white Local."[144] Regarding such discrepancies, Minor Robinson felt that the separate union locals "didn't seem right . . . because the 47 at that time had locked up a lot of the good jobs. They'd sign a contract with a club; they'd only use 47 musicians."[145] As Lee Young remembered, "they had double standards, different rules. The black musicians . . . worked seven days a week when they worked clubs. The white musicians, Local 47, they were not allowed to work but six nights a week, but they got seven nights' pay. That's the way it was."[146]

Even when black and white musicians worked the same type of jobs, Lionel Hampton recalled, black musicians in Los Angeles were paid about one-fifth of what white musicians made.[147] Although the dues were less in the black local, the pay scale was higher in the white local, and Barney Bigard, who had studied in New Orleans under the famed Mexican music instructor Lorenzo Tio Jr. in the quintessentially Creole Seventh Ward, claimed his Creole identity over his "Negro" status.[148]

Mexican Americans were aware of the wage differential between the two Locals. Accordingly, Anthony Ortega joined Local 47 because "it was considered a stronger union, and it was bigger."[149] Since "all the best gigs were [with] the white musicians union," Ortega reasoned, the Mexican American musicians "would join the white union." In short, "If you belonged to the [Local] 47, well, your chances were better."[150] Sesma remembered that "whatever Mexicans there were, when we joined the union we had no problem joining the white union. We passed."[151] Of course, Mexican American musicians were not literally "passing" as white, but their place in the dominant culture's black-white binary is illustrated by the fact that even among wartime "all-girl" swing orchestras, "in some locations, black women passed as Mexican to play in white bands."[152] As Anthony Ortega stated bluntly, "Everybody knew that the white union had more advantage, so if they were able to . . . they were going to join that. They don't want to be held down any more than they already have."[153] Mexican Americans therefore benefited from their membership in an exclusive club, seizing the opportunity to taste the economic, if not all of the social, "wages of whiteness."[154] The Local 47 admission of Mexican Americans tested the boundaries of their broader segregation, and implied a certain complicity with that of African Americans, therefore revealing the often contradictory contour lines of the swing-era multicultural urban civility.

Despite the prevailing preferential arrangements of the day, however, a few African Americans managed to integrate the Hollywood motion picture orchestras during the 1940s, as did the drummer-timpanist Chico Guerrero and the bassist Tony Reyes, two Mexican American Angelenos who worked in the Metro-Goldwyn-Mayer (MGM) orchestra.[155] In 1940, Mexican trumpeter Rafael Mendez moved to Hollywood, where he joined the MGM orchestra, made solo appearances in several films, cut 154 records on the Decca label, appeared on the Bing Crosby radio show, and, in 1945, recorded with Paul Whiteman.[156] Yet, in the case of Mexican Americans, union membership alone did not guarantee full access to the Hollywood studios. Even as Mexican Americans seemingly stepped closer to becoming white ethnic Americans, they still remained a racial other, they still faced some barriers that their Anglo, Jewish, and Italian American peers did not, and they were often forced to make concessions in order to survive in the music business. For instance, Don Tosti was denied jobs several times early in his career because of his surname, Tostado, which translates as "toasted" in English. After forming his first band during high school, he was advised to shorten and Americanize Edmundo Tostado to "Don Toastie," but he resented having to change his name to succeed in the music business, especially when it sounded like a popular breakfast cereal. He compromised by spelling his new stage name like the nineteenth-century Italian composer Paolo Tosti, whose music he had studied.[157]

Another swing-era musician who experienced frustrations with, and discrimination by, a music industry that never knew what to do with Mexican Americans, was Lalo Guerrero. Even though he did not emerge from the same social landscape as Don Tosti, Chico Sesma, Paul Lopez, and Anthony Ortega, the similarities and differences in Guerrero's upbringing reveal the "range of variation" in the Mexican American generation, and, during the course of his career, he made his musical reputation in Los Angeles. Lalo was born in 1917 in Tucson, Arizona, and raised there by his father, Eduardo Guerrero, born in La Paz and raised in Guaymas, Sonora, and his mother, Concepción Murietta, born and raised in Santa Ana, Sonora. In the Tucson barrio, Lalo enjoyed *rancheras*, *corridos*, and *norteño* accordion songs, as well as Burl Ives ballads and Bob Wills and His Texas Playboys. From the Hollywood musicals screening at the local theater, he learned American pop songs and tap-dancing. By age ten, Guerrero had taught himself to play the family piano. In his first public performance, as a fifth grader, he sang and tap-danced "Mammy" in full blackface, with black suit and white gloves, at a public elementary school assembly. When Guerrero was twelve, his music teacher taught him how to recognize the solo instruments in classical music recordings by ear, and when he was fourteen his mother taught him "classic Mexican songs" on the guitar.[158] At seventeen, Guerrero wrote "Canción mexicana" ("Mexican Song"), which incorporated a medley of treasured staples like "Cielito lindo" and "Mi rancho grande," and which became part of the national culture of Mexico after being recorded by Mexican ranchera stars Lucha Reyes and Lola Beltrán. Like his childhood friends, Lalo was also "drawn to" jazz, the blues, and black dance styles at a neighborhood nightclub, particularly "the trumpet and the sax and the electric guitar." He "was captivated by that music," and "night after night" he would stand outside the club, "watching the dancers and listening to the band." Regarding "those black musicians," he said, "their music got into my blood."[159]

In 1934, during seventeen-year-old Lalo's senior year in high school, his father voluntarily repatriated the family to Mexico City. There Guerrero absorbed "a whole new world of . . . tremendous orchestras, beautiful melodies," regional rhythms, and magnificent Mexican composers and singers, including a rhyming, improvising street vocal trio. His fourteen-year-old cousin taught him so many Mexican songs on the guitar that Lalo filled up an entire tablet transcribing them. After three months the family moved back to Tucson, and, to help support them during the Great Depression, Lalo began performing his new Mexico City repertoire for tips in local bars with three other guitarists. Known as Los Carlistas, they "vocalized in harmony." In 1937 and 1938 they tried to make it in Los Angeles, where their local connection, Frank Robles, booked them on a Spanish-language radio station for an early morning remote broadcast from the California Theater on Main Street. Robles met a Hollywood agent named Francisco Miguel, who landed them a bit part singing in a Mexican restaurant scene in a Gene Autry movie and who secured them engagements at the whites-only Cotton Club, which catered to its Culver City film studio clientele, and at exclusive Hollywood nightclubs like Omar's Dome on Western Avenue, and the Trocadero.[160] Los Carlistas also performed for affluent Anglo Angelenos downtown at Club La Bamba, on Spring Street near the original pueblo plaza and Catholic church. At "the Bamba Club," where "95 percent of the customers were Anglo," they played "the Mexican standards that [whites] were familiar with," but then they "added the conga from the Caribbean, and the customers would form long lines and dance around the room and among the tables." After returning to Tucson, then performing in New York City "on one of the most popular radio programs in America, *The Major Bowes Amateur Hour*," while representing Arizona at the 1939 World's Fair, the group broke up. That same year, Guerrero briefly tried his luck again in Los Angeles, singing at El Charro and, with fellow guitarist Lupe Fernandez, serenading customers at Café Caliente.[161]

At first glance, it may not seem that Lalo Guerrero's early career in Los Angeles fits neatly into this book's main arguments. At the height of the swing era and the jitterbug craze, here were Los Carlistas, guitars in hand, wearing bright *serapes* and either white muslin peasant garb—*huarache* sandals with white socks and straw sombreros—or black *charro* costumes, black shoes, and black sombreros, entertaining rich Hollywood Anglos as part of a "Latin" floor show, singing during the intermissions between musical sets, and strolling among the tables in the Mexican mariachi tradition.[162] The Hollywood clubs, and their Culver City and downtown auxiliaries, were symptomatic of, rather than resistive toward, the Anglo cultural domination of Los Angeles. Nevertheless, Guerrero's vocal harmony guitar performances in the heart of both the Los Angeles entertainment and tourist industries became part of the city's urban culture, and his cultural contributions at this time were Mexican in form, content, and presentation, but American in show-business ambition, whether faithfully re-creating "traditional" Mexican music or presenting new compositions in an American context; whether respected as dignified or exoticized as quaint. Unlike the jazz musicians introduced in this chapter, Guerrero consistently maintained strong connections with Mexican and Latin American culture, yet in his working-class, bilingual, bicultural, mass American media upbringing, he was typical of his generation.

When World War II began, Guerrero moved to San Diego to work for Convair Aircraft. At night he sang and performed with a dancer named Lolita, along with bare-legged showgirls, downtown at the Mexicali Club, resulting in local press notices calling him a "tenor troubadour" and a "romantic troubadour." He also sang with Lolita as part of a United Service Organization (USO) group that entertained American troops and recruits twice a week at the Camp Pendleton Naval hospital, and aboard docked aircraft carriers. Guerrero would sing hits of the day, like "Green Eyes" and "Rum and Coca Cola," with one "chorus in Spanish and one in English." Guerrero's USO involvement, deemed "essential war work" by the draft board, led to so many conscription deferments that by the time he was finally drafted, the war ended.[163] Similarly, Guerrero's jazz musician contemporaries, Tosti, Lopez, and Sesma, never saw active duty during World War II, not because their jazz gigs were deemed essential war work but because they were deemed 4-F. Paul Lopez lacked full mobility, Chico Sesma also had polio as a child, and Don Tosti's physical examination revealed a spot on his lungs. Sesma argued that remaining on the home front enabled him and his Roosevelt High cohorts "to break through with a greater facility," and that "the war opened the door for many musicians that otherwise may not have been able to get in."[164]

Indeed, these Mexican American Angelenos were able to cross over into, fit in with, and occasionally stand out in, some of the better-paying, prestigious white big bands of the swing era. For example, in the fall of 1941 Don Tosti attended Los Angeles City College (LACC) to study accounting, but he got his big break while sitting in with the school jazz band on a day that the trombonist-singer Jack Teagarden's orchestra was recording for overseas troops via the Standard Transcription Services on campus. Tosti, who had studied with a German bassist named Arthur Pabst, impressed Teagarden. By 1942, Tosti, then nineteen, was traveling the country playing bass in Teagarden's big band (see figure 9). This led to work with bandleader Bobby Sherwood, who wrote a big band number specifically for Tosti in 1944 called "Tostado," which centered on a bass solo. By the end of the decade Tosti had toured extensively with Charlie Barnet, Les Brown, and Jimmy Dorsey, who was the best man at Tosti's wedding.[165]

Chico Sesma was a sight-reading sideman who, after graduating from high school, enrolled as a music major at LACC, where he made important connections.[166] When he played with LACC's studio staff dance orchestra, "musicians from the studios and name big bands [used to] come in and rehearse us and lead us through charts. . . . Everything was very high tech. The professor was an engineer and had a lot of sophisticated recording equipment so we made a lot of records."[167] These contacts led Sesma to the orchestras of Johnny Richards—who was born Juan Ricardo de Cascales in Queretaro, Mexico, whose mother was a concert pianist, and who was a multi-instrumental musical prodigy as a child—and Jimmy Zito. With both bandleaders, Sesma unsuccessfully attempted to "make it big" in New York during the early 1940s.[168]

Paul Lopez played with the big bands of Ken Baker and Earl Spencer, and he even sat in once with the Benny Goodman Orchestra. Tosti, Sesma, and Lopez thus joined a small but significant group of well-paid Mexican American swing musicians which included the trombonist Jake Flores, who played with Jack Teagarden after Tosti left, and the trumpeter Ernie Figueroa, a fellow El Paso native who played with Charlie Barnet, Benny Goodman, and Hubie Diamond in New York during the early 1940s, and who would eventually secure Tosti a job with Jimmy Dorsey.[169] Another El Paso native, Ruben Leon, spent his teenage years in Lincoln Heights.

9. Don Tosti, publicity still, New York, James Kollar Studios, 1943.
COURTESY DON TOSTI COLLECTION, CALIFORNIA ETHNIC AND MULTICULTURAL
ARCHIVES, DEPARTMENT OF SPECIAL COLLECTIONS, DONALD DAVIDSON LIBRARY,
UNIVERSITY OF CALIFORNIA, SANTA BARBARA.

A brilliant arranger, saxophonist, clarinetist, flautist, and pianist, Ruben Leon played lead alto saxophone in the 1940s with the Earl Spencer and the Charlie Barnet orchestras.

The best-known Mexican American big band musician was Ernie Caceres, a Tejano who played primarily baritone saxophone, but also alto and tenor, as well as clarinet. His brother Pinero was a trumpeter and pianist, and his other brother, Emilio, was a jazz violinist who accompanied Ernie to Detroit and New York, but who also led a popular swing orchestra in San Antonio.[170] Ernie Caceres played with the orchestras of Bobby Hackett, Jack Teagarden, Fletcher Henderson, Benny Goodman, Tommy Dorsey, Woody Herman, and, as a featured soloist, Glenn Miller. He also appeared with the Miller band for three musical numbers in the 1941 film *Sun Valley Serenade*. After serving in the U.S. Army in 1945, he eventually recorded with Eddie Condon, Louis Armstrong, Sidney Bechet, Roy Eldridge, Ella Fitzgerald, Dizzy Gillespie, Hot Lips Page, Frank Sinatra, Muggsy Spanier, Ruth Brown, and the Metronome All Star Band.

Caceres's prominence was particularly significant given the dearth of nationally famous Mexican American swing bandleaders and jazz soloists. As Anthony Ortega explained:

> The door was open for [Mexican American musicians] more than, for instance, a black person, in the earlier days, especially. But even so, I would venture to say that [Anglos] would prefer to have a white guy that could do the job, and maybe a Mexican guy if he was very exceptional, or could blend in, so to speak; wouldn't stick out too much. Ernie Caceres, amazingly so, was a very dark guy, very obviously Mexican, you know? But I'm glad . . . that Glenn Miller didn't hold that [against him]. He was qualified. He was a hell of a musician.[171]

Mexican American jazz fans certainly recognized Caceres as a talented instrumentalist and improviser. For example, Vince Ramírez remembered that when he attended his first jazz concert, a Tommy Dorsey show at the Paramount Theater in downtown Los Angeles, "Ernie Caceres was taking a solo when I walked in."[172]

Mexican Americans' racial position gave them an advantage over African Americans in the musicians union, and in the big-name white swing orchestras, even though both groups were considered inferior by the dominant culture. During and after World War II Mexican Americans continued to "walk the color line," but many were becoming less ambivalent about their status in the United States, particularly in Southern California, where the war effort was priming the pump of the economy.[173] Yet members of the Mexican American generation were once again reminded that no matter how patriotic or law-abiding they were, the average white citizen did not want to hire them, or work alongside them. In October 1941 the newly formed Fair Employment Practices Committee (FEPC) held hearings on racial discrimination barriers to employment in the defense plants of Los Angeles, and in the summer of 1943 an FEPC investigation reported blatant racist practices throughout shipyards on the West Coast.[174] By 1943 there were approximately two hundred thousand people of Mexican descent living in the greater Los Angeles area, but only five thousand of them, the Congress of Industrial Organizations reported, found war industry work.[175] In one case, Henry Savala, a clerk-turned-salesman at Robinson's department store, was turned away from every aircraft plant in Los Angeles without ever being told why.[176] Even skilled Mexican American mechanics had to move to San Diego, where the Consolidated Company opened its aircraft plants to all citizens with a high school diploma and five to ten weeks of retraining.[177]

Nonetheless, 550,000 industrial jobs created between 1940 and mid-1943, coupled with the high number of enlisted and drafted workers, caused an acute labor shortage that forced defense industry employers to hire women and racial minorities as early as 1942.[178] The *California Eagle* reported that "by August 1942 the Los Angeles Board of Education also established training courses in black and Mexican neighborhoods to equip minorities with special skills."[179] Hortencia Esquivel recalled, "There were a lot of jobs . . . if you were eighteen, you went to work for the defense plant," which had "better benefits" and "was a better paying job than anything else." After her brother enlisted in the Navy and completed his tour of duty, he worked for Douglas Aircraft in Santa Monica, as did Esquivel's two female cousins and others in her neighborhood. In short, "there was a lot of work," Mexican Americans "got paid good . . . union wages," and they continued working at the defense plants even after the war's end.[180] In general, many Mexicans shared an advantage over African Americans in the workplace. From canneries to defense industry–contracted corporations, Mexicans were often hired at places that did not hire blacks.[181] Indeed, as blacks "came to dominate" the unskilled workforce in Los Angeles, they pushed ethnic Mexican workers a rung or two up the socioeconomic ladder.[182] After the Second World War, thousands of workers from both groups lost plum jobs in the aircraft plants and ship-yards; however, the war boom and the new military industrial economy ultimately resulted in more advances for Mexican Americans than for African Americans.[183]

From Rosita the Riveters to soldiers, bandleaders, musicians, and jitter-bug dancers, the Angelenos profiled in this chapter were, as the leading historian of the Mexican American generation says, "Americans all," with "a pluralistic world view that stressed coexistence between the material and political rewards of the 'American Dream' and the preservation of their parents' culture."[184] Although they harbored considerable ambiva-lence toward U.S. culture—having witnessed the repatriation campaigns of the early 1930s, the hardships of the Great Depression, and the racism of the Second World War—Mexican Americans, like young people of all ethnic and class backgrounds, became enamored with the lush, swinging sound of the big bands. For many of them, swing was fun to dance to, but it was also "American," and as such it helped them to further differentiate themselves from the traditional Mexican music of their parents' genera-tion. Yet, for some, this attitude would change as they got older, while for others, the melodies and rhythms of Mexico had always been a familiar and important part of their lives since childhood.

For example, in Boyle Heights, as in most mixed-Mexican, and ethnic Mexican neighborhoods, you could walk down the street and hear Mexi-cano music wafting out of homes and neighborhood stores.[185] In East Los Angeles, Hortencia "Tencha" Garibay's "mother used to put the Mexican station with the boleros and [Tencha and her siblings] used to put the swing. There was Harry James and Tommy Dorsey and Glenn Miller . . . we used to listen to that, and we used to listen to [wonderful] American pro-grams." Her mother, Margarita Padilla from Durango, and her father, Hipolito Rodarte from Zacatecas, "just listened to the disc jockey that played the Mexican music."[186] When Vince Ramírez was growing up in East Los Angeles, his parents, Vicente Ramírez from Baja California and Maria del Refugio García from Nogales, Arizona, listened to Mexican music, especially boleros. Vince, whose favorite bandleader was Jimmie Lunceford, and his brothers listened to so much swing music that his "mother could tell the difference between the clarinet played by Artie Shaw and Benny Goodman."[187] In West Los Angeles, Hortencia Esquivel "lis-tened to American music mostly," particularly jazz ballads, and she would buy the latest 78 rpm records to play on the family record player. Her parents, Miguel Aguiniga from Michoacán, and Carmen Mendoza from Morelia, "always listened to Mexican programs" on the radio. Hortencia and her siblings "could play our own music, but mostly we had Spanish music because my parents always had it on."[188]

Another bicultural constant among the different Mexican American Angelenos was the Mexican tradition of Catholic Church–hosted *jamaicas*. Part charity sale and part Saturday night dance, these jamaicas were more like block parties.[189] Vince Ramírez recalled that the jamaicas at Our Lady of Lourdes Catholic Church on Third Street in East Los Angeles were like "bazaars or carnivals . . . you had entertainment, food and games" to raise funds for church programs and activities. Since "they had *folklórico* dancing," the music they played "was mostly Mexican."[190] His fellow East Los Angeles resident María Olivas Alvarez remembered *lotería* and "music, lots of music; no Mexican thing without music. You have music for everything." The music played at the jamaicas differed depending "on which parish you went to," but "they would play both" Mexican and American music.[191] In La Colonia, the Mexican district in the heart of Watts, people would come out and dance to the sounds of rancheras and polkas, but also to Artie Shaw's "Frenesi" and Glenn Gray's "No Name Jive."[192] Hortencia Esquivel depicted the West Los Angeles jamaicas of her youth as Saturday night fundraiser dances "with little stands where they'd sell food." For dancing they provided "a mix, but mostly Mexican music. A lot of Mexican people used to go," but for the younger generation "they played jazz."[193]

Despite repeated exposure to mariachi, guitar trio, bolero, ranchera, and *conjunto* styles, Mexican Americans throughout Los Angeles were "hooked on" and "crazy about" swing bands.[194] As Vince Ramírez simply stated: "I was and the people I pal'd around with were." In other words, he and his Mexican American friends on the Eastside preferred big band jazz music, as indicated by their excursions dancing about town.[195] Moreover, swing dances were held at Sacred Heart High School for girls on Griffin Avenue in Lincoln Heights, and at Cathedral High School for boys on Bishop Road near Chinatown.[196] By listening and dancing to swing, Mexican Americans were neither performing blackness nor assimilating whiteness but forging their own freestyle expression somewhere between the sass of subcultural black music and the schmaltz of mainstream white music. In addition, the jazz musicians espoused a "color-blind" philosophy based on a meritocracy of jazz chops. Nonetheless, despite Don Tosti's insistence that musical talent—and his appreciation of it—knows no color, all of his major musical influences happen to be African American musicians. For example, he picked up the tenor saxophone in high school after hearing Chu Berry, Ben Webster, Coleman Hawkins, and Lester Young, and he switched from saxophone to bass out of admiration for Count Basie's bassist, Walter Page, and especially Duke Ellington's bassist, Jimmy Blanton. Similarly, Paul Lopez's favorite big bands were those of Count Basie and Jimmie Lunceford, while Chico Sesma loved Lionel Hampton, Count Basie, Duke Ellington, and Fats Waller.[197]

Anthony Ortega, who grew up with African Americans in Watts, was influenced by black saxophonists like Charlie Parker, Teddy Edwards, Dexter Gordon, and Wardell Gray, as well as by, to a lesser extent, Ben Webster, Sonny Stitt, and Johnny Hodges. Yet he was also impressed by the Italian American Charlie Ventura, the white Angeleno Art Pepper, and the reed section of the Glenn Miller Orchestra. One of Ortega's earliest influences was hearing Frank Sinatra sing with Tommy Dorsey's big band, but he also remembered his cousin, Ray Vasquez, playing Chu Berry and Coleman Hawkins solos on the tenor saxophone. Ortega himself used to listen to Charlie Parker 78s on his wind-up Victrola, slowing down the machine to better hear Bird's rapid runs.[198] In addition to the radio and the jukebox, record players were conduits for the dissemination of African American jazz culture, and Sesma attributed his cohort's musical preferences to being "born in a cosmopolitan setting." Led by the jazz musicians, swing-era Mexican American Angelenos became modern urbanites. The experience of growing up in a metropolis like Los Angeles helped them to foster a broader cultural outlook, but one without strong musical ties to Mexico.

Due to the influence of black and white instrumentalist improvisers, and of popular Jewish and Italian American jazz singers, Sesma, Lopez, Tosti, and Guerrero each internalized, to varying degrees, a cultural hierarchy that placed mainstream and avant-garde American music over traditional Mexican music. For instance, Don Tosti never liked ranchera music, which he said, "anybody can [play]." Tosti considered this "shit-kicking music" simplistic, and inherently inferior to harmonically complex jazz and rhythmically sophisticated Latin music.[199] In 1935, when he was twelve years old, Tosti played violin with La Orquesta Muro in Ciudad Juárez, but the group was not a typical *orquesta típica*, for although the Mexican musicians dressed in charro outfits, they played a mix of American music and Mexican *música tropical*.[200] Sesma's parents listened to mariachis, boleros, and trios, but he "hated" these "monotonous" styles of music. Although his tastes changed later in life, in his youth Sesma "could not stand" Mexican music because it did not swing.[201] As Paul Lopez lamented, in California "too many Mexicans" play "German music . . . using the same chords—tonic, subdominant, and dominant—and most everybody plays by ear." Lopez thus found ranchera, the Mexican equivalent of country and western, "corny," unlike jazz, where "you learn your chords, you learn to compose, you learn to write. It's a whole growth process that really doesn't ever stop."[202]

These Angeleno jazz musicians have been accused of musical snobbery and "elitism," but as learned practitioners of a highly technical form, they were simply skeptics, and their distaste for traditional Mexican music demonstrated their acculturation as Mexican Americans.[203] As Sesma made clear, "We were very American in our roots, and in our upbringing."[204] Lopez recalled that "we were more American than Mexican in those days. If you came out with the Mexican stuff, they'd say, 'Oh, look at that hillbilly.' Like a hick." And although mariachi music supposedly "stirs the heart of a Mexican," it did not stir that of Paul Lopez. As he declared, "I'm an American. Actually, in my heart, I don't know what the hell I know about [Mexico]."[205] Such sentiments could lead one to argue that these musicians were simply white ethnic participants in a national American musical style who happened to be of Mexican descent. As products of their time and place, they were Americanized in many respects, but their musical creations, made in the idiom of swing and jazz, contributed to both local Mexican American life and national American society, so they must be considered part of Mexican American expressive culture.

Mexican American Angelenos were assimilating on their own terms despite larger structural constraints such as discrimination and segregation in employment, housing, and public recreation, working their mojo and resisting dominant cultural values by embracing African American music and dance, and by retaining their bilingualism and other ethnic connections. Manuel Peña claims that the Mexican Americans of this generation "embraced selected aspects of American culture," even as they were "clinging to" Mexican "symbolic antecedents" like mariachis and rancheras because of their "persistent allegiance to the mother culture."[206] However, while Mexican American Angelenos may have experienced "a frustrated assimilation," this alleged allegiance to the culture of the Mexican motherland was not as pronounced during the swing era, and even less so in the rhythm and blues and rock and roll periods.

In fact, the one musician in this swing-era cohort with the most loyalty to Mexicano culture, Lalo Guerrero, unlike his Los Angeles peers, with their jazz training and big band backgrounds, always remained culturally connected to Mexican trios and conjuntos, sometimes as much out of economic necessity as ethnic authenticity. Yet Guerrero also internalized his own somewhat elitist cultural hierarchy, for when he first came to Southern California he disliked the corridos and rancheras that were popular among the recently arrived Mexican immigrant laborers. Specifically, he felt that the popular Los Angeles Spanish-language radio ensemble, Los Madrugadores (The Early Risers), played "corny" music "for a different class of people—the boozers and brawlers and cantina [types]." In contrast, the music of the working-class Mexican American musicians of his own group, Los Carlistas, was "more refined," cultured, and sophisticated because it was "modeled on the Mexican singers they saw in Mexican movies."[207] In modern fashion, both the American and Mexican culture industries at the height of each country's golden age of studio system cinema filtered his cultural tastes.

Again, Guerrero's biculturalism was shared by, and in part defined, the other members of the Mexican American generation. The expressive culture of the Mexican American generation was not Mexican *or* American; clearly it represented a mix of both. Although jazz and jitterbug predominated, Mexican music was always in the background, and often in the mix at a party, or on the playlist at a dance concert. Not every piece of music that the historical actors in this narrative played or danced to must be labeled "Mexican American jazz," or "Mexican American swing," simply because the musicians or dancers were of Mexican heritage. Indeed, their music may not have had any identifiable Mexican or Spanish-language elements during the swing era, although it would in later eras and in other genres. Still, the musicians played straight-ahead modern jazz as well as more commercialized big band swing, just as the music fans listened to small jazz combos in bars and clubs, while the dancers danced the jitterbug in dance halls and ballrooms. In short, the context of their era, and the reality of their surroundings, meant that they were both Mexican and American. They made inroads in mainstream popular culture and in the larger society, but they still encountered barriers to advancement. Whites still reminded them that they were Mexicans, but their interactions with other ethnic groups throughout the city, on tour cross-country, and at military bases and overseas in the armed forces, only increased their self-esteem, personal confidence, and ethnic pride. Their music should be considered Mexican American music because it reflected the broad interests and diverse influences of this generation.

For example, Anthony Ortega led a band during high school called the Frantic Five, made up of Anthony on alto saxophone, Reyes Gaglio on bass, Chuy Ruiz on drums, Ortega's African American friend Walter Benton on tenor saxophone, and Walter's cousin Jimmy O'Brien on piano. During the wartime musicians union recording ban, Ortega's cousin Ray Vasquez arranged a recording session for the Frantic Five with Rex Records, a small, independent, nonunion Hollywood label owned by a Jewish American businessman named Mory Rappaport. They recorded a song Ortega wrote based on the tune "East of the Sun (and West of the Moon)," which Anthony had heard Tommy Dorsey play, with Frank Sinatra vocals. In a typical Mexican American generation gesture, Ortega's title for the composition, "The Clutching Hand," was inspired by the name of the mysterious, cloaked villain in a low-budget 1936 Saturday matinee detective serial. This tune and its B-side were recorded under the name "Ray Vasquez and His Beboppers," even though Ray never played on it, and none of the musicians' names appeared on it. Worse, they were not paid on that recording date.[208]

The white radio disc jockey Harry Schooler used to hire the band to play at jazz concerts he hosted at ballrooms in Long Beach, Venice, and Santa Monica. In addition to Ortega's group, Schooler would hire the Lincoln Heights–Boyle Heights band of Maurice Vendrel, Ray Lugo, and Bill Trujillo, and a Redondo Beach band led by a black drummer named Melly Glen. These groups would alternate short sets, billed as a "battle of the bands" to attract people. The Frantic Five were also hired by the radio disc jockey Al Jarvis to accompany the up-and-coming white jazz singer Frankie Laine at a couple of Army bases in Southern California. On Sundays the Frantic Five would occasionally be allowed to play at the Streets of Paris, a Mafia-owned nightclub on Hollywood Boulevard at Cherokee Avenue, and one night they even opened for the Gene Krupa Trio. In addition, they performed for enlisted men at the USO center in Watts in 1945. Finally, while still in high school, Ortega and his friends would occasionally sit in on jam sessions at Central Avenue spots like the Downbeat Club, when the more established players, like Teddy Edwards, Hampton Hawes, Dexter Gordon, Sonny Criss, Wardell Gray, Howard McGhee,

Lucky Thompson, and Roy Porter got tired late into the night. The jam session masters of ceremonies would let them sit in more frequently at the Crystal Tea Room on Sunday afternoons, but it was hard to get into after-hours clubs if you were underage. Undaunted, they would sneak in anyway to jam on the bandstand at Jack's Basket Room.[209]

The lifestyles and career paths of the musicians introduced in this chapter involved not only a great deal of touring, especially as sidemen during the heyday of the big band swing era, but also many migratory dislocations to search for steady work. One way to analyze Mexican American membership in the white union Local 47 is to see it as a parallel path toward financial stability, one of several available, such as sports, the armed forces, or education. The musicians' excursions across Southern California and the United States, like their sustained public and private educations, were not entirely typical of their generation, but many Mexican Americans were demanding, and beginning to experience, improved social conditions during the war years. Upward mobility was difficult, and, accordingly, the Mexican American generation in Los Angeles has been marked by a dichotomy between those youths who advocated advancement through education and those who rejected mainstream institutions, acceptance, and assimilation. During the swing era it was statistically more common for a teenage Mexican American to drop out of high school than to graduate, but a growing number of youths pursued educational goals as a means to individual socioeconomic success, and, in line with the middle-class political organizations of the era, toward the racial uplift of the entire group.

For example, the Coordinating Council for Latin-American Youth, founded in 1941, "believed education to be the principal means for young people to achieve social, cultural, and economic integration. Yet it also recognized that the majority of Mexican Americans as a predominantly poor population faced obstacles in the public schools." As Mario García notes, "The Los Angeles system mixed students more, although with increasing segregation patterns," but in "surrounding areas . . . officials widely segregated Mexican origin pupils" into "Mexican schools." As part of a "dual public school system," the Mexican school curriculum emphasized Americanization courses, "intended to socialize Mexican children to the norms and values of American society," and vocational training, intended to track and funnel Mexican students into the bottom rungs of a segmented labor market that "desired cheap manual labor from the Mexican American communities." García concludes that "the school system likewise caused serious cultural alienation among young Mexican Americans as they increasingly felt pulled in two cultural directions."[210]

This dismal school situation, but also educational success stories, existed to the east of Los Angeles in San Bernadino County, where instructive comparisons can be drawn with the urban experiences and ambitious efforts of some Angeleno members of the Mexican American generation. A 1942 study of one rural ethnic Mexican district east of Los Angeles County, in the "Inland Empire" region, where the economy was based mainly on citrus farming, measured the cultural assimilation and educational achievement of thirty-seven Mexican American youths who graduated from either their local high school or junior college from 1932 to 1941.[211] These high achievers, eight of them born in Mexico, were part of a broader community in which "the average father has been, or still is, a laborer in the fruit crops." Nevertheless, even among this parental population, one man had been a paymaster for a large sugar beet factory in the town of Chino, one was a Baptist minister from Mexico, one started a successful father-and-sons cement business, one became a mechanic with the Santa Fe Railroad, and another started a father-and-sons trucking and hauling business.[212]

Among "the second-generation Mexicans" surveyed, the use of Spanish persisted, often based on an attitude that asked, "Why should we use English always? To the Americans we are just Mexicans, regardless of how hard we try to be like them. Why should we accept the language and customs of another race when we have our own?" At the same time, the Mexican American teenage boys went to "the picture shows" every Saturday or Sunday. Moreover, "the young Mexican . . . feels as American as John Jones. He likes swing music, Superman, and Bob Hope. He knows the latest words to the latest hit tune, he can rattle off the records of the leading baseball stars. . . . But, when he goes to get a job, he is told that only 'white boys' are being hired." Indeed, "without exception, the Mexican who was medium or dark [colored] had many stories to relate of racial discrimination. They are banned from public swimming pools, refused service in many restaurants, forced to sit in separate sections in picture shows and at concerts, and in many instances are not permitted even to apply for jobs." Undaunted, the youths in question "often mentioned that they were the only Mexican members of clubs in high school," and that their mere club membership changed the Anglos' minds about Mexicans.

Driven by their "desire to succeed," they felt that each individual advancement would assure "for the Mexicans who come after them a better and fairer opportunity." Hence, regarding the many problems faced by Mexicans, one U.S. Army soldier wrote a letter vowing that "regardless of the outcome of this war, you may rest assured that all of the boys of Mexican origin now serving . . . will never live to see the time when surrender is the order of the day."[213]

The study's author found that through sheer persistence, Samuel Montoyo managed to become a welder—and one of the few Mexicans hired—at the San Diego Consolidated Aircraft Company in the months before the factory opened up its hiring practices, and "he feels that it is the opportunity of his life to break down prejudice against the Mexicans 'by always doing his part and then a little bit more.'" One star pupil, Antonio de Valles, began "studying to become a chemical engineer at the University of California [Berkeley]," while one of his former junior college classmates moved to Berkeley to become a junior high school teacher. Another youth, Aureliano Ruiz, with financial assistance from his father, constructed a small store where, with the help of his sister, he sold groceries and meats at a small profit. Ruiz was studying "business" Spanish in hopes of conducting business with Latin American countries, he was a member of the Claremont Coordinating Council, and he was an active member of "the Mexican Y.M.C.A.," for which he helped sponsor "dances, plays, and sports activities in his Mexican community."[214]

Of the young women studied, several found secretarial work, like the one who, after taking "commercial courses" in junior college, became "secretary to the manager at [the] Padua Hills" theater. Several more were teachers, one of whom also "gave private music lessons after school hours" in Chino. One of the other Mexican American educators had been working since she was fifteen years old, including three years teaching in California schools. After graduating from junior college she worked "with the Padua Theatre group" while completing her education at Pomona College and Claremont College. She "had incurred many debts in order to finish her studies, but these she was happily able to repay the first year, during which she was employed as a teacher in the high school" in Norwalk, just east of the San Gabriel River. Mary Garcia earned a bachelor's degree and a master's degree from the University of Southern California, and then worked at Jordan High School teaching "classes in French, Spanish, and English, having also taught German." Another young woman "completed her education at Santa Barbara State College, specializing in the teaching of small children." She taught "Mexican folk music and dancing to the other pupils in her school as well, often giving programs for other schools and organizations." She felt that she was ideally suited to help her Mexican students "translate their ideas into more facile English, and that since they know that she, too, is a Mexican, her example encourages them to learn."[215]

Henrietta Zamorano obtained her license at an Ontario beauty college and was continuously employed as a beauty operator in Pomona and Ontario. She claimed that since the field began "opening up to Mexican girls," it became "an incentive to an increasing number of" them "to complete their high school education," which was "a required qualification." Virginia Garcia worked as a sales clerk in a Los Angeles dress shop by day and was "taking a nurses' preparatory course in night school," while two other young women used their junior college classes to gain valuable stenographer experience. One of them turned down an offer to become a government stenographer because "it entailed leaving her family for a long time." Having registered with many employment agencies in Los Angeles, she said, "I have had several opportunities, but I want to make the most salary I can. Since I have so much experience back of me, I should be able to make more than a beginner, even if I am a Mexican." One young lady could not accept a job as a court interpreter in Riverside due to an injury, while another passed her civil service examination, but declined "the position since it meant that she would have to move to Washington, D.C."[216] In one incredibly opportunistic example, Florence Guttierez "made an opening for herself out of the misfortune of war" when "she went immediately upon word of the evacuation of the Japanese to the San Fernando" Valley "to take over a contract held by Japanese for the hiring of" asparagus pickers. She successfully assembled her crews and, after the crop season, returned "to the position she has held since her graduation, with a department store in Pomona."[217]

The Second World War therefore produced much spatial and social mobility for Mexican American women, especially taking into account defense industry workers. Yet their increasing wartime occupational and educational opportunities did not correspond to an increased participation in the male-dominated music industry. Due to the gendered economy of the jazz scene, Mexican American women's key role in the production of popular dance and the reception of popular music was not matched by performance as professional, unionized musicians. Still, the experiences of female secretaries, stenographers, court interpreters, beauty salon operators, field labor contractors, department store employees, civil servants, nurses, and elementary, language, and music teachers counterbalance masculinist narratives of Chicano history. In addition, although it was supposedly "unusual" for so many members of the Mexican American generation to be so educated and so ambitious, the small data sample from San Bernadino County, combined with the overall findings from Los Angeles, indicates a general pattern of academic attainment, and pink-collar, skilled, and semiskilled employment. Perhaps such achievements were not as unusual as suspected, considering how much the music educators, high school musicians, big bandleaders, jazz disciples, jitterbugs, go-getters, and college graduates described in this chapter contributed to both the Mexican American expressive culture and the urban civility of the period.[218] They are therefore considered and acknowledged along with the zoot suiters, pachucos, and pachucas, who are the subjects of much more scholarship, and of the next chapter.

the drape shape:

intercultural style politics

When you were at home you had your skirt a little longer, and then when you got into the street you used to roll it up and be in style. . . . I was never a bad girl. It's just everybody was dressing like that.
—Hortencia Garibay, interview by author

There was a pride in being a pachuco. You would not see a lousy looking pachuco. Definitely tailor-made.
—Ed Frias, interview by author

The two Mexican youths . . . were both brown-skinned, about my colour, slender and slightly stooped, with Indian features and thick curly hair. Both wore bagged drapes that looked about to fall down from their waists, and greyish dirty T shirts. They talked in the melodious Mexican lilt.
—Chester Himes, If He Hollers Let Him Go

Set in Los Angeles during World War II, Chester Himes's *If He Hollers Let Him Go* tellingly concludes with the interaction between its African American protagonist and narrator, Bob Jones, a shipyard employee falsely accused of rape by a white female coworker, and two Mexican Americans wearing "drapes," or zoot suit pants, who, like Jones, had been given the choice between military induction or civilian incarceration. The two "Mexican youths" empathized with and respected Jones, calling him "man," whereas the arresting Anglo police officer called him "boy," and their soiled T-shirts, imply that they had been held for some time.[1] According to Los Angeles City Councilman Carl Rasmussen, the Los Angeles Police Department had "been asking draft boards to draft particularly obstreperous" zoot suiters, and "usually the requests are complied with."[2] As Edward Escobar notes, in the war years the LAPD used a new curfew ordinance, along with "field interrogations" and "noncriminal detentions . . . as control mechanisms." In 1943 alone, "more than 2,000 Mexican American youths" suffered from "unjustified and baseless arrests." The police therefore engaged in overarresting of profiled youths, public humiliation, excessive force, illegal beatings, and detention without legal representation (see figure 10).[3]

Blacks and ethnic Mexicans in Southern California often received similar treatment from law enforcement, judges, juries, and the general Anglo public. Examining these similarities, as well as differences, will continue this book's fruitful comparisons between African Americans and Mexican Americans. This chapter analyzes not only the zoot suit, but also pachucos and pachucas, including their unique dance moves, haircuts, and language, while drawing on oral histories to hear what everyday Mexican Americans thought about zoot suiters. I use the term *style politics* because the zoot suit and pachuco/pachuca styles became politicized in a context of police persecution, wartime sensationalism, military and civilian vigilantism, and both working- and middle-class moralizing. As the opening epigraphs suggest, a young woman could dress like a pachuca to "be in style," but she risked being considered a "bad girl." For young men who dressed like pachucos, the drape shape elicited pride and indicated class, in contrast to Anglo stereotypes of slack Mexicans. However, before addressing the zoot suit and its pachuco, pachuca, and black hep cat adherents, we will revisit the city's wartime jazz scene and brewing culture war. The Sleepy Lagoon mass trial, in which seventeen Mexican American youths were wrongly convicted of murder, and the zoot suit riots are milestones, both tragic and defiant, in Chicano history, but they are also part of a wider social and cultural history of Los Angeles. The iconoclastic pachucos and pachucas listened and danced to both white and black swing orchestras, both inside and outside of the barrio. Similarly, since zoot suits, called "drapes" on the Eastside, were usually weekend wear, we will examine the

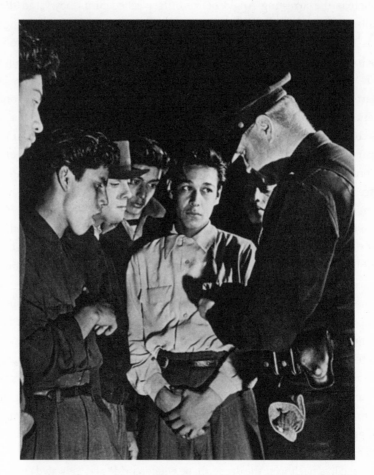

10. Police officer questioning Mexican American youths, early 1940s.
COURTESY AUDREY A. LOGAN.

full scope of everyday Mexican American clothing styles, some just as hip, if not yet as rebellious.

This chapter operates squarely within, yet strives to move beyond, binaries of Mexican/American, pachuco/G.I., and pachuco/square. Thus, I more fully contextualize, and reevaluate, the relatively familiar narratives of zoot suits and pachucos by comparing them to African Americans, the jazz scene, other U.S. cities, and Mexican American "squares" and middle-class organizations. Mexican American pachucos and African American hep cats created two vibrant subcultures with distinctive yet parallel gendered styles that enriched the youth culture of swing music and jitterbug dancing. In doing so, they became the catalysts for a showdown over the public face of the modern metropolis. In short, taking a fresh look at wartime Los Angeles from the perspective of the music scene, and considering zoot suits, pachucos, and pachucas from a wider angle, further develops this book's arguments for a multicultural urban civility and a Mexican American expressive culture, as well as its broader profile—and rethinking—of the Mexican American generation.

In October 1942, the city's racial tensions began to burst through the surface when two hundred Mexican American youths fought with police at a downtown movie theater, and when a crowd of pachuco zoot suiters threw rocks at LAPD officers at a Westside dance hall.[4] During the early 1940s, many Mexican American youths frequented the Nu-Pike amusement park in the harbor community of Long Beach, as well as the carnivalesque amusement piers in Venice, Ocean Park, and Santa Monica. With their roller coasters, bingo parlors, and pedestrian-friendly beachfront boardwalks, the three piers drew locals, both Anglo and Mexican American, from the Westside, and, thanks to round-trip trolley service out of downtown Los Angeles, from all over the city. Swing big bands would play at the Casino Gardens on the pier in Ocean Park, and at the Aragon Ballroom on tiny Lick Pier in Venice. Lick Pier was overshadowed by the adjacent Venice Pier, a much grander "pleasure pier," known as the "Coney Island of the Pacific," which boasted the Venice Dance Hall. During the day, sailors and soldiers on weekend leave, as well as Mexican American youths and other Angelenos would flock to the area.[5] The spring of 1943 produced a number of disturbances on the beachfront, where cocky Mexican American zoot suiters would sometimes walk the boardwalk with arms interlocked, four-wide, forcing the locals to disperse before them.

In May 1943, violence erupted in Venice out of this volatile mix when an angry mob of approximately five hundred sailors and civilians attacked a smaller group of Mexican American boys—most of whom were not wearing zoot suits—and their dates, as they emerged from the Aragon Ballroom after a dance. The mini-riot rushed from the ballroom down the boardwalk, spread north into Santa Monica, and raged past midnight. While no whites were arrested, "many [Mexican American] boys were badly beaten, others thrown into jail for seventy-two hours."[6] In front of two thousand spectators, the police arrested the assault victims, many of them from the Alpine Street barrio, located between the Chavez Ravine and Chinatown, but the charges of disturbing the peace were eventually dismissed due to insufficient evidence.[7]

In downtown Los Angeles, pachucos would stride down the street, five side-by-side, and if white pedestrians would walk around them, they would laugh or stick their legs out.[8] On May 31 near downtown, a dozen sailors and soldiers fought with Mexican American boys, who badly wounded one of the seaman. Three days later, on June 3, 1943, the so-called zoot suit riots broke out when about fifty sailors avenged their buddy. The Chavez Ravine, Alpine, and downtown districts became battle zones as white sailors dragged Mexican Americans out of theaters, bars, jukebox cafes, billiard parlors, and dance halls, assaulted them on the street, cut off their long hair, then stripped off and burned their zoot suits. By the fourth day of violence, thousands of local civilian vigilantes and military personnel from nearby bases joined the fray, as the Anglo mobs took "taxi-cab brigades" to hunt for Mexicans in Boyle Heights, and along Whittier Boulevard into East Los Angeles. By the fifth day, some even took the streetcars into Watts, looking for black and brown youths.[9] As a *Time* magazine story reported, the LAPD "practice was to accompany the caravans in police cars, watch the beating and jail the victims." Regarding this hands-off policy, one of the local police chiefs explained, "Well, we represent public opinion. . . . Most citizens thought it was a good idea anyway. They were against zoot-suiters, the same as most people are against jitterbugs and jam sessions."[10]

Social interactions and intercultural exchanges, along with the swift demographic changes brought on by the war, and the increased social and spatial mobility of racial minorities, threatened not only the idyllic middle-class Anglo-Saxon city that Los Angeles business boosters and bourgeois elites had long advertised, but also the very good life on which this image was predicated. The Mexican population during the war years was approximately 133,000, or 8 percent of the total.[11] This was also a period when many African American migrants arrived in Southern California, and the press excited fears of uppity, free-wheeling blacks and Mexicans, creating a hysteria over zoot-suited "baby gangsters" as the law enforcement and criminal justice systems tried to control the movements of alleged roving hoodlums.

In late June 1943, race riots ignited in Detroit and Harlem. By the end of the summer, they had spread to Beaumont, Texas, and Mobile, Alabama. The Detroit riot was the deadliest, with six thousand federal troops called in, nine whites and twenty-five blacks dead, seventeen of the latter killed by white policemen, seven hundred people wounded, including police officers, and $2 million in property damage. The riots combined with the internment of Japanese Americans the previous March to shatter America's facade of domestic unity and egalitarian democracy. Nationally, there were outbursts between men and women in the workplace, and amongst white workers who refused to allow African Americans to integrate their all-white industrial jobs, unions, and federal housing projects.[12]

Despite such urban conflict and racial strife, the Los Angeles jazz scene engendered cooperative spaces of cross-cultural tolerance and understanding. For example, in the early 1940s the jazz impresario Billy Berg insisted on hiring interracial, predominantly black jazz bands to play for integrated audiences at the series of jazz venues he ran in Hollywood.[13] The saxophonist Sonny Criss described Billy Berg's Swing Club on Vine Street in Hollywood as "the first really cosmopolitan club with a great deal of publicity behind it where Negro and white people mixed without any pressure. It was . . . an atmosphere that embraced people from all walks of life."[14] Another jazz proprietor, Norman Granz, was "determined to feature the best jazz musicians in town, without regard to color, at organized jam sessions" at Billy Berg's, and "by November 1942 the club was entirely nonsegregated and even allowed interracial dancing."[15] In July 1944 Granz made history when he produced the first full-scale jazz concert at the Los Angeles Philharmonic Auditorium, a venerated venue that had previously exhibited only classical symphonies. In addition to establishing Granz's "Jazz at the Philharmonic" (JATP) jam session concert series, this performance represented interethnic solidarity, as the lineup included black and white performers, and the proceeds went to the Sleepy Lagoon Defense Fund. A native Angeleno who attended UCLA and served in the military during World War II, Granz was both a product, and a shining example, of the city's multicultural politics. His JATP concerts would eventually go on the road, and in each city Granz demanded that the participating auditoriums and dance halls be integrated in order for the all-star bands to perform.[16]

On any given weekend during the war years, up to fifty thousand military men spent their leave in Los Angeles, including many southerners unfamiliar with Mexicans and unused to the multiracial nature of the city.[17] Los Angeles boasted the nation's largest ballroom in the Hollywood Palladium, and the largest nightclub in the Hollywood Canteen, which hosted twenty-five thousand servicemen each week at the height of the war. Organized by over forty unions and guilds, including both the black musicians union Local 767 and the white Local 47—which booked volunteer star entertainers—the Canteen was staffed by seven thousand volunteers, including some of the film industry's leading actors. This relaxed atmosphere led to numerous racial incidents, "precipitated by volunteer dance hostesses who struck some as too willing to cross racial lines to entertain servicemen."[18] Attempts to police what Sherrie Tucker calls the "dance floor democracy" of integrated nightclubs indicate that venues like the Canteen and Billy Berg's were out of place in the actual neighborhood of Hollywood, which was, Ted Gioia argues, a "redneck area" in the 1940s.[19]

Due to the social ordering and racial regulation of the era, musicians and their fans encountered prejudice and resentment as they moved throughout the city. For instance, jazz bandleader Lionel Hampton compared the hostile social reality of 1940s Los Angeles to that of the deep South. As he explained, "You had to sit in the back of the bus, go into the white nightclubs by the back door . . . [and] taxis wouldn't stop for you."[20] In Glendale, African American musicians needed to apply for police permits to remain in town after six in the evening, or be subject to arrest. At two in the morning, blacks who performed in Glendale, if they had their papers in order, were promptly provided with squad car escorts from the clubs to the city limits.[21] Similarly, jazz bandleader Roy Porter was once escorted to Pico Boulevard, the supposed southern racial border of the city proper, after a show in Hollywood. Porter felt that "what these red-neck cops didn't realize was that the bebop and jazz that the black musicians were playing was bringing the races closer together."[22] In South Central Los Angeles, representatives of the Newton Street police station realized this all too well, and they "regularly brought in mixed couples for a pat-down on the flim-siest of excuses."[23]

Many of the city's nightclubs and ballrooms excluded African Americans, except as stage performers. The bandleader Horace Heidt's Trianon Ballroom in South Gate established a policy that banned the booking of black orchestras entirely.[24] That same year, a Los Angeles newspaper reporter accused the owners of a Hollywood club of denying entrance to a featured jazz musician's black friends. In his employers' defense, the owners' press agent asked, "What makes [the reporter] think that Negroes are admitted . . . as guests at the Palladium, the Trianon, or any of the so-called white niteries in Los Angeles?"[25] In response to charges of discrimination made by the president of the black musicians union local in 1945, the Hollywood Chamber of Commerce launched an unsuccessful campaign to suspend the licenses of fifteen nightclubs for denying employment to African Americans.[26]

This racially restrictive environment prompted one young bebop singer, Lee "Babs" Brown, to take on the surname Gonzales. Raised in Newark, Babs moved from New York to Los Angeles in 1943. During his stay, his appendix burst. Babs called a taxi to take him to a hospital, but the cab driver stole his wallet and dumped him in front of the emergency room. Lacking identification, he assumed a new identity, becoming "Ricardo Gonzales" to beat the system and avoid "being treated as a Negro." From the hospital he was also able to get a room at the Sheraton Hotel for a night. Like the unionized black jazz musicians we discussed in chapter 1, the singer obviously recognized the different treatment afforded Mexican Americans. Babs Gonzales had flirted with another ethnic identity once before—when he first came to Los Angeles he would wind a turban around his head and, inspired by the East Indian motion picture actor Sabu, call himself Ram Singh.[27] The dark-skinned protagonist of *If He Hollers Let Him Go* toyed with a similar idea while dining in a white restaurant with his light-skinned African American date, to whom he said, "Hell, they probably think we're movie people anyway, or that you're white as it is. I'll tell them I'm an East Indian if you think that'll help. Next time I'll wear a turban."[28] As we saw in the previous chapter, at times it was necessary to circumvent society's racist rules, especially in a white hospital, hotel, or restaurant.

When African Americans and Mexican Americans made their presence felt more frequently in white-dominated public spaces, altercations with Anglos multiplied, not only on beachfront boardwalks and downtown boulevards, but also on streetcars. During the Second World War, Los Angeles boasted one of the most extensive mass transit rail networks in the nation. The fifty-foot long Pacific Electric Red Cars ran alone, or in two- or three-car trains from Redlands and from San Bernadino to Santa Monica, then down the coast to Redondo Beach, as well as from the San Fernando Valley and from Pasadena through downtown to Long Beach, to Orange County, and to Whittier. The smaller Yellow Cars made shorter runs downtown. In the 1930s, passengers and revenue had declined, but rail traffic increased briefly when the city's population mushroomed during the war years, as throngs of people used the system for work, recreation, and sightseeing.[29] Although not as bad as the white bus drivers and streetcar conductors in wartime Birmingham, Alabama, who used fists, blackjacks, and pistols "pretty regularly to maintain order," and to physically eject black passengers, those in Los Angeles did nothing to stop the violence in their vehicles during the riots.[30] Nevertheless, unlike the police, they "were comparatively cool." Thus, even African Americans with cars "often chose to take the #4 Melrose bus between Central Avenue and Hollywood."[31]

Whether on buses or streetcars, in dance halls or ballrooms, there were many racially and sexually motivated encounters in the months leading up to the zoot suit riots. Such a history of violence is an integral part of California, which has been marked by "white male entitlement," from the Spanish soldiers and missionaries to the Anglos who flooded the mid-nineteenth-century Golden State in the name of Manifest Destiny. Poor white workers and ethnic European immigrants bought into a system that compensated them for their material hardships by ensuring privileges and status over the darker groups beneath them, on whom they projected their class resentments and racial hatreds through Indian massacres, Mexican lynchings, and anti-Chinese riots.[32] The Anglo Protestant Midwesterners who migrated to Southern California during the first two decades of the twentieth century brought a blend of Progressive ideals and eugenicist fears of race mixing, and they stubbornly maintained their privileges.

Yet what led enraged white servicemen and civilians to rip zoot suits off of Mexican Americans, then burn the clothes in the street? What was the zoot suit, and why did it provoke so many different reactions, from pride to anger? During the 1930s the zoot suit evolved out of the hustler garb of Harlem hep cats and the dapper stage outfits of African American jazz musicians, especially the popular Harlem singer-bandleader Cab Callo-way, "Mr. Hi-De-Ho." Through his Cotton Club performances, recordings, and 1936 jive dictionary, he was one of the first singers to popularize the hep cats' exaggerated clothes and secret slang. Enjoying its greatest popularity during World War II, the zoot suit was worn primarily by African Americans in Boston, New York, Philadelphia, Detroit, Houston, and Los Angeles, and by Mexican Americans in El Paso, Houston, Detroit, and Los Angeles, where it was also worn by Filipinos, some Japanese Americans, and the occasional European American.[33]

The suit included a broad-shouldered coat that pinched at the waist, then flared downward to about the mid-thigh in the "fingertip" style. It was accompanied by a long-sleeved dress shirt, always wrinkle-free, either with a short, wide necktie or unbuttoned at the throat, collar spread out onto the wide coat lapels. Baggy, pleated trousers, cinched high above the waist by a thin belt or held at the ribs by suspenders, widened to the knee, then narrowed dramatically at the ankle in pegged cuffs. Or, in the hep cats' rhyming slang: a "killer-diller coat with a drape shape, reat-pleats and shoulders padded like a lunatic's cell."[34] More than a flamboyant sartorial style, the functional zoot suit also allowed jitterbug dancers to execute strenuous arm movements, such as spinning and swinging their partner, and to improvise quick swing steps without tripping on their trouser cuffs.[35] Likewise, for dancing, Mexican American zoot suiters wore either expensive "feather weight" leather shoes, or heavy double-soled shoes, called "brogues," that they purchased at Price's shoe store downtown on Main Street.[36] Extreme, more expensive versions of the "drape shape" included a longer, knee-length coat, and accessories such as a wide, pancake-thin brimmed fedora hat, with optional feather, a smaller porkpie hat, or a gold watch chain dangling from the pants pocket down below the knees.

Comparing Anglo and Mexican American teenagers with regard to the zoot suit, one 1942 study concluded, "These are not what the well-dressed American boy is wearing, though they are the goal of most of the Mexican boys."[37] Another study estimated that wartime West Coast pachucos paid at least 50 dollars for draped pants, and up to 125 dollars for a full zoot suit, while Beatrice Griffith, a former social worker and Los Angeles housing project community director, mentioned pachucos buying an entire zoot suit for 65 dollars.[38] East Coast hipsters could buy a full zoot suit, with matching hat, dress shirt, and shoes, for about 75 dollars.[39] In Los Angeles, many young Mexican American men saved a large portion of their wages from their often-menial jobs to buy the latest fashions.[40] "They would save their money," and "some of the guys would say, 'Well, we have to save enough *lana* to spend at least a hundred bucks for our outfits.' "[41] Seemingly every Mexican American in East Los Angeles bought their drapes at Murray's clothing store, a downtown establishment on Third and Main streets, near Little Tokyo.[42] Even though Murray's catered to movie stars like George Raft, the business brought in by young Mexican Americans and African Americans was also welcome.[43] As Chico Sesma recalled, "We all had accounts at Murray's," and all of the local Mexican American swing "bands had their uniforms made there."[44] Curly's, a "little hole in the wall" tailoring establishment on Whittier Boulevard in East Los Angeles, was also "very popular."[45]

The zoot suit had already achieved widespread national popularity by March 1942, when the War Production Board regulated the wartime manufacture of suits, creating a maximum standard for fabric to be used. In response to the continuing demand, downtown clothiers like Murray's, Young's, and Earl's would sell and customize bootleg zoot suits.[46] The federal government even filed an injunction against one of the main Los Angeles stores selling zoot suits on the grounds that it used too much cloth. On June 9, 1943, after the worst of the rioting, the Los Angeles City Council proposed a resolution instructing the city attorney to prepare an ordinance that officially prohibited wearing zoot suits within the city limits, and that made such action not only "a public nuisance," but also a misdemeanor punishable by thirty days in jail.[47] Although this resolution was never officially passed, in part due to questions over its constitutionality, in a hegemonic version of style politics, both municipal and federal authorities sought to criminalize already racialized and politicized garments.

The national media painted zoot suiters as unpatriotic, and many Anglo Americans felt the zoot suiters were bucking the norm of domestic wartime society.[48] One white Angeleno, sixteen-year-old Henrietta Lee, recalled that "L.A. was like a war zone, and the pachucos had just taken over." By driving servicemen from outlying El Toro military base into Los Angeles to fight "zooters," she felt like she was doing her part for the war effort.[49] In 1943, when the Citizen's Committee on the Zoot Suit Riots blamed the media as a factor and cited race as a central cause, Mayor Fletcher Bowron proclaimed that racial discrimination was not the cause, and that "too many citizens" were raising "a hue and cry" about police prejudice. He pledged "two-fisted action" by police against the real cause of the riots: juvenile delinquents.[50] As for the Mexican American and African American youths arrested during the riots, Mayor Bowron said, "They all look alike to us, regardless of color and the length of their coats."[51] In response, an Angeleno named Dan Acosta wrote a letter to the Los Angeles press to ask, "If all this were true, why are we consistently called hoodlums? Why is mob action encouraged by the newspapers? Why did the city police stand around saying very nonchalantly that they could not intervene and even hurrayed the soldiers for their 'brave' action? Not until these questions are answered, will the Mexican population feel at ease."[52]

In the immediate aftermath of the Los Angeles zoot suit rioting, Congressman John Rankin of Mississippi told the House of Representatives that "a badge of distinction" ought to be awarded to the servicemen who participated in the attacks on un-American Mexicans and Negroes.[53] Twenty-four hours later, Eleanor Roosevelt convened a press conference to address the issue, declaring that the riots were due to long-standing discrimination against Mexicans in Southern California. A Los Angeles Times editorial responded by claiming that Roosevelt's accusation "ignore[d] history, fact, and happy tradition," for "we have the largest Mexican colony in the United States and we enjoy fraternizing with them. . . . We like Mexicans and we think they like us."[54] The president of the Los Angeles Chamber of Commerce also replied to Roosevelt, arguing, "Instead of discrimination against Mexicans, California has always treated them with the utmost consideration."[55] Clearly, not every Angeleno agreed with the First Lady when she warned that Americans would sooner or later have to face the fact that "we have a race problem."[56] In Los Angeles, the cultural production and racial interaction of emergent youth cultures threatened to redraw race and class lines. In response, the city's elites, aided by the press, the police, the courts, school board officials, and real estate companies, sought to reinscribe the privileges of whiteness.

White servicemen believed that young, able-bodied black and brown zoot suiters refused to fight, angrily accusing them of draft-dodging anti-Americanism. In reality, during World War II, Mexican Americans joined the armed forces in numbers far larger than their proportion in the total population, a phenomenon fueled by patriotism, and by their having a higher percentage of young people of military age than any other group of similar size in the United States.[57] Mexican Americans' high rate of military service meant that many young pachucos had older brothers fighting in the war, and many became soldiers, sailors, marines, and paratroopers themselves. For example, Raul Morin recalled a typical evening in 1944 after a hard day of boot camp. At Camp Roberts, just north of the Mission San Miguel Arcángel along the old El Camino Real, about thirty Mexican Americans would be playing the guitar, "talking, singing, laughing, and drinking," while "young 'pachuquitos'—who often bragged of being veterans of the Pachuco–Zoot Suit War—would be wrestling, fighting, cursing, and yelling." After he and his comrades returned from overseas duty, "where we had been held in contempt by others who disliked us because of our constant Spanish chatter or our laxity in military discipline, we were now admired, respected, and approved by all those around us, including most of our commanding officers."[58] While in the armed forces, many Mexican Americans "learned how it felt not to be treated like a Mexican," and compared to Negro youths, they were granted more freedom of choice regarding to which branch they were assigned.

Many youths born in Mexico were "turned down when they attempted to enlist," but eventually "even the alien noncitizens in the United States were classified 1A and were drafted. Many . . . were later given the opportunity to become citizens by taking the oath while in the service."[59] In a bitter irony, the very citizens whose loyalty and patriotism were questioned during the war sacrificed the most, as Japanese American combat units distinguished themselves in battle, and many Mexican Americans earned the Congressional Medal of Honor, the nation's highest decoration for bravery above and beyond the call of duty. In wartime Los Angeles, ethnic Mexicans made up about one-tenth of the population, yet, as a random sampling of ten city newspapers revealed, Spanish-surnamed "men of Mexican ancestry" made up about one-fifth of both the casualty and awards lists. In addition, "because Mexican families are usually large, many homes had four or more sons in the service," and "in some homes as many as two or three members were casualties."[60]

The young Mexican American Angelenos coming of age in the late 1930s and early 1940s, having survived the Great Depression, were now trying to live through the Second World War. In addition to this historical context, they were thoroughly enmeshed in their modern, often hostile metropolis, which bombarded them with mixed messages. In response, a growing number of them created a strategy of negotiation centered on African American–derived swing music, jitterbug dancing, and zoot suits. The most alienated among them became pachucos and pachucas. Pachucos created their own hairstyle, as smooth and suave as them, by slicking their thick, long black hair back on the sides toward the nape of the neck, so that it fell in two feathery waves at the collar in the "ducktail," also known as a "D.A.," or "duck's ass," and, by the police and the press, as an "Argentine" haircut. The sociologist Emory Bogardus described young Mexican American men wearing "long coats, generally black . . . and long hair, combed back in 'duck-tail' fashion."[61] According to Carey McWilliams, "Going in for broad-brimmed hats, the boys let their hair grow long and comb it straight back in two black wings that meet at the back of the head. . . . Dolled up in these fancy zoot suits and racing around in cut-down and hopped-up jalopies, the pachuco gangs have occasioned much sensational publicity" (see figures 11 and 12).[62]

African American hep cats wore their straightened hair pomaded long on the top and the sides, often with a ducktail wedge at the neckline, like "the solid cats in their pancho conks" described by Chester Himes.[63] Mauricio Mazón found that "during and after the Zoot-Suit Riots Mexican-American youth were known to have shaven their heads—a kind of scarification that indicated their victimization by servicemen. These youngsters sported their smooth pates as a badge, meaning they had survived contact with the enemy."[64] Pachucos might wear a thin mustache, a single patch of hair under the bottom lip, or a goatee, like jazz musicians and African American hep cats, but unlike the general populace. Also very much against the norm, pachucos in Los Angeles were known for unique black-ink tattoos on the back of the hand between the thumb and forefinger—usually a cross with radiant lines extending outward, but sometimes the initials of their neighborhood or gang—and also for tattoos on their arms, neck, and face.[65] Finally, they were known for a stylized black-letter graffiti. As María Olivas Alvarez remembered, wherever they went, the pachucos would write gang names or street numbers on the walls, and they had their own way of writing. By the early 1940s, the pachucos, whom Alvarez described as "disorderly," "rebellious," "mean," and scandalous, had already created gangs like White Fence in Boyle Heights—the oldest original barrio club—and Sangra in San Gabriel.[66]

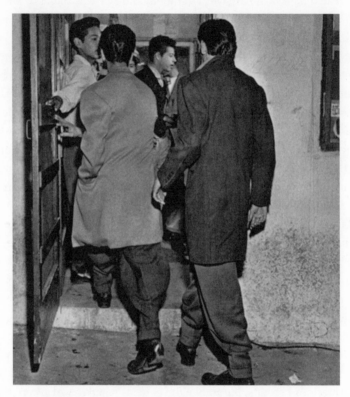

11. Ducktails, drapes, and double-sole shoes, early 1940s.
COURTESY AUDREY A. LOGAN.

12. Mexican American youths in car, early 1940s.

COURTESY AUDREY A. LOGAN.

Many academic attempts to solve what Ralph Ellison called in 1943 the "riddle of the zoot" have centered on the East Coast, and on men. By studying both male and female zoot styles in Los Angeles scholars can try, as Ellison tried, to decode the "profound political meaning" encrypted in the drape shape, but without portraying the zoot suit phenomenon in black and white, and without ignoring pachucas.[67] The Los Angeles pachucas also spoke the Spanglish street slang and wore the zoot clothing style.[68] For instance, many young Mexican American women wore the zoot coat with a shirt, blouse, or sweater, a knee-length skirt, and either ankle-strap heels or leather dancing shoes with mid-calf black bobby socks. The pachucas would often wear "a modified 'zoot suit,' with black skirts and hose, including the broad-shouldered and longer coat of the boy's costume."[69] Beatrice Griffith observed that Mexican American girls wore "a long finger-tip coat or letterman's sweater, draped slacks or a short full skirt," along with "high bobby socks, and huaraches." To complete the effect, "they were usually made up heavily with mascara and lipstick, and the favorite hair style was a high pompadour with flowers and earrings."[70] Some pachucas lightened their hair with peroxide. Hortencia Esquivel noted that while the pachuco and pachuca styles were popular in the Westside barrios, the Mexican Americans in Central and East Los Angeles wore more extreme zoot fashions.[71]

A 1943 *Los Angeles Times* article mentioned three "slick chicks . . . all wearing dark skirts and the long identifying coats of the zooters."[72] As one young Mexican American woman recalled, the Black Widows, from the Maravilla neighborhood in East Los Angeles, were "the best looking ones that dressed nice. . . . they all died their hair black. Some of them had natural little streaks. They were pretty. I used to look at them at the dances, we all used to go to the dances, and they used to come in their little groups . . . from all over."[73] McWilliams described the pachuca look as "black huaraches, short black skirt, long black stockings, sweater, and high pompadour."[74] In a Mexican American exaggeration of the popular pompadour style, the woman's hair was swept up from the forehead in tall bangs, pulled back high on the sides, and left shoulder-length at the back. Like the zoot suit they accompanied, in-your-face styles like the ducktail of the pachucos, and the pompadour and extreme makeup of the pachucas, represented responses to rejection and intimidation which claimed space, drew attention to their wearers, and declared that Mexican Americans were here to stay, so get used to it (see figures 13 and 14).[75]

13. Pachuca style on jitterbugs at Club Los Pachucos, a nightclub opened by Los Angeles civic leaders to combat juvenile delinquency by providing wholesome recreation. November 13, 1942. COURTESY BETTMANN/CORBIS.

14. Pompadour hairstyle, early 1940s. COURTESY AUDREY A. LOGAN.

Regarding the fashion-forward pachuca style, Lupe Leyvas stated:

During the forties we had . . . miniskirts . . . and long jackets that went the same length as our skirts. Our socks would be almost to our knee. Sometimes we would wear white boots with tassels. Our hairdos were high pompadours, flowers in our hair—mostly artificial flowers. When we wore dresses, we'd have like sweetheart necks, very low waisted, and very full at the bottom, so when we turned and danced, there was a lot of room for our knees. A lot of jewelry.[76]

Hortencia Garibay used to wear long white socks, as well as, on other occasions, a blouse, a short black skirt, short black boots with fur on the outside, little gold hoop earrings, and two big flowers in "a big pompadour. I was never a bad girl. It's just everybody was dressing like that."[77] As Carlos Espinoza stated, "You had a lot of us who would . . . double the money and buy our wives, or girlfriends at that time, a suit to match so that when we went down to the dance you would look good in the suit made out of the same material. . . . Sharkskin suits in different colors."[78]

The most daring pachucas donned the men's draped slacks, and even the full zoot suit. For example, Chole Camarena, the Lincoln Heights pachuca who frequented Central Avenue, wore the popular pompadour hairstyle, thin, silver shoulder-length earrings, suede "elf" boots, or ankle-strapped high heels. Tall and slim, Chole received many compliments on her clothes from the young men with whom she danced. In their gabardine, hound's tooth, and sharkskin suits, they could appreciate her glamorous finery. Chole's Mexicano parents, however, could not. At seventeen- and twenty-years-old, respectively, her mother and father immigrated to Los Angeles from Tepatitlán, Jalisco, Mexico in 1900. In 1940 their fifteen-year-old daughter began hanging out with pachucos and adopting the pachuca style. By 1942 Chole was working eight-hour days packing and inspecting fuel pumps at an auto parts store at 12th and Olive streets downtown, taking the streetcar back to Lincoln Heights, then sweeping the neighborhood drugstore until ten at night. Chole's father bought her conventional, pretty dresses, but Chole preferred purchasing custom-made skirts and draped slacks downtown at Murray's with her own money. Her father once tore up one of her zoot suits, and on another occasion, after catching her going out on the town in drapes, he yelled, "I don't want no pachuca in my house!"[79]

One Mexican mother who did not approve of the expensive zoot suits used to tell her son, "Don't you ever try to be a pachuco because '*son marijuanos.*' "[80] In many Mexicano and Mexican American households, parents balked at the hip styles that their sons, and especially at those that their daughters, favored. Leyvas recalled rolling up the waist of her knee-length skirt to make it shorter, but only after leaving her disapproving parents' house. Then after the dance, she would pull her skirt back down before returning home.[81] Similarly, Hortencia Garibay said, "When you were at home you had your skirt a little longer, and then when you got into the street you used to roll it up and be in style."[82] Carlos Espinoza explained that because of parents who did not like the drape style, "some of the guys would go down to their neighbor's house and put the zoot suit on, and then go to the dance. And they would come back and take it off, and put their Levi's on and go home."[83]

The clothing fashions of these young Mexican Americans present historical evidence for a Chicano expressive culture with a versatile aesthetic of stylization, improvisation, and adaptation. For instance, Tomás Ybarra-Frausto outlines a typically Chicano "attitude rooted in resourcefulness and adaptability, yet mindful of stance and style," one "of survival and inventiveness." He identifies an "irrepressible spirit," "underdog perspective," and bicultural, working-class, devil-may-care sensibility "attuned to mixtures and confluence," and to juxtaposition. In particular, Chicano youth cultures utilize "strategies of appropriation, reversal, and inversion," feigning "complicity with dominant discourses while skillfully decentering and transforming them."[84] A key part of this process, as seen in this book, was African American popular music. For example, although the average wartime Mexican American Angeleno followed bandleaders like Benny Goodman, Artie Shaw, and Tommy Dorsey, many pachucos listened almost exclusively to hard-driving black bandleaders like Count Basie and Jimmie Lunceford, whose "hep" music was the best for jitterbugging. These orchestras played "their music," and the neighborhood pachucos made sure that Lucie Brac's father stocked his Lincoln Heights pharmacy jukebox with their favorite black swing tunes. As Lucie recalled, "they all used to dance the jitterbug. And of course they loved black music."[85]

During the early 1940s Lincoln Heights was composed of Italian and Mexican immigrant families, and, like her pachuco friends, Chole Camarena disliked her father's Mexican music, but enjoyed swing music and jitterbug dancing.[86] The pachucos' influence on the development of Mexican American expressive culture, especially in the realm of fashion, slang, style, attitude, and dance, was considerable. For instance, apparently Mexican American youths danced the jitterbug differently than black and white youths of the era. As Don Tosti put it, "We used to dance a pachuco swing, the Mexican kids."[87] Gloria Rios stated, "If I happened to dance with a zoot suiter, I would try to do the pachuco hop, and if I was dancing with a serviceman, I'd just do straight jitterbugging. I mean, you have to adjust to your partner, you know, especially when you're at a dance." Rios added that "the pachuco hop . . . was like a Latin version" of the jitterbug.[88]

Vince Ramírez would see "main bands" at the Pasadena Civic Auditorium, where, for a while "there was a style of dancing that the non-Mexicans used to do instead of swinging the girl and all that. They would stand close together and kind of stomp their feet in a certain rhythm."[89] Ed Frias and his friends all danced the jitterbug, but he remembered that Anglos "had their own little steps."[90] Hortencia Esquivel also noted that by "turning around too much," whites "had a different style, completely. . . . They didn't dance like the Mexicans did, you know, like the pachucos danced." The pachucos "were very good dancers" who would let their female partners "do the turns." The pachucos "had their own style, mostly slow dancing," but "they danced the jitterbug, too."[91] According to Arthur Arenas, unlike the jitterbugs, the pachucos did not exert themselves, nor did they spin. Instead, they executed what documentarian Joseph Tovares calls "stoic moves." At the clubs, a stationary pachuco would strike a pose, extending one hand ever so slightly as the pachuca circled him three times, for he did not want to wrinkle his coat.[92] Chico Sesma noted that the pachucos "had their own style of dancing," in which "the man" stood "in one position and he spun the girl around" without "a lot of body movement."[93] Ed Frias recalled that on the West Coast the jitterbug was called "the Balboa," which, Lucie Brac asserted, was "a little more smooth, a little more cool than the [athletic] Lindy Hop." She remembered that "the guys could just stand still, and they'd keep twirling the girls around, going this way and that way."[94] Although pachucos were considered "the best dancers . . . the male pachuco would stand and really direct the dancing; turn the girl . . . and then another turn, and the girl was doing all the work."[95] According to Vince Ramírez, the pachucos did not twirl the girl or themselves. Rather, the pachuco dance style was about "exaggerating to make a point. A non–zoot suiter would swing the girl and let her go out and bring her back. A zoot suiter would hunch his back and turn his neck and grab the girl close and just kind of jiggle . . . cheek-to-cheek."[96]

Just as Mexican Americans put their own twist on the jitterbug, they also made the zoot suit style their own, in typical Chicano fashion. Yet along with their long, slick ducktail pomades, they also helped pioneer another all-American working-class look: denim blue jeans and leather jackets. For example, a 1942 study describing three groups of Mexican American teenagers in Lincoln Heights, Boyle Heights, and Belvedere reported that although the boys came "from large and often poverty-stricken families[,] . . . expensive leather jackets" costing up to ten dollars were quite popular among them.[97] Beatrice Griffith depicted two young Mexican American men wearing ducktail haircuts, draped pants, and leather coats during the zoot suit riots, and she also described a teenage Mexican American social club in the Alpine Street neighborhood in which "some dressed up, draped out in their zootsuits. Others wore their work jeans with black leather jackets and gloves."[98] In snapshots of the period, quite a few young Mexican Americans can be seen sporting leather bomber and flight jackets.[99] With their tough, working-class look, Mexican Americans originated the cool postwar "rebel without a cause" style a decade before it became part of mainstream fashion (see figures 15 and 16).

The jazz musician Anthony Ortega remembered that denim jeans were in vogue during the early 1940s when he was growing up in Watts. To "the guys at that time, the dirtier your pants were, the hipper it was. Like you would buy a new pair of Levis and wear them for maybe two or three or four months without washing them," until "they would get so stiff they would practically stand up by themselves." That was "the thing . . . with a lot of the guys. And then maybe on the weekend they would wear their creased pachuco pants."[100] Many Mexican Americans wore draped pants, but others owned one zoot suit for special occasions or weekend dancing, thus their regular school-/workweek style often gets overlooked: denim blue jeans with sweaters, varsity letterman sweaters, or leather jackets (see figure 17). Arthur Arenas described the typical non–zoot suit style as "Levi's and a T-shirt and brogues." You would "get your argyle socks, because when you wore Levi's, you've got to show the socks. That was the thing, and you roll up your Levi's on the bottom."[101]

In addition to jeans, leather jackets, zoot suits, and laid-back dance steps, Mexican Americans spoke their own unique language. The pachuco slang, called *caló*, like the encoded "jive" of African American jazz musicians and their hipster followers, displayed creativity, improvisation, and linguistic play, and each idiom was incomprehensible to outsiders and

15. Striking a pose, early 1940s.
COURTESY AUDREY A. LOGAN.

16. Mexican American sartorial range of variation, early 1940s.
COURTESY AUDREY A. LOGAN.

17. Mexican American youths wave white handkerchiefs and "surrender" in front of the Los Angeles Central Jail during the end of the zoot suit riots, June 12, 1943.
COURTESY BETTMANN/CORBIS.

elder generations. From the hep cats' and pachucos' standpoint, "whoever needed the faintest explanation of even the most cryptic gesture or statement was by definition a square."[102] Each subculture was extremely masculine, and, according to one analysis, most of the caló terms fall in the general semantic areas of "grooming, clothing, food, women and sex, recreation and crime."[103] In the largely all-male world of the pachucos, the major speech acts revolved around virility, conquests, "challenges, boasts, insults, reinforcement and requests for solidarity," while many of the brash verbal exchanges revolved around taunts and braggadocio.[104] As Dick Hebdige argues, such unorthodox, alternative vocabularies possess "the power to provoke and disturb."[105] In conjunction with other stylistic elements that also express the values of the group, such as music, dress, dance, and drugs, those who use the code cement their camaraderie, reaffirm their collective masculine identity, and help the members make sense of their world.[106]

Among African Americans, many of the hep cats' terms had been used by jazz artists during the Depression, and many date back much further. Jive, with its emphasis on talent, speed, verbal virtuosity, breadth of vocabulary, and the infinite combinations of words, was the verbal equivalent of jazz, a running set of variations on the theme of rhythm. African American hep cats were the strutting, smooth-talking opposites of stereotypical shuffling, stuttering Sambos, and they referred to each other as "man" at a time when many whites still called black men "boy."[107] Their sinewy slang, like the modern cities from which it sprang, was characterized by "its breathless pace, its vibrant energy, its imaginative richness." Indeed, their fondness for adjectives like *crazy*, *mad*, and *frantic* indicates that they were feeling the effects of modernity, with its "rapid and often cataclysmic urban growth," which disrupts traditional social relationships, and its rampant industrialization, which "speeds up the whole tempo of life." The African American jazz musicians, hep cats, and hustlers fought "to get a grip on the modern world and make themselves at home in it."[108]

The earliest pachucos, many of them Prohibition-era marijuana traffickers, also suffered the hard knocks of modernity in the West Texas borderlands in the early 1930s, when the capitalist economy faltered. These original gangsters from El Paso referred to their hometown as El Pasuco or El Pachuco, and some of them migrated to Los Angeles, where their distinctive styles became firmly entrenched. The first pachucos in *Califas*, as they called California, may have arrived as early as the 1920s. By 1933 they certainly had arrived, having caught rides on freight trains and stopped in Southwestern towns along the way, where they taught other young Mexican Americans their slang. In 1942, a large group of young Mexican American pachucos with long rap sheets were given an ultimatum by the El Paso chief of police: Leave town or go to prison. They hopped trains to Los Angeles, the city that during the war years became the nation's pachuco capital.[109]

Like the jive of the hep cats, caló was an inventive, living language, and thus hard to pin down, but certain key features and typical terms can be detailed.[110] Historically, the name *caló* itself refers to *zincalo*, the language of the Gypsies in fifteenth-century Spain, who brought to Mexico many words, such as *chale* (no, no way), *jaina* (girlfriend, sweetheart), *chavalo* (boy), *entacuchar* (to get dressed up), *tacuche* (suit), *tramos* (trousers), *tando* (hat), and *calcos* (shoes). From an archaic New Mexican regional Spanish dialect came words like *chanclear* (to dance), *vato* or *bato* (dude, man, guy), *güisa* (girlfriend) for "chick" or "broad," and *garras* (rags) for clothes or "threads." In addition, southwestern *rancho* terms were used in modern, urban contexts, such as *arrear* (to ride a herd of livestock) for driving a car, and especially *borlo* or *borlote* for a dance party. As with African American jive, in caló additional meanings were assigned to existing words. For instance, *mayate*, originally meaning "June bug," became slang for a black person, while *grifo*, originally meaning kinky or entangled, became slang for a habitual cannabis smoker, and *grifa*, for marijuana itself. The latter words may have originated from their phonetic similarity to the English *reefer*. In other examples, the term *jura*, for "police," was derived from the Spanish *jurado*, the sworn jury in a trial proceeding, and the word *jefe* (boss) became slang for father, and *jefa*, for mother.

Hispanicized English words or phrases, such as *guachar* (to watch), *ay te guacho* (I'll see ya), *beibi* (baby, girlfriend), *troque* or *troca* (truck), *parquiar* (to park), *lonche* (lunch), *chante* (house, shanty), and *chantar* (to get married, similar to the Spanish verb *casar*), were common. Also typical were Spanish translations of English slang words and phrases, such as *huesos* (bones) for dice, *lechuga* (lettuce) for dollar bills, *cortarse* (cut it out), *pegarle* (beat it), *dar quebrada* (to give a break), and *quebrado* or *quebradón* (broke, without money). In yet another act of cultural borrowing between Mexican Americans and African Americans, caló speakers also incorporated loan words from black vernacular English, particularly jive. For example, in the early 1940s some young Mexican American Angelenos referred to pachucas as "slick chicks" and to pachucos as "mad cats" or "hep cats." Many *pachuquismos* of unknown derivation may be from the streets, bullrings, and criminal underworld of Mexico, the badlands of the U.S.-Mexico border, or the barrios of Ciudad Juárez, El Paso, and Los Angeles. These include *simón* (yes, I agree), *nel* (no), *de aquella* (fine, swell), *firme* (hep, solid), *carnal* (brother), *carnala* (sister), *ruca* (old lady, wife, girlfriend, "chick"), *feria* (money), *mota* (marijuana), *ranfla* or *ramfla* (old car, jalopy), *placa* (squarish graffiti script claiming neighborhood or gang name, or a person's nickname), *tírili* (marijuana smoker, pachuco), *ése* (hey, you, man), the feminine *ésa*, *ése vato* (hey, man), *órale* (right on, all right, that's right), *Q-Vo?* (What's up?), *Que onda?* (What's happening? What's going on?), and *con safos* (leave this alone, don't touch, same to you), which, usually in its abbreviated form, *c/s*, was often written next to placas.[111]

Spanish words were often substituted for similar-sounding English words, as in *birria* (a shredded goat meat dish) for beer, or *carro* (cart) for car, while rhyming words and poetic metaphors were also typical.[112] Finally, this pachuco patois was distinguished by the sonorous nasal drawl that those who were "with it" or "in the know" used when they spoke the slang. As Beatrice Griffith noted, the pachucos speak "with a high nasal sound" in a "sing-song effect," but "greetings and exclamations tend to be in a monotone."[113] Indeed, unlike the fast-paced cadence of black hep cats, which was forged in the urban hustle and bustle of the East Coast, the laconic lilt of the pachucos was born of the relaxed tempo and laid-back lifestyle of northern Mexico, the southwestern United States, and particularly Southern California, where succeeding generations of Angeleno African American homeboys developed a languid "Calabama" drawl.[114] Caló, despite its underground origins, represents "a bona fide linguistic variety of Southwest Spanish spoken by Chicanos and Chicanas from various social and economic backgrounds."[115]

The African American hep cats' style was complemented by that of black slick chicks. Malcolm X described the African American women who packed Boston's Roseland Ballroom in the early 1940s as wearing "wayout silk and satin dresses and shoes, their hair done in all kinds of styles."[116] In the bars and clubs along Central Avenue, the "Harlem" of Los Angeles during the 1940s, fashionable black women dressed up "in frills and feathers and long earrings and hats with things hanging off them, fancy dresses with slits in the skirts . . . black silk stockings that were rolled, and wedgie shoes."[117] The pachucas, on the other hand, with their exaggerated makeup and hair, their risqué all-black ensembles, and their reputations as back-talking fighters, openly defied traditional Anglo and Mexican female gender roles. María Olivas Alvarez remembered pachucas as being "very tough." She "used to ride the streetcar," and when pachucas would come in, "you never knew what was going to happen. . . . You just tried to stay away from them because you were always afraid that they would start something."[118] Catherine Ramírez contends that pachucas "rejected middle-class definitions of feminine beauty and decency," and that they "seemed to betray" both "middle-class standards of feminine respectability, and working-class expectations of the dutiful daughter."[119]

As Sherrie Tucker argues, "the ideology that governed wartime propaganda favored a definition of normal womanhood in which woman meant a white, middle-class housewife who would disappear from the workforce as soon as the war was over."[120] Catherine Ramírez also found that brown pachucas did not fit into the available white wartime feminine archetypes of Rosie the Riveter or patriotic "V-girl." Moreover, Ramírez adds, pachucas embodied "wartime fears of both juvenile delinquency and unbridled female sexuality," and they were consequently portrayed as oversexed and promiscuous. While the middle-class Spanish-language newspaper *La opinión* described pachucas as physically and morally impure, as scandalous *malinches*, or female traitors to the race, the *Los Angeles Evening Herald and Express* emphasized pachucas' sharp style, charm, sex appeal, and extreme miniskirts.[121]

During the height of the zoot suit rioting in 1943, Carey McWilliams recalled, one Los Angeles newspaper described pachucas as marijuana-addicted, venereal-diseased prostitutes. A group of eighteen Mexican American young women responded with a letter that the op-ed pages of the metropolitan papers refused to publish. However, Jewish newspaper editor Al Waxman published it in his *Eastside Journal* on June 16, 1943, along with a photograph of the women. They wrote: "The girls in this meeting room consist of young girls who graduated from high school as honor students, of girls who are now working in defense plants because we want to help win the war, and of girls who have brothers, cousins, relatives and sweethearts in all branches of the American armed forces. We have not been able to have our side of the story told."[122] Still another group of Mexican American young women, all of them pachucas, also "bitterly protested the story in another letter," insisting that they "be examined, as a group, by an officially appointed board of physicians" to "prove" their virginity.[123] Finally, a slanderous "exposé" printed in the *Los Angeles Evening Herald and Express* in October 1943, just a few months after the riots, accused pachucas of engaging in "weird sexual activity." One Mexican American responded, claiming, "Half of us girls were zooters, and the other half Squares. But we were all friends and nobody had a court record." Eager to prove their virtue and uphold their clean reputations, thirty of these young women "wanted to go in a body to Juvenile Hall to undergo medical examinations."[124]

These Mexican American women, both pachucas and squares, protested accusations of deviance and immorality by defending their virginity and respectability. During the late nineteenth and early twentieth centuries, African American women confronted the exclusionary domestic ideologies of womanhood by creating a "politics of respectability" in which they cultivated middle-class manners and morals to subvert stereotypes equating blacks with an absence of mainstream values like inhibition and morality.[125] In contrast, African American hep cats and slick chicks, and Mexican American pachucos and pachucas, challenged middle-class propriety with their public displays of working-class conspicuous consumption and streetwise sexuality, despite their hypersexualization in mainstream representations and the dominant discourse. As Catherine Ramírez points out, pachucas engaged in a politics of style, but, "ironically, even though their makeup and garments may have been signs of disposable income and evidence of class mobility, they marked them as 'trashy' and 'vulgar.' . . . as lower-class and, thus, as sexually available."[126]

Young Mexican American women remained dark others in the imagined community of Anglo Angelenos, particularly among white pundits, politicians, and policemen, who invoked traditional nineteenth-century Anglo stereotypes of ethnic Mexican women.[127] Even empathetic observers were not entirely immune to the popular stereotypes of the day, as they mixed praise with generalizations. For example, in an attempt to analyze the pachucas' tough femininity, Beatrice Griffith exoticized them, noting that "a bravado and swagger accentuated the dark beauty of these girls," who "had an impudence attractive to all males, light or dark." By claiming that many of them were "little tornadoes of sexual stimuli, swishing and flouncing down the streets," Griffith implied that they enticed white sailors.[128] Similarly, Chester Himes described Mexican women as being "very pretty on the whole," with "very expressive eyes," and "the warm disposition usually attributed to Latins."[129] Assertive, defiantly unconventional pachucas had their mojo working, but when they exhibited their expressive culture in the public sphere, more reactionary elements in the city sought to exoticize and criminalize them in order to minimize their importance. Nonetheless, their suave styles put them and pachucos ahead of the hipness curve, jitterbugging and slow posing as an integral part of the swing-era urban civility.[130]

During the 1930s and early 1940s, Douglas Monroy demonstrates, young Mexican American Angelenos became modernized, and Americanized, not just by work and labor relations, but by popular fashion and film as well. For instance, a 1933 survey revealed that action films, from Westerns to Tarzan and gangster movies, were very popular among Mexican American boys. Perhaps they felt some vicarious connection with the wisecracking, pin-striped Italian American and Irish American gangsters portrayed on film, who rose from rags to riches not by dint of wage work and frugality, or by luck and pluck, but by vice and violence.[131] A 1942 report found that 86 percent of Mexican American youths saw at least one movie a week.[132] Like many other second-generation Americans, they consumed the images and lifestyles that flickered at them in darkened movie palaces.[133] As part of young Mexican Americans' "repulsive-attractive" response to a society that promised them exciting new possibilities amid segregation, low wages, and inferior education, Monroy concludes, the zoot suit "symbolized passive defiance of Anglo-American culture."[134] The historical literature on the zoot suit is rich and varied, but whether passive defiance, inarticulate rejection, cultural rebellion, political statement, badge of defiance, or emblem of estrangement, zoot suits worn in violation of wartime cloth rationing definitely offended the silent majority.[135] Whether or not the zoot suiters themselves ascribed ideological import to their clothes, given the context of segregation, discrimination, and criminalization, the style became politicized, especially outside of barrios and mixed-race neighborhoods. Indeed, zoot suiters created a commanding presence that challenged the boundaries of segregation, demanded first-class citizenship on the domestic front, and declared that Mexican Americans would not remain subservient or marginal.

One wartime study portrayed the era's zoot-suited, jitterbugging cross-racial affinities as "confused efforts" or failed "attempts at Americanization [which] too frequently adopt only the worst of the new, its brashness and crudity."[136] Actually, these types of intercultural interactions represented a different kind of Americanization, one that was more culturally inclusive than state-sponsored efforts. The pachucos and pachucas had in fact already maneuvered around that very "duality of assimilation and secession."[137] According to Lucie Brac, the pachucos "were the smartest ones—they knew they weren't going to be assimilated, so they all formed their own ethnicity, their own language, their own style, their own country."[138] Rather than fully assimilating or fully resisting the dominant culture, pachucos and pachucas helped create a modern, assertive Mexican American culture. Another member of the Mexican American generation argued that "they had the best of both worlds," and that while "the families that were more recent . . . would accept what was given to them, what society would say . . . the pachucos, the youngsters . . . were not going to accept that."[139] The pachucos and pachucas symbolized a defiance "designed to offend those whom they saw as their oppressor—especially figures of authority such as the police."[140]

While the zoot suit may have shamed and embarrassed middle-class blacks and Mexican Americans, or alarmed and puzzled visiting Mexicans like Octavio Paz, many working-class Mexican Americans perceived pachucos as "classy," and admired their tastefully tailored suits. For example, according to the trumpeter Paul Lopez, "In those days [Mexicans] looked sharp. You looked dap, man, going out Saturday night with your maroon tie, a new black suit, and a lot of shit in your hair . . . [looking] like Tyrone Powers."[141] In this chapter's second epigraph Ed Frias, who was raised in Boyle Heights by his Mexican-born parents, recalled that "there was a pride in being a pachuco," and that the pachucos' zoot suits were "definitely tailor-made. . . . You could get some drapes off the rack, but it would still have to be altered."[142] Similarly, Lalo Guerrero stated that the pachucos "prided themselves" on always being impeccably pressed. "You wouldn't see a wrinkle in a shirt or suit. And the shoes nicely shined."[143] Of course, "the pachucos were very careful not to mess up their clothes." Furthermore, the zoot suit "used to be out of reach for the average person, but they were so proud of how they looked. . . . It was a wonderful era for the young people that wanted to demonstrate to the rest of the world, and to the Anglo society, that we were here and we were valued."[144]

Even though some older Mexican Americans felt that pachucos made all Mexicans look bad, in reality, just as the black hep cats' style refuted ethnic notions of black bodies, the pachucos' sharp, clean look, and Mexican Americans' higher profile in the Los Angeles economy and culture, confounded stereotypical perceptions of Mexicans as dirty, dangerous greasers, itinerant farm hands, or invisible lumpen laborers. This involvement increased as the younger generation sought a way out of working poverty, some of them dreaming of the plush mansions and deluxe automobiles of the stars, some excelling as students and athletes, and some taking advantage of their military service in order to get their fair share of the California good life. Others looked for often extralegal angles, while the majority simply sought a decent living wage to support themselves and their families. During the early 1940s Southern California underwent a renewed industrialization, as the federal government poured millions of dollars into local contracts.[145] Despite halfhearted enforcement by the Fair Employment Practices Committee, and hence continued workplace discrimination, shipbuilding and aircraft industry war production jobs enabled young working-class Angelenos of color, especially Mexican Americans, to find steady employment in high-paying assembly plant jobs with medical benefits.

This new purchasing power and minority consumer ethic privileged immediate gratification over bourgeois notions of respectability and fru-gality.[146] As Himes's black shipyard worker reflected, "I'd never had two suits of clothes at one time in my life until I got in this war boom."[147] Suddenly young men and women of color were even more visible, in smart clothes and new cars that smacked of success. For Himes's protago-nist, the only thing worse than getting fired from his job would be losing his automobile. He said, "My car was proof of something to me, a sym-bol."[148] Working-class men of color driving nice cars angered white people because these status commodities signified that racial minorities were no longer beneath whites at the bottom rung of the socioeconomic ladder.[149] On Central Avenue, the Newton Street precinct patrolmen once hauled in the African American jazz vocalist Billy Eckstine "simply for having a new Cadillac with New York license plates."[150]

Any leveling of the social playing field or "equality of appearances" became apparent to the many white civilians who helped Anglo sailors and soldiers drag draped Mexican American and African American boys out of movie theaters and streetcars, beating them, stripping them, burning their zoot suits, and leaving them in the gutter for the police to jail.[151] The ducktail hairdo particularly offended sailors and other enlisted men, who shaved it off of young Mexican Americans' heads in these sidewalk specta-cles. Draped out in their finest attire, zoot suiters carried themselves with greater self-confidence, a fact noticed by whites of all classes. In their efforts to keep Los Angeles Mexican Americans in line, Anglo Angeleno vigilantes undoubtedly agreed with the man who wrote New York Mayor Fiorello LaGuardia after the 1943 Harlem riot, complaining that "the nig-ger can afford to dress 'and strut' far better than a lot of whites."[152] As this "rough parity of appearances emerged," zoot suiters participated in an "American democracy of clothing," in which men and women dressed as though they felt they were as good as the next person.[153] Having suc-cumbed to one of consumer culture's cardinal features, "the democratiza-tion of desire," young zoot suiters were typically modern in that their clothes revealed few clues as to their vocation.[154] As Robin Kelley writes, the musical subcultures in which drapes flourished rejected the values of the work world for those of the dance hall, where zoot suiters dressed up, "escaping the degradation of work and collapsing status distinctions be-tween themselves and their oppressors."[155]

As seen in chapter 1, young Mexican Americans in particular ranged far and wide throughout the city to follow their favorite bands. In a 1942 study surveying 213 "Mexican boys" aged thirteen to eighteen, the majority of respondents "indicated no serious handicap in their search for amusement, except . . . at certain public beaches, because of their Mexican appearance," while 76 percent "felt that there were enough good places to which they could take a girl to dance." Yet the other 24 percent encountered racist resistance, and in this same study 63 percent of the respondents "felt that the police treated Mexican boys more unfairly," while 51 percent claimed to have "been taken to the station for questioning when they had done nothing wrong." Even though Mexican Americans were relatively freer to move about a wider range of the city than African Americans were, doing so exposed them to further police discrimination. For instance, "even those with a fine school record, possessing leadership, dependability, and honesty, reported in interviews that the police had at some time treated them with brutality, on no other grounds than that they resented being called a 'dirty Mexican' or 'another crooked Mexican,' when stopped on the street by policemen."[156] Officers would frequently tell Mexican Americans, "You're way out of your district," or, "You don't belong in this part of town." As a police station desk officer informed the Hollywood Pacific Sound Company personnel manager after two of his Mexican American employees were arrested, it was departmental policy to keep Mexicans and blacks out of Hollywood. The manager was told, "They've got to stay in their own neighborhoods, where they belong."[157]

Yet Mexican American youths were admitted to the Hollywood Palladium if they wore trousers with mildly tapered cuffs, as was the style, but not if they wore zoot suits, and certainly not if they were pachucos. For example, in 1942 several Mexican American youths "decked out in their finest 'pachuco' dress" were "politely informed" by the Palladium management that they were not dressed like the "other Americans" in attendance. When the boys returned later with more conservative attire and ducktailless haircuts they were admitted without question.[158] Even accomplished, respected African American musicians ran into white resistance, such as the time Snooky Young and Gerald Wilson were denied admission to see Tommy Dorsey's orchestra at the Palladium in 1943. However, after Young and Wilson disputed the box office cashier's and the manager's claims that they were wearing zoot suits by demanding that he measure their trouser cuffs, they were sold tickets. Wilson suggested, "Snooky Young and I may have been the first two blacks to ever buy a ticket at the Hollywood Palladium."[159] Thus, the zoot suit and jazz dance culture of wartime Los

Angeles represented an alternative civil society that the rioting servicemen and Angeleno civilians neither wanted nor fully understood, although pachucos and pachucas were excluded from certain better-class venues. Regarding the nondraped Mexican American youths who frequented the Palladium, they had not totally abandoned their Mexicanness, for their identity was a mix of Mexican and American cultures.

The pachucos and pachucas also created a hybrid culture, but their caló tongue and defiant attitude rendered them outcasts. As Arthur Arenas recalled, "You couldn't get into the [Hollywood] Palladium without a tie, and you absolutely couldn't get in with a pair of drapes. The cops would take you out."[160] Carey McWilliams noted that "while the fancier 'palladiums' have been known to refuse them, even when they have had the price of admission, there are other dance halls, not nearly so fancy, that make a business of catering to their needs. . . . Knowing that both as individuals and as a group they are not welcome in many parts of the city, they create their own world and try to make it as self-sufficient as possible."[161] Arthur Arenas agreed, stating that "a lot of guys would dress up in zoot suits and go to the nightclubs in Boyle Heights. That's where all the zoot suits were, and all the fights. And the cops."[162] While brown-on-brown violence was definitely a problem, in East Los Angeles, police officers "routinely raided parties," "broke up outdoor games and gatherings," "chased young people out" of public parks after sundown, or arrested them for loitering, then beat them "while in custody until they confessed their guilt."[163]

During World War II, Mexican Americans responded to violations of their civil rights, such as police harassment, intimidation, and brutality, by fighting for social, economic, and political advancement. In short, they pushed for a "Double Victory" over white supremacy abroad and racial discrimination at home.[164] By the early 1940s, Mexican American activists participated in Congress of Industrial Organizations–affiliated labor unions, which developed Latinos in leadership positions, and in the short-lived but significant Communist Party–affiliated El Congreso del Pueblos que Hablan Español (Congress of Spanish-Speaking Peoples), which fought for workers' and women's rights while advocating for Latino studies curricula and bilingual education.[165] El Congreso brought an end to the practice of officers arresting Mexican American women and demanding "sexual favors."[166] El Congreso also demonstrated outside the California State Building in Los Angeles to protest the suicide deaths of two Mexican

American boys at the Whittier Reform School, pressured the police department to stop unjust arrests and beatings, and organized a boycott of local stores that refused to hire Mexican Americans.[167] Even the most bourgeois organization, the League of United Latin American Citizens (LULAC), defined Americanization as acculturation, but not cultural assimilation. Other middle-class leaders from this generation also espoused an ideology of "cultural pluralism" and promoted a kind of dual cultural citizenship that they hoped would result in the full acceptance and integration of Mexican Americans into all levels of U.S. society as first-class citizens, without the loss of their cultural heritage and ethnic identity.[168]

In symbolic opposition to the Mexican American middle-class professionals arguing for a bicultural assimilation stood the pachucos and pachucas. Many Anglo Angelenos believed that zoot suiters were juvenile hoodlums, but only a small number of them were actually hustlers, criminals, or gang members. The hard-core hustler has been described as a cynical, nihilistic man who wore "his face like a mask," "lived 'for kicks,'" and tried to remain "beyond the law."[169] For many young pachucos, *la vida loca* (the crazy life) meant to live fast and get thrills in the here and now. Adopting the attitude that "the laws are against us but we can outsmart them," pachucos considered petty theft "smart if the thief is not caught." The average pachuco "has had enough contact with American urban life not to want to work the way his father has." As a result, he "works only to accumulate enough money to maintain his personal prestige and 'style' and to have a high time." In other words, pachucos want "to get what they want from society without having to suffer its penalties."[170]

Hustlers lived on the margins of mainstream capitalism, conducting business in an informal economy where, as Robin Kelley states, "money was primarily a means to avoid wage work and negotiate status through the purchase of prestigious commodities."[171] Hep cats and pachucos did not endorse white Protestant cultural values of propriety, yet neither did they articulate a structural critique. Moreover, lest the hustler lifestyle be romanticized, Kelley notes that hep cats and jazz musicians' resistance to wage labor was often achieved by preying on women—especially black women—who were seen as another commodity. In fact, hep cats took pride in their ability to live off of or pimp women.[172] This general attitude was shared by pachuco hustlers. According to George Barker, "the pachuco accepts little or no responsibility about the girls he takes out with him. His main concern is that [they] don't squeal. . . . The smart pachuco gets the girl to pay for his dinner."[173] Leading up to the "zoot war," the media hyped up Mexicans' alleged criminal activity and drug use, yet some barrio youth glamorized these same actions. Pachcucos and hep cats shared a love of dance and a mentality of working to live on the weekend, rather than living to work during the week—or better yet—working as little as possible. During World War II, the influence of the pachuco and hep cat subcultures could be felt throughout Los Angeles, as evidenced by the young Mexican American who told Beatrice Griffith, "Now the town's really loose on marihuana, and not just our side of town. Young kids in the west-side high schools use it too."[174]

As Joan Moore's research reveals, the pachucos from the hardscrabble barrio El Hoyo Maravilla in East Los Angeles wore drapes and ducktail haircuts, smoked marijuana, and tattooed themselves with various symbols that designated their allegiance to their girlfriends, their barrio, or their race. Indeed, they took pride in their Mexican heritage and rejected assimilation into American culture. They spoke primarily in caló or in Spanish, and ridiculed any Mexican American who spoke *gabacho*, a derisive term for white *norteamericanos* that they used to denote the English language.[175] In early 1943, some pachuco Angelenos had reportedly been " '[de]pantsing' the cops and making life miserable for them" in retaliation for harassment and brutality. In more seditious actions, during the war pachucos had torn down posters promoting the war effort, and, on this and one other occasion, had even burned the American flag.[176]

Even as young pachucos danced to that most modern of music, jazz, and listened to the latest hit records on the jukebox, they still continued earlier Mexican traditions, such as playing the acoustic guitar and composing corridos "for the purposes of song and gang gossip" (see figures 18 and 19).[177] Beatrice Griffith transcribed the Spanish lyrics and English translation of a corrido that details the police shooting death of the seventeen-year-old Faustino Sánchez in August 1939.[178] The East Los Angeles resident José González, whose older brother, Salvador, was a pachuco, recalled that every time a Mexican American was killed by the police, the "homeboys" and "pachuquitas" would write a corrido about it.[179]

Tomás Ybarra-Frausto argues that "the disenfranchised subgroups within the Chicano community" gave voice to "a defiant Otherness," and certainly the tough pachucos and pachucas of wartime Los Angeles fit his description.[180] Griffith was correct in describing pachucos as fearless fighters who followed a code of personal honor, yet her account ignores

18. Mexican American youths around a jukebox at a neighborhood social club, early 1940s. COURTESY AUDREY A. LOGAN.

19. Mexican American youth with guitar at a neighborhood social club, early 1940s. COURTESY AUDREY A. LOGAN.

Anglo *machismo* and male bravado in the dominant American culture.[181] No less masculinist and sexist than the larger mainstream culture, the pachuco and African American hipster subcultures were also crucial in expressing a new, confident attitude. As a youth worker named Henry Marin attested, "these youths rebelled against the notion that whites could use Mexicans as 'a bunch of clowns.'" As a young attorney, Manuel Ruiz Jr. had defended many pachucos, and he found they "were not bad at all." Ruiz realized that by wearing their zoot suits they could "articulate their dissatisfaction" with the discrimination they endured daily. Edward Roybal felt that Mexican American zoot suiters "ran afoul of the law . . . because they insisted on defending themselves." In short, by fighting for respect and demanding equality in employment and entertainment, the pachucos and pachucas rose up "against traditional forms of discrimination and subordination."[182] In this context, their acts of self-determination rendered their styles political, but not for everybody.

Even though many contemporary adults lumped all zoot suiters together, there was a clear distinction between those young men and women actually involved in gang activity and those who wore zoot suits "as a symbol of sophistication" to indicate that they were hip or "modern."[183] As Griffith stated, "The majority, the hundreds of girls who dressed in the Pachuco style (when it was 'hep' to do so) affected the dress in a spirit of adventure. They wanted to be considered . . . up to date and not old-fashioned."[184] Chole Camarena, who wore zoot suits, did not engage in any illicit activities, and hence did not consider herself a pachuca.[185] Griffith remarked that although a few short-lived girl gangs sprang up at the time of the zoot suit riots, usually the "girls who hang around together . . . do not follow the patterns of even the most casual gang, except that they seek each other's companionship, and lend clothes or money when necessary."[186] Thus, while not all Mexican American zoot suiters were pachucos or pachucas, the trendsetting pachuco style was disproportionately influential considering the small number of youths involved in the rough-and-tumble subculture.

Lucie Brac remembered a range of draped Mexican American youths, from the gangsters to those on the "fringe" who were "straight" and "dressed normal": "There were some that wore the drapes that just liked the music [and] the style; they liked belonging, and they would hang out with the other guys—the more hard-core, the dealers, the pushers, and the druggies." Unlike the pachucas and pachucos, Brac and her friends at Sacred Heart High School were "goodie-goodies" who never adopted the draped style. They were "squares" in that they "felt assimilated" and "had a little higher aspirations" for themselves. Nevertheless, in Lincoln Heights and Boyle Heights "everybody knew everybody," and "everybody got along."[187] Outside observers like George Barker and Beatrice Griffith perceived a rivalry between pachucos and the squares, those Mexican Americans who studied hard in school, or dressed like and hung out with Anglos. Some pachucos reportedly called such youths "Pepsi-Cola kids" or "Pacoimas."[188] Griffith mentioned pachucos taunting squares by calling them "teacher's pet" or "big shot." One Mexican American teen dreamed of a college education, and during the course of his schooling he became a community leader at a local recreation center. Yet the neighborhood pachucos followed, beat, and persecuted him so much that he eventually suffered a nervous breakdown. But many squares lived side-by-side with the pachucos on friendly terms. One high school senior, a varsity letterman, said, "A lot of my Pachuco friends who have 'records' tell me they wish they had another chance. . . . The kids I used to hang around with dropped out . . . but they know I'm on the football team and like it."[189]

In another example, "less serious minded" neighbors sarcastically accused the local squares of "putting on airs." As a result, "the young people confess that this small minority of their own people causes them more embarrassment than the few Americans who discriminate against them." One boy even moved out of his neighborhood to escape the cynical attitude of some in his community who called him a "big shot," and asked where his "white collar job" was.[190] One wartime "square" was Julian Nava, who grew up in East Los Angeles and eventually went on to become a U.S. Navy aviation machinist, East Los Angeles College student body president, Pomona College graduate, Harvard University history PhD, California State University, Northridge, history professor, Los Angeles Board of Education member, U.S. ambassador to Mexico, and Los Angeles mayoral candidate.[191] Nava was fifteen years old during the zoot suit riots, but, as he said, "Our parents disapproved of the zoot suits and we never wore them." Still, Nava maintained, "It wasn't all negative. Quite frequently, as in the case of the beatniks later, it was not simply rebelliousness, but a searching for something new and more meaningful."[192]

As one aspect of a similar search, during the late 1930s and early 1940s some young Mexican Americans chose to become politically active in organizations like the Mexican American Movement (MAM). As George Sánchez illustrates, MAM pushed education as the key to acceptance by the larger society, to transcending the limited confines of the barrio, and to increased socioeconomic mobility. From a self-help group geared mostly to boys, the organization expanded after 1940 to include professionals committed to working with all ethnic Mexican youth. Sánchez comments that despite its leadership training institutes, regional conferences, and "inspirational" newspaper, the group was too optimistic, portraying discrimination as an obstacle any individual could overcome, and simplifying a complex problem in a city where "part Indian" Mexicans were legally segregated in education. He concludes, therefore, that MAM did not represent the majority of Mexican American Angelenos. Certainly, their politics of racial uplift and self-improvement could not help every ethnic Mexican in Southern California, even though, like the educational success stories from the end of chapter 1, these high achievers felt that social mobility "promoted not only personal advancement but progress for Mexican American people as a group." However, it is impressive that MAM included enough credential-earning graduates to form a Mexican American Teachers' Association, and that its 1940 Mexican American Girls' Conference increased female participation in all aspects of the group's work. The leadership opportunities provided by MAM proved especially appealing to ambitious young women, for whom careers in sports, music, and the armed forces were extremely unlikely.[193]

Many working-class members of the Mexican American generation were already adopting an American identity without abandoning their Mexican heritage, just as the middle-class political organizations advocated. Hence the Coordinating Council for Latin-American Youth "called on Mexican-Americans to be proud of their ethnic origin," supported "a pluralistic approach to ethnicity," "stressed that integration could be accompanied with degrees of cultural retention," and "drew distinctions between Mexican Americans and Afro Americans as a way of trying to avoid the stigma of racial inferiority imposed on blacks."[194] The young Mexican American professionals in the "distinctly middle-class" council engaged in community organizing "as a response to growing youth alienation in the barrios." Founded in 1941, the council was led by Executive Secretary Manuel Ruiz Jr., a dynamic and articulate bilingual attorney who had been among the first Mexican Americans to receive a law degree from the University of Southern California, and who ran a successful law firm specializing in international commerce. The reformist council "believed in elite leadership and in the responsibility of the small Mexican American middle class to uplift their poorer constituents." After establishing and operating two boys and girls youth clubs in East Los Angeles, by 1945 the council sponsored fourteen youth groups throughout Los Angeles, as well as in San Fernando, Pacoima, and Canoga Park. In conjunction with the Mexican Athletic Association of Los Angeles, the council also supported youth athletic teams in a variety of sports. The council provided counseling services to youth, especially gang members, and the Los Angeles County Board of Supervisors assigned several probation officers to work full-time in the group's activities. In addition to "rehabilitating youth," the council urged local and state agencies to provide adequate playground and recreation centers to improve conditions in East Los Angeles and other Mexican American communities.[195]

Besides the formal middle-class political groups, there were also grassroots organizations. For example, many high school and junior college graduates formed athletic clubs, organizing young boys into teams, and coaching them in baseball, football, and basketball during after-school practices. Other graduates organized a junior college boys' club called "Los Colegentes Mexicanos" to encourage Mexican American youths to continue their educations beyond high school. The Mexican Teachers Organization brought together ethnic Mexican public school teachers to encourage Mexican youth in the secondary schools to prepare themselves for teaching positions. Finally, by April 1942 a general conference was being held every spring for all of the Mexican clubs throughout the state.

It is unknown how many Mexican Americans were impacted by the middle-class groups, clubs, and organizations, but many individuals placed a premium on education because the knowledge gained in school made them sure of themselves in life, like the young man who promised, "Believe me, my children are going to have all the education they want."[196] According to Ed Frias, although all of his friends came from the same economic background, with hard-working parents stuck in menial jobs like housecleaning, painting, and construction, those who went to the right school and who had the support of their families were "exposed to higher goals [and] higher education. And that's what happened to us." At Cathedral High School, Ed's classmates included well-to-do Anglos from Pasadena and Alhambra. Frias estimated that the student body at the private Catholic school "was about 5 percent Mexicans," and that their Mexican parents "wanted better for their kids, so they felt that a high school educa-tion would open doors, which it did, for many."[197]

Just as George Sánchez argues that the Mexican American Movement "reflected the cultural outlook of a certain segment of Mexican American youth," Mario García contends that the Coordinating Council for Latin-American Youth "contributed to the making of a particular Mexican Amer-ican generational view."[198] Consequently, focusing exclusively on pachu-cos at the expense of middle-class political leaders and upwardly mobile squares, or vice versa, ignores the vast majority of Mexican American youths who operated on different points along the middle of the cultural spectrum. Moreover, it is difficult to determine which kind of politics was ultimately more effective in improving the lot of Mexican Americans as a whole: the style politics of the pachucos and pachucas, or the racial uplift politics of the educationists. Even without truly comparing their impacts, clearly each form of politics manifested a new kind of culture, one both Mexican and American, but with many other influences as well. As the pachucos created a powerful, lasting expressive culture critical of the dom-inant society, the squares worked hard, played by the rules, and went to school. In other words, both the pachuco and square cohorts in the Mexi-can American generation tried to work the system, as each overcame its respective obstacles.

At this time, Mexican Americans were still relegated to attending only one day of the week at certain public roller rinks, nightclubs, and swim-ming pools. While María Olivas Alvarez went freely to public beaches in Long Beach and Santa Monica, she still remembered seeing newspaper want ads for apartments that read, "For Rent: Pets OK, no kids, no Mexi-cans," and she heard about job ads that ended with "No Mexicans."[199] Vince Ramírez was never turned away from any establishments, but, as he said, "I was afraid to go to certain places, a real proper dance hall in Montebello. I wouldn't go in the swimming pool either. . . . I'd go some places, but I was made aware of it. Like I'd go into a store where there was a security guard there, and he's sitting down relaxed. I'd come in and he stands up and gets alert."[200] Anthony Ortega stated that "most of the time I felt accepted, but . . . sometimes it would be mostly all white kids, and then you'd get the feeling that maybe you're kind of not as good as some of the kids." As Ortega added, you could "get the resentment through the way you were talked to, or addressed, or maybe ignored, not paid that much attention to one way or the other." Ortega's older brother overcame racial discrimination in large part by his confident attitude, which derived from the fact that "he was pretty smart in school." Conversely, "if you feel less confident in certain things it kind of takes away from you doing better in other things."[201] After graduating from Cathedral High School, Ed Frias could have attended either Loyola Marymount University in West Los Angeles or the University of Notre Dame, but he turned them both down because he lacked the money to buy clothes in "the Ivy League look." Even though his monsignor offered to pay for his tuition, Ed knew that the overwhelming majority of students would be rich whites, and he "was shy—probably . . . self conscious, [with an] inferiority complex."[202] This nagging lack of self-esteem both fueled and hindered the Mexican American generation's socioeconomic success and expressive culture, and it reflected and perpetuated the members' bicultural duality.

Of the Mexican Americans who came of age during the zoot suit/war years, Griffith commented, "the older brothers of these teen-agers were away in the services; their parents were working in the factories. . . . They are Americans, but to the fifth generation they are known as 'Mexicans,' if their skin is dark or they bear a Spanish name." As a result, many among them said, "We're Americans for the draft, but Mexicans for getting jobs."[203] Accordingly, most of the people from this generation simply referred to themselves as Mexican, but Hortencia Garibay, for instance, would say that she "was a Mexican American."[204] Hortencia Esquivel would "say 'Mexican American' because we were born here, but we are of Mexican descent. . . . I would use that: Mexican American." Other times she would simply say Mexican. "A lot of people wouldn't say it . . . but we did. We were proud of being what we were. . . . We were raised very Mexican. . . . we spoke Spanish in the home."[205]

María Olivas Alvarez said of her family, "we always thought of ourselves as Mexicans . . . but it wouldn't feel like inferior." Alvarez heard the term *Mexican American* while growing up, and some of her neighbors would "say they are American," but if somebody asked them, "What are your parents? . . . they'd say, well, Mexican."[206] Lalo Guerrero remembered his mother declaring, "Soy pura chicana. Yo soy chicanita" ("I'm pure Chicana. I am a little Chicana").[207] Anthony Ortega recalled much "variation" in one's self-designation, including the term *Mexican American*. Ortega claimed that "some people were offended" by the term *Chicano*, but for others it "was accepted," and it was not as derogatory as *cholo, greaser,* or *beaner*. In fact, the pachucos used to call each other Chicano, using the word to mean "more like a homeboy," especially during the zoot suit riots.[208]

The rebellious, noncomformist aspect of the Mexican American generation was certainly reflected in the image of the pachucos as hep, proud tough guys, wielding knives and using drugs with no regard for the law, and in that of the pachucas as slick, defiant gangster molls, wielding razors and running wild with no parental guidance. Yet for both Mexican Americans and African Americans, the "way out" zoot suit look stretched dominant constructions of masculinity and femininity until they were called into question. For example, the black hep cats on Central Avenue wore jewelry and cologne, with shiny shirts and diamond stickpins, while some Anglos perceived an air of effeminacy in the pachucos' painstakingly coifed hair and detailed accessorizing.[209] Compared to typical business suits, the men's rather androgynous drape jacket "utilized a more overt symbol of female fashion" in its length and shape.[210] According to Emory Bogardus, "some wearers claim that [the zoot suits] are 'attractive,' 'easy to dance in,' and just as 'becoming' as the delimited attire worn by women who frequent night clubs."[211] Conversely, the broad-shouldered coats and pleated trousers also lent Los Angeles pachucas an androgynous air. In the early 1940s, nice girls did not wear trousers, especially in the ethnic Mexican community. As Catherine Ramírez argues, "cross-dressed" pachucas who wore the entire zoot suit engaged in a rather "butch," or masculine, public display.[212] Some of the hard-core pachucas would tattoo "teardrops on the lower outside corner of their eyes, to represent the number of years of separation from their vato, because of imprisonment, or death," while some pachucos "would also wear earrings (taboo for men of the era), necklaces, and rings."[213]

The zoot suiters' cultural assertiveness was threatening because they appropriated "the dress codes of white male status and normality, playing with the images of an Anglo popular culture's own masculine 'outsiders'—the southern dandy, the Western gambler, the modern urban gangster."[214] Mexican Americans who wore extreme zoot suits exhibited the sartorial splendor and fastidious flair of a subtly subversive icon, the dandy, a masculine figure that subordinates the respectability and conformity of conventional moral authority.[215] The national press demeaned black and brown zoot-suiters as draft-dodging dandies, while many local Anglos must have perceived well-dressed pachucos as Mexican Zip Coons

—uncouth urban "darkies" who sought to mimic the clothes of their social betters. Or, as the journalist William Davenport put it, "The zoot suit is strictly Filipino houseboy on his day off."[216]

The racial connotations, moral usurpations, and gender ambiguities of the zoot suit, along with the outlaw status of the pachucos and pachucas, limited the appeal of the drape style, especially for ambitious young Mexican Americans. Ed Frias, for instance, credited basketball with giving him an opportunity "to excel in something, but at the same time to be a team with [mostly Anglos and Italians], and get to know other nationalities."[217] Athletes enjoyed their arenas for performance of physical prowess, and, like the pachucos, had uniforms and codes of honor. Neighborhoods like Lincoln Heights and Boyle Heights produced their share of Mexican American athletes, even though UCLA and USC never noticed, much less recruited athletes from the Eastside until the 1950s.[218] In addition to the U.S. military, athletics and professional music were the other major avenues of masculine expression and cultural assimilation.

As Griffith recounted, in school pachucos most often excelled in music, athletics, and woodshop, and if a square was adept at these pursuits, "he [was] considered less of a teacher's pet or a 'paddy, who's afraid to get his hands dirty.'"[219] In Chico Sesma's words, "The musicians kind of had a special station in [their] existence between the mainstream and the pachuco element." Although the musicians never socialized with the pachucos or "assumed their lifestyle in any degree," the pachucos liked musicians, and the two groups "mixed well."[220] As Don Tosti recalled, "I didn't belong to any gangs, and nobody bothered me because I was a musician, and I had a swing band in school."[221] Similarly, in Watts the neighborhood pachucos always showed respect for Anthony Ortega. The pachucos would sometimes line up on the streets and pick fights with unsuspecting pedestrians, but Ortega was never bothered, especially while carrying his saxophone case.[222] Paul Lopez remembered that pachucos were always broke, in trouble, and "more concerned with the way they dressed." Lopez could not relate to or communicate with pachucos because, in his opinion, "they didn't know anything about music."[223] The pachucos loved to dance and party, but violence often surrounded them, with Sesma mentioning "a lot of conflict within our own people, the Mexican Americans, not so much at school as there was at the weekend dances." Gangs from different areas would go to the various ballrooms where Sesma and Lopez worked, "and the evening would hardly ever transpire where there wasn't a fight of some kind, and blood usually flowed."[224] In contrast, Himes succinctly noted in 1943, "Negro youths in Los Angeles county are not organized into gangs, nor do they belong to the Mexican pachuco gangs."[225] In Watts there were no black gangs yet, but Mexican Americans from La Colonia would fight other Mexican Americans from 103rd Street, and from the Eastside barrios of Maravilla and Clanton. Anthony Ortega described the Mexican Americans from Watts and those from the Eastside as "rivals. If you were from Watts, you'd better watch it if you go to East L.A., and vice versa," if you were in a gang.[226] As Ed Frias related, "I never got bothered, and I lived right in the middle [of Boyle Heights]. But I wasn't stupid enough to go wandering around in other parts of the city . . . because they would always say, 'Where are you from?' "

Many Mexican Americans picked up the zoot style but were not pachucos and did not even consider themselves zoot suiters. "The zoot suit I never wore," said Ed Frias. "I never was a zoot suiter. I wore drapes, but I wasn't a zoot suiter. The only suit I did have was a [drape]. We all had drapes—not excessive, just nice. Mostly the guys had their two, three pairs of drapes: gabardine, sharkskin, little thin belts, suede shoes."[227] Edward Manuel Rodriguez was a sixteen-year-old Angeleno in 1942 who followed the drape style, buying zoot suits with cash he earned working on his own. His mother, Jessie Rodriguez, born in Aguascalientes, Mexico, in 1908, came to the United States in 1913. Her son Edward's expensive wardrobe did not bother Jessie, and she turned down his offers to give her his money. Consequently, the young man owned "different suits in different colors, [with] shoes to match [and] everything."[228] When Chico Sesma played in the Sal Cervantes Orchestra alongside classmates from Roosevelt High School, he explained, "We had the fifteen-inch cuffs and twenty-five-inch knees, and the fingertip jackets, but we were not pachucos. In spite of our little three-, four-, and five-dollar gigs, we still had tailor-made suits—three changes."[229]

Although both Mexican American and African American Angelenos wore zoot suits, the black hep cats' clothes were, like their East Coast counterparts', more flamboyant than the pachucos, who preferred black, sharkskin, or charcoal gray, and dark blue or brown with pinstripes. According to Lucie Brac, the pachucos' tasteful suits were made of beautiful fabric. They "dressed sharp, but their colors were more reserved. I think the blacks were a little louder."[230] Mary Hernandez, who lived in Watts during the war years, did not remember many pachucos with wide-brimmed, floppy hats, or long chains down their pants pockets. As Lucie Brac stated, "You didn't see the [big] hats on the guys that much. I think maybe that was more black."[231] Even though Chole Camarena would wear powder blue drapes and purple or green suede boots, she still insisted that African Americans were too fond of bright shirts, and were therefore a little more extravagant than pachucos.[232] Looking back on the period, Rudy Leyvas, the younger brother of Sleepy Lagoon defendant Hank Leyvas, stated, "Frankly, we didn't consider ourselves zoot suiters because we didn't wear the extreme zoot suits that the blacks wore."[233] As one Eastside resident recalled, "there were great extremes in zoot suits—the peg of the trousers, the length of the coat, how much shoulder padding, how wide the hat brim if you wore a hat."[234] In lieu of the zoot coat, many young Mexican American Angelenos would also wear dark sweaters or short-sleeved, soft-collared, pullover knit shirts with their draped pants. Apparently African American zoot suits were more colorful and Mexican American drapes more muted (see figure 20). Whereas African American hipsters in both New York and Los Angeles favored loud, bright colors, thick chalk stripes, and bold plaid patterns, Mexican American Angelenos preferred gray or black drapes.

Any distinction of loud versus reserved remains one of degrees, for both pachucos and hep cats operated on the margins of mainstream culture. Beatrice Griffith contended that "pachucos as a rule feel closely allied with Negro youth, and their attitudes are friendly except where outside leadership has consciously tried to change it."[235] During the long, hot summer of 1943, a columnist for the *Pittsburgh Courier*, one of the nation's leading African American newspapers, went even further. Before warning African Americans that they might be the next victims "of the patriotic lawlessness of men in uniform," the writer claimed that due to their mutual "affinity . . . in Los Angeles Negro and Mexican zoot suiters are closer together than they are to members of their own racial group."[236] In fact, the two groups did not always get along, as suggested by Himes's character, Bob Jones, who said, "Two little Mexican slick chicks passed; I caught them looking at me and they turned up their noses and looked away disdainfully."[237] Nonetheless, there were specific instances of sporadic social solidarity, especially during times of crisis. Just as the cross-cultural jazz dance scene facilitated interethnic connections between the young men of color who wore drapes, external forces often encouraged alliances between them as well.

20. Frank Lopez in dark drapes, San Fernando, 1944.

For example, during the worst of the zoot suit rioting, a car full of draped youths ran down a police officer who tried to question them; stone-wielding pachucos pelted a Pacific Electric train transporting sailors as it approached Long Beach; twenty-five black and Mexican American zoot suiters were arrested for stoning a Pacific Electric Red Car in Watts; and 125 draped youths clashed with Marines in Watts, where military police and LAPD reserves were called in to stop the fighting.[238] There were probably other such incidents of rebellion, since, along with Mexican Americans "and some Filipinos," the only other people attacked on the streets of Los Angeles were African Americans, like the black defense worker whose eye was gouged out with a knife after he was pulled off of a streetcar by a crowd of whites.[239] On June 7, 1943, the fifth day of the riots, some Mexican American youths heard a radio broadcast reporting that the evening's sailor convoy was going to converge just past downtown on Central Avenue.[240] Fifteen-year-old Rudy Leyvas was approached by a black man he had never seen before, who asked him, "Are you coming to fight the sailors?" When Rudy replied yes, the man lent him his car, with a full gas tank, at a time when gasoline was being rationed. He told Rudy, "Take it, use it, when you get through, leave the keys in it and put it any place on Central Avenue, and I'll pick it up. All I want you to do is get one of them white guys for me."[241]

As a result, Rudy recalled, "All day we were just transferring guys from the neighborhoods into the city. The black people loaned us their cars to use." About five hundred reinforcements were gathered for this down-town defense squad, and when night fell, sailors and civilians in U.S. Navy trucks pulled up to the intersection of 12th Street and Central Avenue. About twenty young pachucos lured the truck brigade down an adjacent alley behind a theater into a large lot, where their hidden comrades sprung the trap. After a half-hour rumble, which included chains and baseball bats, the retreating servicemen and civilians were rescued by "busloads of police," who quickly arrested "dozens of Mexicans." Rudy said, "They were surprised. It was the first time anybody was organized to fight back. Lots of people were hurt on both sides."[242] The next morning, senior military officials designated Los Angeles off limits to service personnel.[243] This coordinated resistance by Mexican Americans was made possible in large part by the assistance of African Americans.

"This joining together," Emory Bogardus noted, represents one racial minority group uniting with another "against common 'enemies.' "[244] In another instance, late one Saturday afternoon during the rioting, a young black man was walking down the street "with three Mexican lads. A cab drove up to the curb and four Marines hopped out. One of the Marines said, 'let's give these 4-F zoot-suiters some combat training.' " In the ensuing fistfight, the four youths more than held their own, but then the police came and took them into custody. As the African American youth recalled, "My guilt as a zoot-suiter was determined by a careful measurement of my trousers! My trousers proved me innocent. However, one of the officers phoned my mother and warned her that I should not be seen in public with Mexicans who apparently were zoot-suiters." Three months later, the man was inducted into the segregated U.S. Army.[245] Bob Jones, Himes's black protagonist, could have easily been speaking for a dezooted pachuco when he said, "I felt buck-naked and powerless, stripped of my manhood and black against the whole white world."[246] Despite individual zoot suiters' free will and personal choices, they all too often received similar treatment from Anglo Angelenos, the police, and the criminal justice system.

This harsh reality was seemingly lost on "respectable" middle-class Mexican Americans, to whom zoot suiters represented an impediment to assimilation into American culture. The unwelcome publicity surrounding pachuco hoodlums and gangsters during the war years exposed "a community gap that began dividing Mexican Angelinos during the 1930s," for "although most Mexicans in Los Angeles were poor, a small contingent of the community was decidedly geared toward career advancement and economic security."[247] In 1936 just under 10 percent of married Mexican men claimed to have "skilled" jobs, while over 13 percent listed their job as either "white collar" or "small business ownership."[248] By 1946, 62 percent of employed Mexican American heads of households were "skilled" workers.[249] Older, conservative white-collar Mexican Americans like municipal judge Arthur S. Guerin considered draped youths like Alfred Barela "a disgrace to the Mexican people."[250]

While pachucos and other draped Mexican Americans vexed their middle-class counterparts, they perplexed visiting middle-class Mexicans. For instance, while visiting Los Angeles during the war years, the Mexican poet and intellectual Octavio Paz was struck by how far many Mexican Americans had strayed from any recognizable Mexican culture. Echoing the white Los Angeles press, Paz generalized about "the" pachuco, "a sinister clown" engaged in "grotesque dandyism," and about U.S. "Negroes," who all "try to 'pass' as whites."[251] Implicitly portraying Mexico as a static source of traditional customs, Paz lamented the plight of pachucos, "orphans" who had lost the cultural "inheritance" of their Mexican "forebears."[252] Yet even as Paz bemoaned the Mexican Americans' lack of officially sanctioned *mexicanismo*, U.S. pachuco and pachuca style began to influence not only regional Mexican American culture but also the national culture of Mexico.

Specifically, in 1943 a brash young Mexican comic named Tin Tan burst onto the stage in Mexico City. Born Germán Valdés in Ciudad Juárez, Tin Tan learned caló in the pachuco quarters of his hometown and its U.S. sister city, El Paso. He began his career as a disc jockey on a Juárez radio station, where he was known for using pachuco slang.[253] He then toured northern Mexico and the southwestern United States with a vaudevillesque *carpa* comedy troupe, after which he took his routine to Mexico's capital, where he quickly became a headliner at the most popular theaters and a regular over the airwaves of XEW, Mexico City's powerful radio station, "the RKO of Latin America." One of his troupe members, Meche Barba, copied her stage persona, including snug sweater, short black skirt, black socks, pompadour, and dark makeup, as well as her dance moves, from pachucas she had seen in Ocean Park at the Casino Gardens nightclub.[254] Although Mexico has its own tradition of rapid verbal wordplay and clever double-entendres, with his fast talk and loud suits, Tin Tan also modeled his stage persona after Cab Calloway, and coupled with his caló slang, he represented an archetypical Americanized *pocho*.[255] To a still-modernizing Mexico his troupe thus brought an American zoot style, which Tin Tan disseminated through an international Spanish-language movie market in 1945, when he began making a series of Mexican films in which his character displayed a jazzy, improvisational language, as well as an "unrestrained wardrobe."[256] Indeed, Mexican zoot suiters were called pachucos, and sometimes *tarzanes*, after the Hollywood *Tarzan* films starring Johnny Weismuller, because in addition to wearing drapes, they wore their long hair slicked back to their shirt collars in the ducktail fashion.

To his credit, Paz was correct when he wrote that *"pachuquismo* is an open society."[257] The pachuco lifestyle was occasionally adopted by non-Mexicans in Los Angeles, such as Anglo kids who "would hang out with" their Mexican "friends that lived in the same area."[258] There were white youths who absorbed aspects of the pachuco subculture, such as Victor "Bobby" Rodman Thompson, the lone Anglo arrested and convicted along with the draped Mexican Americans of the "38th Street Gang" in the Sleepy Lagoon trial. Thompson, who was twenty-one years old in 1942, grew up in Vernon, where he "had become completely Mexicanized."[259] Beatrice Griffith claimed that in racially mixed or predominantly Mexican neighborhoods "you find youths of Scotch-Irish Protestant, Jewish or Italian, Russian or Negro backgrounds who have learned to speak Spanish with Pachuco emphasis, [and] wear the traditional Pachuco clothes and haircuts." Griffith even described "one blue-eyed Irish boy living in a Mexican community who [had] so completely adopted the Pachuco culture pattern that he [sang] and create[d] corridos."[260]

Exploring music, dance, clothing, and speech styles reveals more cross-cultural borrowing of this kind, as Los Angeles was both a very segregated city and a site of hybrid identity formation. George Barker suggested that in Los Angeles during the 1930s the original pachucos borrowed the style from Filipinos.[261] Young Mexican Americans may have been influenced by young Filipinos' "McIntosh" suits—a sportier version of the typical business attire.[262] Japanese Americans also wore drapes, a habit no doubt acquired in neighborhoods like Boyle Heights and Watts. In fact, at the Amache internment camp, rural Nisei were shocked to see the Nisei boys from Los Angeles strutting around in zoot suits and proudly carrying knives. The zoot suit must have served the same transformative function for these hip, urban Japanese Americans, who considered their nondraped rural peers "country hicks," as it had for a young Malcolm X, and for countless young working-class urban Mexican Americans, who differentiated themselves from poor rural Mexicans.[263]

Perhaps some Japanese American zoot suiters had more in common with other draped Angelenos of various ethnicities than with their own rural "cousins," and vice versa, as suggested by the wartime tale of Ralph Lazo, a Mexican American who grew up in the mixed, but heavily Filipino area along Temple Boulevard north and west of downtown Los Angeles. Lazo voluntarily registered as a Japanese during the internment because so many of his friends were being forcibly relocated. "My Japanese-American friends at Belmont High were ordered to evacuate the West Coast," he said, "so I decided to go with them. Who can say I haven't got Japanese blood in me? Who knows what kind of blood runs in their veins?" After two years of internment, Lazo left the Manzanar Relocation Center in August 1944 and joined the U.S. Army.[264]

In the end, the system manages consent and co-opts resistance, so that rowdy working-class street styles like the zoot suit eventually become appropriated. Even the drape shape itself ultimately became bastardized and decontextualized by the mainstream postwar fashion industry. Dubbed the "bold look" in 1948, this toned-down zoot suit was, according to the president of the International Association of Clothing Designers, designed "to give an aggressive look to the American male."[265] As for the original pachucos and hep cats, however rebellious they were in their youth, as they aged they inevitably slowed down and changed styles, including caló, or "pachuco." For example, a Tucson teen, nicknamed "Goat," claimed that " 'respectable married people' don't approve of the pachucos, and that boys forget Pachuco after they get married." Alex, who became a pachuco while attending Jordan Junior High School in Watts, shed his earlier style and slang when he returned from World War II, got married, and settled down.

Similarly, Enrique learned pachuco talk in 1942 as a sixteen-year-old at Roosevelt High School in Boyle Heights, but on returning from the Army and moving back to Tucson, he spoke Spanish at home with his parents and sister, and "both English and Spanish with his friends," reserving caló "for occasions when he [wanted] to amuse them."[266] As Griffith noted, describing "delinquent" pachucas, "When the girls grow older many of this small group 'wise up,' get jobs and sometimes get married."[267] Even though Griffith did not consider that perhaps some of the "delinquent" pachucas were in fact already "wise" to their place in the larger power structure, former pachucas could seemingly assume a new "square" identity by finding jobs and husbands. In short, Mexican Americans could become respectable by adopting new clothes and hairstyles, socializing in proper circles, and speaking less caló. Despite the power of the zoot suit, the pompadour, and the ducktail as strategies of negotiation, these youth styles could eventually be cast off.

The pachuco style and attitude, the colorful dialect, and the hep swing-era Mexican Americans exerted a strong influence well into the postwar period. In particular, the wartime similarities and cultural compatibilities between Mexican Americans and African Americans continued, with notable exceptions, during the rhythm and blues era. Neither the zoot suit nor swing music suddenly disappeared in 1945, but by the early 1950s both had fallen out of fashion and segued into their successor forms. The pachucos and pachucas gave way to the cholos and cholas, who created a new style, but one that still retained elements of the drape shape. Big band swing gave way to a new style played by stripped-down, jumped-up small groups. This grittier, bluesier music, and its role in the development of the next phase of both Mexican American expressive culture and the urban civility culture wars over popular music and the local citizenry, is the subject of the next chapter.

boogie woogie breakthrough:

the rhythm and blues era

Participation of all groups in enjoyable social and recreational activities
. . . is particularly important in building wholesome community life. Rec-
ognition of common interests and the development of informal friendly
relationships can do much to dissipate traditional prejudices and can
serve as a base for cooperative action.
—Robert C. Jones, "Mexican American Youth"

In [the early 1950s], those groups [at the Angelus Hall] could play anything.
They would play jazz . . . blues, swing, and you just went with it. . . . Our
weekend was our weekend, and we're going to party, have a good time,
and then Monday back to [work].
—Ed Frias, interview by author

It is music that inspires dancing, and Americans are a very musical
people and just as much a dancing people as any African tribe.
—"The Champions of Hollywood: Dancers in a Great Tradition,"
Newsweek, June 23, 1952

In 1944, a 30 percent federal excise tax, later reduced to 20 percent, was levied against "dancing" nightclubs. As the jazz drummer Max Roach recalled, "Club owners, promoters, couldn't afford to pay the city tax, state tax, government tax."[1] After the Second World War, business dropped sharply at hotels, ballrooms, nightclubs, and one-night locations. Many venues cut back from seven to four or five nights a week, sometimes to weekends only, while many promoters suspended their operations. By the late 1940s, as jazz gradually lost its dancing audience, many swing performances were offered less in ballrooms and dance halls, and more in sit-down theaters and concert halls. Unable to maintain their large payrolls and high overhead, big bands either broke up or reorganized with fewer members. By the end of 1947, the orchestras of Benny Goodman, Woody Herman, Artie Shaw, Tommy Dorsey, Jack Teagarden, Benny Carter, and Cab Calloway had dissolved, while many commercial sponsors canceled dozens of swing radio shows.[2]

As a result, for the purposes of this book, the period from 1945 to 1955 is defined as the rhythm and blues era. Mexican Americans from this generational cohort witnessed anticommunist Congressional witch hunts at home and fought in the Korean War abroad. They heard the big bands of their zoot-suited, jitterbugging older siblings as children and adolescents, but they grew up on a new kind of sound that, as Ed Frias noted above, drew from blues and swing music. In 1945, Louis Jordan recorded the hit song "Caldonia," Oklahoma-born, Los Angeles-based Joe Liggins recorded "The Honeydripper," and the Boyle Heights native Hadda Brooks recorded "Swingin' the Boogie." By 1946, when Oklahoma-born, Los Angeles-based Roy Milton and His Solid Senders scored hits with "R. M. Blues" and "Milton's Boogie," swinging, stripped-down combos playing bluesier styles like boogie woogie epitomized the new music, and an even more uptempo style called "jump blues" developed based on the eight- and twelve-bar blues form, with a prominent 2/4 backbeat, piano triplet rhythms, "honking" tenor saxophones, and "shouting" lead vocals. In 1947, the hand-clapping energy and inviting pulse of jump blues burst from singles like "Good Rockin' Tonight," recorded by both Wynonie Harris and Roy Brown. By 1949, *Billboard* magazine began using the catchall label "rhythm and blues" to rename what was then its "sepia" music chart. In the segregated music and radio industries, black recordings made by and for black people, whether distributed by major or independent labels, had traditionally been called "race records," but a new marketing term arose that was less offensive to blacks and more appealing to whites, hence rhythm and blues, or R & B. As *Newsweek* magazine noted, "Americans are a very musical people," but the national pop music scene was changing, as the magazine's white, middle-class readers must have surely sensed. In the context of a 1952 article on professional ballroom dancers in Holly-wood, the *Newsweek* claim that Americans are "just as much a dancing people as any African tribe" seemed to implicitly acknowledge the legacy of jitterbug dancing, as well as the potential cultural impact of the rhythm and blues genre.

Los Angeles politicians and municipal arts administrators, reacting to the popular music and dance scenes, created the Bureau of Music in order to encourage patriotic citizenship, prevent juvenile delinquency, and bring proper music to the people of the city. As this chapter's opening epigraph indicates, social and recreational activities were recommended for "build-ing wholesome community life," and for improving intergroup relations. The Southern California rhythm and blues scene facilitated cross-cultural affinities and allegiances, with black artists performing on the Eastside, and white disc jockeys promoting concerts on the radio and serving as masters of ceremonies for events in Southeast Los Angeles, as white youths caught on to the new sounds, then downtown, and then the rest of the city at large. The urban civility became more racially diverse in the R & B era, and therefore more threatening to the status quo. Ultimately, the educational infrastructure, cultural production, and grass-roots initia-tives of musicians, promoters, and fans brought music to more people, and brought more people from different neighborhoods together, than the official middle-class music programs of the city government did.

After World War II, mobile racial minorities were still kept in line, and in "their districts," as the African American trumpeter Howard McGhee, who lived in Los Angeles from 1945 to 1947, learned when he was ha-rassed by the Los Angeles Police Department after going with his white wife, an ex-model, to a movie theater.[3] In a 1945 incident, thirty-five home-owners, including the African American musician Russell Smith and the actress Hattie McDaniel, were sued by their white neighbors after moving into the part of the West Adams district known as Sugar Hill. At the time, the Puerto Rican trombonist Juan Tizol, who co-composed the songs "Caravan," "Conga Brava," and "Perdido" with Duke Ellington, was also living in West Adams, an area just northeast of the University of Southern California. Due to his racial status as an Afro-Latino, Tizol was included in the lawsuit as a "Negro." The black bandleader Benny Carter had faced a similar lawsuit earlier that year in the exact same neighborhood.[4] In 1948, after Nat "King" Cole's pathbreaking extended engagements at the elite Hollywood Latin club the Trocadero supposedly proved that he had been "accepted" into mainstream society, he moved into Hancock Park, an upper-crust area on the Westside, only to have his wealthy white neighbors burn crosses on his front lawn.[5]

The postwar years in Los Angeles marked a transitional period both musically and demographically, as illustrated by the swing-era cohort of musicians introduced in chapter 1. For example, Don Tosti, like Anthony Ortega, studied under local music instructor Lloyd Reese in the mid-to-late 1940s. Tosti said: "Charlie Mingus was a friend of mine. We studied with the same black teacher, Lloyd Reese, in the black town. I didn't care what color, if they were good, I wanted to learn. And [Lloyd Reese] used to come and see me at the Sombrero. I studied with him, and I was a big orchestra leader. I wanted his knowledge. I wanted him to develop me so I could get better." Tosti thus maintained his jazz skills and, like Ortega, also played at the Streets of Paris nightclub in Hollywood.[6] In 1947 Paul Lopez played in a jam session with Charlie Parker after Bird's release from the Camarillo State Hospital, and later that year Paul was mentioned in the jazz maga- zine *Down Beat*. In 1948, after playing with nightclub house bands in Los Angeles, Lopez left town to perform in Chicago with the Freddy Slack band, and from there to New York, where he would work, off and on, for the next decade.[7] Chico Sesma, meanwhile, played trombone with the Boyd Raeburn Orchestra, and then worked with the Russ Morgan Or- chestra for a year and a half in the late 1940s, when it was the house band of the luxurious Regal Biltmore Hotel at Fifth and Grand streets. Morgan's society band would accompany acts like Al Jolson, Danny Thomas, and the Andrews Sisters, and would also occasionally record in Hollywood for motion pictures.[8]

By the mid-1940s, Tosti, Sesma, Lopez, and others from the swing-era cohort were working steadily and earning decent salaries. Tosti in particu- lar was living comfortably off of his stints with the big bands, and swiftly climbing the socioeconomic ladder. In 1944, he bought his aunts a two- story house in City Terrace, even though the Anglo owner, a Mr. Polsen, originally tried to persuade Tosti to buy a home in Santa Ana. Polsen wanted $7,500 for the house, but he settled for Tosti's offer of $5,000 cash. By the war's end in 1945, large numbers of Jews began moving out of Boyle

Heights and City Terrace, settling in the Fairfax district along Beverly Boulevard, as well as in Beverly Hills, Bel Air, and the San Fernando Valley. Symbolically, Canter's famous delicatessen moved from Boyle Heights to Fairfax Avenue in 1948.[9] William Phillips, the owner of Phillips' Music Store, saw at least six of his Jewish neighbors from City Terrace move either to the Westside or the San Fernando Valley. Some, like the King brothers, became Hollywood film producers, while others invested their mercantile shop earnings in banking and real estate. In 1955, Philips moved to Beverly Hills.[10] Most of the better vacant houses in Boyle Heights and City Terrace were then purchased by Japanese Americans who had returned to the Eastside, and by upwardly mobile Mexican Americans. Depending on what they could afford, Mexican Americans began buying the remaining homes or renting in the beautiful new apartment buildings on City Terrace Drive.[11] The wartime relocation of Japanese Americans, a postwar exodus of Jews, a concomitant movement of ethnic Mexicans from Watts and South Central Los Angeles, and a steady stream of *braceros* eventually left Boyle Heights less multicultural and more Mexican than it had been at the beginning of World War II.

Again, such demographic changes were matched by corresponding musical changes, as new postwar genres emerged to satisfy a working-class public that still demanded dance music. For instance, much to the chagrin of the staff writers at *Down Beat*, as jazz clubs began folding throughout Hollywood, "barn dances" and "hoe-down" performances emerged to replace them. In short, although the poor white Dust Bowl migrants had been derogatorily called "Okies" and "Arkies," even by other whites, their tastes, and those of their children, were influencing popular music and dance in Los Angeles, and horrifying elitist Anglo jazz journalists by the late 1940s.[12] As western swing and "hillbilly" music surged in popularity, "square dance" nights at the Beverly Hills Hotel and the Pasadena Civic Auditorium drew larger crowds than any other night. Noting the commercial viability of local favorites like Spade Cooley and Tex Williams, one jazz writer lamented, "It appears that barnyard bounce is about the only form of music that will pay off consistently in [Hollywood]."[13]

Although the swing orchestras faded in the R & B era, some Southern California Mexican Americans who had grown up during the big band era continued attending jazz concerts throughout the 1940s. For example, Hortencia Esquivel used to see Les Brown at the Hollywood Palladium, and she and her husband remained swing fans. Her husband, Nemorio, was born in West Hollywood when it was still called Sherman, and when it used to have "a lot of Mexicans," but he was raised in West Los Angeles. The Esquivel family had been in Los Angeles since the nineteenth century, and Nemorio was a World War II veteran and a member of the American Veterans, or AmVets. Each Veterans Center Post had a social club, and Nemorio was voted "commander" of the Culver City post. In the postwar period each social club would organize fundraising dances, hiring the bands of Charlie Barnet, Harry James, and Xavier Cugat. Sometimes two or more posts would combine for a dance. Each post also had a women's auxiliary, made up of the wives of the AmVets. Hortencia Esquivel recalled that the veterans' wives used to take things to the soldiers' homes, visit them for company, render aid, and order flowers for funerals. They would also march in patriotic parades and organize separate dances for the women, as well as some dances combined with the men's social clubs.[14] In addition, Hortencia's old Westside spots still swung, though they also exhibited anti-Mexican prejudice. Evidently, in 1948 Don Tosti and his Mexican American fiancée were once denied entrance to the Casa Mañana in Culver City, but the couple went directly to the Casino Gardens in nearby Ocean Park, where they danced the night away.[15]

Another swing-era member, Anthony Ortega, also attended straight-ahead jazz shows in the late 1940s. Ortega and his friends would leave their Watts neighborhood and see bands like those of Gene Krupa, Stan Kenton, Lionel Hampton, Duke Ellington, and Count Basie, not only on Central Avenue, but also at downtown theaters like the Orpheum and the Million Dollar.[16] Ed Frias and Lucie Brac, who came of age in Boyle Heights and Lincoln Heights during the swing era and the beginning of the rhythm and blues era, attended many jazz performances during their courtship. In 1947 at the Carousel, a nightclub by the Los Angeles Coliseum that showcased African American stars to a mostly Anglo audience, they saw the pianist Errol Garner play, and they heard Sarah Vaughan sing with "glamorous, velvet-voiced" Billy Eckstine's talent-packed orchestra.[17] They also danced downtown at the Avedon Ballroom, where local swing bands like Phil Carreon's still played to largely Mexican American audiences, and in East Los Angeles at Our Lady of Lourdes Catholic Church, where the Armenta Brothers and the Sal Chico band played swing, rhythm and blues, and boleros every weekend for a mix of "cholos" and "straight kids."[18] Almost every weekend throughout 1950 and 1951, Ed and Lucie also danced at the Hollywood Palladium to bands like those of Tex Beneke,

Louis Prima, and Les Brown. It mattered little that the audience was "mostly white," for as Ed explained, the Palladium still "had the big band sound, and we loved to dance."[19]

During this transitional period of big band swing, small-group jazz, western swing, and jump blues, two members of the swing-era cohort, Don Tosti and Lalo Guerrero, created an exciting style of music—pachuco boogie woogie—that expanded both the Mexican American generation's collective mojo and the city's urban civility. Ironically, the blending of pachuco slang with popular music started on Olvera Street, the two-block strip of shops and vendor booths between Union Station and the Plaza.[20] After the Second World War, Guerrero moved to Los Angeles, where he went from singing and playing guitar at La Golondrina restaurant on Olvera Street to singing as a featured vocalist with the house band at nearby Club La Bamba. Singing solo and with the band, then serving as master of ceremonies for the floorshow, Guerrero was in his element, on the microphone, in front of an audience. In 1946, Manuel Acuña, the artists and repertoire man for Imperial Records, a local label, signed Guerrero to record with two other musicians. Known as the Trio Imperial, they achieved local popularity playing corridos, romantic rancheras, and comical songs.[21]

Guerrero quickly made a name for himself as the lead voice, and songwriter, in the Trio Imperial, and sometime in 1946 he wrote a polka called "Nuestro idioma" ("Our Language"), "making fun of the way that the pachucos were destroying the Spanish language." Since Guerrero had a knack for writing humorous songs but no stake in either the pachuco subculture or the zoot suiter fashion, his "original objective" was "simply to make fun of the pachucos in music." However, after the owner of Imperial Records, Lew Chudd, persuaded him to write another pachuco song, Guerrero responded with "La pachuquilla," a novelty polka with caló lyrics describing the clothes of a girl from the Maravilla barrio. It sold sixty thousand copies throughout the Southwest within a few months. Guerrero quickly followed by writing "El pachuco," a caló polka about the pachuca's boyfriend, who jealously protected her, then "El pachuco y el tarzán," about a rival from Mexico City who tried to come between them, as well as "La boda de los pachucos" ("The Pachucos' Wedding"), among others in the series.[22] Rather than for dancing, "these songs were just for listening and laughing." Guerrero even wrote a tragic caló corrido called "Los dos carnales" about two brothers who fell for, and fought over, the same girl—

21. "Lalo Guerrero, Exclusive Imperial Recording Artist,"
publicity still, ca. 1947. COURTESY DAN GUERRERO; LALO GUERRERO
COLLECTION, CALIFORNIA ETHNIC AND MULTICULTURAL ARCHIVES,
DEPARTMENT OF SPECIAL COLLECTIONS, DONALD DAVIDSON LIBRARY,
UNIVERSITY OF CALIFORNIA, SANTA BARBARA.

with one brother ultimately killing the other. Allegedly inspired by a true
story, the song's poetic stanza structure followed typical corrido patterns,
but its lyrics were sung "in pachuco."[23] In fact, Guerrero "would skip from
English to Spanish to caló in the same song and sometimes even in the
same sentence," just as the pachucos themselves switched linguistic codes
(see figure 21).[24]

While Guerrero was the lead singer of the Trio Imperial, the label also
recorded him singing romantic Spanish-language ballads as a soloist. His
solo records were so well-received that Lew Chudd recorded Guerrero
singing in English as "Don Edwards" to see if the entertainer could
achieve success with an Anglo audience. Guerrero consented, for as he
said, "Ever since I was a boy . . . I wanted to cross over into the English-
language market." Unlike fellow Mexican American generation members
Andy Russell and Vicki Carr, whose light complexions and Anglicized
names helped them become musical successes, Guerrero's first English

love ballad sold poorly, and Imperial quickly abandoned the experiment.[25] In high school, Guerrero's "idols" were singers like Rudy Vallee, Al Jolson, Eddie Cantor, and Bing Crosby. As Guerrero noted, "I wanted to be like them. I sang only in English. I could sing Mexican music . . . but I wanted to be just a plain old American vocalist. There was also more money to be made in American pop music."[26] Back then, he added, "I used to call myself 'Eddie Guerrero, the Jazz Singer.' " Guerrero's crossover dreams of becoming a mainstream crooner were never realized, according to him, because Anglos "wouldn't buy a Mexican group singing American music. . . . That's why we had to resort to Mexican music to make a living."[27]

Although the first popular songs utilizing pachuco slang were actually Guerrero's guitar-trio polkas, Don Tosti jump-started the formation of a pachuco boogie sound in 1948, when he combined African American boogie woogie with Mexican American caló. In between tours and still under contract with the Jimmy Dorsey band, Don Tosti recorded two original compositions—"Pachuco Boogie" and its B-side, "Güisa gacha" ("Stuck-Up Chick")—at Radio Recorders studio in Hollywood for a local independent record label, Discos Taxco, owned by William Castillo. However, due to an American Federation of Musicians recording ban, Tosti had to record under his father's name as "Don Ramon and His Orchestra," or risk losing his job with Jimmy Dorsey.[28] In "Pachuco Boogie," which Don Tosti described as "boogie woogie blues," pianist Eddie Cano displayed the classic boogie woogie piano style with its bouncing ostinato figure of continuously repeating two-pulse bass patterns played by the left hand, and its "rhythmically and melodically playful" jazz phrases improvised by the right hand.[29] On "Pachuco Boogie," drummer Raul "Lito" Diaz maintained a steady brush shuffle beat and sang a soulful scat solo like a jump blues shouter, while Bob Hernandez blew breezy, melodic saxophone lines, and Don Tosti spoke in pachuco.

With local airplay from the Spanish-language disc jockeys Eddie Rodriguez and Milton Nava, as well as broader exposure by the Anglo disc jockey Al Jarvis, "Pachuco Boogie" gained popularity first in California and then throughout the Southwest, becoming a favorite among pachucos and also reaching curious English-speaking listeners. Consequently, "Pachuco Boogie" reportedly became one of the first million-selling "Latin" songs.[30] Tosti and his "Pachuco Boogie" session musicians quickly capitalized on their success by recording another hot-selling Tosti song, "Wine-O Boogie," a bluesy boogie with a full-throated Raul Diaz scat solo, and with a

Tosti line about the pachucos enjoying "música *locota*" (crazy music) on Main Street, as well as its uptempo B-side, "El tírili" ("The Marijuana Smoker"), a *guaracha*. One of three main rumba rhythms, the guaracha was originally "a topical song form for chorus and solo voice, with improvisation in the solo," and its modern version employed "a fast rhythm" while maintaining the traditionally "racy and satirical" lyrics.[31] The pachucos used the word *Chicano*, so in 1948 Tosti wrote "Chicano Boogie," a rocking boogie woogie romp complete with Spanish-caló lyrics, scat singing, and R & B saxophone. In 1948 Tosti also wrote and recorded "Los blues," a traditional blues with Spanish-caló vocals, "Güisa guaina" ("Wino Chick"), a light, smooth, Nat "King" Cole–style piano/guitar/bass jazz trio song with Spanish-caló lyrics, and "Loco," a swinging blues shuffle with a walking baseline by Tosti and love-song vocals by Diaz that opened in Yiddish—"Ich bin meshuga" ("I am crazy")—then switched to Spanish, and then to English lyrics. Performing in Los Angeles as the Pachuco Boogie Boys, they would often "incorporate Duke Ellington and Count Basie tunes within the course of a set," exemplifying what Raul Diaz called "Chicano jazz" (see figure 22).[32] Disregarding the genre rules of the music industry, they managed to break through into the mainstream by juxtaposing spoken caló with shouted scat, and by melding Mexican Spanish and pachuco slang with jazz, blues, Latin, and R & B rhythms.

Meanwhile, by 1948 Lalo Guerrero's success as a soloist enabled him to leave the Bamba Club and organize his own band, Lalo y Sus Cinco Lobos (Lalo and His Five Wolves), which performed in other local Latin clubs. In 1949 Guerrero and his band forayed into swing and boogie woogie styles when they recorded "Marihuana Boogie," an ode to the pachucos' favorite high that blended boogie woogie piano with swing arrangements. In "Marihuana Boogie," the clarinet and muted trumpet "doubled the melody," playing the same pitches to create an airy, lilting effect. These opening and closing statements evoked the sound that Glenn Miller perfected by having a tenor saxophone play the melody in harmony with the clarinet. Guerrero's pianist drove the rhythm in the typical boogie woogie style, the bassist thumped out a steady pulse, and the drummer spiced up his brush-shuffle with snare and bass drum fills. Finally, Guerrero gave the song a uniquely Mexican American flavor with his Spanish lead vocals mixed with English and caló passages.

Around this time, the band also recorded other Guerrero pachuco-themed slang songs like "Vamos a bailar" ("Let's Dance") and "Los chucos

22. "Raul Diaz, Philmos Recording Star, featured with Don Tosti and His Orchestra," publicity still, ca. 1948. COURTESY DON TOSTI COLLECTION, CALIFORNIA ETHNIC AND MULTICULTURAL ARCHIVES, DEPARTMENT OF SPECIAL COLLECTIONS, DONALD DAVIDSON LIBRARY, UNIVERSITY OF CALIFORNIA, SANTA BARBARA.

suaves" ("The Smooth Pachucos"). In 1950, Guerrero recorded "Chicas patas boogie" ("Chicano Boogie"), in which he borrowed the melody and basic rhythm from a popular recording released that same year by Capitol Records, the Kay Starr song written by Louis Prima, "Oh Babe!" However, Guerrero Mexican Americanized the Kay Starr version, replacing the forgettable English lines with Spanish-caló ones that took the listener on a pachuco dance culture tour, complete with a roll call of culturally connected barrios, from the Rocky Mountain and Southwestern states through California's Central Valley. Moreover, Guerrero jumped up and spurred along this clever, catchy song with saxophone and trumpet solos, a walking bass line, rollicking piano flourishes, hand clapping, and shouts of "Hey!"[33]

Considered as a whole, the pachuco boogie songs were a clear example of the creative expressive culture of a bilingual, bicultural generation loyal to swing but hip to new African American and Afro-Latin popular styles. The use of Latin rhythms further distinguished the pachuco boogie sound from the African American R & B of the era, as evidenced by "Vamos a bailar," a swing number with a *danzón* interlude, and "Los chucos suaves," an inviting guaracha driven by Guerrero's maracas and Spanish-caló vocals, Nacho Barranco's trumpet melodies, and Pete Alcaraz's impressive Latin piano solo. Similarly, Don Tosti's "Güisa gacha" was based on a typical guaracha and contained commanding piano work by Eddie Cano, whose playing "incorporated the block chord harmonies of Errol Garner with the *montuno* of Noro Morales."[34] Lastly, Tosti's guaracha "El tírili," a paean to pot with Tosti rapping his Spanish-caló lyrics and even scatting, was powered by bongo drums, Mexican maracas, and Eddie Cano's memorable Latin piano.

In typical Mexican American fashion, Tosti, Guerrero, and their musicians effortlessly fused their multiple musical influences with pachuco attitude and slang. Guerrero stated that throughout the Southwest he "became a hero" to the pachucos, who "loved" the songs describing their lifestyle. The general public liked the songs because they were "happy," "danceable," and "sort of comical."[35] Guerrero, like Tosti, gained greater representation by conveying certain aspects of a distinctly Mexican American zeitgeist. In particular, Tosti's vocal delivery sounded more like laid-back streetcorner or dance hall conversation than sung lyric, as he stylishly exaggerated the pachucos' mellifluous, drawn-out drawl. After "Pachuco Boogie" became "an underground anthem," young Mexican Americans "began following Tosti because of the *calo* raps he did and the urban tales he told on the 78 rpm discs."[36]

The pachuco boogie lyrical content centered around interrelated features of *la vida loca* (the crazy life) that embodied a particular mentality rooted in the city's mean streets.[37] For example, Guerrero's "Marihuana Boogie" slyly employed slang terms in the line, "Mi jaina se llama Juana . . . pero ya todos los vatos le dicen marijuana" ("My girl's name is Juana . . . but now all the guys call her Mary Jane"), while lyrics like "Marijuana, como te quiero yo" ("Marijuana, how I love you") expressed a value system that would be instantly recognizable to pachucos and anyone familiar with their ways. The song contained other double-entendres, such as "Ya estoy volador" ("Now I am a flier") or "aviador" ("aviator"), both pilot terms evoking flight. Given that the dominant society had used "loco weed" as a pretext to deport Mexicans in the early 1930s, and had federally criminalized it in 1937 with the Marihuana Tax Act, Mexican Americans' mores were countercultural, particularly regarding a plant with such a long history of use in Mexico and the U.S. Southwest.[38] Indeed, because of the strong connection between marijuana and Mexicans, many African

American jazz musicians referred to joints as "Mexican cigarettes." During the war years, the Los Angeles newspapers ran sensationalistic articles about reefer-peddling zoot suiters, and there were highly publicized crackdowns on marijuana use in Hollywood, where racial mixing at jazz clubs provoked intense police surveillance.[39] In the late 1940s, Tosti played his pachuco boogies and rumbas at the Paramount Ballroom in Boyle Heights, which was owned and operated by a Mexican American named Ray Rodriguez and his brother.[40] Guerrero would perform downtown at El Hollo—a true hole-in-the-wall dive—on Macy Street near the Plaza, to audiences composed primarily of pachucos, who could appreciate what a postwar Los Angeles mariachi corrido called the "poesia del tírili" ("poetry of the marijuana-smoking pachuco").[41]

Moreover, Tosti's jazz trio jaunt, "Güisa guaina," was inspired by the national Mexican love song "La borrachita" ("The Little Female Drunkard").[42] Even when Lalo Guerrero sang with the Trio Imperial, he wrote rancheras like "Borracho busco un amor" ("Drunkard Looks for a Love") and "Borracho y enamorado" ("Drunk and in Love"), as well as a polka called "El pachuco guaino" ("The Wino Pachuco") and comical songs like "El borrachito" ("The Little Male Drunkard") and "El tírilongo."[43] Similarly, in the caló slang of the day, the name of Tosti's song, "El tírili," meant "the pachuco," since many pachucos referred to themselves as tírilis or tírilongos, but it also meant "the pot lover," "the reefer man," or "the marijuana dealer." These songs could be perceived as playing on white stereotypes, airing Mexican Americans' dirty laundry, or ridiculing the drunks and grifos in the community, but they humorously commented on everyday characters from real barrios. Placed in their proper context, the "tírili" and "guaino" songs existed in the same earthy tradition as earlier African American swing songs about smoking reefer, and as the many urban blues and R & B songs popular at the time about drinking booze. Like the African American songs, the tone struck by the pachuco tales of drug and drink was neither community pride nor moralistic shame but bemused acknowledgment.

The pachuco songs certainly expressed an element of música vérité, with their lyrics about getting crazy, shaking one's hips, getting down, giving it one's all, getting into it, tearing it up on the dance floor, being turned on, exciting one's heart, getting high, and being hungover. In addition to veiled references to pot, for example, Guerrero's "Marihuana Boogie" contains sexual double-entendres, such as "Vamos pues a tronarlo las—manos digo yo." In this case, "tronar las manos" means to clap one's hands, but since *tronar* means "pop," and is also a pachuco slang term for sexual intercourse, the first half of the line "Let's go, then, to pop the—" alludes, in Guerrero's momentary pause, to "popping" some "babes."[44] Among pachucos, the phrase *tronarlo* also meant to "spark up" a marijuana joint, to "pop" a pill, or to fire a gun, but in this case, the line reflected the machismo of the pachuco lifestyle. As we saw in chapter 2, caló was transferred from El Paso to the rest of the Southwest via the railroads, but it was also transmitted via records by radio disc jockeys and on local jukeboxes, traveling east from Los Angeles back toward El Paso, while also emanating north toward the San Joaquin Valley, Oakland, and Sacramento. Thus, radio transmitted and popularized both black and pachuco hipster slang to black, white, and Mexican American youths. For instance, teenage Mexican American boys in Tucson would often crowd around the jukebox for hours, straining to catch the slang in songs like Tosti's "Pachuco Boogie," with its caló lyrics about getting in the groove, showing off one's clothes, taking a spin, getting charged up, and coming down. In the end, the pachuco boogie songs lent instant visibility to an entire generation of Mexican Americans who not only enriched popular culture but also made it their own. The popular pachuco party songs powerfully articulated an identity and a dialect at odds with the square, monolingual dominant society.

In assessing the pachuco boogie style, Manuel Peña argues that, unlike the "musical genius" Guerrero's "brilliant attempts" at innovative musical synthesis, Tosti's songs were ambiguous "cultural compromises," and that Tosti appropriated "the pachuco-as-cultural-icon" for profit, embracing, "in a commercial sense, the lifestyle of the pachuco."[45] In reality, Guerrero appropriated the pachuco lifestyle first, as his initial comical pachuco songs were driven not only by his ear for linguistic wordplay and his flair for funny lyrics, but also by Imperial Records owner Lew Chudd's eye for an untapped market. As Guerrero admitted, "As a matter of fact, I was commercializing. I mean, I have to tell the truth. [The pachucos] inspired me to write this kind of [music]."[46] Guerrero wrote "Marihuana Boogie" because the pachucos "smoked a lot of . . . grifa or yerba. . . . I didn't use it but, just to fit the pachucos' image of me as one of them, I let them think that I did."[47] In short, "I wanted them to think I was hip like they were."[48] Tosti had a more legitimate claim to pachuquismo due to his youth in El Paso's Segundo Barrio. Young Tosti learned "pachuco talk" from the neighborhood gang members, and later, from listening to Tin Tan's Ciudad Juárez caló radio show. Furthermore, he arrived in Los Angeles dressed "to the extreme," with high-waisted black-on-gray "fantasy" pants, pointed Florsheim Cuban-heeled shoes, and shirts with French cuffs and stiff, detached collars.[49] Regarding "Pachuco Boogie," Tosti stated: "I wrote this novelty tune to make money and I succeeded!"[50]

Although Tosti tasted the money and prestige of the big bands during his jazz touring heyday, staying in plush hotels and sporting expensive suits, Guerrero was, in his own way, no less upwardly mobile. A talented songwriter who wrote over sixty compositions during his six years with Imperial Records, Guerrero possessed the will and the drive, the *ganas*, typical of his generation, despite being cheated by the label.[51] In Tosti's opinion, "Lalo made a millionaire out of Lew Chudd. Guerrero got very famous, but [Chudd] made the money." Don Tosti exhibited his cohort's business savvy, joining the musicians union, getting top dollar as a sideman, receiving royalties as a composer and arranger, and paying his musicians well when he was the bandleader. At one point, when he was writing arrangements for Guerrero at Imperial, Tosti threatened Chudd with a small-claims lawsuit in order to receive the amount agreed to in their contract. In his subsequent dealings with Imperial, Tosti made sure he was paid in advance. As Tosti said of Guerrero's fame, "I'm not as well known," but "nobody screwed me." Despite Tosti's songwriting successes, he never became a household name among Mexican Americans, who, he insisted, mistook him for an Italian. He even allegedly started a trend in Los Angeles of Mexican American singers and musicians "Italianizing" their names to achieve greater mainstream success. Two examples were Chico Guerrero, who changed his name to "Chico Palomo," and Chico's brother Joe Guerrero, who changed his name to "Joe Como" soon thereafter, just as Italian American crooners were becoming major stars in popular music.[52]

Don Tosti and Lalo Guerrero adapted boogie woogie to speak to their own cultural sensibilities, reporting on the pachuco lifestyle without adopting it. Thanks to the continuing postwar cultural capital of the pachuco throughout the Southwest, they garnered great success with these pachuco songs. However, by the early 1950s, times were changing, and both men moved into the "postpachuco" phases of their careers, with Guerrero embarking on some lucrative Southwestern tours with his band, and Tosti writing several popular boleros and performing in Los Angeles before the Pachuco Boogie Boys broke up in the mid-1950s. The protean musical explorations and strategic business decisions of Tosti and Guerrero mirrored the moves made by other members of the Mexican American generation who, despite continued oppression, increased their political assertiveness and social mobility. As Mario García contends, "The Mexican origin community in Los Angeles had become even more dispersed" as "residential stability, increased education, better employment opportunities due to a war and cold war economy, all contributed to a new Mexican American state of mind and being. Not all shared in these changes, but enough [did] to release new political energies."[53] In particular, after the Second World War, Mexican Americans engaged in what García calls "the politics of rising expectations," which included postwar labor union campaigns for just wages, workplace safety, fair benefits, and job seniority, as well as postwar civil rights campaigns to desegregate schools and public facilities, publicize housing segregation and police brutality, and combat offensive media stereotypes through economic boycotts.[54]

The trajectory toward greater Mexican American visibility and activism could also be seen in the careers of labor leader Bert Corona and political leader Edward Roybal. After being discharged from the U.S. military in 1945, Corona, a former president of the International Longshoremen and Warehousemen Union Local 26 and former chair of the Committee to Aid Mexican Workers of the Congress of Industrial Organizations Los Angeles Council, moved into the Ramona Gardens housing projects and formed the Mexican-American Committee for Justice in Housing, along with community leaders, returning war veterans, and other former union organizers. Roybal, a college-educated World War II veteran and director of health education for the Los Angeles County Tuberculosis and Health Association, narrowly lost his first race for the city council in 1947. He rebounded from this defeat by founding and becoming the first president of the Community Service Organization (CSO), a political activism group that recruited one thousand members and registered over eleven thousand Mexican American voters in 1948. The organization's efforts, along with those of Roybal's campaign manager Roger Johnson, culminated in Roybal's historic 1949 election to the Los Angeles City Council, where he was often the only voice speaking out for labor, equal rights, affordable housing, and civil liberties. The CSO continued mobilizing the local Mexican American communities, with the steelworkers union leader Anthony Rios as the vice president, the garment worker union activist Maria Duran as treasurer, the garment worker union business agent Hope Mendoza on the executive board, Fred Ross as full-time organizer, and Saul Alinsky's Industrial Areas Foundation providing outside funding.[55]

In an era of national postwar prosperity, many Mexican American Angelenos purchased homes and started small businesses. For example, in ethnic Mexican communities there began springing up "malt shops, hot-dog stands, little hamburger 'joints,' trucking outfits, dry cleaning, tailoring, and florist shops, grocery stores, small cab companies, crate produce houses, machine shops, radio repair shops and garages, plumbing stores as well as small restaurants and beer and taco 'joints.'" Not all of these shop owners were former servicemen, but as one young veteran of five European campaigns said, "American guys had a lot of dreams when they went away to war, but the Mexicans didn't. Most of our lives we just had trouble. . . . But we figure we learned more overseas than in all our school years together. . . . So we came home with a lot of ideas and plans."[56] The G.I. Bill helped many Mexican Americans follow through on these plans, as it entitled World War II and Korean War veterans to not only a college or vocational school education, but also government loans to establish businesses and, bypassing Federal Housing Authority racism, to build homes.[57]

During the postwar period, a group of Mexican American World War II veterans, who had attended college through the G.I. Bill and become white-collar professionals, founded the Mexican American Youth Foundation (MAYF), an equal rights organization sponsored by local Catholic churches and represented by cells throughout the Los Angeles area. By 1948, Lucie Brac from Lincoln Heights had become so Mexican Americanized that during her junior year in high school she was elected president of the MAYF. As president, Lucie organized fundraisers and camp retreats in the Malibu Hills, where members planned strategies for the achievement of Mexican American equality.[58] Although many military veterans, and others, advanced economically and socially, they knew that not all of their peers received the same opportunities, hence the need to fight for basic civil liberties.

In 1946 alone, police obtained confessions from four male Mexican American minors "by force and violence," while in a Los Angeles junior high school, sixteen-year-old Esther Armenta complained to her mother, Catalina, that her Anglo classmates "would spit on her . . . and call her a 'dirty Mex.'" After being charged with the use of "bad language," the juvenile court sentenced Esther to the Ventura School for Girls, a notorious "correctional" institution, where one of the matrons whipped her until she had "black and blue marks on her arm." The San Fernando Valley Council on Race Relations charged that the police broke into Mexican homes without search warrants, that they beat, threatened, and intimidated Mexican juveniles, and that they habitually conducted indiscriminate, "wholesale roundups and arrests of Mexican-American boys." A deputy sheriff in Montebello shot a thirteen-year-old Mexican American boy in the back, killing him. The boy, Eugene Chavez Montenegro, had been an honor student at St. Alphonsus parochial school, and his parents were a highly respected middle-class couple whose neighbors, Anglo and Mexican American alike, all testified to the boy's excellent reputation. As usual with such cases involving ethnic Mexicans, no formal inquiry was ever convened, nor did the internal police investigation result in any disciplinary action against the offending officer.[59] In 1948, Roybal, then chairman of the CSO, complained about the "unwarranted beatings of Peter Castro, Peter Silva, and Paul and Melvin Walker . . . at the East Los Angeles sub-station by Deputy Sheriffs Cludy and Serrano" to County Sheriff Eugene Biscailuz, who himself participated as a "Californio" in "La Fiesta" civic parades.[60]

Instead of World War II leading to a double victory over racism abroad and at home, discrimination continued to pervade many sectors of life: "as late as 1949 insurance companies in California were refusing to issue Mexican-Americans, as well as Negroes, policies for insuring their automobiles."[61] And in 1951 the persistent police brutality culminated in the "Bloody Christmas" incident at the Hollenbeck police station, where LAPD officers yanked seven young Mexican American men out of their cells and viciously beat them. This time the public outcry forced the courts to indict and jail some of the officers. Even after Mexican American troops had again made the ultimate sacrifice for their country, "over there" in the frozen mud of Korea, back home their comrades continued to fight for social justice. In 1953, La Alianza Hispano-Americana (The Hispanic-American Alliance) took on the case of David Hidalgo, a fifteen-year-old Mexican American beaten by two Los Angeles sheriff's deputies. Two years later, Hidalgo's stepfather, Manuel Domínguez, won a civil lawsuit and one thousand dollars in damages.[62]

As early as the mid-1940s, the Chicago-based American Council on Race Relations (ACRR) had denounced police misconduct and other forms of U.S. racial discrimination in studies like "Police and Minority Groups,"

"The Problem of Segregation," "Negro GI's Come Back," and a pamphlet titled "Hemmed In," which exposed the "ABC's of restrictive covenants."[63] As illustrated in a 1947 report sponsored by the ACRR and the Haynes Foundation, "The Problem of Violence: Observations on Race Conflict in Los Angeles," Mexican American responses to such obstacles included not only economic advancement and cultural pride but also anti-Negroism and anti-Semitism. The "Race Conflict" report revealed that in Watts, "threats of violence are common and have been made equally by Mexicans and whites against the expanding Negro population."[64] Moreover, "in the older, more settled sections of Watts . . . returning Mexican veterans, resentful over the striking changes which have occurred during their absence, have in some cases threatened to band together to expel the Negro invaders from the community." Yet in "the surrounding 'lily-white' communities [like Willowbrook and Compton] which fear and resist Negro infiltration," merchants "discourage any Negro or Mexican trade." Mexican youths from Watts and white youths from neighboring Lynwood insulted and physically assaulted one another, until the Anglo adolescents mounted "a gang attack on the Mexican residents of Watts."

Meanwhile, in Boyle Heights, a "series of violent Negro-Mexican disorders" erupted after "an altercation between two Junior High School girls, one Mexican and the other Negro, who had formerly been close friends." Paradoxically, "rioting broke out" between the Mexicans and Negroes of Boyle Heights even though "the major discord," the "basic tension" is "between middle class Jews and working class Mexicans," as well as between "lower-class Mexicans" and the police, whose methods resulted in "brutality, intimidation, and complete disregard of civil rights." The report also examined "the drive of the middle-class Mexican for status and acceptability."[65] For example, in the "solidly middle-class" neighborhood of West Jefferson, just west of the USC campus, between Baldwin Hills below and West Adams above, white-collar Mexican Americans, Japanese Americans, and African Americans overcame restrictive racial covenants in order to live among Anglos.[66] In Los Angeles, Mexican American lawyers, businessmen, and newspaper editors created the Pan American Optimist Club (PAOC), "an association of young business and professional people of Latin American extraction." The PAOC in turn sponsored a social club for Mexican American adolescents, but only for those of the "higher type." Another middle-class organization, the Mexican Affairs Committee, "oppose[d] cooperation with Negro groups, believing that the Mexican caste advantage would be compromised by any identification with Negroes. The committee, competing with middle-class Jews for social prestige, [was] outspokenly anti-Semitic as well."

In Watts, the Catholic Church kept ethnic Mexicans and Negroes apart by building a segregated church for the increasing number of black Catholics, and by locating new parochial schools in predominantly Mexican areas. Catholic welfare organizations followed a similar policy of self-help and segregation. For instance, sports teams sponsored by the Catholic Youth Organization (CYO) "are not allowed to play against teams which are composed of both Mexicans and Negroes," and CYO officials challenged "the eligibility of a member of one of their own teams when it was discovered that one of his parents was an 'Anglo.'" In Watts, the interracial character of the local branch of a social group called the Teen Agers Club was "virtually destroyed" when its Mexican members seceded to the CYO.[67] By July 1946, over five thousand Mexican American boys and girls had enrolled in CYO clubs in athletics, orchestral music, dramatics, art, and dancing, with ninety-one gangs represented.[68] The 1947 report on "Race Conflict in Los Angeles" concluded, "the Mexican is often motivated by a drive for caste superiority to the Negro. . . . For the Mexican there is a more complex set of alternatives than for the Negro. His caste disadvantages are not so great and the temptation to seek individual escape is therefore greater."[69]

In fact, U.S. Census results indicate that the number of Mexicans in Los Angeles had doubled between 1940 and 1950, which led to "the geographic dispersal and expansion of existing Mexican communities."[70] The greater Eastside barrio population swelled due to natural increase, residential segregation, and continued migration from rural inland communities, other Southwestern states, and Mexico. With new houses selling for from twelve thousand to fourteen thousand dollars, working-class Mexican Americans fanned outward into respectable neighboring communities and, searching for their own version of the California good life, even farther northeast and southeast from East Los Angeles. Moreover, an unknown number of Mexican Americans living near downtown or in South Central Los Angeles probably tried their luck in the West Jefferson district, in South Bay towns like El Segundo and Torrance, in the San Fernando Valley, or in Orange County. However, as mobile Mexican Americans discovered when they ran into staunch discrimination, many of these areas remained stubbornly white.[71]

For example, in January 1947 the Los Angeles County Committee on Human Relations fielded numerous requests for information on restrictive housing covenants "from the Pasadena Council of Social Agencies, Pasadena Council of Churches, several groups in San Fernando Valley, and individuals in Alhambra, Eagle Rock, South Pasadena, and El Monte." The Committee learned that "M. Craig Friel and Associates," a company from northern California, was spreading covenants in Canoga Park, Reseda, North Hollywood, Pasadena, Compton, and Willowbrook, through its working relationship with the "Title Insurance and Trust" Company and "the chambers of commerce in these communities."[72] Indeed, the proportion of Los Angeles area municipalities with covenants prohibiting Mexicans and other people of color from purchasing houses had climbed from 20 percent in 1920 to 80 percent in 1946.[73] Technically, restrictive housing covenants were declared unconstitutional by the Supreme Court in 1948, but racial discrimination in housing sales continued afterward, as explicit covenants gave way to gentlemen's agreements between realtors and buyers. In towns absorbing a postwar surge of Mexican American homeowners, most whites' racial attitudes had not changed much by 1951, as illustrated by the blackface minstrel shows put on at the Whittier Kiwanis Club, the El Monte Elks Club, and Torrance High School.[74]

The large-scale demographic and geographic movements of the postwar years led not only to race conflicts between whites, blacks, and Mexican Americans, but also to intraethnic class differences within "the" community. One history of Mexican Los Angeles argues that in the late 1940s "a substantial segment of the Mexican community moved from downtown and Eastside barrios into the city's emerging post-war suburbs," where "large Mexican communities" soon "developed their own sense of suburban identity." When "more fortunate" Mexican Americans working in skilled trades relocated to "blue collar suburbs," recent Mexican immigrants moved into the now-vacant low-rent apartments in "the city's older barrios." This "community division," the authors contend, left "a deepening rift between upwardly mobile, rapidly acculturating Mexican Americans and their working-class peers, both native-born and immigrant."[75]

Such an interpretation, however, is rather dichotomous, considering that many of the more established, assimilated "native-born" Mexican Americans were still either working class, lower middle class at best, or the sons and daughters of Mexican immigrants, or all three. In addition, even though not all working-class ethnic Mexicans were "upwardly mobile," they too had been "rapidly acculturating." To survive economically, Mexican Americans took advantage of every opportunity, but their gains were not always at the expense of blacks, and they were not necessarily trying to be white. Furthermore, they did not receive the same benefits and second chances as the Anglos and white ethnic European Americans of this period, who formed what has been called "the welfare generation."[76] In short, not every member of the Mexican American generation who bought a home was becoming middle class, and not every member who joined the middle class was becoming white.

In the years after the Second World War, Mexican American Angelenos had their mojo working, increasingly on their own terms, from socioeconomic advancements, political candidate elections, and community activist campaigns to cool expressive cultural creations like pachuco boogie woogie singles with Latin B-sides. The inevitable internalizations of materialism, individualism, ethnocentricism, and a distinctly Mexican anti-Negroism were mitigated by the powerful popular music and dance scenes. In the general white imagination they remained largely an insignificant, alien racial other, and they continued to suffer the real-life consequences, such as housing discrimination and police brutality. Yet they rebelled against the dominant American conservatism and supposed Anglo superiority by participating in jazz and rhythm and blues, as part of a larger dialectic between competing, parallel visions of the city's civil society.

In response to the multcultural urban civility, Los Angeles officials created their own version. In August 1944, the city council established the Los Angeles Bureau of Music as part of the Municipal Art Department.[77] Emphasizing the need to recognize "the personal and social power of music," proponents such as Arthur Leslie Jacobs, a musician and member of the Church Federation of Los Angeles, argued that "the Bureau of Music has an important function in city government as it brings people together to make music, and in so doing makes them better neighbors and citizens." To win the support of the Los Angeles City Council and Mayor Fletcher Bowron, the Music Bureau's founding fathers employed the rhetoric of civic responsibility, claiming that music should receive the same support given schools, libraries, and museums. Artie Mason Carter, founder of the Hollywood Bowl, articulated the bureau's raison d'être, insisting that music, like education, is one of the "community necessities of daily life and should be brought easily within the reach of all."[78]

With its official slogan of "More Music for More People," in 1947 the bureau began a program that soon became its signature feature: youth choruses, adult choruses, and community singing, followed by talent show–style local entertainment.[79] *Los Angeles Times* reporter Lee Shipey stated that "in one district a Mexican group and an Anglo-Saxon group combined with such perfect teamwork that all their friends and relatives grew friendlier when they gathered to applaud them. In (another) chorus there are Negroes, Nisei, Chinese, Russian, Spanish and Anglo-Saxon singers creating harmony, both musical and social." Praising the bureau's efforts in the Chavez Ravine area for the magazine *Music of the West*, Isabel Morse Jones reported, "This Palo Verde district has been a center of city tensions between the Mexicans and the surrounding neighborhoods. The chorus is helping to relieve those tensions and bring harmony."[80] In contrast, an article of February 1948 described how attempts "to put on community choruses under the auspices of the Los Angeles Bureau of Music in the Palo Verde neighborhood" were met with "outright hostility" by "older teen-agers," whose "idea of community singing is a get-together in the Elysian Park hills with a few bottles of liquor, a box of marijuana reefers, and a guitar. To participate in community singing is 'sissy stuff,' and the younger children, who otherwise might cooperate . . . were it not for this attitude by their slightly older friends, instead shy away from consistent attendance at the weekly chorus sessions."[81]

A journalist from the *California Eagle* attested that in the East 14th Street neighborhood, just south of Pico Boulevard, people no longer worried about juvenile delinquency because from four hundred to six hundred children, and their parents, turned out for the events sponsored by the Bureau of Music. Despite initial reservations, "the community sings caught on and now neighborhood youths are staging their own acts to supplement the Monday night programs." Mayor Bowron also lauded the bureau's ameliorative effects, and reaffirmed its overall mission, declaring that because "the people of this city should have music in their lives, the Music Bureau has endeavored to carry music to all the people. Through the remarkable organization of youth choruses . . . thousands of our growing boys and girls in all sections of this vast community . . . will be better citizens and ours will be a better city in which to live."[82] The portrayal of the Music Bureau as a deterrent to juvenile delinquency reveals a faith in both cultural determinism and progressive reformism. That it was also depicted as a means toward racial harmony reflects a belief in liberal integrationism. As David Theo Goldberg notes, however, although the integration model purported to improve race relations and minority social conditions, "the central values continued to be defined monoculturally."[83] Accordingly, the bureau's attempts to expose all young people to the character-building glories of Western musical masterpieces were flawed by its own cultural biases.

For example, as the *Music Journal* reported in 1952, the Music Bureau presumed that "in an impoverished area where little familiarity with great musical traditions is found among the youngsters," people did not really want such exposure to the arts anyway. By this logic, the various community sings were deemed successful precisely because they are tailored "to the wishes of the participants. Thus there is no attempt to force a group of Mexican children of little musical experience into the preparation of a Bach cantata for a youth chorus festival program. (Talented members of any chorus naturally have the opportunity to audition for any of the Bureau's several concert-type choruses.) On an occasion when folk songs were a feature of such a festival they had a starring part, however."[84]

Apparently, the music bureaucrats felt that low-income Mexican residents were fit to perform only their quaint folk songs and that they possessed neither the aptitude nor the desire for classical music (see figure 23). Yet as we saw in chapter 1, the teenage Don Tosti served as concertmaster of the Los Angeles All City High School Symphony Orchestra, and two Mexican American Angelenos played in the MGM studio orchestra. Chico Sesma "wanted to be a classical musician, but the field for a classical musician is very narrow," and a livelihood much less "available."[85] The pachuco boogie pianist Eddie Cano argued that Mexican American and African American musicians had to earn a living right out of high school, and therefore could not afford the extensive musical training necessary to get hired in the symphony orchestra. Cano began classical piano studies at the age of five, and in addition to his daily piano practice, he would perform solfeggio lessons and informal recitals for his grandfather, who had been first cellist in the Sinfónica Nacional de México. Don Tosti, who was more than qualified, auditioned for the Los Angeles Philharmonic in the early 1940s, but was not accepted. Cano recalled that the city's premier cultural institution, its official orchestra, was "locked up" to skilled Mexicans like Anthony Ortega and Ruben Leon. By the 1950s, a Mexican American clarinetist and "one or two blacks" had been hired, but they "had a hell of a time getting in there."[86] Nevertheless, in the

23. Jessie "Jesusita" giving her daughter, Jessica, piano lessons at home, 1949. COURTESY SHADES OF L.A. ARCHIVES, LOS ANGELES PUBLIC LIBRARY.

Music Bureau's hierarchical cultural scheme, which made clear distinctions between "the 'highbrow' music-lover" and "the person of little musical knowledge who enjoys community singing," there were no classically trained Mexican musicians, and Mexican folk songs did not impart any true musical knowledge or experience.[87]

In addition, the Music Bureau relegated the city's rich tradition of ethnic Mexican community singing to the periphery, devaluing a poetic oral culture in which traditional lyrics are sung in unison, across generations, at baptisms, *quinceañeras*, weddings, anniversaries, and other social gatherings. For instance, Eddie Cano vividly recalled that, when he was a child growing up in Chavez Ravine during the 1930s, "his uncles and family friends perform[ed] traditional Mexican music on the porch of his grandfather's house on Sundays."[88] Growing up just south of downtown Los Angeles, Jaime Corral's first musical love was Mexican music. His immigrant mother, who worked as a seamstress downtown but had starred in a musical and sung on the radio in Nogales, Sonora, would sing rancheras with Mexican neighbors on her front porch or at house parties, with somebody invariably accompanying her on acoustic guitar. In 1944, at the age of six, Corral started singing the popular rancheras of Jorge Negrete and Pedro Infante before this audience of neighbors, one of whom taught him the basic chords on the guitar.[89]

The Los Angeles Music Bureau never fully incorporated these unofficial community sings, or the diverse cultural practices of Mexican Americans, but it did offer more than one hundred summer concerts a year on a rotating basis in public parks, including Lincoln Park and Hollenbeck Park, both in neighborhoods fast becoming majority ethnic Mexican, and in solidly Mexican Belvedere Park on East Third Street. In an attempt to consider the people's varied tastes, the Los Angeles Symphony and Civic Center orchestras were contracted, but also the Mexican Típica Orchestra, which, with its singers, dancers, and conductor José Córdova Cantú, was "extremely popular in East Los Angeles."[90] Nonetheless, apparently these free concerts never came to any predominantly black neighborhoods, nor were existing South Central orchestras or Local 767 musicians invited to perform. In this case, the act of acknowledging Mexicans but ignoring blacks casts doubt on the assertion that the city's "music program reaches all of its citizens," from the San Fernando Valley to the San Pedro Bay, from Westwood to Lincoln Heights.[91]

If Mayor Bowron, the city council, and the music bureaucrats wanted a working model for successful public music programs, supplemented with private support, that stimulated interest in the arts while linking the diverse citizenry of Los Angeles, they needed to look no further than the multiethnic urban cultures of Boyle Heights and South Central Los Angeles. The music curricula and orchestras at Roosevelt, Jefferson, and Jordan high schools, as well as the local music schools and private instructors, were still years ahead of their time, and still turning at-risk youths toward lives of continuing education and study, while honing the craft of neighborhood amateurs and working professionals alike.[92] However, when proponents of the Los Angeles Music Bureau spoke of bringing music to the people, they did not mean all the music, or even all the people. The Music Bureau assertion that "Los Angeles is actively using music as a moving force in drawing together the scattered communities which comprise this metropolitan area of more than 2,000,000 people" ignored a listening, dancing, and performing public already participating in musical expression, and already connected through both organized and informal networks.[93]

While the local dance music scenes had already successfully achieved a functional integration, the bureau, depicting itself as an equal-opportunity vehicle for uniting Los Angeles, pursued a policy of scientific management that included the appointment of a "city music coordinator."[94] The twelve different community sings were decentralized and autonomous, but also subject to coordination, supervision, oversight, and administration.[95] Furthermore, unlike the private sector venues, the bureau enjoyed a city budget that expanded from four thousand dollars in 1944 to one hundred thousand dollars in 1952, and several of the community sings even had their own bank accounts.[96]

The youth choruses and community sings, along with the civic symphony and public park performances, were evidently popular, boasting impressive attendance figures that expanded from just under 6,000 in 1945 to almost 419,000 in 1952.[97] Yet surely the incalculable jazz, swing, R & B, and Latin music performances in and around Los Angeles since the middle 1930s must have drawn together more people from more neighborhoods than municipal and county music programs. Still, when the Los Angeles County Board Supervisor John Anson Ford wrote in 1948 about providing young people "with a priceless opportunity to grow in their . . . understanding of a great and noble art," he was referring to the Los Angeles Philharmonic's Symphony Concerts for Youth, not the city's public school music programs and orchestras or its neighborhood music schools and instructors, and certainly not its social clubs, nightclubs, dance halls, and ballrooms.[98] Tellingly, the majority of the Los Angeles County Music Commission's funds supported the Hollywood Bowl, the Los Angeles and Long Beach Philharmonic orchestras, the Civic Light Opera, the Guild Opera, and other highbrow cultural activities, consciously avoiding "a destructive competition with commercial entertainment in the area."[99] Municipal and metropolitan music programs were indeed competing with an urban popular culture that increasingly blurred the lines between high and low, but local politicians and arts patrons, in their efforts to imbue their fellow Angelenos with cultural refinement and virtuous citizenship, could not see past their own ideological preconceptions.

In this postwar battle for the hearts and minds of the people, the city's elite did not form a monolithic bloc but included both conservative and liberal factions. The conservative faction was represented by politicians, corporate leaders, urban planners, "redevelopment boosters," and downtown realtors interested in economic expansion, highway construction, and the removal of urban "blight," as well as by the Los Angeles City Council, which continued its wartime jumble of politics and morality.[100] For example, the city council voted against a proposed 1949 ordinance that would have made it illegal for the white musicians union local "to refuse membership to Negroes." Contentious councilmen rushed through and defeated the measure "to avoid trouble" with the black community, and to avoid "dissension," which they warned "is exactly what the Communists want."[101] In support of conservative politicians and businessmen, and representing a propertied silent majority, Los Angeles law enforcement agencies provided the muscle to regulate the dancing bodies of residents in a vain attempt to control the widespread race mixing that accompanied the city's "musical miscegenation."[102]

The liberal faction was represented by John Anson Ford, who championed racial integration and subsidized music, and by the Music Bureau, which countered "attacks made by various taxpayers' groups . . . opposed to municipal support of the arts."[103] Music continued to be presented as the perfect tool to produce enlightened citizens, but by 1948, a contingent within the liberal faction also promoted a broad concept of "recreation" that excluded many public amusements, but included athletics and dancing. Hence Mayor Bowron, John Anson Ford, and the other county board supervisors consistently advocated parks and recreation programs, in tandem with officially sanctioned social activities, as a means to defeat juvenile delinquency. Jaime González Monroy, program director of the East Los Angeles Young Men's Christian Association, argued that recreation was not only the "means of bringing youth of all groups together," but also the medium through which "many of the evils of racial misunderstanding and conflicts would certainly be lessened." However, even though recreational programs were offered as panaceas against prejudice, and as positive alternatives to the temptations of street life, some observers, such as USC student Kiyo Umeda, noted that many Los Angeles social agencies discriminated against people who were pachucos or suspected gang members.[104]

While the municipal music proponents stressed genteel cultural enrichment, some of the recreation advocates emphasized physical and emotional release, including social dancing. Thus, in 1952, the Los Angeles Metropolitan Recreation and Youth Services Council extolled the benefits of "wholesome" recreation for young people, listing "dancing and other social events," as well as "music and rhythmic activities" as two of its official categories. Recreation, the council explained, releases the tension of "mental and emotional strain," providing "opportunities to use abilities, muscles, impulses, tendencies, not permitted use during work," while "discharging aggression" and "satisfying social hunger." In addition, recreation "maintains emotional balance," granting "temporary escape from intolerable realities."[105]

African Americans already possessed a long tradition of refreshing the body and relaxing the mind after a hard week's labor. As Robin Kelley theorizes, in darkened dance halls, blues clubs, and jook joints, black workers, in spite of occasional fights, reinforced a sense of community and expressed an often socially circumscribed sexuality. By reclaiming their overworked bodies for pleasure, they undermined capitalist labor discipline and the Protestant work ethic, and by "dressing up," they constructed "a collective identity based on something other than wage work."[106] As Rosa Linda Fregoso argues, dance, with its "ritual properties," is also "central to the everyday life of Chicano and Chicana working-class culture," not just as "an end in itself," but as a pleasurable and meaningful "means to express one's relation to the world through stylized movement."[107] In Los Angeles, the communal, emotionally engaging vernacular traditions of Mexican Americans and African Americans almost certainly reached more people, and better reflected the multiracial character of the city, than the official ersatz version of expressive culture.

Rather than wait for the city's Music Bureau to bring music appreciation to a public park near them, or for the County Board of Supervisors to fund their social activities, many Mexican American and African American communities drew on their own resources. Mexican American neighborhood associations sponsored weekly dances, while informal "home parties" drew adults and youths and often included African Americans, Italian Americans, and Irish Americans, thereby "maintaining social cohesion and developing community ties."[108] In 1950, a cross-cultural "Twilight 'til Dawn" benefit dance to raise money for the Boy Scouts of Los Angeles was held at El Sombrero, a downtown Latin nightclub owned by a wealthy Mexican couple. With members of the "Alta Qualidad Club" assisting the local black hostesses, and with Joe Adams, the first African American disc jockey in Los Angeles, as the master of ceremonies, this philanthropic community event illustrates the kind of "grass-roots" multicultural urban civility that sprouted in between the nightclubs, auditoriums, and stadiums, independent of the music industry and the city government. Revealing the breadth of popular styles missing from the municipal music programs, the evening's entertainment included a jazz contest for local musicians, "nimble swing . . . square dancing," solo performances by classical and jazz vocalists, a rhythm and blues vocal harmony group, and a Latin band.[109] In the years after the Second World War, Mexican American car clubs organized dances and "battles of the bands" in which Mexican American groups "played R & B and Latin music," while enterprising youths hired rhythm and blues groups for neighborhood concerts at American Legion halls throughout the city, and at the Laguna Park playground gymnasium in East Los Angeles.[110]

These grass-roots initiatives complemented the bustling late-1940s commercial dance scene that blended black musical styles like swing, boogie woogie, jump blues, gospel, and urban blues into the new genre called rhythm and blues. In fact, from 1945 through the early 1950s, Los Angeles was home to the largest number of independent R & B labels in the country, including Modern, 4 Star, Exclusive, Excelsior, Aladdin, Specialty, and Imperial.[111] For several years in the mid-1940s, at least half of the nation's best-selling R & B recordings came out of Southern California.[112] Nevertheless, the concept of music participation advanced by the County Board of Supervisors and the Los Angeles Bureau of Music did not encompass the exciting "race music" that circulated throughout the urban soundscape via record retailers, jukebox operators, and especially white disc jockeys. In the 1930s, Al Jarvis had been the first disc jockey in Los Angeles to play jazz on his long-running radio program, *Your Make-Believe Ballroom*. Hunter Hancock followed in 1943 with his one-hour show, *Holiday in Harlem*, and its opening refrain: "From blues to ballads, from bebop to boogie, featuring the very best in Negro entertainment." In 1948, Hancock became the first disc jockey to play an all–rhythm and blues format with his daily three-hour program, *Harlem Matinee*, which was quite popular among Mexican Americans and African Americans, as was the pioneering black disc jockey Joe Adams's 1948 R & B program, *For Dancers Only*.[113]

During an age of stifling domestic regimentation, the rhythm and blues scene facilitated musical and social experimentation, and Johnny Otis, the veteran Central Avenue swing drummer, bandleader, and songwriter, helped to spearhead this process. By late 1947, Otis cut down his big band, hired blues singers, and switched from drums to piano and vibraphone. In 1948 Otis, along with three co-owners, opened the Barrelhouse, a "pure R & B club" located along the railroad tracks at Wilmington Avenue and

Santa Ana Street in Watts. The first Los Angeles nightclub to feature rhythm and blues exclusively, it offered full shows, with strippers, dancers, comics like Pigmeat Markham and Redd Foxx, vocal groups, blues shouters, torch singers, and instrumentalists. Hancock served as the master of ceremonies, Thursday night was amateur talent night, and Otis led the house band until 1950. After scoring three number one R & B hits in 1950 with his Barrelhouse discoveries Little Esther Phillips and the Robins, Otis began conducting wildly successful cross-country rhythm and blues "Caravan" tours in 1951, and by 1952 he had recorded a total of ten top ten R & B songs.[114]

In 1948, even before his chart-topping run, during which Otis became one of the hottest recording and performing R & B artists in the nation, he brought the gutbucket grooves and jump blues of the Barrelhouse to Boyle Heights. At the Angelus Hall, just east of the Los Angeles River at First and State streets, Otis started headlining Sunday evening shows every week. Ed Frias of Boyle Heights remembered Mexican Americans and African Americans from "different segments of the city" gathering from 1949 through 1951 to see Joe Liggins and His Honeydrippers, as well as the local black "honking" tenor saxophonist Cecil "Big Jay" McNeely.[115] In this exuberant, swaggering style, the "honkers" would make their saxophones squeal and bleat high notes, or growl, or honk, hitting one low note repeatedly in extended solos that worked the crowd into a frenzy. Big Jay McNeely, along with two other regular Angelus Hall acts, Johnny Otis and the Armenta Brothers, consistently attracted enthusiastic fans through 1955.[116] The Mexican Americans and African Americans who met in Boyle Heights were the primary rhythm and blues fans in Los Angeles, but despite many cultural affinities, their social interaction was limited.

For instance, Ed Frias recalled seeing "black guys with Anglo girls, but you did not see black guys with Chicana girls. That was a no-no . . . among the Mexicans."[117] In 1951 and 1952, Chole Camarena, who had gone dancing on Central Avenue in the war years, would see Joe Liggins and His Honeydrippers at the Angelus Hall, where she and her Lincoln Heights friends would chat with Mexican Americans from other neighborhoods over pitchers of beer. Among the regular patrons were two young African American men who would ask Chole and her Mexican American friend Mable to dance. The two young women always said yes, but the exchange was limited to the dance floor, for as Chole said, "We did not socialize with them or bring them home with us." Nonetheless, the young women's willingness to dance with black partners earned them "bad reputations" as "nigger lovers."[118] Whether expressed to reject or elevate their supposed place in the body politic, the antiblack prejudice of Camarena's Mexican American companions was stronger than, but compatible with, their love of African American culture. In essence, any symbolic separation from the cultural influence of African Americans, any physical separation from actual black people, went hand-in-hand with a profound affection for, and loyalty to, black music and dance.[119] Ironically, Chole Camarena, who had been disdainfully called a pachuca by many of her elders, ended up being the only woman in her neighborhood to marry an Anglo man, raising a biracial family with Leslie Ray in her childhood neighborhood of Lincoln Heights.[120] Chole had crossed the color line again, but this time it was more acceptable back in the barrio.

In addition to frequenting the Angelus Hall, Ed Frias and his buddies would often drop off their dates, then hit the after-hours spots on Central Avenue, which offered jazz and R & B music until five in the morning. In 1949, Ed even took Lucie Brac to Jack's Basket Room. However, Lucie argued that even though Mexican Americans came from different areas of Los Angeles to hear black music on Central Avenue, they still "didn't want to *be* with blacks. You really didn't see many inter[racial] relationships." She and Ed saw Ella Fitzgerald in 1950 because "we just liked the sound of that music, but we didn't try to integrate with them, or be a part of the black people."[121] Ed Frias never met or befriended any blacks at any of the clubs he visited on Central Avenue, but as he noted, "we were in black territory and nobody bothered us," since "everybody was there to have a good time."[122]

Yet Mexican Americans did not just consume black music, they assimilated elements of African American expressive culture into their own, for inspiration and modification, and they also engaged in personal, professional, and educational relationships with black Angelenos. Within the wider social, economic, and political context of the postwar period, although some Mexican Americans internalized racism and classism, integrating into U.S. society, engaging with mainstream popular culture, and even asserting their Americanism may not have necessarily represented a tendency toward white middle-class cultural norms and values. On the contrary, the two racial minority groups fueled an alternative frame of reference that increasingly drew in Anglo Americans, Jewish Americans, and Asian Americans. At the heart of this countercultural set of values beat the African American–Mexican American connection, which, despite its imperfections, became more intense when Southern California led the music industry turn toward jump blues and R & B.

As Art "Tudy" Brambila stated, in the early 1950s, while songs like Kay Starr's "Wheel of Fortune," Patty Page's "Tennessee Waltz," and Theresa Brewer's "Music, Music, Music" topped the pop charts, on Clover Street in Lincoln Heights "it was Johnny Ace and 'Pledging My Love,' 'Cherry Pie,' and 'All Night Long.' "[123] These young Mexican Americans preferred the African American Ace, a Memphis native whose pensive, vibraphone-heavy ballads hit the rhythm and blues charts from 1952 to 1955, over mainstream white singers like the former "hillbilly" vocalist Kay Starr. Chole Camarena and her husband, Leslie Ray, would go dancing at the Airliner bar and grill on North Broadway in Lincoln Heights, and also at the Riverside Rancho, where they would see the orchestra of bop-turned-R & B saxophonist Earl Bostic.[124] Los Angeles Mexican Americans also supported "Little" Richard Penniman, as they represented a significant portion of his fan base early in his career. A native of Macon, Georgia, Little Richard cut his first two record sides for RCA in 1951, then recorded blues songs for Peacock between 1952 and 1955. After signing with Specialty Records in Los Angeles, and recording in New Orleans, Little Richard burst onto the national music scene with "Tutti Frutti" in 1955. Yet even before he hit the charts, Mexican American music fans were hip to Little Richard's evolving style, which was already "raunchy, furious, fast and highly sexual."[125] For example, Ed Frias remembered seeing Little Richard perform regularly in East Los Angeles at Sebby's on Whittier Boulevard and Soto Avenue.[126]

By the mid-1950s, many other African American performers had established themselves in Los Angeles, including the jump blues shouters Wynonie Harris from Omaha and Big Joe Turner from Kansas City, the blues shouter-crooner Jimmy Witherspoon from Arkansas, the mournful blues balladeer Percy Mayfield from Louisiana, and, from Texas, the electric guitarists T-Bone Walker, Pee Wee Crayton, and Johnny Watson, and the pianists Amos Milburn and Charles Brown. Collectively, these artists created "a new urban dance music" that incorporated uptempo boogie woogie, Texas blues, honking tenor saxophones, and even southwestern swing.[127] With its diversity of styles in a sunny California setting, "West Coast" R & B has been deemed "more classy and laid back," with "a more mellow and sophisticated flavor," and a "smoother, more urbane performance style."[128] As a vital part of this history, disc jockey Tom Reed notes, "Mexican/Chicano support of early Los Angeles–created Black music and artistry has been ongoing."[129]

Mexican Americans could not get enough of the African American artists performing in Los Angeles, and the feeling was mutual. Hence in 1952, Chuck Higgins, a former area high school band trumpeter, Club Alabam tenor saxophonist, and Los Angeles Music Conservatory student, recorded the single "Pachuko Hop."[130] Once disc jockey Hunter Hancock "broke" the honking tenor sax instrumental on his *Harlem Matinee* show, Higgins became a local star, especially among Mexican Americans, who attended his live shows and bought copies of "Pachuko Hop," with its jump blues B-side, "Motor Head Baby." As Jim Dawson remarks, "Considering the importance of East L.A.'s *barrio* to the popularity of R & B in Southern California, it's surprising that it took until 1952 for a black artist to dedicate a tune to the pachucos."[131] At the time, Higgins had been living in the Aliso Village housing projects in Boyle Heights, and after he released "Pachuko Hop," the neighborhood gangs would follow his band wherever it played. Moreover, during Higgins's frequent performances throughout East Los Angeles, the large Mexican American audiences wanted extended, jam session versions of his songs.[132]

In the next two years, Higgins recorded the Mexican American–inspired instrumental singles "Tortas," "Boyle Heights," "Beanville," "Bean Hop," "El Tequila," and "El Toro," all for the local Combo label, as well as, in 1955, "Pancho" for Aladdin Records, and "Wetback Hop" for the black-owned Dootone record label.[133] Higgins claimed that Walter "Dootsie" Williams, owner of Dootone, suggested the name "Wetback Hop," but since the pejorative word in the title refers to an "undocumented" foreign national, or so-called illegal alien from Mexico, the song failed with his "core audience."[134] Another local African American saxophonist, Jack McVea, a veteran of the Club Alabam and of Lionel Hampton's big band, appealed to an increasing postwar ethnic Mexican influence with his 1954 baritone sax instrumental recording, "Tequila Hop."[135] In particular, Mexican American car club members embraced rhythm and blues records, as "honking" saxophone tunes became the cruising anthems of neighborhood low riders.[136]

By 1949, the once ubiquitous Red Car mass transit lines had been dismantled, the streetcar era was over, and the automobile reigned, from stock-car and drag racing to demolition derbies and car shows. After the war, car customizing spread from Sacramento to southern California, where it was practiced by Mexican Americans, particularly military veterans who had picked up mechanical skills in the tank corps, the motor pool, hangars, and shipyards, as well as civilians working assembly lines in Los Angeles automotive factories. They combined early modifications such as filling in the body surface seams and lowering the roof for smoother lines, with their own innovations. Mexican Americans would typically "detail" a used Chevrolet sedan or Fleetline coupe by adding baroque original upholstery from Tijuana and double rearview mirrors, as well as shiny chrome exterior extras, window glass etchings, and acrylic enamel or lacquer paint jobs. These moving works of art were lowered in the back by filling the trunk with sandbags. With their wide "Mickey Mouse" whitewall tires and big hubcaps, these voluptuous "bombs" carried on the pachucos' clean, classy aesthetic, and pride in appearance.[137] In Boyle Heights, the owners of corner service stations and auto repair shops lent their facilities, tools, and advice to local car clubs, encouraging the boys "to turn out 'custom jobs.'"[138]

Unlike Anglo hot-rod racers, Mexican Americans cruised slowly, with the driver slumped down low behind the wheel, in a movement that mirrored "the laid back, methodical walk characteristically employed by cholos."[139] As this new style took off in Southern California, Mexican Americans found themselves at the forefront of both car culture and popular music. For instance, one night in 1950, Big Jay McNeely, the "king of the honking tenor saxophonists," drew so many cars to neighboring drive-in theaters at Whittier and Atlantic boulevards in East Los Angeles that traffic was blocked "in every direction." According to the then-novice disc jockey Dick "Huggy Boy" Hugg, "the place went so crazy the sheriffs had to come out to control things."[140] In their low rider cars, Mexican Americans demanded unconditional recognition and claimed public space in defiance of police surveillance and harassment. In their McNeely mania, they influenced other Angelenos, and their taste for rhythm and blues "was greatly responsible for the music's early exposure to and acceptance by young whites around Los Angeles."[141] In fact, Huggy Boy, an Anglo American, was introduced to African American music by Mexican Americans while working and living in East Los Angeles during the late 1940s.[142]

By the summer of 1950, white Angelenos were discovering the raucous R & B of McNeely, whose band typically included his brother Bob on baritone saxophone; drummer Jimmy Wright, a white hipster who cruised his customized convertible with Huntington Park car clubs; the white guitarist "Porky" Harris, an ex-sailor who usually played in hillbilly bands; and on occasion, the Mexican American saxophonist Jess Rubio, from Anaheim. McNeely became very popular in white, working-class towns in Southeast Los Angeles such as Huntington Park and South Gate, as well as in Bell, which Britt Woodman, an African American trombonist from Watts, described as "prejudiced," and in Bell Gardens, which had been derisively labeled "Billy Goat Acres" because of the many "Okies" who settled there in the 1930s.[143] These communities "became bastions of rhythm and blues fever very early, thanks in part to the car clubs and the kids' growing love of honking saxophonists."[144]

Once African American R & B caught on among working-class Mexican Americans and European Americans in East and Southeast Los Angeles, it was not long before the music reached a broader, citywide audience. This process advanced apace in the early 1950s, when the jazz promoter and radio disc jockey Gene Norman would throw R & B "Jubilees" featuring Wynonie Harris and Big Jay McNeely at the Shrine Auditorium. In downtown Los Angeles, Al Jarvis put on shows by Jimmie Lunceford and Louis Jordan at the Orpheum Theater, Huggy Boy promoted Big Jay at the Orpheum Theater, and Hunter Hancock hosted McNeely at the Olympic Auditorium, both to mixed Anglo and Mexican American audiences. As McNeely asserted, "the authorities were trying to shut me out of Los Angeles. They didn't like me playing at the high schools or the theaters, 'cause I was bringing whites and Spanish and black kids together and rilin' 'em up." During this time McNeely also played in the Orange County town of Fullerton, and in the recently developed San Fernando Valley, where "the audience would be all white."[145]

Emotionally expressive African American rhythm and blues called out to white youths in a context of increasing suburbanization. After World War II, housing shortages, postwar prosperity, population growth, and white flight from the central city, among many factors, led to a suburban homeowning boom that complemented the national baby boom. Yet in the new subdivisions of identical tract houses along the Los Angeles periphery, such as those in the city of Lakewood, near Long Beach, many youths were raised in a monotonous cultural environment characterized by racial homogeneity and social conformity.[146] In contrast, black music and dance, which emphasize "personal stylization" and "individual improvisation . . . within a communal tradition and collective setting," appeared very appealing, as did the "back-and-forth interaction" between spectators and performers typical of African American celebration.[147] The ecstatic crescendo of wildly hypnotic honking tenor saxophone solos in general, and Big Jay McNeely's bottom-heavy tone and full vibrato technique in particular, induced a heightened emotional state.[148] As a new generation of white Angelenos discovered how "black social dancing circulates social energy," rhythm and blues opened a new front in the culture war over virtuous citizenship and proper civil society.[149]

Southern California's R & B music and dance scene culture brought young people together, even more than the 1940s swing scene. By 1950, when the large record stores downtown and in Hollywood would not even stock records by black artists, an African American entrepreneur, John Dolphin, purchased late-night airtime on a local radio station and hired black disc jockeys to broadcast from his twenty-four-hour record store, Dolphin's of Hollywood. The store was actually located at East Vernon and Central avenues in South Central Los Angeles, but Dolphin reportedly reasoned, "If Negroes can't go to Hollywood, then I'll bring Hollywood to Negroes." Dolphin even built a small, professional-quality recording studio in the back of his store so that he could record new songs from local artists, press the records on his own label, then sell them right on the premises.

In late 1953, Huggy Boy began hosting a live, late-night rhythm and blues program from the large front window of Dolphin's establishment. The biggest stars of R & B gave interviews in the storefront window to promote their latest singles and local club dates, with the radio broadcasts reaching as far away as Arizona. In late 1954, Huggy Boy began playing the Texas-born, Los Angeles–based honker Joe Houston's "All Night Long" as the show's theme song, yelling "Keep alive and listen in!" over the blaring tenor saxophone, and inviting all of his listeners to turn their cars around and drive to "Vernon and Central, Central and Vernon." As a result, R & B musicians, actors, and Mexican Americans from the Eastside gravitated to John Dolphin's record store on weekend nights, making it "the most happening place in Los Angeles." After hours, cars lined Vernon Avenue bumper to bumper, while Huggy Boy addressed the people cruising outside the store, his voice echoing from their automobile radios. Restless whites from throughout the city and suburbs—even from thirty miles away in the San Fernando Valley—also drove to Dolphin's to buy hard-to-find R & B records and participate in the exciting urban nightlife.[150]

Rhythm and blues had crossed over to a young white audience on an unprecedented scale, and this was perceived as a serious problem by Los Angeles law enforcement. Since 1950, Chief of Police William H. Parker had been transforming the LAPD into a professional, mobile, aggressive force.[151] More than any of his predecessors, Chief Parker crusaded against race mixing and inner-city vice, to the point of using inflated crime statistics and dubious racial theories to scare up funding resources and amass political power.[152] In the name of fighting juvenile delinquency, drugs, and gangs, police officers zealously reinforced the racial status quo by patrolling the boundaries between areas. For instance, Newton Street Division policemen would enter John Dolphin's store, turning Anglos away or escorting them from the premises with the warning that "Central Avenue was too dangerous for white people." According to the *Sentinel*, an African American publication in Los Angeles, one night a dozen officers formed a human chain at the front door, "terrifying Caucasian customers . . . and rousting them from the neighborhood." Huggy Boy recalled that after two o'clock in the morning when the bars closed, Dolphin's and the neighboring barbecue restaurants would be packed, but uniformed police officers "would chase away the white kids," while undercover agents would search blacks on suspicion of selling drugs. In late 1954, Dolphin gathered a petition of one hundred and fifty black business people from the neighborhood protesting these tactics. Sergeant George Restovich countered that the gatherings violated a ten o'clock curfew, and that other businessmen complained about teenagers assembling on sidewalks while Dolphin's outside loudspeaker blared music onto the street.[153]

In short, when whites joined Negroes and Mexican Americans in greater numbers, the rhythm and blues scene was deemed subversive. As the leading independent label distributors reported to *Billboard* magazine in 1952, "a major portion of the R & B sides now being sold are bought by Spanish and mixed-nationality buyers," due largely to promotion by Los Angeles disc jockeys.[154] In 1954, so many white teenagers were buying rhythm and blues records that it caused a national moral furor over allegedly "obscene" lyrics. In Long Beach, after a local radio station banned R & B records, the Sheriff's Department went even further, banning "offending" records from all area jukeboxes. In 1955, twenty-five leading Los Angeles disc jockeys gave in to pressure from censors at the Junior National Audience Board by agreeing to "avoid public airing of records which [were] believed objectionable."[155]

While the forces of mainstream morality tried to disrupt the threatening music scenes and stem the tide of R & B, Mexican Americans continued to develop their expressive culture, social identities, and conflicted relationships with whites, blacks, and Mexicanos. For example, while acts like Big Jay McNeely were bringing down the house at the Angelus Hall in the early 1950s, a few blocks farther east in Boyle Heights, recent Mexican migrants were dancing to Mexican music at Pontrelli's Ballroom. As Ed Frias stated, "We didn't go there because that was not our music. Their music was too different. We liked jazz. . . . we liked to rock. But the [Mexican] immigrants . . . would tend to [stick] together."[156] Like Don Tosti, Paul Lopez, and Chico Sesma, Frias heard both Mexican music and swing in his youth. Like his Boyle Heights fellows from the swing era, Frias preferred the big bands to mariachis and rancheras, and as he became old enough to go nightclubbing, his preference remained with African American music over Mexican music. Indeed, for Ed Frias and many of his peers, jazz and blues-based music was as much a part of their community as authentic, traditional Mexican music.

Thus Mexican American Angeleno José González's favorite musical acts included rhythm and blues artists like Ruth Brown, Lloyd Price, and Fats Domino, as well as locals like Big Jay McNeely and the popular vocal group the Platters. Born in 1937, González grew up with relatives in New Mexico and Texas before finally settling in East Los Angeles. José's older brother, Salvador, was a pachuco during the war years, and his older sisters, Sadie and Rufina, were both jazz enthusiasts. José's mother and grandmother listened exclusively to Spanish-language radio stations in the house, and José remembers hearing corridos, rancheras, polkas, and *canciones* throughout his youth. However, like the Mexican American swing kids before him, José preferred African American dance music, in his case, the swing and jump blues he heard on the radio, and on his sisters' records. José González represented many members of the Mexican American generation when he asked, "What did I know about Mexico? I was born and raised in the U.S.A."[157]

However, despite increasing Mexican American assimilation in the postwar period, not all members of the rhythm and blues–era cohort disassociated themselves from traditional Mexican music. In addition, not every Mexican American listened to rhythm and blues or Latin music in the 1950s. For instance, Virginia Vital was raised in East Los Angeles, where she listened to American pop singers Edie Gorme and Andy Russell, as well as Mexican singers Javier Solís and Trio Los Panchos. Vital and her three siblings saw Hollywood movies at the Strand Theater on Whittier Boulevard every Sunday as youths, but in 1949 fifteen-year-old Virginia began accompanying her parents to Eighth and Main streets downtown, where the California Theater screened Spanish-language films featuring Mexican stars like María Félix and Pedro Infante.[158] Similarly, María Olivas Alvarez from East Los Angeles saw Spanish-language movies at the Million Dollar Theater, the California Theater, and the Paramount Theater, but she also saw English-language movies at Grauman's Chinese Theater in Hollywood. She even saw Sammy Davis Jr. perform with the Will Maston Trio at the Million Dollar Theater, yet, like other Mexican Americans throughout Los Angeles, she felt the pull of Spanish-language Mexican music and culture.[159]

For Jaime Corral, as we saw earlier in this chapter, mariachis and rancheras were his first musical loves. Corral sang Mexican music throughout his life, but he also drew from African American cultural influences. He spent his youth downtown on Maple Avenue at 23rd Street, in a community composed mostly of Mexicans and Anglos, with a sprinkling of blacks and Asians, where "everyone got along just great, [with] absolutely no racial tensions whatsoever."[160] Corral's friend, James "Jimmy" Diego Vigil, called the neighborhood "the center of the center" of the city, where downtown ends and "South Central" Los Angeles begins.[161] Despite the fact that African Americans did not dominate the area geographically, a black grammar school teacher named James Thompson influenced Corral and Vigil greatly. For Corral in particular, whose father had left his mother after they settled in Los Angeles, Thompson became like a "surrogate father." This same teacher also molded another of his pupils, the future Los Angeles disc jockey Joe Adams, and the two remained lifelong friends. Both Corral and Vigil went to John Adams Middle School on West 30th and Main streets, where they continued to interact with black teachers and students. For example, Corral's eighth-grade class of three hundred elected him president and African American students as vice president, secretary, and treasurer.[162]

Although Vigil went to Excelsior High School in the Southeast Los Angeles neighborhood of Norwalk, in 1953 Corral became part of an extremely mixed student body when he attended his local high school, Los Angeles Polytechnic. On Washington Boulevard between Flower Street and Grand Avenue, two blocks south of the Olympic Auditorium, "Poly" was the second oldest high school in town, and also, according to Corral, "the most integrated [and] diverse high school in the city." In contrast, to the North, between Third Street and Beverly Boulevard, stood the predominantly Filipino Belmont Senior High; to the Southwest, near the Memorial Coliseum, the formerly all-white, but increasingly black Manual Arts; to the Southeast, near Compton Avenue and 41st Street, the largely black Jefferson High; to the East, in the heart of Boyle Heights, the mostly ethnic Mexican Roosevelt High; and to the West, on West Olympic Boulevard, the still-white Los Angeles High School. Polytechnic therefore reflected its surrounding neighborhood, as no single ethnic group enjoyed a numerical majority. In addition to its own internal diversity, out of the entire unified school district, only Poly had a sizable population of international foreign exchange students. Despite many Angelenos' fears of social disorder, this heterogeneous environment led not to urban violence but rather to relaxed attitudes. Corral and his Poly schoolmates even used their own hip racial labels, calling Mexicans "Beans," blacks "Spooks," Anglos "Fades," Filipinos "Flips," and Japanese "Buddha Heads." Back then, when talking to his African American friends in high school, Corral would never refer to someone as "black" for fear of offending or insulting them. However, it was perfectly acceptable to describe that same person as a "spook," or, if you wanted to "really get down," a "spliv."[163]

During their high school years in the early-to-middle 1950s, Corral's circle of friends liked various musical styles. For instance, Vigil's older sisters, who had hung out on Central Avenue in the 1940s, exposed him to jazz. With them, he saw Count Basie, Duke Ellington, and one of his early favorites, Illinois Jacquet. Moreover, his sisters often attended Norman Granz's Jazz at the Philharmonic, and he occasionally tagged along. Vigil remembered them all seeing Buddy Rich, Gene Krupa, and Illinois Jacquet at these Los Angeles JATP concerts. Yet as Vigil got older, rhythm and blues captured his ear, more than jazz or Latin music. While his high school buddies frequented jazz clubs downtown and on Central Avenue, or danced to Latin music at the Zenda Ballroom downtown, Vigil caught R & B acts downtown at the Avedon Ballroom, and at a club called the Sons of Herman. Corral had been surrounded by Mexican music, and he listened to a little rhythm and blues, but he preferred jazz, to which he was also introduced at a young age. Two of Corral's neighbors, Robert and Ralph Mendez, always played jazz on the radio whenever he would visit their house. Soon Corral and the Mendez brothers, who were a little older than Corral, would shop for jazz records, sneak in to see Hampton Hawes and Dizzy Gillespie at jazz clubs like Le Cris on Central Avenue, and see local and visiting jazz players in East Los Angeles at the Digger on Atlantic Boulevard. Another classmate, Tommy Saito, like most Japanese American youths his age, listened to jazz, and he would often take the streetcar from his neighborhood into bordering downtown to hear live jazz music.[164]

At the same time, as we will see in chapter 5, Corral and fellow Poly students Tommy Saito, Richard Barrientos, Kay Nomura, and two of their African American pals, William Roach and O'Dell Lomax, all became enamored with Latin music. Corral and his friends certainly assimilated aspects of African American culture after coming up with black schoolmates like Roach, Lomax, the disc jockey Joe Adams, and the drummer Billy Higgins. As Corral argued, "You just couldn't help it. . . . You start partying with them and you start talking like them, you adopt mannerisms and language and things like that without even knowing it. We just picked that up. . . . It was part of our culture." In their high school days, Corral, Saito, and Nomura sounded just like young African Americans.[165] Nomura, a second-generation Japanese American, walked and talked like his black neighbors, but as Vigil explained, Nomura's body language and black verbal cadence "is not affected" because he just "doesn't know any other way."[166] For Corral and Saito, "talking black" came so "naturally" that they could turn it on and off at will. In the end, high schools like Polytechnic, Belmont, Roosevelt, Jefferson, and Jordan produced an urban citizenry with multiple cross referents, from social dancers and loyal concertgoers to professional musicians.

African American culture was not the only point of reference or interest, as many of the urban encounters resulted in jazz musicians' and impresarios' dating, and often marrying, Mexicanas. African American music producer and club owner Bardu Ali dated a Mexican woman named Tila who owned a restaurant two doors down from the Club Alabam on Central Avenue. Los Angeles musicians who married Mexican or Mexican American women include the Jewish American Rene Bloch, the Japanese American Tommy Saito, the Mexican-Filipino American Richard Barrientos, and the African American Gerald Wilson. For Wilson, who relocated from Detroit to Los Angeles in the early 1940s, the appeal of Mexican culture was particularly strong, and it began well before he met his wife, Josefina Villaseñor. As he said, "I have been into the Mexican culture for a long time. I have been exposed to it very extensively. Just listening to it can get you somewhere, but you have to be exposed to the people." Wilson did more than just listen, as illustrated by his "Mexican-influenced music," including his famous instrumental ode to a Mexican bullfighter, "Viva Tirado," and other lesser-known homages like "El Viti."[167]

Conversely, for Los Angeles Mexican Americans, jazz and rhythm and blues created strong new connections with African Americans, as well as continuing contact with Jewish Americans and Anglo Americans. For example, the musical careers and creations of Anthony Ortega and Gilbert "Gil" Bernal represented part of a collective Mexican American expressive culture, one which made significant national, and eventually international, contributions. Although Bernal was born in Watts in 1931 to a Sicilian father and a Mexican mother, as he explained, "my mother raised me and I took her name and always considered myself part of her culture not his."[168] Until he was five, Bernal heard the boleros of Cuba and Mexico on the Tijuana-based Spanish-language radio station to which his grandmother listened, but by age eleven he idolized the swing trumper Harry James, having heard a song by James on a downtown Los Angeles Mexican restaurant jukebox.[169] In 1945, Ortega saw the fourteen-year-old Bernal impersonating comedians, actors, and singers at a Jordan High School talent show assembly. Ortega, who was already taking private lessons and performing with the Junior Hep Cats school swing band on alto saxophone, befriended the younger Bernal. As they listened to swing instrumentalists on Ortega's record player, Bernal would "imitate the solos note for note" by voice, without missing an inflection. He "had good rhythm, and he could hear the intervals." Impressed, Ortega encouraged him to take up the saxophone. After Bernal's mother bought Gil a tenor saxophone, Ortega began teaching him a few scales. Between Ortega's tutelage and band classes at Jordan High, Bernal learned fast. He was, Ortega recalled, "very talented, very quick, and very musically inclined."[170]

Once he graduated from Jordan in 1948, Bernal landed his first professional job, a nonunion gig performing with a ten-piece band at the Majestic Ballroom in Long Beach, followed by another nonunion job working with Scatman Crothers at the Manchester Club near Watts. In 1950, Bernal's high school English teacher, an African American woman who had played with Louis Jordan and Lionel Hampton, secured him an audition with Hampton's orchestra. After singing a ballad live with the band onstage at the Million Dollar Theater, and with the approval of Hampton's manager/

24. Gil Bernal in tenor saxophone battle with Johnny Board, Lionel Hampton Orchestra, Paramount Theater, Los Angeles, September 23, 1952. Photographer: Dave Ramirez. COURTESY GIL BERNAL.

wife, Gladys, nineteen-year-old Bernal got the job.[171] Hampton, a vibraphonist, drummer, and entertainer, was one of the few bandleaders to maintain a successful big band during the postwar years, and he always drew a full house with backbeat-heavy crowd favorites like "Flying Home" and "Central Avenue Breakdown." In concert, Gil Bernal would take center stage in tenor saxophone battles with bandmate Johnny Board during the song "Air Mail Special," from Los Angeles to the Apollo Theater in New York City (see figure 24). Bernal's vocals were featured on "I Only Have Eyes for You," as well as on the ballad "September in the Rain," which he also sang on a Hampton recording for Decca Records in 1950. After Hampton's pianist, Milt Buckner, wrote Bernal a "Latin-tinged show business" arrangement of the Miguelito Valdés song "Babalu," it became his signature production number. After Bernal's tour roommate, the trumpeter Quincy Jones, wrote him an arrangement of the Cole Porter song "Love for Sale," it became his new production number, and "it always went over especially well with the ladies."[172]

In 1951, Anthony Ortega returned to Los Angeles after three years in the U.S. Army, and Hampton's band happened to be in town.[173] Bernal soon contacted Ortega, informing him that Hampton needed a replacement alto saxophonist for the orchestra, which used about five saxophones, five trumpets, and four trombones, and which featured some of the best African American musicians in the country. Ortega sat in with the band for a month, performing limited engagements in Los Angeles, as well as one-nighters in Santa Ana and, in northern California, San Jose. Finally, Hampton hired Ortega to join the orchestra and tour the United States.

Hampton played many southern ballrooms in which blacks were cordoned off from whites. Ortega found such blatant Dixie Jim Crow "hard to believe" because "the band was performing for everybody." Still, Ortega had witnessed racial discrimination all along Central Avenue, and he had himself been repeatedly stopped and his person and his car searched by law enforcement officers in East Los Angeles. For instance, one evening after he and his cousin Ray Vasquez had been pulled over, the officer shined a flashlight in their faces, but Vasquez had already pulled out a flashlight from the glove compartment, and "he flashed it in the cop's face." Like many in the Mexican American generation, sometimes Ray "would rebel. He didn't want to take any of that stuff."[174] One night after a Lionel Hampton show in the Deep South, Ortega and Bernal were walking down the sidewalk with Quincy Jones and two other African American bandmates when a police patrol car pulled over to the curb. Shining their flashlights on Ortega and Bernal, the passenger-side officer asked them, "What are you white boys doing with these niggers?" As Ortega recalled, "I knew there was a prejudice thing against Mexicans, so I thought right away to say, 'Oh, we're not white boys, we're Mexicans.'" On hearing this, the other officer replied, "Oh, that's the same as a nigger," then drove away.[175]

In this exchange, the southern white policemen considered Mexican Americans colored, yet on two separate occasions Bernal was told by African American promoters, "If you could pass as black we could all make a lot of money."[176] Bernal never tried to pass as black, but, he said, "Many of the musicians that I worked with, at first, thought I was part black . . . by the music that I played, and the way I played it." He had already sponged up the bop-influenced saxophone sounds of Dexter Gordon and Wardell Gray on Central Avenue, but he began absorbing rhythm and blues when he traveled with Hampton's band, staying in the black hotels in the black neighborhoods, and, after the shows, hanging out in black bars and at black parties. He had received encouragement while on tour, but he had also been warned by his bandmates that he would have to move his wife and children to New York City if he hoped to find steady jazz work. Bernal did not heed his fellow musicians' advice, and when he left Lionel Hampton's band in 1952, he could not find many jazz jobs in Los Angeles. Accordingly, he began to emphasize the aggressive attack of R & B, which he had added to his repertoire. Since there were no nonblack musicians playing in that style around Los Angeles, it was easier for him to find work, especially in Hollywood and West Los Angeles. Playing just enough R & B and pop songs to keep the club owners and the patrons happy, he would still "go between R & B and jazz ideas."[177]

A few years earlier, Bernal had met some of the white musicians—as well as a Mexican American musician named Mike Valdez—playing what would soon be coined "West Coast jazz," a variant of early 1950s "cool" jazz, at Los Angeles City College. He had jammed with these college friends in the San Fernando Valley, and had recorded, as a saxophonist and a singer, "progressive jazz" with them, as well as with Art Pepper and Chet Baker. As a result of these connections, when he formed his own combo in Los Angeles he hired the drummer Shelley Manne and the trumpeter Shorty Rogers. In 1954 Bernal and his bandmates were recruited as studio session musicians for Spark Records, a fledgling label founded by the songwriting team of the lyricist Jerry Lieber and the pianist Mike Stoller, who would go on to write dozens of best-selling R & B songs for African American artists. Of Polish-Russian heritage, Jerry Lieber was raised in segregated Baltimore, where his widowed mother ran a grocery store near a black neighborhood in the early 1940s. After hearing African American music, Lieber "identified with the blacks." According to Lieber, "I imitated black cultural attitudes for so long as a child that it became second nature to me."[178] After his family moved to Los Angeles in 1945, Lieber's cultural conversion intensified at John Burroughs Middle School, near Highland Avenue and Sixth Street. Although located in the affluent Anglo neighborhood of Hancock Park, the school was integrated. While attending Fairfax High School, the seventeen-year-old Lieber worked at Norty's Record Shop on Fairfax Avenue in the heart of the Jewish district, but he became hooked on R & B while hearing it on the radio as a busboy at a Filipino restaurant.[179]

Mike Stoller grew up on Long Island, took piano lessons from the stride piano master, James P. Johnson, at age eleven, joined a Harlem social club at age fourteen, and even sneaked into Fifty-Second Street jazz clubs. After Stoller moved with his family to Los Angeles in 1949 at age sixteen, he attended Belmont High School. His high school friends back on Long Island were all middle-class whites, but at Belmont the students were mostly Mexican American, Filipino American, and African American. Stoller "learned the pachuco dances and joined a pachuco social club" in East Los Angeles, where he played piano with a local band led by saxophonist Blas Vasquez, learning Mexican American interpretations of Anglo, African American, and traditional Mexican musical styles.[180] When a former high school classmate introduced Lieber to Stoller, they found they both shared a "taste for the blues." As Stoller recalled, "We responded to black records and to white people who lived a black life-style."[181] In fact, both "had black girlfriends and were into a black lifestyle."[182]

Stoller's musical upbringing demonstrates the wide-ranging allure of African American expressive culture, and it reveals the often hidden role Mexican Americans have played in the history of popular music. Bernal met and befriended Stoller in 1950 at Los Angeles City College, where both were studying music. When Lieber and Stoller started Spark Records in West Hollywood in March 1954, Stoller brought in Bernal's combo to back up the Flairs, a vocal group out of Jefferson High. For Spark Records, Bernal also recorded a few of his own compositions, such as "King Solomon's Blues," a sinewy, slurred-note lament, and "Easyville," a melodic, mid-tempo honker. His single, "The Whip," received radio airplay by Los Angeles disc jockeys, and by Cleveland disc jockey Alan "Moondog" Freed, who used it as the opening theme to his late night R & B program, excitedly announcing Gil Bernal's name to white teens in the Midwest. Then listeners heard "The Whip," a rousing, rapid-fire stinger that rode single notes but also fluidly ran the range of the saxophone.

Bernal blew away the lines between jazz, jump blues, R & B, and rock and roll. In 1954 and 1955 he again recorded for Spark Records, this time playing saxophone in the studio with another local African American vocal harmony group, the Robins, who were veterans of Johnny Otis's house band at the Barrelhouse. Bernal's saxophone shines on such Robins songs as "Riot in Cell Block #9," with his sultry solo lending emotional punch to the surly, radio serial–inspired prison story, as well as on "Framed" and "Smokey Joe's Café," both stop-time blues numbers (see figure 25).[183] These songs were written by Lieber and Stoller, two Jewish American

25. Gil Bernal recording vocal single with the Robins backing, Los Angeles, ca. 1954. COURTESY GIL BERNAL.

"white Negroes," recorded at the Jewish American sound engineer Abe Robyns's Master Recorders on Fairfax Avenue, circulated by the Jewish American distributor Abe Diamond, and played by the Anglo disc jockey Hunter Hancock, thus showing how Jews, along with white disc jockeys, often became the middlemen for the introduction of black styles to white Angelenos. In 1955, when Atlantic Records hired Lieber and Stoller as independent producers, they, and the Robins, moved to New York City, but Bernal stayed in Los Angeles.

The pachuco subculture momentarily crossed over into the mainstream with the pachuco boogie songs, but Bernal broke through in a different way during the rhythm and blues era, and his facility with jazz, pop, and R & B broadened the palette of the Mexican American generation. The life stories of Gil Bernal and Anthony Ortega illustrate some of the ways that Mexican Americans sustained multicultural public spaces in and beyond Los Angeles, while achieving professional success and expanding Mexican American expressive culture in and beyond the community. For instance, when Bernal left Lionel Hampton's big band in 1952,

26. Anthony Ortega with Lionel Hampton Orchestra, 1951.
COURTESY ANTHONY ORTEGA.

Ortega remained, performing in Cleveland, Philadelphia, and in New York at the Apollo Theater, where Redd Foxx and Slappy White performed stand-up comedy between acts. In 1953 Ortega accompanied Hampton on the bandleader's first European tour. The orchestra now included Clifford Brown, the Jefferson High alumnus Art Farmer, and the fellow Jordan High alumnus Clifford Solomon. From the Deep South to Harlem and Europe, Ortega received support and encouragement from his black bandmates, especially the lead alto saxophonist, Bobby Plater, behind whom he played. Lionel Hampton was so impressed with Ortega's playing, particularly on clarinet, that he gave him solos on many songs, and once told him, "There are two clarinet players: You and Benny Goodman" (see figure 26).

In November 1953, Ortega left Hampton's orchestra, then traveled back east with the organ trio of the former Hampton pianist and arranger Milt Buckner. He flew to Oslo to marry his fiancé, Mona Ørbeck, a Nor-

wegian pianist, then the newlyweds moved to El Monte to live with Ortega's mother. The Los Angeles jazz scene moved at a slower pace, as
Ortega played a few weekend performances with his own quartet at the
Red Feather club on Western Avenue, where Redd Foxx took the stage
between jazz sets, and accompanied the organ trio of African American
female singer-organist Perry Lee at Dynamite Jackson's on Central Avenue. Ortega also played at the Memory Lane on Santa Barbara Avenue,
near the Memorial Coliseum, with Luis Rivera, a light-skinned, wavy-
haired African American organist originally from Columbus, Ohio, who
Hispanicized his birth name, Louis Washington, while living in San Antonio, Texas. In early 1954, Ortega toured Norway and Sweden, and recorded a government-sponsored radio broadcast with a group of Norwe-
gian musicians as his first album, *The Anthony Ortega Quartet*, in Oslo (see
figure 27). In late 1955, he toured the East Coast with Luis Rivera, before
settling in New York City for several years.[184] Ortega's organ trio jobs, his
European trip, and his first album, as well as Bernal's jazz ballad tour
singing, and his sensual sax solos around town and on R & B hit singles,
signified not only the forays of two jazz-trained musicians into postwar
popular styles, but also the eclecticism and creativity of the Mexican American generation (see figure 28).

To further illustrate this generation's cultural range of variation, just
as chapters 1 and 2 ended by mentioning the go-getters, educationists,
squares, and political leaders, this chapter takes a parting glance at some of
the upwardly mobile Mexican American aspirants of the immediate postwar era. At James Garfield Senior High School in East Los Angeles, which
was about "half Armenian and half Mexican" in the late 1940s, with a
sprinkling of other whites, Hortencia Garibay remembered how "some
Mexicans would go with the Anglos . . . like a bunch of friends and they
would ignore the rest of the Mexicans. . . . Most of them were *güeros* . . .
I think they were trying to [be] wannabes."[185] In 1948, a Mexican American senior at the University of Southern California said, "I am ashamed of
my group. So many of my Mexican friends claim to be Spanish in the
university. We are Americans in the sense of ancestry and pioneer background, and as to our Indian ancestors we may be proud of their glorious
culture."[186]

Ortega, unashamed of being Mexican, insisted that joining the U.S.
Army was "really good" for him because he suddenly "met guys from all

THE ANTHONY ORTEGA QUARTET

27. *Anthony Ortega Quartet* album cover, 1954. COURTESY ANTHONY ORTEGA.

28. Anthony Ortega with alto saxophone and clarinet, France, 1954. COURTESY ANTHONY ORTEGA.

over the country," while Ed Frias noted that when he was discharged from the Army following his service in Korea, his friends were "a German, Jewish, an Irish," and a Mexican American "who denied he was Mexican."[187] In 1953, Frias graduated from the police academy and became a LAPD officer, but he quit after only two years because "he had a hard time dealing with the racism" on the force. By the mid-1950s, there were "a lot of Mexican American cops" who "acted white," and, in their minds, "were accepted as white," but Frias felt that because people judge one another by skin color, you can act as white as you want, "but you're not white, you're Mexican."[188]

However, in the music world of Los Angeles, Mexican Americans were technically white. In January 1950, the white union Local 47 made a physical and symbolic move, relocating from downtown to 817 North Vine Street, above Melrose Avenue in Hollywood, where much of its membership had a stranglehold on some of the best-paying jobs. The city's double-standard system continued until April 1953, when the two separate and unequal American Federation of Musicians locals "amalgamated" after a campaign waged by African American and Jewish American activist musicians.[189] The union amalgamation affirmed the swing-era Mexican American musicians' membership in the white local, which had indeed enhanced their economic position. As part of the book's generational narrative, these tangled relationships between Mexican Americans, class, and whiteness will be unraveled further in the next two chapters.

Finally, since this chapter opened with a discussion of pachuco boogie, it closes with a snapshot of post-pachuco style and Mexican American expressive culture from 1945 to 1955. For example, in late 1947, when East Los Angeles College, then in its third year of existence, was still located on the campus of Garfield High, Vince Ramírez remembered seeing a few neighborhood pachucos strolling about in full zoot suits with hats. Nevertheless, some time near the end of the 1940s and the beginning of the 1950s, the zoot suit finally fell out of fashion.[190] The hard-core pachucos' successors, the cholos, forged a new style in the barrios. In Mexico and Latin America the term *cholo* historically referred to "a partially and incompletely acculturated Indian or mestizo."[191] The derogatory word had been used by New Spain *criollos* to denote a Mesoamerican *mestizo*, and by nineteenth-century Californio *gente de razón*, or "people endowed with reason," to describe the local former missionized Indians and the rural migrants—mostly poor mestizos from northwestern Mexico and second-

or third-generation "Hispanicized" Indians from Baja California—who worked as their house servants and *vaquero* ranchhands, or as unskilled laborers and craftsmen in the pueblos.[192]

Like the pachucos, the Southern California cholos were "strongly associated with street gangs," and their style was rapidly adopted by other urban Mexican American youths.[193] Whereas the drape shape depended on expensive, tailor-made suits, the cholos "used readily . . . available items in distinctive combinations."[194] Army-surplus khaki pants, or "chinos," worn with a loose white cotton crew-neck undershirt, or a tight white ribbed-cotton sleeveless muscle shirt, came into vogue. Although the pachuco drapes were gone, the cholos continued wearing high-waisted baggy trousers. After World War II, some pachuco *veteranos* had reportedly worn Army-issue shirts with pegged Army pants and thick-soled shoes.[195] Reflecting Mexican Americans' continued participation in the armed forces, along with khakis, cholos incorporated military-style black web belts with silver buckles, highly polished black leather shoes, and black knit stocking caps, or "beanies."

Cholo casual-wear components also included long-sleeved Pendleton plaid flannel shirts, worn buttoned up to the throat, or with only the top button fastened, or folded lengthwise and draped neatly over one forearm; a hair net for keeping their slicked-back hair in place; suspenders; inexpensive, flat rubber-soled, black canvas slip-on shoes, nicknamed "winos"; and de rigueur squarish black sunglasses with extremely dark lenses. Ben Davis and Dickies workpants became fashionable, along with the ever-popular khakis, each of which could be cut off or hemmed just below the kneecap, and worn with knee-high white athletic socks during the summer months. Cholos followed the earlier sharp, clean look by pressing a single crease down their trousers, and they even ironed their white T-shirts.[196] Many other residual pachuco elements remained constant, like fedora felt hats; the ducktail haircuts; mustaches and goatees; caló slang; customized low rider cars; gang hand signals; black, gray, and navy blue colors; and a love of African American music. In addition, cholos still practiced the prewar "barrio calligraphy," inscribing their stylized *placas* on neighborhood walls, fences, freeways, and other public spaces to mark territorial boundaries.[197] Finally, they also began expanding the minimalist tattoos of the pachucos into black-ink body artwork, from Catholic and Mexican visual icons to the development of an elaborate Old English lettering.[198]

The swing-era Mexican Americans sometimes decried the casual new look, particularly the wearing of undershirts in public, yet the macho, working-class cholo chic symbolized, and helped create a broader rebellious attitude. Lewis MacAdams argues that cool as a way of life, a political stance, and a secret knowledge did not truly emerge until after World War II, amid "the paranoia and conformity of the Cold War."[199] In the stylistic landscape of postwar Los Angeles, cholos were the epitome of cool. Hanging out on local street corners, they would "play the wall," striking various poses, such as squatting on the balls of their feet, with an elbow on each knee, or standing with knees and heels together, feet pointing in opposite directions. The latter pose had been perfected by both the pachucos and, as early as 1940, by East Coast black zoot suiters who, in order to more dramatically showcase their draped outlines and swinging chains, "would 'cool it'—hat dangled, knees drawn close together, feet wide apart, both index fingers jabbed toward the floor."[200] Like the cholos, the cholas were associated with gangs, and they too influenced Mexican American expressive culture. Cholas maintained the tough sexuality of the pachucas, lightening or streaking their hair with peroxide, teasing or "ratting" their hair into tall bangs, shaping their eyebrows into thin arches, and wearing dark eyeliner, lipliner, or lipstick.[201]

In ethnic Mexican neighborhoods after the Second World War, non-cholo and non-chola styles existed. As Ronald Arroyo contends,

> In place of the zoot suit, young batos were picking up on one button roll suits, white shirts with Mr. B [Billy Eckstine] collars, knit suspenders and matching tie, and Marine Cordovan dyed shoes. Their chicks kept their hair high, but put aside the suits for black sweaters and black skirts sometimes split on the side, a gold or silver cross decorated their breasts, bobby socks and low saddle shoes replaced the high heels. These cool pairs dug jazz now called bop.[202]

By the late 1940s, for black hep cats the zoot suit "had begun to outlive its usefulness as a symbol of black consciousness. It had crossed over to 'whitey.' " In response, some young African Americans assumed the intellectual look associated with bebop's fashion trendsetter, Dizzy Gillespie: "the heavy-rimmed spectacles, the berets and goatee beards, the turtleneck sweaters and crumpled suits."[203] Those African Americans closer to the hustler end of the social spectrum borrowed heavily from the cholo style, as they led the development of a new working-class black street style. In 1953, East Los Angeles had 5,481 African Americans out of a total population of 90,850, although blacks were 65 to 68 percent of the residents of the Aliso Village, Aliso Village Annex, Pico Gardens, and Estrada Courts housing projects.[204] The concentration of blacks in Eastside housing projects led to African American cholos like the postwar welterweight boxer from East Los Angeles nicknamed "Geronimo."[205]

The dynamic between African Americans and Mexican Americans continued into the rock and roll era, as did the cholo style and this generation's socioeconomic and political struggle. An exciting transitional cohort of young Mexican Americans took the energy and emotion of rhythm and blues to new heights, gaining greater representation and recognition. Several of the swing-and R & B–era musicians also achieved more mainstream exposure and acceptance playing jazz, pop music, Latin, and motion picture soundtracks. Finally, the multicultural urban civility expanded its scope and impact in the face of increased opposition by conservative social and political forces, in the intensifying culture war over competing visions of civil society.

come on, let's go:

the rock and roll era

It wasn't so much an outlaw thing, it was more an extension of the culture and our culture being able to break into the mainstream of society. We all had our heroes in the barrio, but when they were able to get acceptance out of the barrio, that was the ultimate.
—*Rudy Salas, quoted in Don Snowden, "The Sound of East L.A., 1964,"*
Los Angeles Times, *October 28, 1984*

I like to expand the—stretch out the song. What I like to do is, when I improvise something, like if it's a standard tune. . . . I try to stick pretty much to that, so it's recognizable, like if I'm recording, and then start drifting out. In other words, don't sock 'em all at once, you see? Let 'em kind of like dwell into the thing a little bit, and then start searching, where they get a little accustomed.
—*Anthony Ortega, interview by author*

I often lay back in my garage room, listening to scratchy records of Willie Bobo, Thee Midnighters, War, and Miles Davis. Sometimes oldies; the "Eastside Sound" revues, old Stax and Atlantic rhythm & blues: Wilson Pickett, Rufus Thomas, Solomon Burke and The Drifters. And of course, Motown. . . . For the most part, the Mexicans in and around Los Angeles were economically and socially closest to blacks. As soon as we under-

stood English, it was usually the Black English we first tried to master. Later in the youth authority camps and prisons, blacks used Mexican slang and the cholo style; Mexicans imitated the Southside swagger and style—although this didn't mean at times we didn't war with one another, such being the state of affairs at the bottom. For Chicanos this influence lay particularly deep in music: Mexican rhythms syncopated with blues and ghetto beats.
—Luis Rodríguez, Always Running

From the mid-1950s to the Chicano Movement, Mexican American Angelenos expanded their eclectic expressive culture, including their mutual affinities with, and borrowings from, African American style, language, and music. Luis Rodríguez's autobiography describes "blacks" and "Mexicans" as being "at the bottom" during this period, and certainly many Mexican Americans remained in low-paying jobs or slipped a rung or two back down the economic ladder, yet others moved on up and out of the working class. Rodríguez also notes that both Latin and jazz artists remained popular, as did performers of R & B, a genre now increasingly called "soul" music. As the East Los Angeles musician Rudy Salas's epigraph reveals, Mexican American musicians found even wider acceptance, even though jazz improvisers like Anthony Ortega did not receive their just due. This chapter introduces new players, follows familiar figures from the swing- and R & B–era cohorts, and profiles socially mobile and politically active Mexican American Angelenos, as part of the geographic and cultural frameworks through which the musical movements, interethnic exchanges, and assertive agency of this generation must be understood. Mexican Americans still had their mojo working, as their cool style —and ethnic Mexican culture in general—influenced both whites and blacks in Southern California more than ever before, and as more of their musical performers than ever gained national recognition during the rock and roll era.

In 1955, black artists such as the gospel-inspired pianist Little Richard and the country-inspired guitarist Chuck Berry reached nonblack audiences, while the cross-pollination between R & B and country and western music led to the rise of white "rockabilly" guitarists and singers such as Bill Haley, Elvis Presley, and Carl Perkins. As part of this national paradigm shift, the urban blues performers Bo Diddley, Muddy Waters, Jimmy

Reed, and Howlin' Wolf experienced crossover popularity from 1955 to 1958, as did the vocal harmony, or "doo wop" groups the Penguins, Platters, El Dorados, Cadillacs, Five Satins, and the Teenagers, as well as the R & B singer Etta James and the pianist Fats Domino, the gospel-tinged singers James Brown and Sam Cooke, and the pianist Ray Charles. By 1958, music industry marketing categories were hopelessly blurred by the continuing success of Chuck Berry, Elvis Presley, and Little Richard, and by the mainstream popularity of the rockabilly guitarists Buddy Holly and Gene Vincent, and the pianist Jerry Lee Lewis. With their emotionally exciting vocals and prominent dance rhythms, these artists helped contribute to a hybrid style. In its early years, rock and roll was also called "the big beat," due to its simplified, hard-driving 2/4 rhythm with the accent on the back beat. Lyrically, many of the new songs would abandon the mature themes of the blues and R & B for references to adolescence and innocent love.[1]

Still, the ascendance of rock and roll as the music of choice for the nation's young consumers, both urban and suburban, led to what one historian calls "a profound shift in cultural values on the part of mainstream youth" toward African American sensibilities. Postwar economic prosperity allowed more people to buy into the status-symbol commodity lifestyle of the middle classes, producing unprecedented leisure time and disposable income for baby boom teenagers. Yet American workers' "happy middle-class existence" and newfound "affluence concealed an unrewarding lifestyle," hence their suburban children were drawn to the music's spirit and energy.[2] Indeed, as popular music, rock and roll contained enough residual elements of the ribald, roughneck boogie woogie and jump blues styles to counterbalance the values of the regimented, bureaucratic dominant culture. Robert Palmer argues that "as a musical idiom" the new genre contained "a spark of freshness, an attitude of adventure and exploration."[3] At first, "with its sexuality and blackness," it "brought out fears of miscegenation," but the music quickly came to symbolize youthful white rebellion, particularly after teen-targeted Hollywood films like *Blackboard Jungle* (1955) and *Rock around the Clock* (1956) became hits, and after Elvis Presley was dubbed the "King of Rock and Roll."[4]

The African American slang term *rock and roll* had long described sexual intercourse in blues lyrics. In that tradition, Jimmie Lunceford recorded a song called "Rock It for Me" in 1939, while Cab Calloway recorded "I Want to Rock" in 1942, and in the mid- to late 1940s, the word *rockin'* could be found in jump blues lyrics and song titles. Since 1951, when the black vocal group the Dominoes used the term in their suggestive R & B song, "Sixty-Minute Man," Alan Freed had called his Cleveland R & B radio program the "Moondog Rock 'n' Roll Party." After Freed began broadcasting from New York City in late 1954, he helped spread R & B and black-based rock and roll, playing the original songs by African American artists rather than the white cover versions pushed on disc jockeys by the corporate major record labels. Anglo radio disc jockeys in Los Angeles, like their taste-making counterparts in New York, Chicago, and Memphis, introduced musical styles, announced local concerts, promoted new talent, and conducted on-air interviews with musicians, swinging open the door to increased acceptance of black music in the process.[5] By the mid-1950s, the advent of rock and roll resulted in teenage throngs converging at different dances, hops, and jamborees throughout the city and county of Los Angeles. In 1956 alone, Mexican Americans led the way, particularly East Los Angeles "teenage clubs" for young men, such as the Gents, Honeydrippers, and Jesters, and those for young women, such as the Incas, Las Damas, Athenas, Heart Menders, and Persians.[6] Some were both car clubs and social clubs, like the Jesters. East Los Angeles also produced the Eagles, the Lourds, and the Road Burners, as well as the Starlets, and the Road Burnerettes.[7] At Jordan High School in Watts, the Rock and Roll Fan Club included members of Mexican American social clubs like the Gay Gents from South Los Angeles, and the Charmers and Cheaterettes from East Los Angeles.[8]

In the R & B era, the city music bureaucrats had tried to supplant the popular music scene by funding a more wholesome, state-sanctioned version. After 1955, the culture war over competing visions of civil society entered a new phase, as disc jockeys, dance promoters, and independent record store and record label owners began attracting even larger numbers of white youths to rock and roll. In response, law and order enforcers intensified the antagonism as they continued to suppress the race mixing in their midst. More than ever, radio became a forum facilitating the legitimization of rock and roll, as well as the development of a unique Mexican American expressive culture. For example, among the local disc jockeys, Huggy Boy played more risqué songs than his rivals, much to the delight of his young listeners, who soon began to engage in an entirely new kind of music participation. In particular, Mexican Americans, both male and female, made up a large part of his audience, requesting songs on Huggy

Boy's dedication shows, declaring their love and broken hearts, and representing their neighborhoods, during the night's broadcast.[9]

Another white disc jockey, Art Laboe, became the first on the West Coast to play only rock and roll records, including those by white artists like Carl Perkins, when he debuted in 1955 on the Los Angeles radio station KPOP. Laboe was also one of the first, along with Huggy Boy, to welcome Mexican Americans onto his program, playing their dedications on the air. As a result, by 1956, Laboe's show was the number one radio program in the metropolitan area, and his live remote transmissions from Scrivner's Drive-In Restaurants in Hollywood and midcity attracted such a legion of low riders that Scrivner's built a two-hundred-car capacity hilltop restaurant at Western Avenue and Imperial Boulevard in South Los Angeles to accommodate his following. Teenage Mexican American car customizers finally found a place where they could congregate, and a medium through which their voices could be heard, as Laboe aired twenty-five thousand dedications from the restaurant remotes in the first five years alone.[10]

While young people found new outlets for self-expression, the powers that be cracked down on allegedly obscene cultural influences. For example, by 1955, Johnny Otis hosted a daily radio program on KFOX, through which he showcased and popularized black vernacular styles. His immediate broadcasting success led to other ventures in 1955, such as a record store on Western Avenue and his own short-lived record label and recording studio. In addition, local television station KTTV hired Otis to host a weekly, half-hour live musical variety program featuring the members of his band, and special guest stars like the Drifters and Ray Charles.[11] However, in response to whites socializing with blacks, Mexican Americans, and Asian Americans, police officers would "hassle the kids standing in line to get into the television show." Despite rumors of impending racial strife or gang violence, as Otis remembered, "we never had any trouble, the people got along great."[12]

Nevertheless, he encountered stiff opposition from "major record companies, publishing firms, radio and TV stations, ballrooms, and police departments," as well as "church and parent groups" alarmed about the negative effect of black music on white youth. Undaunted by the arbiters of morality, Otis continued to use his weekly television show and his daily radio program to promote the Southern California dance parties he staged with business partner Hal Zeiger. According to Otis, "As the music grew in

popularity, more and more white kids came to our dances, sometimes . . .
even dancing with African American and Mexican American teenagers."
Glaring officers who "hated to see white kids attending the dances with
Black and Chicano youngsters . . . would stand around . . . harassing [the
teens] with bullshit questions, checking their ID's." As this campaign of
intimidation intensified into one of sabotage, the policemen even invoked
obscure Progressive-era laws designed to restrict underage dancing.[13]

In a parallel development, a 1956 report by the Los Angeles Metropolitan and Youth Services Council pointed out that among the "minority
group residents" of Boyle Heights and Watts, teenagers "wish for nice,
large dances away from school." The council urged "agencies and schools"
to "cooperate with youth in such planning if a suitable multipurpose facility were available in or near each community," noting the "need for recreation staff" at "the self-organized teenage clubs now coming to the playgrounds, but getting no supervision."[14] That same year the Los Angeles
County Board of Supervisors, voting on an existing law which mandated
that all public dance areas be walled, rejected a new licensing code amend-
ment that would have allowed parks to sponsor dancing in the open. Even
John Anson Ford, the longtime liberal politico, objected to liberalizing the
rule, warning that it "would lead to a lot of dancing in the darkness," and
thus "might contribute to 'increased juvenile delinquency.' "[15] Whether
Ford's reservations reflected a fear of actual criminal acts by minors or
merely a fear of youth sexuality, the board effectively outlawed dancing by
young people in public parks, even as civic resources in poorer neighborhoods began dwindling. Twenty years earlier, in 1936, three East Los Angeles elementary and junior high school playgrounds had been successfully lit up and filled to capacity until 9:30 P.M., six nights a week, for
activities that included semimonthly dances and musical recitals, as well
as "occasional local talent entertainment." As the Brooklyn Avenue School
night playground director, A. A. Levine, noted at the time, "juvenile delinquency, by means of a properly supervised program, catering to the needs
and desires of our youth, is materially curbed and noticeably lessened."[16]
Instead of simply illuminating local parks and playgrounds again, the city
and county failed to provide adequate dance facilities for recreation.

In Los Angeles, on the other hand, a strictly enforced city ordinance
stipulated that public dances in the city limits involving minors under
eighteen must obtain permits from the Board of Education, effectively
limiting the dances to school grounds. By 1955, this limitation on all-age

dances, along with disruptive police harassment, spurred promoters like Johnny Otis and Art Laboe to move their events outside of Los Angeles.[17] For instance, nineteen miles south in Long Beach, three thousand to four thousand teenagers at a time would pack the Civic Municipal Auditorium to enjoy the steady backbeat and ribald lyrics of African American artists, while Otis and his partner Zeiger "often paid off the firemen and police" to avoid trouble.[18] Otis also initiated Saturday night dances at the American Legion Stadium in El Monte, a blue-collar city twelve miles east of Los Angeles on the San Gabriel River, starring his band, his current recording artists, his newly discovered talent, and popular local acts. Drawing up to two thousand black, white, Asian American, and Mexican American teenagers, linked from far and wide by radio stations and freeways, these concerts at the El Monte Legion Stadium became a community-driven cultural institution until the late 1960s.

As Matt Garcia's research reveals, at a time when interracial dating "was unacceptable," at El Monte in the mid-1950s, Marta Maestas remembered, "it was Latina women with a black man. It was black girls with Latino boys. But, it was kind of an easy mix." Richard Rodriguez, from the nearby town of Duarte, claimed that by the late 1950s at the El Monte Legion Stadium dances, you would see "more blacks dating white girls and Chicana girls," and "every now and then you might see a white man with a black girl or a white man with a Mexican girl, or vice versa."[19] As Rodriguez recalled, "When I went to El Monte, I felt that I could date anybody I wanted to; I could dance with anybody I wanted to." However, he added, "it might have been accepted there at the dances, but . . . if you dated a black girl, your parents would probably move out of the area."[20] While racial interaction still had limits, a new cohort increasingly participated in cross-cultural socializing, as well as occasional drinking and fighting in the parking lot, where young people also engaged in necking, and more, in the backseats of cars, confirming John Anson Ford's worst fears of dirty dancing and delinquent behavior after dark.[21]

In 1956, the El Monte City Council revoked the dance permit it had issued to Zeiger on the grounds that "rock and roll creates an unwholesome, unhealthy situation." Undeterred, Otis fought back against what he called "racism, under the guise of all-American morality." Arguing that the decision was designed to prevent youth race mixing, Otis, joined by Al Jarvis, Hunter Hancock, the National Association for the Advancement of Colored People, representatives of the American Civil Liberties Union, and representatives of the recently integrated musicians union Local 47, successfully pressured the council into rescinding its ban.[22] Since the 1920s, blues and jazz had provided artistic and personal "freedom of expression" and had "served as a crucial alternative" to bourgeois concepts of "Culture" and "Civilization."[23] In postwar Southern California, the culture clash that started with swing, jitterbug, and the zoot suit riots raged in the rock and roll era, as each side stood its ground based on opposing views of proper civil society.

For example, in a 1958 *Music Journal* essay, Los Angeles Mayor Norris Poulson lauded community orchestras' annual concerts and the Los Angeles Philharmonic's season of regional, downtown, Hollywood Bowl, school program, and "Symphonies for Youth" performances. The Municipal Arts Department's Bureau of Music was still on its mission of "citizenship through music," and Poulson touted the bureau's "project to provide more music for more people." Praising the "civic and cultural satisfaction and enjoyment" gained from the city's highbrow musical citizenship efforts, the mayor reported on the continued success of not only the city-sponsored youth choruses, which had begun airing local telecasts the previous year, but also the community sings, which had been functioning as free neighborhood "service clubs," and the municipal bands, which had "played approximately 1,100 [Sunday afternoon public park] concerts in Los Angeles to a total of more than 2,200,000 persons in the past decade."[24]

Despite these impressive figures, the city's homegrown multicultural urban civility must have still reached more people, and certainly more accurately represented the full diversity of its citizenry. The data would be conclusive if one could calculate the total number of ethnic Mexican family parties and barrio church *jamaicas* since the 1930s, pachuco social club weekly dances since the early 1940s, Mexican American social club and car club dances since the late 1940s, the myriad black and mixed-race R & B concerts presented last chapter, Mexican American neighborhood singing/acoustic guitar collectives like the 1956 Lincoln Heights group Los Reyes, and the rock and roll performances analyzed in this chapter, not to mention the countless jazz and Latin music shows, since a decade before the Los Angeles Music Bureau's inception in late 1944.[25] Indeed, venues like the Long Beach Municipal Auditorium, the El Monte Legion Stadium, and, from the swing through the mambo years, the Hollywood Palladium, each consistently drew two thousand to four thousand people per event. For many Southern California youths, the Music Bureau youth choruses and community sings must have paled in comparison to the El Monte Legion Stadium's "raw sexual energy," lively music, and social dancing.[26]

In this charged atmosphere, El Monte audiences were thrilled by regular performers like the Penguins, Jesse Belvin, Don and Dewey, the Carlos Brothers, Rene and Ray, Rosie and the Originals, and Sal Chico, as well as the Masked Phantom Band, a group put together by Hal Zeiger that featured saxophone sensation Bobby Rey (né Reyes). As a child in East Los Angeles, Rey's uncle, a clarinetist with the Los Angeles Philharmonic, trained him, as did an Italian conservatory professor. At twelve, Bobby abandoned the clarinet for the saxophone, and at fifteen he received lessons from the African American saxophonist Earl Bostic, a technical wizard. Soon Rey, who had grown up on the African American honking tenor saxophone style, was competing against his idols Big Jay McNeely, Chuck Higgins, and Joe Houston in "battles of the saxes" in Hollywood, North Hollywood, and West Los Angeles. Another favorite at the El Monte shows, "Handsome" Jim Balcolm, became popular locally for his 1958 single, "Corrido Rock," with its dual saxophone Mexican harmonies, rock guitar solos, and double-time polka beat.

In 1958, the Anglo Angeleno group the Champs recorded "Tequila," which topped the national pop charts for five weeks on the strength of its memorable saxophone solo, played by the song's Mexican American composer, Danny Flores, under the stage name of Chuck Rio. The Champs followed "Tequila" with "El Rancho Rock," a big beat version of the Mexican song "Allá en el rancho grande."[27] Just as Johnny Otis's popular radio and television programs helped him promote his El Monte concerts, Art Laboe used his popular radio show to promote the dances he had been holding at the Shrine Auditorium and the Orpheum, United Artists, and Paramount Theaters in downtown Los Angeles.[28] Laboe had also been renting the Long Beach Municipal Auditorium, but by 1958, the year his television dance party program aired on the KTLA station, Hal Zeiger invited him to emcee live shows at the El Monte American Legion Stadium every other week, thereby further solidifying his connection to Southern California Mexican Americans.[29]

The weekend evening El Monte Legion Stadium concerts provided rock and roll and doo wop groups with a stable venue that drew young people, many of them from the eastward Mexican American diaspora in the San

Gabriel Valley. In the process, the El Monte dances became associated with a "golden age" of Los Angeles doo wop. One study of the street-corner, a capella vocal harmony genre describes a "classical doo wop era" from 1955 to 1959, in which flourished a gospel-, jazz-, and R & B–influenced black style marked by nonsense syllables, melisma techniques, falsetto-driven harmonies, instrumental backing, innocent adolescent love lyrics, and a fresh excitement that was in turn offbeat, humorous, and sentimental. From 1959 through the genre's waning years in the early 1960s, doo wop experienced a crossover pop period during which white and Italian American, as well as both black and white all-women vocal groups reached a wider audience, achieving success beyond the rhythm and blues charts.[30] In Los Angeles, doo wop groups sprang up in local high schools, and they were recorded by black independent record label owners like Dootsie Williams and John Dolphin.[31] For example, out of this postwar scene emerged a doo wop quartet named the Jaguars, composed of the African Americans Herman "Sonny" Chaney, from Texas, and Charles Middleton, from Louisiana, the Mexican American Manuel "Manny" Chavez, from Los Angeles, and the Polish-Italian American Valerio "Val" Poliuto, from Detroit. The Jaguars, one of the first integrated vocal groups, met in South Central Los Angeles while attending Fremont High School. After appearing on Hunter Hancock's popular local CBS television program *Rhythm and Bluesville* in 1955, they became an instant Southern California success. Carrying popular music to all corners of the area, the Jaguars played not only the El Monte Legion Stadium and the Long Beach Municipal Auditorium, but also, by 1958, the Pacific Ocean Park amusement park, and, crossing into Los Angeles Music Bureau territory, the Hollywood Bowl.[32]

Fremont High School also produced Cleveland "Cleve" Duncan and Dexter Tisby, both of whom, along with Bruce Tate and Curtis Williams from Jefferson High, formed the Penguins. In 1954, the Penguin's song "Earth Angel" went to number one on the R & B charts, and to number eight on the pop charts. Curtis Williams wrote "Earth Angel" and its flip side, "Hey Señorita," originally called "Ese chiquita."[33] The Diablos released "Adios, My Desert Love" in 1954, while Don Julian and the Meadowlarks, a predominantly black vocal group from Fremont High, recorded "Ay, Sí Sí" in 1955 and, after performing thereafter for Mexican American audiences, "Low Rider Girl"/"Everybody Let's Cruise" in 1966. By 1967, black groups had recorded as many as thirty-six doo wop songs about exotic Spanish-speaking women—most of them Mexican—with titles such as "Down in Mexico" and "Dance Señorita."[34] In the mid-1950s, the local African American vocal group the Platters were so popular on the Eastside that when they played the Paramount Ballroom on Brooklyn Avenue, Mexican American youths lined up "20 deep on the sidewalk and around the block twice!"[35]

The writer Don Snowden argues that "the romantic style of the doo-wop groups . . . played right into the traditional ballad and harmony orientation of Mexican folk music."[36] According to the East Los Angeles record store owner John Ovalle, Mexican Americans in the 1950s were "partial to" the a capella doo wop style and its many love ballads.[37] These original vocal harmony R & B singles exerted a strong attraction for California Mexican Americans as "oldies," as did later songs like the "Gangster of Love" Johnny "Guitar" Watson's "Those Lonely, Lonely Nights" (1963), James and Bobby Purify's "I'm Your Puppet" (1966), and Brenton Woods's "I Think You Got Your Fools Mixed Up" (1967), among many others. In fact, as the African American Angeleno disc jockey Tom Reed states, "it was El Monte Legion Stadium, with its large Mexican American following to this day, generation after generation, that has helped keep this music alive."[38] During the mid-to-late 1950s, telephone poles in Santa Monica advertised each El Monte *baile* on black signs with brightly colored print, next to fliers for boxing and wrestling matches, to an assumed Mexican American audience.[39]

Doo wop definitely influenced Little Julian Herrera, one of the regularly featured performers at the El Monte Legion Stadium. For Johnny Otis's Dig Records, Herrera recorded typical doo wop ballads in the black vocal harmony style, including "Lonely Lonely Nights," a local hit in 1956, as well as "Symbol of Heaven" and "Here in My Arms," in 1957. Otis argued that Herrera "was not much of a singer, but he knew what to do with what he had." A dynamic dancer with a sensational stage show, Herrera became an Eastside heartthrob.[40] Accordingly, Otis featured Herrera to attract Mexican Americans, who represented a significant segment of the dance audience.[41] As Otis recalled, Mexican Americans "were the most loyal and responsive, and they would show up everywhere we went."[42] Ironically, Little Julian Herrera was born Ron Gregory in Massachusetts to Hungarian Jewish parents, from whom he ran away at the age of eleven. He eventually hitchhiked to Los Angeles, where a Mexican woman took him into her Boyle Heights home. Moreover, his hit song was cowritten, produced, released, and promoted by Otis, whose parents were Greek immigrants, but who chose a life in African American music, and considered himself "black by persuasion."[43]

The intercultural affinities that produced Johnny Otis and Little Julian Herrera also shaped the first Mexican American rock and roll star, Ritchie (originally "Richie") Valens, who expanded both Mexican American expressive culture and the larger urban civility, while achieving unprecedented recognition. Valens was born Richard Steve Valenzuela on May 12, 1941, to Steven Valenzuela, a World War I veteran born in California, and Concepcion "Connie" Reyes, born in Arizona. After his parents separated when he was three, Richie Valenzuela moved from San Fernando to adjacent, semirural Pacoima to live with his father. The produce- and citrus-producing southwestern San Fernando Valley already had sizable populations of ethnic Mexicans and Japanese, then after World War II, many African American defense workers and discharged soldiers moved into the area's new houses. During the 1940s and 1950s, therefore, Valenzuela lived in the only mixed-race towns in the predominantly white Valley. Valenzuela's father had always encouraged him to play musical instruments, and by the age of five he played a homemade guitar crafted from a cardboard box and a broom handle. At his mother's house Valenzuela heard mariachi music, at his father's, he heard flamenco, blues, jump blues, and R & B, and he also played and sang along to records, especially those by the "singing cowboys" Roy Rogers and Gene Autry, as well as by Herb Jeffries, a jazzy country and western balladeer. When Valenzuela was ten, his father died of complications from diabetes, after which the boy lived for spells with relatives in Long Beach, Norwalk, and Santa Monica.

Despite a lack of formal musical training, as a youth he learned to play the guitar and the drums by ear, and he was exposed to a range of music by family, friends, and older neighbors. For example, across the street from his Aunt Ernestine's lived an African American military veteran and long-time musician, Bill Jones Sr., who taught young Valenzuela how to tune a guitar and fret a few chords. While attending Pacoima Junior High School from 1955 to 1957, he modified his first electric guitar in his woodshop class, and he often played and sang at impromptu lunchtime concerts, at school rallies, and in jam sessions with his peers.[44] As his schoolmate Manny Sandoval remembered, "the Mexican kids . . . used to call [us] *falso* . . . because we liked to be with everybody. . . . So they wouldn't come around that much to group into the music thing with us. It would be the Blacks, some of the whites, and a few Chicanos."[45]

After his fellow Mexican American students called him fake or phony, while attending San Fernando High School, one of his older friends, an Anglo neighbor named Louis "Skip" Raring, invited Valenzuela to play private parties for the local white car clubs/gangs, the Lost Angels, the Igniters, and the Drifters, whose members were won over despite some initial racist reservations. In 1957, Valenzuela joined the Silhouettes, a local band that included the vibraphonist Gil Rocha, the pianist Frankie Gallardo, the drummer Conrad "Nino" Jones, the trumpeters Dave Torreta and Armando "Lefty" Ortiz, the saxophonists Ray Lerma, Bill Jones Jr., Walter Takaki, and Sal Barragan, and vocalists Phyllis Kay, Emma Franco, and Walter Prendez. Valenzuela played doo wop, Fats Domino, and corrido rhythms, and he would often write original material for the band. The Silhouettes' practice sessions seemed more like spontaneous dances as neighborhood teens gathered outside of Conrad and Bill Jones's garage, and Valenzuela's popularity increased as the band performed in the San Fernando and Pacoima American Legion Halls and Recreation Parks.[46] While still a member of the Silhouettes, Valenzuela continued to play solo at parties for both the Lost Angels and the local Mexican American car club, the Lobos, and, according to Walter Takaki, "Ritchie actually got the two gangs, the Lobos and the Angels, a little bit closer together. Whenever he was playing, they would get along just fine."[47]

In May 1958, Valenzuela came to the attention of the independent record producer Bob Keene, a swing clarinetist and former bandleader who had just scored a number one crossover hit on his short-lived Keen Records with the black soul singer Sam Cooke. As the artist and repertoire man of his new Del-Fi label, he was looking for fresh talent. Keene became Valenzuela's manager, then promptly produced the rhythm rocker "Come On, Let's Go" in an effort to capture the young guitarist's high-energy performance style on tape. For the B-side, Valenzuela recorded Lieber and Stoller's "Framed," which he had frequently covered live, replacing Gil Bernal's saxophone solo from the Robins version with his own blues guitar, and replacing the original vocals with a slower delivery that conveyed the injustice of being railroaded by the interlocked systems of law enforcement and criminal justice. Before pressing and distributing the 45 rpm record, Keene added a "t" to Valenzuela's first name, then persuaded the youth to shorten his family name. Keene, who had Anglicized his own surname, Kuhn, warned Valenzuela that pop radio station disc jockeys would read the Spanish name on the label, assume it was Mexican mariachi or Latin mambo music, and throw it away without ever listening to it.[48] Keene then took Valens's first single to the most popular radio station in Los Angeles, KFWB, where his contact there, disc jockey Ted Quinlan, "broke" the song, and where fellow station disc jockey Gene Weed got behind it all the way to number one on the charts in Los Angeles.

In the summer of 1958 Valens promoted his first single by appearing on rock and roll radio programs, including Quinlan's popular all-night show, on the television dance shows of disc jockeys Al Jarvis, "Jolly" Joe Yokum, and Art Laboe, at hops and radio station–sponsored listener house parties, and on a San Francisco television program. With "Come On, Let's Go" peaking on the national *Billboard* singles charts at number forty-two, and on the R & B charts at number eleven, Keene released Valens's second single, "Donna," a lovelorn R & B ballad based on a real-life schoolmate named Donna Ludwig, whose father forbade her from dating a Mexican.[49] Keene left a copy of "Donna" with the program director of KFWB, who immediately put the song on the air. As disc jockeys discovered the B-side, "La Bamba," radio listeners called in to request both songs, first in Southern California, then across the country. Ritchie decided to forego his senior year at San Fernando High in order to promote "Come On, Let's Go." In the fall of 1958, Keene took Valens on a short tour that stopped in Chicago; Cleveland; Buffalo; New York City, where he appeared on Alan Freed's rock and roll teenage dance show; Philadelphia, where he made his national television debut on Dick Clark's *American Bandstand*; and Washington, D.C., and Baltimore, where he played on local television music programs.

Back in Los Angeles, both the new single and its Spanish-language flip side were creating a buzz, and Valens combined radio station and personal appearances with recurring performances at the San Fernando American Legion Hall, Pacific Ocean Park, Long Beach Municipal Civic Auditorium, Disneyland, and the El Monte American Legion Stadium. Ritchie also performed in Azusa and headlined a Teen Kan Teen high school "Youth Rally" in West Covina, along with Sam Cooke and the Hollywood Flames. In addition to these promotional efforts, Keene engaged a top booking agency, General Artists Corporation, to ensure that Valens achieved national exposure. After playing in Washington state and in Honolulu, Valens returned to Hollywood to record songs for his first album. Orders for "Donna" were pouring in, and with a one-thousand-dollar royalty advance from Keene, Valens made a down payment on a new house for his mother.

Although he always dreamed of a home with a swimming pool in Beverly Hills, Valens settled for a modest pink stucco tract house with turquoise trim in Pacoima.

In December 1958, General Artists Corporation arranged for Valens to work a weeklong engagement with Alan Freed's Christmas Jubilee at Loew's State Theater in Manhattan, to play a one-night show at the Apollo Theater in Harlem, and to appear again on Dick Clark's *American Bandstand* during prime time hours to perform "Donna." In addition, Valens sang "La Bamba" live and in color on NBC's Sunday night prime time rock and roll television program, *The Music Shop,* and he played concerts in Buffalo and Toronto. Such a mix of national visibility and local performances paid off so much that when Valens returned to Los Angeles in early January 1959, "Donna"/"La Bamba" was emerging as a double-sided hit, with "Donna," a 750,000 copy–selling gold record, eventually reaching number two on the *Billboard* singles chart, and "La Bamba," number twenty-two. In Great Britain, Valens's popularity soared, with an English rocker's version of "Come On, Let's Go" on its way to cracking the British top ten, "Donna" hitting the top thirty, and an English cover of the ballad hitting number three.

Before Valens could stop long enough to enjoy his career success, after only two weeks in Los Angeles, he hit the road again, embarking on a very poorly run "Winter Dance Party" tour of Minnesota, Wisconsin, and Iowa. On a tour bus with no heating in subzero weather, a cold, exhausted, and homesick Ritchie wanted to skip the final concert dates, go home, rest, and regroup. Instead, on the evening of February 3, 1959, Ritchie Valens was killed, along with Buddy Holly, J. D. "The Big Bopper" Richardson, and pilot Roger Peterson, when their single-engine plane crashed in an Iowa field during a snowstorm.[50] His star continued to rise, however. His eponymous first album (see figure 29) reached number twenty-three on the charts; his posthumously released single, "That's My Little Suzie," reached number fifty-five; and, in a celluoid "farewell appearance," he displayed his charisma for two tantalizing minutes in Alan Freed's youth rock and roll movie, *Go Johnny Go!* (1959), playing guitar and singing "Ooh! My Head" for three blushing teenage girls.

After eight action-packed months of professional recording and touring, the seventeen-year-old had only just begun to plumb the depths of his creativity. His unique sound revolved around his inventive guitar playing and his direct, honest vocal delivery, which ranged from joyous to

29. *Ritchie Valens* album cover, 1958.

lonesome. Although he had played so many Little Richard cover songs that his early fans called him "Little Richie," and "Little Richard of the Valley," even Ritchie's version of Little Richard's "Ooh! My Soul," the Valens rocker "Ooh! My Head," with its pounding rhythm and swaggering, throaty vocals, or his teen love ballad "Little Girl," with its loose blues groove and falsetto vocals, or his cover of the doo wop duo Robert and Johnny's "We Belong Together," with its timeless romantic lyrics, were never simply pale imitations of black music.[51] As a child, Valens would ride horses on the ranches his father was working, dreaming of becoming a "singing cowboy" like his "western heroes," and he "used to sing a lot of country-western" in his youth.[52] Stylistically, this country influence can be heard in Ritchie's vocal timbre and inflections on the song "Hi-Tone," and in his twangy, cowboy rhythm guitar line on his cover of Ersel Hickey's rockabilly song, "Bluebirds over the Mountain."[53] Sartorially, Valens's favorite performance ensemble consisted of black pants accompanied by a rhinestone-studded black vest, and a puffy-sleeved, shiny blue satin shirt with a broad collar and leather laces drawing together a V-neck. He purchased this outfit at Nudie's in North Hollywood, where singing cowboy, western swing, and country and western performers, as well as rock and roll stars like Elvis Presley, shopped for their stage attire.[54]

During his youth, as family and friends would sing and play guitar on neighborhood front porches and at backyard barbecues, Richie's uncle, John Lozano, and his cousin, Dickie Cota, taught him Mexican songs, including the traditional wedding song "La Bamba." The song is a prime example of the *son jarocho* style that derived from the strong African legacy in Mexico, and originated on the Veracruz Atlantic seaboard.[55] Valens's interpretation introduced the average American, and the world, to Mexican folk rhythms on guitar, combining them with a swinging rhythm section, and a clear, percussive clave beat.[56] Initially, Valens was hesitant to record "La Bamba." According to Bob Keene, "Ritchie felt it would demean his culture. It was a national folk song and he was afraid it would be exploiting his ethnic music." Valens's aunt, Ernestine Reyes, reassured him that anybody could play "La Bamba," and she eventually provided him with the Spanish lyrics.[57]

At the time of his death Valens had been working on a follow-up to "La Bamba" called "Malagueña." One demo version of the song, with piano accompaniment, sounded like "España cani" ("Spanish Gypsy Dance"), a traditional bullfighter arena *pasodoble* written in 1934 by Spanish composer Pascual Marquina. The main version of the song, a hypnotic, commanding guitar solo demo, merged the flamenco march of "España cani" with the melody from "La malagueña" ("The Woman from Malaga"), a classical acoustic guitar tune written in 1927 by Cuban composer Ernesto Lecuona that had also been popular in Mexico.[58] Valens's "Malagueña" would have injected flamenco into American popular music, but by rocking the Lecuona classical guitar melody, Valens also pointed in another musical direction. His fingered tremolo technique, a rapid alternation between two notes of a chord, a third apart, emerged in flashes on "Malagueña," as it did in the opening riff on his version of Larry Williams's "Boney Maronie." On his original "Fast Freight," a rocking instrumental, Valens and the session band anticipated by three years Dick Dale's first blistering instrumental "surf guitar" recordings, which, along with the Beach Boys' harmonic soft rock, spawned Southern California surfer-themed music for white teenage consumption in 1961.[59] Tellingly, the Mexican cultural influence in Southern California was evident on the 1963 Beach Boys hit, "Surfin' U.S.A.," which imagines everybody across the country wearing "baggies" and "huarache sandals too," as well as on Dick Dale's 1964 Mexican-tinged instrumental, "Taco Wagon."

Ritchie Valens thus synthesized diverse sources while prefiguring new sounds. A ruggedly handsome, shy-yet-tough Mexican American with prodigious talent, charming personality, ambitious drive, and family support, Valens also beat the odds with the help of his manager Bob Keene's insider connections and business instincts. Ironically, Keene, who considered the Spanish surname Valenzuela a liability in the music industry, convinced Ritchie to record and release "La Bamba," a song sung entirely in Spanish. The African American studio musicians with whom Valens recorded his hit songs also played a key role in helping him convey his musical ideas to the fullest, while retaining the feeling and excitement of a live performance. For example, Earl Palmer propelled all of his Del-Fi recordings on drums and percussion, the jazz bassists Buddy Clark and Red Callendar lent their input, as did the rhythm guitarist Rene Hall, who arranged the charts for the session band, played the solo on "Come On, Let's Go," and even chose the recording studio, located at Santa Monica Boulevard and Vine Street in Hollywood. Co-owned by Dave Gold and music engineer Stan Ross, Gold Star Studios pioneered the use of an echo chamber, which created an electronic reverberation effect that gave Ritchie's ballads a melancholy mood, and his rockers a thicker, heavier sound.

Bob Keene may have mentored and marketed the seventeen-year-old Mexican American wunderkind, but Valens did not succeed solely because of an Anglo svengali. There is no studio editing or engineering on Ritchie's original demos, unarranged takes, and live recordings. On each of his songs, Valens's voice and guitar picking achieved clarity, and he was an improvisational blues guitarist who could rip rapid licks or play pensive, bent notes, who could create a crying effect or an eerie instrumental.[60] In short, the contributions of the session musicians or the studio producer do not lessen Valens's legacy or reduce his achievements, and despite his mainstream acceptance, Valens was not, as one scholar has argued, "co-opted" by the music industry, nor were his working-class ties necessarily "diminished" by "commercialization."[61] In reality, the working-class music of Mexican American Los Angeles included cowboy, rockabilly, and rock and roll tunes, Mexican folk songs, and a wide range of black styles, from the amplified guitars of urban blues to the vocal harmonies of rhythm and blues. These were Valens's influences and they all came back out of him, surged through him, as part of his overall unique style and personal expression. The eclectic experimentations of Valens and subsequent rockers, therefore, not only reflected the postwar configurations of Mexican American cultural identity, but also the modern music of the Southwest, as the members of the Mexican American generation attained greater representation and recognition.

Although Valens never hid or denied his Mexican heritage, it has been suggested that his racial identity was somewhat ambiguous to, and debated by, his national fans until after his death.[62] On meeting Valens, Earl Palmer's first impression was of a "short, stocky boy, Mexican-looking right down to the little curl in front." At Gold Star Studios, Palmer even tried to put the nervous teenager at ease by singing him the traditional Mexican song "Cielito lindo," which Palmer had learned as a child in El Paso.[63] Los Angeles–area teens undoubtedly knew Valens was Mexican American, but their ethnic notions about Mexicans were dispelled at his live shows. As Charlie "Carl" Bunch, the drummer for Buddy Holly on the Winter Dance Party tour, recalled, "When Ritchie walked on stage . . . it was like you stuck your finger into a light socket. The crowd was electrified that way. . . . The music was so powerful that he would bring you to your feet."[64] Moreover, his performances in concert, on television, and on the big screen, and especially his Mexican folk-rock hit "La Bamba," left little doubt as to his ethnicity. Gil Rocha remarked that "when Ritchie was back east, he represented the Mexicans," that the easterners "found out what he was," and that, "back then, he gave us the conviction that a Mexican could make it in a white man's world."[65] In the end, Valens's journey from humble origins to national success, his heartfelt love ballads, and his three-chord rock songs gave an entire cohort of Mexican American youths the confidence to start their own bands and express themselves through music.

By the mid-1960s, a new rock and roll music scene coalesced in the greater Mexican American area east of the Los Angeles River, from Lincoln Heights and El Sereno down to the City of Commerce, and all the way out to Pomona. Much has been written about Chicano rock and roll from East Los Angeles, also known as the West Coast Eastside sound, brown-eyed soul, and even pachuco soul. Many important stories have already been told about the music producers Eddie Davis and Billy Cardenas, and the remarkable bands the Premiers, the Romancers, the Blendells, the Mixtures, the Rhythm Playboys, Cannibal and the Headhunters, Thee Midnighters, Little Ray Jimenez, Chris Montez, Ronnie and the Casuals, the Blue Satins,

Thee Ambertones, the (Arvizu) Sisters, the Atlantics, Mark and the Escorts, the Medallions, Little Ray and the Progressions, the (Eastside) Jaguars (featuring the Salas Brothers), and the Heartbreakers, among others.[66] The musicians found artistic inspiration in the vocals of doo wop and R & B, the blues shouts and funky rhythms of James Brown, the down-home, gospel-flavored soul of Atlantic and Stax Records, and the sleek production values and sweet harmonies of Motown Records, "the sound of young America." Indeed, Rubén Guevara even argues that Motown united African Americans and Mexican Americans more than any other music.[67] The Beatles were particularly influential, but many Mexican Americans preferred the blues-based sound of the Rolling Stones. Added to the party music mix were extended instrumental jams and romantic, slow "grinders."

From 1964 to 1968, East Los Angeles became "a veritable rock 'n' roll factory" during a productive period of sustained musical creativity in which concerts were held at the Big Union Hall in Vernon, Salesian High School in East Los Angeles, the Golden Gate Theater and Kennedy Hall, both at Whittier and Atlantic boulevards in the heart of the Eastside, and, farther east on Whittier Boulevard, the Montebello Ballroom, as well as El Monte American Legion Stadium, the Shrine Auditorium, and some white suburban venues.[68] As in the earlier grass-roots tradition, predominantly ethnic Mexican union halls, churches, Catholic high schools, teen centers, and local social and car clubs held weekend neighborhood dances and staged battles of the bands. The pianist Eddie Cano followed in the swing-era music education tradition, working as a music teacher at Abraham Lincoln High School in Lincoln Heights, while training was also provided by Bill Taggart at Salesian High School, and in music courses at Garfield High School. Record stores with listening booths, like the Record Inn and the Record Rack, played a crucial part, as did Wolfman Jack, a new white disc jockey who broadcast late-night blues and obscure R & B from a radio station in Tijuana, Mexico, and Godfrey, an Irishman-turned-Chicanoized Angeleno who followed in the footsteps of Huggy Boy, who himself still aired Mexican Americans' dedications and broke singles by local bands.

The Eastside sound phenomenon included the Premiers' garage rock, Frankie "Cannibal" Garcia's soul singing, and Thee Midnighters' jazzy horns, as well as Willie Garcia's mature lyrics and emotionally moving delivery on ballads like "Dreaming Casually" and "Making Ends Meet," both released in 1967.[69] In their musical upbringing and cultural production, these talented musicians and charismatic entertainers reflected their times, yet they also represented a transitional cohort between the Mexican American and Chicano generations. As in the swing and R & B eras, Mexican Americans were hip—but not beholden—to mainstream trends, interpreting the latest music while remaining independent and innovative. The singers, musicians, fans, dancers, producers, promoters, and disc jockeys were products of the city's urban culture, but the civility of the rock and roll era was becoming less multicultural, and less subversive, worn down in the culture war over proper civil society. Mexican Americans had spearheaded the larger mixed-race rock and roll music scene, from Long Beach to El Monte, but they also created their own scene by and for themselves, as the state pushed them out of the city limits. For example, after 1962, when a Los Angeles law prohibited dances for people under eighteen unless the proceeds were donated to charity, the police effectively shut down for-profit underage dances, forcing concert promoters like Billy Cardenas to pay a fine.[70] At the same time, Mexican American expressive culture circulated, as the Eastside sound bands reached more people than ever by breaking into the top of the popular music charts, appearing on televised teenage dance programs, touring the country, opening for the Beatles and performing at Shea Stadium, the Hollywood Bowl, and the Rose Bowl. Collectively, the bands enriched Mexican Americans' cultural lexicon, from gang nicknames and barrio car culture to cherished oldies played at quinceañeras, weddings, and house parties.

Histories of postwar Chicano music in Southern California have been dominated by doo wop oldies, Ritchie Valens, the El Monte American Legion Stadium concerts, the Eastside sound, and the different venues that supported the rock scene. However, focusing only on these aspects obscures other figures in the frame. Following the careers and accomplishments of the jazz player Anthony Ortega, the singer-saxophonist Gil Bernal, and the singer-guitarist Lalo Guerrero into the 1960s reveals a wider range of variation in the Mexican American generation. For instance, from 1955 to 1958 Ortega lived in New York City, where he worked with top-notch artists including Dizzy Gillespie, Max Roach, and Clifford Brown, and recorded with Johnny Hartman, Dinah Washington, Maynard Ferguson, Billy Taylor, Herbie Mann, and Wild Bill Davis. Moreover, Oscar Goldstein repeatedly hired Ortega to play in the Monday-night jam sessions at Birdland. In 1955, Ortega recorded his first U.S. album as bandleader, *Jazz for Young Moderns*, which included the Ortega originals "Bat Man's Blues" (which featured Ortega on tenor saxophone, clarinet, and flute) and "Tune for Mona" (a cool swinger with an outstanding trombone solo by Jimmy Cleveland), as well as the standard, "These Foolish Things," on which Ortega's evolving alto saxophone style still evoked both the nimble, fluid Charlie Parker and the lush, bluesy Johnny Hodges. For the album's B-side, a second recording session with only violin, trumpet, bass, bassoon, bass clarinet, French horn, and Ortega on alto saxophone, clarinet, and flute produced jazzy chamber music. Like the progressive big band style of Claude Thornhill, with whom Ortega had also worked, this sound, particularly given its absence of drums, probably registered as softer and less forceful than the prevailing "hard bop" of the time. As a result, when this imaginative album was released in 1958, three years after its original recording date, it received unfavorable reviews in *Down Beat*. Hamstrung by a delayed release, corny album design, and poor distribution, sales were negligible.

In 1958, Ortega and his family moved back to Los Angeles, where the once "intense improvisational jazz scene" had become "stifling," and where, "instead of an art form," music had become "more of an entertainment form." Many of the old Central Avenue nightclubs had moved toward Western Avenue, and those that remained only hired small combos on the weekends. Organ trios, vocal groups, revues, and dancers were in vogue, but many club owners invested in jukeboxes rather than live music. Ortega remembered "struggling just to make a living in music, period . . . just to play my horn to make some money to support my family. . . . I was busy trying to survive." Out of necessity, Ortega sometimes backed up rhythm and blues singers in Los Angeles as a tenor saxophonist, but as he was once told by a bandleader who wanted "a raunchy sound," his tone was "too pretty." During this time, Ortega played with Howard Rumsey's Lighthouse All-Stars at the Hermosa Beach Lighthouse Café, one of the headquarters for the white "West Coast" jazz scene.[71] The six-month substitute engagement consisted of two weeknight shows and a Sunday matinee, but "it just wasn't the same as New York," which was "more hardcore." The owner of the Lighthouse, a Mr. Levine, refused to lend Ortega an advance once, fearing that the money would be used for drugs, and one night Howard Rumsey, the businessman bandleader, told Ortega not to take so many choruses on his solo or else "people might get too bored." At Rumsey's suggestion, Ortega moved to Hollywood, where he quickly found work. In 1959, he catered to a general audience, playing on Sunset Boulevard with the house band at the Cloister, "where all the Hollywood

30. Anthony Ortega, *A Man and His Horns* album cover, 1961.
COURTESY ANTHONY ORTEGA.

celebrities used to come out and dance."[72] That year, the vibraphonist Red Norvo invited him to play a six-week quintet engagement at the Sands Hotel and Casino in Las Vegas.[73]

In 1961, Ortega recorded his second American jazz album, *A Man and His Horns*, with the beboppers Hank Jones on piano, Addison Farmer on bass, and Edmond Thigpen on drums, with Nat Pierce writing the arrangements (figure 30). On this album, a musically mature Ortega displayed his mastery of the alto, tenor, and baritone saxophones, as well as the clarinet, bass clarinet, and flute. He overdubbed all of the sax parts like a complete section and layered in a dual clarinet and bass clarinet line for a full-bodied, tone-blending sound. On his composition "Strolling through the Casbah," Ortega cast a dreamy spell with opening and closing dual flute figures. With this album, Ortega kept alive the soaring swing spirit and swift chord changes of the bop-influenced, straight-ahead jazz tradition, as heard on his original "Happy Day," and on the Billy Taylor tunes "Titoro," which also used Afro-Cuban rhythms, and "Birdwatcher." An advanced improviser with an unpredictable style, Ortega's beautiful tone, poignant voice, thoughtful sensitivity, and melodic inventiveness shined through on the ballads "Handful of Stars," "Memories of Spring," "They All Laughed," and "We'll Be Together Again." Herald Records put out the album, but despite its considerable charms and virtuosity, it did not sell many copies.

In 1962, Ortega and Ruben Leon played on a recording session for Ortega's cousin, the singer Ray Vasquez, who began performing under the name "Ray Victor" in hopes of using his vocal talents to land recording contracts or movie parts. Although he never met these goals, on this album his songs were backed by a forty-piece Hollywood studio orchestra, conducted and arranged by George Hernandez, and produced by Oliver Berliner (see figure 31).[74] Later that year, Ortega moved to Lake Tahoe to work with Ray Victor, who was the master of ceremonies and intermission vocalist in the South Shore Room at Harrah's casino, where Ortega backed up Polly Bergen, Sammy Davis Jr., Liberace, and a young Barbara Streisand. By completely suppressing his improvisational instincts and jazz creativity to perform the same show tune sheet music every night, Ortega had, in his own estimation, finally gone all the way commercial.[75] Disheartened, in 1964 he moved back to Los Angeles, where he immediately joined Gerald Wilson's respected big band, in which he was "able to start exploring again."[76] In 1964, his old Hampton orchestra roommate Quincy Jones had moved to Los Angeles and was writing film scores in Hollywood. Jones gave Ortega his first break into the Hollywood studios by inviting him to perform on the soundtrack for *The Pawnbroker*, a Sidney Lumet film about Jewish Holocaust survivors in a New York ghetto.

For years Ortega had been trying to get into the studios by going to rehearsals at Local 47, but the key was to know one of the studio music contractors. Ortega realized that "each studio's music department had one contractor in charge of getting the musicians. They decided who would work and who would not work." They also recommended individual musicians to film-score composers and to other bandleaders. Based on Quincy Jones's recommendation, the composer Lalo Shifrin started calling Ortega to play on movie soundtracks, as did Bobby Helfer, the contractor at Universal Studios. As Ortega recalled, "I was starting to get a reputation as a different type of jazz soloist. It didn't do me that much good at first, but this far-out sort of approach was finally kind of coming into vogue," although, ironically, it led to recording dates for a 1966 Chrysler commercial, and for a 1966 television situation-comedy, the latter also secured by Quincy Jones.

31. Chico Sesma, Ruben Leon, Anthony Ortega, Ray Vasquez, George Hernandez, 1962. COURTESY CHICO SESMA.

During the 1940s, Chico Guerrero and Tony Reyes had played at MGM, but they left for New York by 1948, and therefore did not stay long enough to bring any of their *compadres* into the fold. Thus, by the mid-1960s, the Mexican trumpeter Raphael Mendez was still playing in the studios, but there were no Mexican American musicians, except "maybe Hal Espinosa," who had "played with Les Brown's band for many years."[77] According to Horace Tapscott, "the whole push toward [merging the musicians union locals] was to get black guys into studio music," and indeed, the "amalgamation" of the black and white locals "did open doors of opportunity for talented black musicians."[78] Progressive Jewish Americans like Alfred, Emil, and Lionel Newman at Twentieth Century Fox, Jerry Fielding, David Klein, Georgie Stoll, the musical conductor at MGM, and Ray Heindorf, the musical conductor at Warner Brothers, used their connections to bring African American musicians into the studio orchestras. As Ortega saw the situation, "It was very limited for Latinos or Mexican-descent musicians to get into the studios, because . . . [white musicians] figured, well, 'The guy probably can't read [music]' or 'The guy doesn't have a very good tone' or . . . 'He's going to be late because he's lazy,' or a number of things along those lines that are stereotyped."[79] In contrast, Bill Green and Buddy Collette, two African American musicians active in Hollywood, were, by 1968, in positions to call Ortega to substitute for them on certain jobs. In another example, when Buddy Collette was working on *The Flip Wilson Show*, he would bring Ortega along with him to the NBC studios.

Ortega told Al Lappin, the music contractor at NBC, "I think I'm being held back because of being a Mexican American. . . . I don't see any Mexican Americans in any of the studio bands, and I know in my case I'm capable of doing whatever they are doing." Soon thereafter, Lappin called Ortega for television specials by Don Knotts and Elvis Presley, and to occasionally substitute in the *Tonight Show* orchestra. Ortega's show-band stint in Lake Tahoe and his occasional forays backing up black R & B and ethnic Mexican Latin bands frustrated him creatively, but his work in the Hollywood studios was entirely different because it continued to pay off over time. By performing on those recordings, with reruns Ortega received small annual residual checks from the phonograph and film industries. In short, Hollywood studio work was well-paying and "steady, but then lucrative in the long run."[80] Mexican Americans' membership in the Local 47 musicians union in the years before the black-white union "amalgamation" paid dividends during both segregated and integrated periods, but only for a select few, and it did not protect accomplished players like Ortega from being treated like Mexicans.

Meanwhile, every Sunday night for two years Ortega played in the house band led by his pianist wife, Mona Ørbeck, at a Compton after-hours club called Clem's. Yet even as the black community supported both Ortega and his wife, he learned that the racial terrain of South Central Los Angeles jazz clubs could be quite slippery for Mexican American musicians. For example, Ortega had played with a couple of organ trios at an all-black club named Marty's, but during an extended engagement there with Luis Rivera, Ortega was "fired because [he] wasn't black," even though Marty's son Ronnie, who ran the club, had once stated that Ortega was "the only" Mexican who could keep up with the black musicians. Ortega suspected that some African American customers must have "wanted to see a black saxophone player instead of a Mexican guy," and that perhaps the Mexican owner, Martin Zuniga, was "prejudiced against his own kind," for instead of defending the bandleader's choice of personnel, he reneged on the original contract. Ortega's experiences illustrate that, parallel to the younger cohort's rock and roll scene, in jazz nightclubs and Hollywood studios, a wider urban civility existed, one which indicated the orientation of the swing-era cohort, and one in which tolerance, and intolerance, cut across racial lines.

In addition to his movie orchestra and organ trio work, Ortega always played modern, progressive jazz, and his music was part of the Los Angeles jazz avant garde. For example, in 1958, when he first returned home from New York, Ortega sat in with Paul Bley's quartet, which also featured the trumpeter Don Cherry, at a little jazz venue on Western Avenue below Wilshire Boulevard called the Hillcrest Club. Bley's music was "pretty far-out" and his band played very advanced original material. Bley "was impressed" by Ortega, so he asked the saxophonist to join the group. Five months later, Ortega left the ensemble, his place taken by Ornette Coleman. From 1958 through 1965, Ortega's unusual timing and interesting phrasing stood out in the big bands of Quincy Jones, Don Ellis, and particularly Gerald Wilson, with whom Ortega recorded the Mexican bullfighter instrumental, "El Viti," "a slow, beautiful number with very dissonant harmonies in the background," live at the Hermosa Beach Lighthouse. Ortega also "started experimenting quite a bit with an atonal type of approach" during these years. As he put it, "I had finally gotten to a point playing jazz that after a while things kind of just started to sound the same . . . like these certain bebop licks or the certain chord structures . . . I kind of wanted to break out of that restricted mode and try to just pick up notes here and there."[81]

Such postbop alchemy found expression during October 1966 and January 1967 in the Northeast Los Angeles neighborhood of Mount Washington. There, Ortega recorded duo and trio sessions that were released as the albums *New Dance* (1967) and *Permutations* (1968), on the local independent label Revelation. Each of the eight songs exemplified group spontaneity, especially the free-drum-and-bass Ortega original, "New Dance I + II," on which the musicians improvised from a sketch arrangement. Ortega still drew on the influence of Charlie Parker, which was like a root "deep at its core," but he had finally found his voice. The melancholy ballad, "The Shadow of Your Smile," and the Ortega original ballad, "Sentimentalize," an alto sax–acoustic bass tête-à-tête along a fluid series of major and minor chord changes, revealed him at his searching, introspective best. Ortega's stretched out, elliptical solos, unexpected turns, "asymmetrical" phrases, and use of "free-time" song structures lent his playing an abstract quality, as did his half-step bending of notes to maneuver across different keys on his composition "Conversation Piece." *New Dance* and *Permutations*, on their respective releases, disappointed commercially, but the jazz journalist Ross Russell gave *New Dance* an excellent review, and the *Down Beat* critic Don Nelsen praised the way Ortega's duets with the pianist Chuck Domanico created "moments of serene beauty."[82]

Even as Ortega created truly original, improvisational work, some black musicians did not accept him, Ortega felt, "because they figured, 'A Mexican guy, well, what the hell does he know about jazz?' " He had also been kept out of certain opportunities on occasion "in the white venue," where they figured, " 'Well, a Mexican guy? What the hell? He plays boleros; he plays cha chas.' " The very fact that jazz music is "a black art" invented by African Americans, according to Ortega, "kind of held me back. In other words, say, if I'd had been black, maybe I'd have made it, like a bigger name in jazz. Maybe, maybe not. Or if I'd been white, possibly." In his opinion, if he had been white, he could have gotten more bandleader recording dates, like alto saxophonist Bud Shank or some of the other West Coast cool jazz musicians. Because Mexican Americans were "right in the middle" between black and white, Ortega argued, they were never seen as innovators in jazz.[83] Due to the impact of both black nationalism and American whiteness on white jazz critics and on music historians, Ortega has received scant recognition in black-and-white jazz histories, unlike fellow Angelenos Ornette Coleman, Eric Dolphy, and Don Cherry, his African American "free jazz" contemporaries. As an artist, by furthering the collective improvisation at the heart of jazz, Ortega virtually ensured his own limited mass appeal in the United States, but he nevertheless cemented his long-term reputation, especially in Europe, where he is critically acclaimed and commercially popular.

Another gifted but unheralded Mexican American swing-era Angeleno, Ruben Leon, was a talented jazz soloist, arranger, and conductor who had played in the Earl Spencer, Charlie Barnet, and Miguelito Valdés orchestras. When Leon first moved to Los Angeles from El Paso he used to watch Don Tosti practice music, but Leon eventually surpassed Tosti both as a jazz improviser and as a Latin arranger. Leon, a *güero*, married a *güera* Angelena named Soledad, or "Chole," and to support their children after the swing era ended, Ruben played Latin gigs while pursuing advanced educational studies. Leon, who as a teenager had transferred from Lincoln

High School to a school for "incorrigible youth," became the principal of Lincoln High for a time, obtained a PhD in psychology from USC, then became the director of a child psychology center in northern California, and eventually a professor at California State University, Los Angeles.[84] Yet Leon also helped shape the jazz developments of the 1960s, forming the Black and Brown Brotherhood Band with Buddy Collette, and performing free weekend South Central concerts in Horace Tapscott's innovative band, the Pan-Afrikan Peoples Arkestra, which featured "black cats playing and Mexican cats playing as well."[85]

Meanwhile, Paul Lopez was playing at Birdland in New York City, where he lived for most of the 1950s, and where he studied composition at the Julliard School of Music in Manhattan. Despite his talents, Lopez could not find steady jazz work in Los Angeles, and he could never break into the Hollywood studio orchestras. To earn a living by his trumpet, he even worked in both the house and relief bands at Las Vegas casinos. After finding success performing and composing Latin music in New York, in 1958 Lopez joined the Latin music scene in Los Angeles, but he also played in Don Ellis's large, temporally experimental jazz orchestra in the mid-1960s.[86] Like Paul Lopez, the former pachuco boogie pianist Eddie Cano successfully switched from jazz to Latin music during the 1950s and 1960s. Don Tosti, in contrast, began performing more frequently in Las Vegas and Palm Springs during the late 1950s, after the pachuco boogie woogie, guaracha, and bolero phase of his career. In 1961, Tosti moved to Palm Springs, where he played as a solo pianist in posh desert hotels throughout the decade.[87]

In 1955, the singer-saxophonist Gil Bernal's working association with Spark Records had just ended, with the Robins, Jerry Lieber, and Mike Stoller moving to New York. Around this time, other than sporadic jobs with a few R & B artists, Bernal made a living as a solo performer in Los Angeles, where, in Ortega's words, Bernal "used to sing and was quite an entertainer, as well as a very good jazz player. He was a good-looking young man, and he took advantage of it . . . moving more into the popular vein, the commercial vein."[88] Of his own versatile style, Bernal said, "I wasn't a complete honker or a complete cool jazz player. If you wanted a Lester Young groove, I could do that, if you wanted it funkier, I would play that. When people really listened more carefully, they would say, 'Wow, what is that?' That's how I used to get my gigs." For example, Bernal sat in at a dance hall in Long Beach and the owner, Morley Turner, hired him on the spot. Bernal originally billed himself as "formerly with Lionel Hampton," but one night Turner put a sign out front promoting "Sex on the Sax: Gil Bernal and His Quintet." Bernal began drawing a full house of female fans, who would sit around the piano bar while he blew his blue notes.

Bernal earned his next engagement, at La Madalon nightclub on Sunset Boulevard in West Hollywood, by first sitting in with the house band. After Bernal created "a different feel" by "throwing in" sounds from South Central, the owner, Sam Einstaus, hired him as a sideman. Soon Bernal was asked "to become the leader since he was already up front announcing, singing," and playing his horn. Einstaus, who had seen an advertisement for Bernal's Long Beach performances "in the papers," changed the marquee to "Starring Gil Bernal, Sex on a Sax." La Madalon was "a dive," and the audience consisted of "hustlers, pimps, gamblers, gangsters" like Mickey Cohen and Johnny Stompanato, movie stars like Mamie Van Doren, Lana Turner, and Marlon Brando, whom Bernal met and befriended through a Filipino friend of Brando's, as well as entertainers like Liberace, who flirted with Bernal and offered him a job.[89] Mexican Americans like Ed Frias also attended La Madalon to see Bernal (see figure 32).[90]

After playing in South Gate and Norwalk, Bernal performed at a club on Hollywood Boulevard and Western Avenue, where he was seen by Spike Jones, the swing-era novelty tunesmith who had put out pop albums of Charleston, polka, and country and western songs, all written with "satirical arrangements." Bernal played in Las Vegas with Jones for several years, but when Jones was not working, Bernal would assemble a jazz group and secure jobs in Los Angeles billed as "Mr. Sex on a Sax, Currently with Spike Jones." In essence, Gil Bernal allowed nightclub owners to market him as a sex symbol in order to feed his family, just as he played "Night Train" with "a little bump and grind . . . to keep working."[91] As part of Spike Jones's farcical revue band, the City Slickers, Bernal sang, played saxophone, did impressions, "and acted as straight man for the comics," including Billy Barty.[92] Across from the Hollywood Palladium Ballroom, Jones and His City Slickers played the Moulin Rouge, a huge restaurant-theater with a pit orchestra, a conductor, a singing chorus, and a dancing chorus of twenty-five "showgirls." Bernal would jump off the stage and into the audience, finding the lap of a famous actress or pretty woman to sit on, playing all the while. He "would sit in Jayne Mansfield's lap and blow macho jazz [with] dry ice in the bell of [his] horn so that it would be smoking." Backed by an all-white orchestra, Bernal performed

32. Gil Bernal, head shot, ca. 1955. COURTESY GIL BERNAL.

his interpretation of the sultry, theatrical tenor saxophone style for an audience of affluent Anglo Angelenos. Yet according to Bernal, "When I played, man, I played . . . hard jazz. It wasn't Mr. Cool." As he saw it, he was playing more in the mold of Illinois Jacquet than of Big Jay McNeeley, much less Stan Getz or Paul Desmond.[93]

Ever the showman, Bernal reproduced his nightclub "honker" act on Spike Jones's television programs on CBS and NBC in the late 1950s, bringing the growling R & B sax sound and crowd-pleasing stage show to a national audience. The band would play some cornball songs with sound effects and comics, but when Bernal performed his featured jazz numbers with the rhythm section, and with trumpets and trombones playing riffs behind him, "it was the real thing." After succeeding as a jazz singer, by the end of the 1950s, as Bernal recalled, "I used to do . . . a little showbiz shtick and it kept me working."[94] At one point in the late 1960s, when Bernal had stopped playing saxophone and "was just singing," RCA Victor tried "to make a Tom Jones–type out of" him. Bernal preferred jazz ballads, but he "went into different kinds of singing" on a couple of unsuc-cessful Tom Jones–style albums.⁹⁵

In the rock and roll era, Lalo Guerrero surpassed his own postwar pachuco boogie regional success, achieving his greatest commercial hit with a parody of an all-American song. In 1955, a popular Disney television program about Davy Crockett, "the king of the wild frontier," sparked a national obsession with coonskin caps, Indian fighting, and the Alamo, and for thirteen weeks the show's theme, "The Ballad of Davy Crockett," topped the music charts. After hearing two Mexican boys from his neigh-borhood singing the ubiquitous song, Guerrero wrote a Spanish-language parody, "Pancho Lopez," about a fictional Mexican hero. Using the catchy melody from the television theme song, Guerrero's version conveyed a moral about not living life too fast. The song was a smash throughout the southwestern United States, hit the top ten in most of the Latin American countries, and became so popular in Mexico that it inspired a Mexican feature film by the same name. At the suggestion of a Hollywood record distributor named Al Sherman, Guerrero wrote an English-language ver-sion of "Pancho Lopez." The new English lyrics described a grinning, lazy Mexican migrant who takes siestas snoring in the sun, fights along-side Pancho Villa, joins "the wetback movement," swims across the Rio Grande, tries picking crops in the fields, then, after opening a taco stand, "his troubles they stop," and he becomes "The King of Olvera Street."

Guerrero's music-industry contact Sherman gave it to a local disc jockey, Alan Ameche, who broke the single, which eventually sold more than five hundred thousand copies throughout the United States. Guer-rero had finally reached a mass American audience. To promote the song, Guerrero appeared in a sombrero, serape, and haurache with socks, per-forming on national television programs like Steve Allen's *Tonight Show*, the *Art Linkletter Show*, Peter Potter's *Platter Party*, and the *Al Jarvis Show*, introducing, a few years before Ritchie Valens, a stocky, mestizo mas-culinity into the culture industries, in contrast to a slim, blond standard of beauty. Guerrero had released the "Pancho Lopez" records on Discos Real, a short-lived Pasadena-based label he cofounded with the recording engi-neer Jimmy Jones and the businessman-investor Paul Landwehr. How-ever, they never received clearance from Wonderland Music Publishing, which owned the rights to the original music. Consequently, they were summoned to a meeting at the Burbank offices of Walt Disney, where they met the corporate magnate and his attorneys. Disney made an offer that

Guerrero and his two business partners did not refuse: split the profits or face litigation.[96]

By 1956, Guerrero followed his mainstream breakthrough hit by writing original songs like "Pancho Rock," putting a Latin spin on the Mickey Mouse Club Theme with "Mickey Mouse Mambo," recording "Señor Sueño" to the tune of "Mr. Sandman," creating the English-language "Tacos for Two" to the tune of "Tea for Two," and parodying "Take Me out to the Ballgame" as "Take Me out to the Bullfight." His 1965 "Elvis Perez," about an acoustic guitarist–mariachi singer who switches to electric guitar and rock and roll singing, itself switched between ranchera and rock. During the song's three rockin' interludes, Guerrero belted out a few verses of three miniparodies: the interlingual "Nothin' but a *Perro*," in which he declared, "You ain't never had a taco and you ain't no amigo of mine"; "Heartburn Hotel," in which, instead of the line, "I get so lonely I could die," Guerrero crooned, "Without guacamole I would die"; and "Don't Be Cruel," in which he implored, "Don't wake me up until noon." "Elvis Perez" reached number two on the "Latin American" charts in the United States, number eight in Buenos Aires, and number two in Mexico City.

That same year the Trio Los Panchos added to the Mexican songbook when they recorded "Nunca jamás" ("Never Ever"), a bolero Guerrero had written from a battered woman's point of view. In a 1957 Mexican Americanized version of the poem, "Twas the Night before Christmas," Guerrero recorded the song "Pancho Claus," about Santa's sombrero-wearing cousin from south of the border who flies a burro-powered sleigh and brings toys to a house in which the mother makes *masa* for tamales and bakes enchiladas, the father dances the mambo and the cha cha chá, while the children listen to Elvis Presley. In a nod to Lieber and Stoller, the songwriters of "Hound Dog," Guerrero also recorded "Pound Dog," about a chihuahua. In addition to the bicultural "Ranchero Rock," in the song "La televisión," Guerrero poked fun at the TV cowboy Roy Rogers and at the 1950s Western shows *The Lone Ranger* and *Gunsmoke*. In 1959, reacting to both the post-Sputnik space race and a popular Spanish-language song about Martians who arrive dancing the cha cha chá, Guerrero wrote "Un marciano en la tierra" ("A Martian on Earth"), which became a hit across Latin America, reaching the top ten in Peru, Argentina, Columbia, and Cuba.

In 1960, he Mexicanized the pop novelty hit, "Itsy Bitsy Teenie Weenie

Yellow Polka Dot Bikini," with his "El bikini de Tia Trini," and he responded to the Chubby Checker dance craze with his "El twist de Luis." By 1960, Guerrero had earned enough money from "Pancho Lopez," despite splitting his half of the proceeds, to stop touring and open a nightclub on the Eastside. In 1962, he led a trio of squeaky-voiced, Spanish-singing "squirrels" in his song, "Las tres ardillitas," which sold well throughout the American Southwest. Also in 1962, Imperial Records rereleased some of its late 1940s singles, including six by Guerrero, on a compilation album called *Mexican House Party*, and Guerrero wrote a parody of Tony Bennett's "I Left My Heart in San Francisco" called "I Left My Car in San Francisco." Throughout the decade, he released a string of "Ardillitas" children's songs similar to the English-language Alvin and the Chipmunks, although his eventually became popular in Mexico and Cuba. He also wrote numerous boleros, rancheras, and polkas with typically Mexicano titles like "Lágrimas de amor" and "Virgen morena," as well as "El corrido de Delano," about the United Farm Workers grape boycott, and comedic songs like "El brujo," "Carta de un bracero," and "El güiri güiri." Finally, in the late 1960s, Guerrero's wry, Spanish-language commentary about the new miniskirt fashion style, "La mini falda de Reynalda," became a *norteño* rock and roll hit in Mexico.[97]

A self-described "entertainer," Guerrero specialized in covering "topical" subjects. He summarized the appeal of his music by saying, "most of my material is upbeat . . . light . . . comical and happy."[98] In his own inimitable style, Guerrero put out scores of songs in Mexican, Latin, and American musical formats. When he composed in traditional Mexican genres, Guerrero typified "the aesthetic value" of Mexican music: "All the beauty that songs have to offer; the melody, the poetry, rhyme, the graphic interpretations that the lyrics present, and other images that one creates when listening to songs."[99] In other words, Guerrero kept the "Mexican" in Mexican American, but at the same time, he used humor to repudiate the hyphenation of being "Mexican-American." By "embracing both identities," Guerrero created truly bilingual, bicultural, and quite witty songs that chronicled "the everyday joys, sorrows and absurdities of Mexican American life."[100]

The trials, tribulations, successes, and failures of the performers from the swing and R & B cohorts shed new light on Mexican Americans' shifting relationships with white, black, and Mexican cultures, and with the economy of the culture industries. Moreover, analyzing the ways that Mexican American style influenced both the local and national cultures helps to more profoundly assess the rock and roll era. Connected across the city's topography of interracial music and dance scenes, and on the cutting edge of stylistic trends, male and female Mexican American hipsters predated the Beats, rebels, and "bad girls" of the "other 1950s."[101] For example, Richard "Cheech" Marin argues that the quintessentially "cool" Mexican American Angeleno style was appropriated by Hollywood in 1955's *Rebel without a Cause*, popularized in the guise of James Dean's Anglo angst.[102] As we saw in chapter 1, Mexican Americans had been wearing leather jackets and cuffed denim jeans since the early 1940s, yet the same "tough guy" image looked different when projected back at them by smoldering method actors on the big screen. As Tudy Brambila recalled, "We couldn't relate to James Dean or Marlon Brando. Our heroes were our fathers, uncles and older brothers who fifteen years earlier had shown their independence in zoot-suits."[103] While rebels of the 1950s liked to race souped-up hot rods and motorcycles, urban Mexican Americans preferred to cruise lesiurely while high on marijuana, socializing with their homeboys and looking for women to meet. Increasingly, many Southern California white youths were attracted to "the cholo image of a controlled, calm, and cool demeanor," and to the Mexican American "male image of being deliberate in talk and gestures."[104] In other words, the "studied disinterest and cultivated detachment affected by cholos" became "the most accessible model of 'otherness' for middle-class white youths."[105] In short, Mexican Americans' cultural capital of cool, their slow, sinuous style, signified a knowing hipness to many Anglos and white ethnics in Los Angeles.

Some cholos still wore the pachucos' distinctive "ducktail" hairstyle, which had so offended sailors and civilians during the zoot suit riots, and rebellious white youths who appropriated it as their haircut were called "hoods," and eventually, "greasers," the derogatory word for Mexicans that Anglos had been using since the nineteenth century.[106] Across the Atlantic, the pomaded ducktail was adopted by English "rockers," described by Dick Hebdige as slick-haired and "overtly masculine."[107] In postwar Los Angeles, though, not all white youths took their style cues from working-class Mexican Americans. Hence Lincoln Heights resident Tudy Brambila reminisced that "while the white kids played with their hoola hoops, we played our guitars at the Downey [Recreation Center] singing 'Corazón Solido.' While they wore Davy Crockett coonskin caps, we wore pachuco ducktail haircuts, khaki pants and spitshined French toe shoes. While they customized their hotrods, we were working on our homemade Saturday Night Specials."[108] This discrepancy can be seen in Victor "Butch" Brac, a Mexican Americanized Anglo who grew up in Lincoln Heights. In 1955, after his parents divorced, Butch moved with his mother and two siblings to Highland Park, where he got kicked out of Catholic school and joined a cholo gang during junior high school, even though he was a "paddy"—the term some Mexican Americans used for whites. After too many trips to juvenile hall, Butch was sent to live with his father in the desert community of Mojave, California. He arrived "in his ducktail and his khakis, and his walk"—the cool cholo saunter—but his new schoolmates were all wearing buzz haircuts and Levi jeans rolled up at the ankle. He soon abandoned the cholo style, and he eventually became not only a star football player at the high school, but also student body president.[109]

In Los Angeles, by 1957, the year that the honking tenor saxophonist Joe Houston recorded an instrumental tune called "Chicano Hop," wearing "khaki trousers, leather jackets, [and] flat-top hair with curly ducktail" was considered a "typical" look for Mexican American boys. One meeting of such youths organized by "Group Guidance of County Probation" in the Flats neighborhood in Boyle Heights turned up a number of clothing styles, "from light gray flannel sports suit to typical khakis with leather jacket; hair style ranged from crew cuts to long and carefully arranged waves."[110] At El Monte American Legion Stadium rock and roll dances, most Mexican American young men wore khaki pants with either short-sleeved Sir Guy leisure shirts or long-sleeved Pendleton plaid shirts, with French-toe (square-toe) shoes, in contrast to the black R & B performers' "Continental" look of pompadours and suits with a narrow lapel and tapered slacks. In general, Mexican American men created their own version of the Southern California casual style, whereas African American men sported a flashier look of tailored suits with velvet or satin trim along the lapel and sleeves.[111]

Mexican American young women at the dances "had stacked hair and wore [flat] white shoes called 'bunnies,' black tight short skirts, and feathered earrings," along with short-sleeved blouses.[112] Chole Camarena remembered Mexican American women wearing bobby socks and oxford saddle shoes, while Johnny Otis recalled that his 1950s Mexican American audiences "liked exactly what the black audiences liked," except that the Mexican American women, with their "beehive hairdos" and "fuzzy sweaters," had their own style.[113] A few Mexican American men, like Jerry

Castellano, even affected the "collegiate" look favored by many Anglo teens. Castellano wore cardigan-style letterman's sweaters in an effort to appear successful at El Monte concerts, and also to distinguish himself from other Mexican Americans. Growing up during the 1950s in Pomona, on the eastern boundary of Los Angeles County, Castellano admired rosy-cheeked, clean-cut Ricky Nelson. Watching Nelson sing and play guitar on the television program *Ozzie and Harriet*, Castellano thought, "If he can do it, so can we!"[114] The bassist Jimmy Espinoza cut his hair and "went completely Ivy League" in the early 1960s while attending the half-white East Los Angeles College campus bordering suburban Monterey Park, and he also played in a surf music band at weekend fraternity parties.[115] In the rock and roll music scene, all clothing styles were represented, with some exceptions. For example, fliers for Eastside Sound concerts would include the line, "Dress Sharp or Don't Bother," or "No Capris," while on the radio Art Laboe would announce, "We're Gonna Rock, We're Gonna Roll . . . at the El Monte Legion, No Levis or Capris, Please."

In addition to fashion, Mexican American Angelenos followed both black and white dance styles, but also created and maintained their own original moves. For instance, at El Monte Legion Stadium, an older African American dance, the hully gully, and an older Mexican American dance, the pachuco hop, still thrived. In a nod to the pachucos' stylistic laid-back edge, the Mexican Americans who danced the pachuco hop in El Monte considered it unmanly for the male dance partner to energetically improvise, as was the norm. Rather, the men kept their cool, minimizing their movements and suavely leading their female partners, who demonstrated creativity and talent.[116] As seen in chapter 1, many pachucos were exceptional dancers, but the hard-core hep cats among them had perfected a near-stationary style of dance. By the 1950s, the cholos continued this blasé demeanor, as they were too cool to exert themselves. At local dances, and particularly at house parties, Mexican Americans displayed a "closed" style of dancing that was quite different from the popular rock and roll style derived from "wide open American ballroom swing." Thus, rather than throwing their partners or flashing acrobatic moves, the men shuffled in a small circle, arms held closely to their torsos, while twirling their partners. If someone was especially uncoordinated on the dance floor, their fellow Mexican Americans would accuse them of "dancing like a *gabacho*."[117]

Many Anglo teens copied both the clothing styles and the dances at El

Monte Legion Stadium, where multiracial dance contests produced a new dance, the corrido rock.[118] Based on the fast-paced popular song "Corrido Rock," the dance consisted of two or three lines of about two hundred people arm-in-arm, each row taking four steps forward, then four steps back until the lines slammed into each other in youthful physical contact and energetic release. In typical Mexican American manner, "an evening at the Legion always ended with tight slow dancing, called scrunching, usually to ballads." After the shows, the party continued in the parking lot, where members of the Boyle Heights car club, the Jesters, wearing blue- or green-tinted, square wire-framed T-Timer sunglasses, would cruise in their lavender-, maroon-, or gray-primered cars.[119] To customize their Bell-flower Buicks and Chevy Impalas, Mexican Americans would "chop" the roof and windows, cut or clamp the spring coils, and fill the trunk with metal blocks, then add the "tuck and roll" stitched leather or plush Tijuana upholstery, chrome "spinners" on pinstripe whitewall tires, Smitty twin mufflers, drag exhaust pipes, and colored lights on fenders and skirts. In 1958, too many low riders scraping the pavement led to the creation of California Vehicle Code 24008, which outlawed any car caught with any part lower than the bottom of its wheel rims. By 1959, Ron Aguirre, a young Mexican American from San Bernadino, using hydraulic pumps salvaged from a surplus B-52 bomber, installed a secret adjustable suspension system that allowed him to lower and raise his "ride" at the flick of a switch.[120] Mexican American low riders actively claimed public space and visibility in the face of coercive containment, and this culture-war dynamic continued throughout the rock and roll era. Indeed, in an inevitable ritual every weekend, the police would eventually break up the evening gatherings in El Monte, and everyone would "caravan back to the Foster's Freeze at Whittier and Mott or to Johnnies' at Whittier and Ditman."[121]

Cholas cruised the scene as well, and they were not merely passengers in their boyfriends' cars. On the contrary, all-female car clubs were instrumental. The producer Eddie Davis recalled how the "cholita" members of a girls car club, the Chevelles, who "used to follow the Premiers," created a "live" sound on the band's 1964 studio recording of "Farmer John," helping to propel the single to number nineteen on the *Billboard* charts.[122] Moreover, in a corrective to male-dominated histories of Chicano expressive culture, Dionne Espinoza notes that "girls' social clubs often sponsored dances, designing and handing out their own flyers." Having their own social clubs and car clubs signified their increased "social independence" and mobility despite "constraints within the family." Indeed, as "a growing number" of urban Mexican American women "obtained positions at the lower end of the white-collar scale as clerical workers, bank tellers, insurance saleswomen, and key-punch operators," more of them were able to cruise Whittier Boulevard with their homegirls in their own low riders. In addition, young Mexican American women helped introduce the British mod style, which promoted a more "feminine" look for men, and "higher visibility for women," into the Eastside. As Espinoza argues, just because young Mexican American women consumed youth culture fashions did not necessarily mean they were "buying into" white culture and the Anglo value system. Similarly, in the new Mexican American hair politics, the decision to rat one's hair into a huge beehive required another, whether or not to peroxide it, and the act of bleaching one's hair could be interpreted as internalizing racism, accessing whiteness, responding to young Mexican American men who found blondes and güeras more attractive, or simply rebelling against parental restrictions.[123]

Keta Miranda contends that the mod style signified a rejection of the cholo image and style during "a moment when economic mobility was a real possibility," when "a new social class outlook and sensibility could be formed."[124] Even though "many of the Mod girls bleached their hair blonde" and "used concealer cream on their lips before applying pink lipstick," Miranda insists that they were not "acting white or attempting to pass." By the same token, their "participation in consumerism" did not indicate "a desire to assimilate." For example, when Thee Midnighters' 45 rpm single, "Whittier Boulevard," came out in 1965, Mexican American women performed a distinct dance to it, one which borrowed from African American "cake walk" steps and Mexican *folklórico* toe-heel steps. Many Mexican American women switched from big bangs, beehives, and hair spray to the mods' straightened hair, brow bangs, miniskirts, and bold, striped minidresses. When America was overcome by Beatlemania, young Mexican American rock bands transformed their look from R & B–style suit coats with velvet trim to "mop-top" Beatles bangs and suits with nearly collarless coats, skinny neckties, and tight trousers. British black leather, ankle-high "Chelsea" boots with wedge block heels and elastic, slip-on sides completed the ensemble.[125] Mexican American musicians thereby ushered in the "fastidiously neat and tidy" English mods' "more furtive and ambiguous sense of masculinity."[126] As Romeo Prado said of Thee Midnighters, "We were the first band from East L.A. to grow long hair, and for that we suffered the consequences: ridicule, fights, and people yelling 'faggots' as we walked down the street."[127] In the end, upwardly mobile Mexican American mods tapped into an international style, incorporated it into their own, and thereby pushed the boundaries of the entire generational cohort's expressive cultural repertoire, while symbolically reflecting a social and economic broadening of Mexican American Angeleno communities in the 1960s.

Accordingly, just as the preceding chapters profiled the Mexican American go-getters, educationists, squares, political leaders, small shop owners, and upwardly mobile war veterans, this chapter analyzes the employment, educational attainment, and continued spatial, social, and economic movements of the Mexican American population. Mexican Americans' economic positions fluctuated throughout the period, as they remained vulnerable to the vagaries of the boom and bust cycle, yet their boats had also been lifted by the increased hiring of the wartime defense industry and the postwar private sector. Many members of this cohort, including but not limited to military veterans, pursued specialized training, higher-skilled jobs, or post–high school education. Moreover, since many of them had greater housing options, particularly when Veterans Administration and Cal Vets mortgage loans facilitated homeownership, not all Mexican Americans lived in all-ethnic Mexican barrios.

For instance, one 1956 report described Watts as "predominantly Negro with little islands of Spanish-speaking people scattered throughout the area." The Hollenbeck community, it was explained, "has done much to overcome tensions due to differences in background, language, and culture. Cultural groups live in separate pockets. Racial groups include Negro from the rural South, Mexican-American and Japanese-American. The Jewish group is gradually leaving." The report concluded that the Boyle Heights neighborhood needed to "continue to develop inter-cultural understandings through cooperative community ventures (festivals, dances, music)."[128] Another 1956 report concluded that "Watts is somewhat below the county average in home ownership, while Hollenbeck is far below. . . . In Hollenbeck families tend to move out as soon as financially able to do so, and many leave when their children enter their teens. There is much more mobility than ten years ago, and . . . Jewish families are gradually moving away.[129]

In Lincoln Heights, a section dense with Victorian houses and some of the oldest churches in the city, one quarter "of all housing units were either dilapidated or deteriorating," and 90 percent "of the housing was built before 1939." Lincoln Heights had been "a comfortable middle class community" of Midwestern Anglos during the 1920s and 1930s, when Italian immigrants began spreading out into the area from the traditionally working-class, immigrant neighborhood of Dogtown, which bordered the Los Angeles River and spanned both sides of the railroad tracks. Before Mexican Americans established themselves in smaller barrios like Clover and Happy Valley, they were, like the Italians before them, concentrated in Dogtown. Mexican American property owners had been "nearly nonexistent" before 1940, but their numbers increased eightfold from 1940 to 1950, as Italians moved out of the neighborhood and into suburban homes. Still, although almost 75 percent of the population had Spanish surnames in 1960, only about 32 percent "of the property owners were Spanish surnamed." Most of the Anglo and Italian property owners did not live in the neighborhood, but property records also indicate Spanish-surnamed landlords who lived "in the suburbs." During the postwar period, Mexican Americans "moved in equal numbers to the suburbs and to other areas of the city."[130] As Tudy Brambila noted of Lincoln Heights, "in the later '50s while the locura still existed with the Clover teenagers, while the Boys' Club and Downey [Recreation Center] continued their struggle to bring us to our senses and encourage a better future for us, our folks were looking to upgrade their lives by moving to our version of 'Beverly Hills': El Sereno and San Gabriel."[131]

One 1957 study compared the city's older "downtown barrios" to predominantly Mexican American neighborhoods in East Los Angeles, and to integrated Anglo–Mexican American suburbs, thereby revealing the many faces of this generation. For instance, the barrios just east of the river experienced a postwar influx of "Japanese and Negroes," which led to "job competition" and to "Mexican resentment," particularly toward the "Negroes moving into the downtown areas." These neighborhoods were also crippled by heavy industry and freeway construction, and marked by juvenile gangs and narcotics. As seen in a group of teenage Mexican American girls at a Catholic Youth Organization recreation center, many of the barrio youths came from poor, "broken" homes, and they resented the raw deal that their parents and society gave them. Some of them formed gangs whose young members refused the dominant culture's laws and rejected "middle-class values of conformity," as symbolized by their "large leather jackets" and ducktail haircuts. The gang members reported that the police stopped them for questioning when they were "only cruising the drag," or "just out to see what Beverly Hills looks like."[132]

Compared to the older barrios near the river, East Los Angeles boasted a higher proportion of homeowners, although the majority of its residents were renters. Most of the men in East Los Angeles worked as "common laborers," but a much higher percentage of people owned small businesses, typically groceries, photography shops, drug stores, and service stations. In the younger, American-born families, many wives worked outside the home in sales or in "the sewing factories," while the bilingual parents increasingly insisted "that their children be fluent primarily in English." On average, one-half to two-thirds of school-age children attended public schools, with the remainder attending parochial grade schools and local Catholic high schools. More Mexican American teenagers than in previous generations finished high school rather than leaving early to work full-time, with a growing number attending college, especially East Los Angeles College, which reported a 50 percent Mexican American enrollment. Finally, the Eastside experienced a postwar increase of low-income Anglo and Negro families moving into the area, particularly as many younger Mexican American families moved out.[133]

Unlike African Americans, who had more limited housing choices in Southern California, an entire cohort of Mexican Americans moved from the older Eastside neighborhoods to the developing suburbs, where they could raise their baby-boom children "far from the noise, dirt, smog, and traffic of the big city." With approximately thirty thousand World War II veterans, and thousands more Korean War veterans leading the way, Mexican Americans started over, moving northeast to Monterey Park, east to Montebello, and, in the San Gabriel Valley, to Whittier, West Covina, Claremont, and Pomona, as well as southeast to Pico Rivera, Norwalk, Santa Fe Springs, and, in northern Orange County, to La Habra and Buena Park. Although they represented less than half of the total residents in these towns, surely they must have been partly responsible for the more than doubling of the population of Norwalk and Whittier between 1950 and 1956, and for a steady growth in Montebello, as well as a more dramatic growth in West Covina. Thousands of young Mexican American families earned easy credit terms on G.I. home loans, then financed mortgages for postwar ranch-style, one- or two-bedroom tract homes with a two-car garage, small backyard, new television set, and modern appliances. Despite some attempts at discrimination, "Anglo and Mexican-American families were interspersed among the tracts" in "integrated" communities.

The Mexican American men worked in construction, and in car and aircraft assembly plants, using the Santa Ana and San Bernadino freeways to commute to and from Los Angeles, or else worked at local facilities like the tire manufacturing firm near Montebello. About 10 percent of the Mexican American women worked outside the home; the rest were suburban housewives caring for their average of three-to-five children.[134] These parents, in their twenties and thirties, spoke so much English at home that their children had to take Spanish-language courses in junior high school or high school. For the parents, a college degree had always been a luxury, but their better incomes enabled them to pay Catholic-school tuition so that their children could finish high school and pursue higher education. Television provided the main family recreation, followed by weekend drives to parks and beaches, and camping trips, including summer visits to Yosemite and Lake Tahoe. According to one Catholic parish priest, "some of the more prosperous ones are even buying cabins up in the mountains."[135] Many of these families attended Sunday mass, became active in their local churches and in their communities, and sent their children to parochial schools.

For example, in 1950 Frank Garcia, born in El Paso to Mexican American parents and raised in Boyle Heights, and his wife, Rose, born in Boyle Heights to New Mexican parents, graduated from high school, got married, and moved to Montebello.[136] Directly east of East Los Angeles, the predominantly white city of Montebello had recently been pressured by the Community Service Organization, City Councilman Ed Roybal, and others to reverse its policy of refusing G.I. home loans to Mexican Americans.[137] Frank Garcia had forced "a showdown with a real estate agent" who first tried to tell him that the newer tract homes were "all tied up," but who then admitted that only the real estate boards could dictate such an exclusionary policy. As Frank argued, "Many of our people take a defeatist attitude. They won't fight something like this; and wonder why they're often kept out of the nicer districts. If you stand up for what you've got coming, you'll win out in the end." Rose recalled that both of their families "were disappointed" when they moved out of Boyle Heights, but "we sure didn't want to raise our kids to grow up and be pachucos." The Garcias raised four out of their five children to speak English, and not Spanish, so that they would not have "two strikes against them . . . speaking English with a Mexican accent." By 1956, Frank, who had worked for twenty years in a downtown camera shop, was " 'a little better off' compared to many Mexican-American families," while Rose, who had studied typing at "a commercial school," worked at home two-to-four hours a day per week for "a large firm in the city."

Another couple, Ed and Stefana Valencia, moved to Pico Rivera after living for fourteen years in Vernon, which had become "heavily industrialized" and hence "a low-status housing area." As Ed said of Vernon, "It was getting too black." Ed, who now worked in a chain store warehouse near Pico Rivera, insisted that he did not "mind colored people," and that he had "a lot of good colored friends," but that he "was thinking of [his four] kids." Although Ed counted Anglo friends among his neighbors and fellow church members, many of the other Mexican American families in the neighborhood kept to themselves rather than mix with Anglo families. Like many of their generation, Ed and Stefana were bilingual, but they never taught their children Spanish. Finally, another Mexican American couple from the 1957 study moved to Santa Fe Springs, sent their children to the neighborhood public high school, then had to fight the local Anglo residents' attempts to gerrymander and redistrict their children out of the school. In general, the downtown and Eastside barrios had a higher percentage of foreign-born Mexicans, larger families, and lower standards of living. In contrast, the suburban "areas of low density" had a "predominance of native-born Mexican-Americans," smaller families, and a higher standard of living.[138]

Mexican Americans like María Olivas and her siblings, who were raised in Chihuahua, Mexico, and East Los Angeles, became postwar homeowners as well. All three of Olivas's brothers served in the U.S. Army, the two oldest in World War II, the youngest in Korea, they worked for years for Bethlehem Steel, and bought their homes with help from the G.I. Bill. María's sister, Jeannie, started at the bottom in a sewing factory, but eventually became a fashion designer's assistant, and bought her own house. In 1957, María herself worked in a Robinson's department store, where "they didn't even want us to speak Spanish." Some of her Mexican American coworkers would even say they were Spanish when asked by Jewish American coworkers. María understood that "a lot of people didn't want to admit they were Mexican because they thought they were going to be treated differently," but she told her Jewish American colleagues, "You know, there aren't that many Spaniards here. . . . We [Mexicans] come in all colors," and, "This Mexican . . . feels very proud." Even María's Mexican immigrant parents eventually moved from East Los Angeles to Montebello.[139]

In 1955, in the County of Los Angeles, a real estate board "expelled two of its members" for selling homes to an Italian-Spanish family and a Mexican American family.[140] Yet in the city of Los Angeles, "Spanish-surname" residents were "more segregated from Negroes than from Anglos," and for Mexican Americans, who earned a "somewhat higher income than Negroes," the path to integration seemed strewn with fewer obstacles.[141] As a California Department of Industrial Relations report stated, "the 'ghettoization' of Mexican Americans in Los Angeles is not as complete as in the case of Negroes." In 1960, only one-fifth of the Spanish-surnamed metropolitan population was concentrated in East Los Angeles, compared to half of all African Americans concentrated in South Los Angeles.[142] For instance, Cheech Marin's father, Oscar Marin, a thirty-year veteran of the Los Angeles Police Department, and his mother, Elsa, both born and raised Angelenos, moved the family from South Central Los Angeles to Granada Hills, a suburb in the San Fernando Valley.[143] In contrast, María Olivas remembered having some Mexican American friends who still owned homes in Watts throughout the late 1950s and early 1960s. One of these friends told Olivas, "Nobody ever bothered us. On the contrary, whenever we'd go on vacation or something, they take care of our place."[144]

Nevertheless, the African American musician William Woodman noted, "after the war . . . blacks from the South . . . came down there, and the environment just changed. And then a lot of the Mexicans began to what you call migrate."[145] Perhaps, as La Colonia became overwhelmed with southern black migrants after the Second World War, some Mexican Americans moved from Watts to adjacent South Gate, despite continuing racial discrimination in the housing market. For example, Becky Nicolaides's research reveals that in 1950, "fully 72 percent" of South Gate's "moderately prosperous" Mexican Americans owned their own homes, although by 1960 the percentage had declined to 47 percent. By 1963, Jordan High School in Watts was 99 percent black, while on the other side of the railroad tracks, South Gate High School was 97 percent white. Some of these "white" students must have been Mexican Americans, for by 1970, "Spanish-language" persons totaled 17 percent of the population in the predominantly white suburb.[146]

Mexican Americans also began moving into Monterey Park, a suburban area northeast of East Los Angeles, during the 1950s. For example, in 1956 Vince Ramírez bought his house in a white track with two Mexican families and one Jewish family. Up the hill, a nearby Monterey Park subdivision used to have a large billboard in the 1930s that read, "Exclusive Community: No Minorities Allowed." Even though Vince Ramírez had moved to the hills of Monterey Park, he and his third wife, Edna Enriquez Ramírez, still participated in ethnic Mexican culture, as well as in mainstream urban culture. Edna, whose family had emigrated from Sonora to Arizona in 1945, moved to Los Angeles in 1956, and she and Vince wed in 1963. In the early 1960s, they heard "fun music" at the Cine Grill in Hollywood, danced to a mix of jazz, rock and roll, and cha cha chá at the Palladium in Hollywood, saw Harry Belafonte at the Greek Theater in Griffith Park, danced to live swing and rock and roll at the Nu-Pike Amusement Park in Long Beach, and attended Dixieland concerts at Disneyland in Anaheim, and at the Knickerbocker Hotel in Los Angeles. On two occasions, a policeman friend of Vince and Edna's took them to Elysian Park dances that were held at the Los Angeles Police Academy and sponsored by La Ley, the Mexican Police Association. At the height of the rock and roll era, Edna attended traditional Mexican dances at La Casa del Mexicano in East Los Angeles, and at events sponsored by groups like Las Hijas de las Américas and Las Señoritas de las Américas. Edna participated in a social club for Sonorans and attended their dances at the Catholic Youth Organization at Brooklyn and Gage avenues near City Terrace. The Club Sonorense was the first social club to hold its annual Mexican dance downtown at the Biltmore Hotel, where their band played norteño, ranchera, polka, bolero, and cha cha chá. Edna also took Vince to the Sunday Supper Club, a series of live weekend music concerts at First and Boyle streets put on by the International Club, a government agency–sponsored social club for recent immigrants from Europe and Mexico.

Vince Ramírez and his two older brothers attended Garfield High School, listened to jazz during the swing era, and were World War II veterans who served proudly in the U.S. Army Air Corps. Each used the G.I. Bill to advance his career. While they attended school, Vince's two brothers worked in their father's machine shop on weekends and during summer and winter vacations. Ron Ramírez became an artist, starting as a helper and ending up as vice president of a company, while Armando Robert "Bob" Ramírez became a "landscape architect." Vince went to East Los Angeles College, then to USC, becoming a licensed civil engineer and part of the first generation of Mexican Americans to be hired by Cal Trans, the California Department of Transportation.

By 1955, Vince recalled, "I was an engineer and I'd work on construction jobs, and I'd walk around with my clipboard and people, whites, Anglos would ask me, 'What are you? What nationality are you?' And I'd say, 'My roots are Mexican.' And they'd say, 'Oh no, you're not Mexican.' And they'd point to the laborers and say, 'They're Mexican, you're Spanish.'" Vince attributed his and his brothers' success to their parents, but he also argued, "Without the G.I. Bill a lot of us would still be in East L.A., would still be doing pick and shovels jobs." Whether military veterans or not, many members of this swing-era cohort became one of the first racial "minorities" on their suburban block. Like other successful Mexican Americans in the 1950s, Vince and Edna's compadre, Nick Rodriguez, who used to attend the African American stage shows at theaters along Central Avenue, bought a house in Monterey Park with his Mexican American wife, Annie.[147]

Mexican Americans thus left South Central Los Angeles, with its freeways and its paucity of public parks, and East Los Angeles, with its five far-flung parks, three of them separated by the 710 and 60 freeways, and its large cemetery, to integrate, or infiltrate, formerly all-white cities like Monterey Park, with its ten parks and its golf course, and Montebello, with its six parks and its large country club. In 1965, out of the approximately 160,000 Mexican American Angelenos who lived in tracts in the upper third of the socioeconomic scale, 130,000 of them lived in tracts with less than 22 percent total Mexican Americans.[148] In other words, many Mexican Americans were moving up the socioeconomic ladder and into formerly all-white suburbs. In addition, they were moving into formerly all-white occupations. A 1965 Census survey revealed that 16 percent of the male respondents in Boyle Heights, City Terrace, and East Los Angeles worked as "craftsmen" or "foremen," while 5 percent of them worked in "professional and technical occupations." Of the area's female respondents, 24 percent were employed as "clerical workers."[149] Finally, more Mexican Americans were attending predominantly white universities. For example, even in the rock music world, Eastside singer Steve Salas spent three semesters on scholarship at Stanford University, and Frankie Garcia attended college to study nursing.[150] However, in the early 1960s, not enough Mexican Americans, and not nearly enough Mexicanos, obtained quality education, skilled employment, decent housing, and satisfactory health care, despite their hard-working legacy in California for generations, and their strong presence in Los Angeles.

A California Fair Employment Practice Committee report, based on 1960 Census Bureau figures, established that "white persons of Spanish surname" comprised 9 percent of the state's total population, compared to 5.5 percent for Negroes, whom they outnumbered in all metropolitan areas except the Oakland–San Francisco Bay Area. While 44 percent of the state's Spanish-surname population resided in the Los Angeles–Long Beach–Orange County metropolitan area, 80 percent of them were born in the United States, and 46 percent of their parents were also American-born. Tellingly, more than half of the Spanish-surname men and almost half of the women aged fourteen and older had not gone beyond the eighth grade in school, and 60 percent of all employed persons of Spanish surname worked in manufacturing, trade, and agricultural industries. In particular, while Spanish-surname men represented nearly 9 percent of all employed men, they comprised half of all men employed as farm laborers and foremen, and while Spanish-surname women represented 6.5 percent of all employed women, they comprised more than 28 percent of all female farm laborers. Moreover, the 1959 median income of Spanish-surname men was lower than that of all whites, but higher than that of nonwhite men, while the 1959 median income of Spanish-surname women was lower than that of both white and nonwhite women. In short, "hundreds of thousands of Mexican-Americans are relegated, like nonwhites, to inferior jobs and poverty-stricken neighborhoods," and subject to discrimination because of their dark skin and Spanish tongue. The report, which attempted to identify the third- and later-generation descendants of Mexican immigrants, as well as newcomers, also pointed out that statistics do not tell the entire story, since "not all persons of Spanish surname suffer social and economic disadvantages."[151] As in previous chapters, the Mexican American generation's range of variation spanned divides of class, nation, and generation, as did its community politics.

For example, in 1963, the Community Relations Educational Foundation (CREF), a Los Angeles nonprofit organization that promoted "harmonious racial, religious, and ethnic relations through educational activities," sponsored its own report on Mexican Americans, which found that one of every nine persons in the Los Angeles region bore a Spanish surname, including "braceros" who "married American women" and obtained either U.S. citizenship or "Green Card" permanent residency. It also confirmed that Los Angeles ranked second only to Mexico City in concentration of people of Mexican descent. In one of the densest areas, Boyle Heights, the 1960 Census revealed that three out of four of the residences were built prior to 1939, and that seven out of ten homes were owned by absentee landlords. Forty-three dwelling units were lost between 1956 and 1960, despite 2,574 more people moving to the area, resulting in deterioration in the quality of the existing housing." Indeed, throughout the Southwest, Mexican Americans rented more than Anglos, but received less for their money, and much of the housing they occupied was "dilapidated and overcrowded," "segregated and sub-standard."[152]

In Southern California, the report described "a fragmentation of public health services in the Mexican American community," with "agencies at work in the field" plagued by "language barriers, impatience, indifference or outright hostility" due to "a lack of understanding." City Councilman Edward Roybal and other Mexican American leaders held community conferences to address health topics, including the problem of narcotics, while participants in a 1963 conference at Occidental College, in the Eagle Rock area of Northeast Los Angeles, proposed a barrio family health center as a pilot project. With regard to education, a 1961 conference by the Council of Mexican American Affairs "stressed the need for specialized counseling and guidance service in elementary and secondary schools, after-school services for youth," outreach to "special needs" parents, and "more dynamic and functional curricula" that offered Spanish-language instruction and covered Mexican "cultural traits" in social studies, art, music, and home economics courses. The Occidental College conference "recommended that school curriculum include recognition of the cultural heritage of the Mexican American," especially in the primary grades.

With regard to employment, the report cited a 1962 conference at Stevenson Junior High School in East Los Angeles, cosponsored by the East Central Area Welfare Planning Council and the Los Angeles County Department of Community Services, as well as a 1963 Youth Training and Employment Project, launched by the Youth Opportunities Board of Greater Los Angeles and funded by the federal Manpower Development and Training Act. In addition to these community efforts, the report underscored "the great unfulfilled need . . . for an affirmative program of merit employment and for adequate vocational training." According to the report's author, Martin Ortiz, "Although an ever-increasing number of Spanish surnames are now evident in the professions of law, medicine, education, architecture and social work, and many are leaders in the fields of business and government, the great preponderance of Mexican Americans are in the lowest economic strata of our community. There has been very little upgrading to white-collar jobs with supervisorial responsibility."[153] Ortiz noted an early 1960s rise in "federal, state, county and city appointments to public office of persons of Mexican descent," then argued that "for every successful man or woman of Mexican descent, there will be innumerable others who will be inspired and motivated to move ahead." Finally, Ortiz observed that "pride in their cultural heritage has been met with public respect," but he concluded the report by warning that "serious lags exist in the utilization of their employment potential, in the education of their young people, in the housing available to them and in the accommodation of public health and social services to their needs."[154]

The FEPC and CREF reports illustrate the realpolitik context in which some Mexican Americans finally achieved some upward mobility, including hard-won success playing the jazz, pop, rock and roll, and soul music of the period. Despite some significant gains as individuals, as a group they still faced disproportionately high unemployment and incarceration, as well as poor education, particularly for at-risk youth. For example, in January 1964, in typical Mexican American generation fashion, articulate spokesmen from local organizations, along with individual professionals, testified before the California State Assembly's Industrial Relations Committee hearing on "special employment problems of the Mexican-American." These witnesses demonstrate that Mexican Americans not only recognized their own problems, but also asked the legislators to make particular programs a funding priority, and to continue funding effective existing programs. Although Mexican American generation members proffered pragmatic social solutions and preventive measures that could potentially improve their conditions, they lacked the financial means and political clout to follow through on their own specific policy recommendations.

For instance, William Acosta, the Community Services Coordinator for the Youth Training and Employment Project in East Los Angeles, proposed that industrial employers give workers a one- or two-year notice before their jobs become automated to allow for retraining. He noted that since the dropout rate at the three local East Los Angeles high schools ranged between 20 and 25 percent, and since the median schooling completed by the area's twenty-five and older adults was less than the ninth grade, this working population was increasingly "less qualified for employment" and hence vulnerable to technological advances like automation. Since the city's only public vocational training institution, Los Angeles Trade Tech, was located just south of downtown, Acosta advocated establishing a comparable facility, which would also offer "intensive courses in remedial education" and "highly individualized instruction," in East Los Angeles and other predominantly minority "pocket areas." Furthermore, since most state employment services were located at one downtown office, he proposed decentralized, local centers for employment services.

Since "the ratio of students to counselors in the schools remained at approximately 665 to 1," Acosta called for an increase in the number of counseling and guidance personnel, preschool teachers, and special staff to work directly with parents and families of students. He argued that an increase in services could stimulate "motivation for higher education" and "personal goal formation," and he urged that "such programs as currently functioning . . . be expanded and more widely financed." For many East Los Angeles youths, "minor delinquency incidents during their early adolescence" led to "repeated rejection or disqualification with potential employers because of their arrest record" during later adolescence or young adulthood. Given the large number of former prisoners (*pintos*) in the barrio, Acosta proposed "that all civil service commissions, general industry, management, labor unions, and particularly the defense and aerospace industries, as well as the armed forces, consider modification of their hiring policies relating to arrest records, or being on probation or on parole . . . to minimize any kind of second class citizenship." In a bitter denunciation, he added, "It also seems rather ironic that as citizens and taxpayers we spend billions of dollars in rehabilitation and training programs within our corrections systems, and then we find that on release to the community, having paid their debt to society, and trained for some type of work, these people, in reality, have little or no chance at all for employment."

In Los Angeles County, the unemployment rate among Mexican American youth stood at six times that of the national average, and the median annual income for Mexican American families, at $2,000 less per year than the rest of the county population. In East Los Angeles, 38 percent of the workforce was involved in "unskilled" labor, compared to nearly 19 percent in Central Los Angeles, 10 percent in Van Nuys, and 3 percent in Hollywood. Conversely, only 1.5 percent of the Mexican American population was involved in professional or managerial work, with a lower-than-county average percentage of workers in semiskilled and skilled job categories. To reverse this imbalance, Acosta recommended "that civil service and private industry consider more practical qualifications and criteria" than certificates or special testing, which were being "over-emphasized and misapplied considerably." What's more, potential employers could easily extend a probationary period contingent on newly hired young people or adults finishing their high school education or two years of college, depending on the job requirements. Considering the "strong feeling among most of the Mexican-American population that" they were still the "last to be hired and the first to be fired," the Youth Training and Employment Project recommendations were meant to enable "the work force of the Mexican-American population in achieving and maintaining . . . human dignity through being able to work and thus . . . sustain their own respective families without dependency on public assistance and other forms of aid."[155]

Another hearing witness, William Gutierrez, a consultant to the Los Angeles County Commission on Human Relations, highlighted two ends of the employment spectrum. On one end, "the Mexican-American . . . has traditionally the highest rate of school dropouts, and when he drops out of school, he may be a functional illiterate" and hence "untrainable." On the other end, even educated, qualified applicants have been discriminated against in various fields, especially "in civil service." Gutierrez pointed out the need for Mexican Americans "to exert their civil rights on employment matters," and "to make complaints about abuses against" them, as well as the need for them "to take a survey of employment in any civil service agency to determine if" they "are working in government in proportion to their numbers in the general population," and if "they hold a substantial number of positions of any importance." As Gutierrez declared, "some grants have been allocated to study the Mexican-American, but Mexican-Americans themselves have not been part of the research." By way of contrast, he added, "At least the Negro has the Urban League."[156]

Sam Hamerman, administrator of urban affairs for the City of Los Angeles Board of Education, sketched "the immediate problem" by citing a recent survey "in the Lincoln Heights, Boyle Heights, City Terrace and surrounding adjacent areas by the Youth Opportunities Board of Greater Los Angeles," which "showed that 2400 young people between the ages of 16 and 21 . . . have been out of school six months or longer, out of work, and in many cases," almost out of chances to "make good." For this population, Hamerman cited the need "for remedial programs in English and basic mathematics," adult education programs, and instruction "in the mechanics of applying for and holding a job." By 1964, individual educators at different schools and in many classrooms had created and conducted innovative, grass-roots programs "with their own funds and on their own time." The Youth Opportunities Board of Greater Los Angeles and the Office of Urban Affairs, under the jurisdiction of the Los Angeles Unified School District, formalized these community efforts into the Extended Day Program, consisting of after-school instruction, tutoring, and student leadership activities, and the Compensatory Program, consisting of regular school-day remedial and English-language instruction.

Pilot programs to prevent "dropouts and unemployability" multiplied, with approximately "200 students enrolled in basic reading classes at three junior high schools and two senior high schools," another 200 attending more advanced classes in "reading improvement," and 100 enrolled in "power reading classes" for "the college catering children." Regarding the "academically oriented student," Hamerman referred to "spot surveys" which indicated "that better than 50 percent of the graduates of East Los Angeles high schools will seek some type of a post high school education." For "the student who is not going to college," and "who may never finish school," in addition to "keeping libraries open after schools close," community "evening counseling" was instituted. Moreover, a pilot program was started "at Lincoln High School where 100 dropouts will be counseled to return to school, [and] where specialized programs will be prepared, leading them to employment or further training." In short, the city validated the hands-on methods of the community, in a civic attempt to bridge the old "pachuco-square" divide, but because of "voter resistance" by "resounding margins" to higher taxes, legislation providing specific assistance for such programs needed to be enacted, and education funding in the state budget needed to be increased.[157]

The committee also heard testimony from Dionicio Morales, who was not only the executive director of the Equal Opportunity Foundation, a nonprofit institution dedicated to promoting equal opportunities in employment and education for Mexican Americans, but also a labor union representative of the Amalgamated Clothing Workers of America. Morales noted that between 1950 and 1960, the Mexican American population increased by 88 percent, and that ethnic Mexicans were exploited in oppressive agricultural fields, in "cruel" garment industry sweatshops, and in certain factories which hired and fired them en masse. Not only did they lack job security, but they were grossly underrepresented in higher paying jobs. Thus, even though "two out of three laborers" were Mexican American, and union membership consisted mostly of laborers, two out of three union officials were not Mexican American. Similarly, even though Mexican Americans made up 10 percent of the California population, only 2 percent of them worked in state civil services agencies. In particular, only 4 percent of Mexican Americans worked for the County of Los Angeles, compared to 24 percent of Negroes, even though "the population proportion in Los Angeles" was "two Mexican-Americans for every Negro."

Although roughly 15 percent of the Los Angeles metropolitan area population was Mexican American, a study of selected private companies holding contracts with the federal government showed that only 4.3 percent of their employees were "of Mexican extraction." In an "even more glaring" discrepancy, while 7.5 percent of their employees were officials or managers, only 0.6 percent of their Mexican American employees "hold such important positions." In contrast, 13 percent of their laborers were Mexican Americans, while only 4 percent of all employees "worked in such capacity." Finally, the California State Department of Employment assigned more than one hundred "minority specialists" to the Los Angeles area, yet not one specialist had been assigned "to East Los Angeles or other areas of high Mexican-American density." Too many Mexican Americans were "economically displaced," that is, "chronically unemployed or underemployed," and they were "the first to be hit by recession unemployment." To try to remedy the situation, Mr. Morales called for "a minimum wage for agricultural workers," a "system of unemployment insurance for agricultural and other seasonal, low-income workers," the empowerment of the state FEPC to more easily "initiate investigations of possible discrimination," and the creation of a "Mexican-American Institute under the auspices of the University of California."[158]

Despite such far-sighted and feasible proposals, based in many cases on already proven programs, judging by social indices such as housing, employment, health care, and education, there was still much work to do by the mid-1960s. Nevertheless, the Mexican American generation doggedly fought for equal education, living wages, and fair treatment under the law, as well as for personal freedoms and civil liberties. Creating a cultural counterpart to concurrent labor and political efforts, the rock and roll era cohort claimed public space across the region with their low riders and dance concerts, pirated radio airwaves with their dedications and requests, influenced surf culture in Santa Monica, Venice, and Orange County, and integrated Hollywood nightclubs and motion picture and television studio orchestras. They rocked América's television sets, parodied the dominant popular culture, and improvised avant-garde jazz. Their collective push for full economic opportunity and freedom of expression, speech, and assembly had advanced well beyond the city limits by 1968, considering the popularity of the El Monte concerts, and especially the national success of Mexican American rock and soul artists.

Ultimately, "the entire East Los Angeles community was undergoing a fundamental change as the American-born Chicanos began moving out and were replaced by more recent immigrants from Mexico who preferred traditional rancheras and corridos."[159] Moreover, the escalating Vietnam War took a terrible toll on the rock and roll scene, as the young Mexican Americans "who played in the bands, ran the social clubs that staged the dances, and formed the audiences . . . were being shipped overseas."[160] In Rubén Guevara's opinion, "towards the late 1950s, serious gang problems began to surface between blacks and Chicanos, and in the 1960s affirmative action programs often wound up pitting us against each other for jobs. . . . The relatively friendly relations between blacks and Chicanos that had existed in the immediate postwar era had been deteriorating for some time. The civil rights movement had, in some ways, awakened us to the reality that our two cultures were very different."[161] In the wake of the 1965 Watts riot, new political and cultural identities temporarily fragmented the mixed-race tolerance of the rock and roll era, as multiracial venues declined. Clearly, Mexican Americans' affinity for African American music had not disappeared, but both groups looked increasingly inward. By the late 1960s, "the fading of the local record labels and independent radio shows," the commercial emergence of white psychedelic rock, the economic decline and neglect of the Eastside barrios, and the political rise of Chicano cultural nationalism all hastened the closing of the one-time rock and roll "factory."[162]

Although the rhetoric of black power radicalism signaled a shift in the relationship between African Americans and Mexican Americans, ethnic nationalism represented a response to reactionary state repression, but not necessarily an all-out rejection of multicultural mixing. The hostile postwar political conservativism of Mayor Poulson, City Councilmen, the LAPD, the Sheriff's Department, urban renewal experts, freeway planners, business boosters, and those who preached the eminent domain gospel impacted the wax and wane, the ebb and flow of the urban civility, yet the popular music and dance scenes still managed to connect the different areas of the region.[163] The powers that be successfully kicked the rock and roll concerts out of the city, suppressing the decades-long effort to establish racial democracy in Southern California, but they never truly won the culture war.

In conclusion, despite a climate of racial segregation and social regulation, the rock and roll music scene catalyzed a black-brown running dialogue, produced both interactions and intolerance, and drew white youths from the suburbs, even as many Mexican Americans were themselves moving out of the inner and eastern city. In a society that never really wanted, nor truly appreciated them, Mexican Americans continued to make moves, from modest, middle-class homes to grass-roots social, economic, and educational programs, from local performances to cross-country concert tours. The next chapter will cover the swing, rhythm and blues, and rock and roll eras again, analyzing the coexisting Latin music and dance scenes through which Mexican Americans responded to a different kind of blackness, while crafting an alternative to whiteness. With the explosion of new Latin styles after the war, Mexican Americans produced a parallel multicultural urban civility and put a new spin on their expressive culture.

5

con sabor latino: latin jazz, the mambo, and latin holidays in los angeles

Its impulses are primitive, its rhythms are frenetic, its pace is frantic and it is called the mambo. It is the most dynamic new Latin dance to appear in the U.S. since the rumba challenged the Lindy hop during the early 30s. . . . The mambo lends itself to variations as readily as American jitterbugging and can be learned easily by anyone.
—"Mambo King . . . ," Ebony, September 1951

There's no time like the present—let's all "Go Latin." It's easy with Cha Cha Cha!
—Donald Duncan, liner notes, Eddie Cano, Time for Cha Cha Cha, 1958

[Mexican Americans] loved it . . . There was música that really moves.
—Hortencia Garibay, interview by author, September 15, 2004

This chapter's first epigraph, from a 1951 *Ebony* article on the "Cuban Negro" Pérez Prado, foreshadowed the impact of the mambo on African Americans, several years before the general white population tried to "go Latin" by dancing first the mambo, then the cha cha chá. Once again, Mexican Americans were hip to the latest thing, for they represented the bulk of the Latin dancing public in Los Angeles, along with a smaller number of Latinos, some African Americans and Jewish Americans, and a sprinkling of Asian Americans and Anglo Americans. As the third epigraph notes, Mexican Americans loved to go out dancing, to let Latin music make their bodies move. In their fine suits and dresses, older former jitterbugs anchored and enlivened the postwar Latin music scene, which, unlike the rowdier swing, R & B, and rock scenes, involved no white youths, and therefore brought no police harassment. Still, like their counterparts in the music scenes analyzed in previous chapters, and in the context of the culture war over proper civil society, Mexican Americans in the Latin music scene increased their recognition, improved their representation, asserted their right to first-class citizenship, and insisted on their own run of the city.

From the 1950s through the middle 1960s, many Mexican Americans took a "holiday" or vacation from their designated place in the social structure, and in the city, by participating in a sophisticated Spanish-language cosmopolitanism. In particular, they rejected an Anglo-imposed identity as labor commodities, flirting instead with an appealing *Latinidad* (Latinness), while creating a parallel, urbane civility with Latino *sabor* (flavor or character). Embracing Latin jazz artists, Cuban musical genres like the bolero and the mambo, and Hollywood high society Latin styles, they merged ethnic Mexican pride with suave elegance to create their own social spaces during an age of Anglo cultural conformity. Musicians, singers, disc jockeys, impresarios, fans, and dancers had their collective mojo working as they drew on a deep tradition of cultural commingling to enrich and expand Mexican American expressive culture. This chapter shows how they produced and consumed various Latin American styles, seized new economic opportunities, and challenged Anglo stereotypes, thereby revealing a wider range of variation and completing this book's portrait of the Mexican American generation.

As seen thus far, rather than claim to be "Latin" or "Latin American," most Mexican American Angelenos simply referred to themselves as "Mexican." Yet in the tradition of California's mythical Spanish fantasy heritage, the film and television industries disseminated a generalized image of "Latins," along with a bland, deracinated Latin music, into the nation's culture and consciousness. Meanwhile, actual Mexican Americans maintained individual and group ties to Mexican culture, even as they dabbled in Latin music. George Sánchez has documented the Los Angeles Mexican immigrant community during the ultramodern 1920s, including a Mexican market for mass culture consumer products, a downtown district of theaters and nightclubs, a Spanish-language music industry of Mexican record label owners, disc jockeys, and impresarios, and a transformation, via experimentation and commercialization, of "traditional" Mexican music. In addition, Sánchez has described how Anglo city officials harassed Mexican disc jockeys, and how immigrant entrepreneurs created a wide range of business enterprises to service the city's growing Mexican population.[1] By the late 1930s, two Los Angeles Spanish-language radio stations, KALI and KWKW, played Latin music on weeknights, and a traditional Mexican music scene, which itself incorporated Cuban and Latin American "tropical" music, coexisted with a high society Latin scene.[2]

Society bands, which typically emphasized "sugary" melodies and "vanilla" chords instead of group improvisation and polyrhythmic density, dominated the recording and performing of Latin music.[3] The Boyle Heights trumpeter Paul Lopez called this international Latin American sound "society rumba," but it could be called "Hollywood Latin" due to the influence of the local culture industries.[4] At the time, society orchestras performed such "lite" Latin music, particularly milder versions of Cuban styles like rumba, conga, bolero, and danzón, at resorts, casinos, and hotels in Miami, Havana, Mexico City, and Tijuana.[5] In the Los Angeles neighborhood of West Hollywood, on the "Sunset Strip," affluent whites were entertained at Latin clubs by "an American band and a rumba band," with elaborate floor shows between sets.[6]

A 1.7-mile portion of Sunset Boulevard between Crescent Heights Boulevard to the east and Doheny Drive to the west, the Sunset Strip had been a dining, drinking, and dancing playground for the rich and famous of Hollywood and Beverly Hills since the 1920s.[7] By the late 1930s, it boasted exclusive Latin supper clubs like Ciro's, owned by Herman Hover, at Crescent Heights Boulevard, and, a bit farther west, the Mexican-themed Mocambo, a dance-until-dawn establishment with an aviary of macaws and parrots. The Café Trocadero, owned by the *Hollywood Reporter* publisher William Wilkerson, was located between Sweetzer and Harper avenues, and the Crescendo, owned by Gene Norman, at La Cienega Boulevard. At the Crescendo and at Ciro's, Paul Lopez recalled, "The movie stars, especially the women, would get a few drinks in 'em, and they liked to get all exotic with that rumba music."[8] Although Mexican American Angelenos did not patronize these elite, extravagant clubs, when Josefina Fierro, the Mexican-born, American-raised labor organizer and executive secretary of

El Congreso, was a student at UCLA in 1938, she would often watch her aunt sing at a Hollywood Latin nightclub.[9] In February 1945 Duke Ellington became the first African American to play the Sunset Strip when his orchestra appeared at Ciro's, while in March of that year Benny Carter became the second when he appeared at the Trocadero.[10] By the mid-1940s, the trumpeter Felipe Lopez, from Phoenix, and the pianist Jerry Galian, from Mexico, both played at Café Trocadero with their respective bands, and local Mexican American society bandleaders Chuy Reyes and Bobby Ramos consistently worked the Sunset Strip venues.[11]

In downtown Los Angeles, upscale, Hollywood-style nightclubs like El Sombrero, at Main and 18th streets, owned by a wealthy Mexican couple, Manuel and Josefina Rivera, and El Babalu, on Sixth Street, owned by a Mexican man named Paul Mirabal, presented Latin society orchestras and, during breaks between sets, floor shows and Mexican guitar trios playing among the tables.[12] According to Paul Lopez, the Latin band at El Babalu played "watered-down salsa," or "West Coast Latin," for "Anglos and movie people."[13] Also popular was Club La Bamba, where, as mentioned in chapter 1, Lalo Guerrero's guitar quartet played Mexican standards, and the customers danced the conga line, in 1938. As we saw in chapter 3, Guerrero became floorshow master of ceremonies and featured solo singer in 1946.[14] Before the Second World War, 95 percent of Club La Bamba patrons were Anglo. Afterward, the ratio was 60/40 white/Mexican, and the audience included Hollywood actors like John Garfield, Ida Lupino, Ann Sheridan, Anthony Quinn, and Ricardo Montalban.[15] Paul Lopez called Club La Bamba a "Mickey Mouse" extension of the Hollywood scene, complete with flamenco dancers, and Don Tosti added that although "hip for a while, it was for high-class Mexican tourists."[16]

Other downtown Latin music spots included the nearby Casa Olvera and La Golondrina, the popular Mexican restaurant on Olvera Street. As we saw in chapter 1, during World War II Mary Gonzalez lived with her father in Watts, worked at the Firestone tire factory in Florence, and danced the jitterbug. After her suitor, Gene Hernandez, sailed to the Pacific theater with the U.S. Navy, Mary would dance to Latin music, usually with two older Mexican American sisters from the Firestone factory. Mary and her work friends would take the Red Car to La Golondrina. There they would mingle with Mexican American and Anglo sailors and civilians, then walk to nearby downtown nightclubs in their hats and high heels. After the clubs had all closed, they would catch the Red Car back to Watts.[17] Although Don Tosti described La Golondrina and Casa Olvera as "tourist traps" that "hip Mexicans" avoided," Mexican American dancers were drawn to them, as well as to other, more working-class downtown Latin nightclubs, such as El Janitzio on Broadway near the Million Dollar Theater. Owned by a Mexican American former musician named Eddie Guerrero, El Janitzio was, in Don Tosti's judgment, "a second-class place" that played "all Latin" music.[18]

Compared to the Hollywood scene, the downtown scene enjoyed more ethnic Mexican participation and representation befitting the important role of Latin music in Mexico and the U.S. Southwest. Yet, as this book has shown, traditional Mexican music also remained a part of Mexican American expressive culture and social dancing. For instance, in 1944, Lucie Brac would go to *tardeadas*, or "afternoon socials" next to the lake boathouse at Lincoln Park, where she and her Mexican American girlfriends would dance to corridos and rancheras with older *bracero* workers from Mexico. Even zoot-suited swing dancer Chole Camarena attended these Lincoln Park tardeadas. Chole and her Mexican American girlfriends found Mexicano immigrants too macho, and therefore never considered marrying them, while Lucie found the Mexican men "possessive." Still, Lucie's best friend and neighbor Alice married an older man from Mexico whom she had originally met at one of the Lincoln Park dances while she was still in high school.[19]

Lucie Brac also attended Sunday afternoon tardeadas downtown at the Zenda Ballroom in 1949, just after she graduated from high school. These tardeadas lacked any pachuco-cholo element, as it "was not their bag. This was the straight kids, and a lot of the Mexican kids that came across the border." Lucie and her Mexican American girlfriends would get dressed up and have a great time dancing away their Sundays with Mexicanos, yet the young women's own aspirations and perceived status, coupled with the mores of the times, constrained their social contact with the Mexican migrants. As Lucie stated, "We were in an age where you never went, or even exchanged numbers, with a guy after you met him at a dance. You knew that these weren't the guys you wanted to be with." Lucie and her friends, who worked as secretaries, considered themselves "a cut above in that [they] were not factory workers," and once a month they would treat themselves to dinners at upscale West Los Angeles restaurants. On several occasions they encountered the same young Mexican men with whom they had danced at the Zenda Ballroom tardeadas, now busing tables at the restaurants. As Lucie explained, "We were embarrassed for them. The poor guys weren't even the waiters. We would all pretend we didn't recognize one another, which was hard."[20]

In the end, when these single, service-industry Mexicanos and these single, pink-collar Mexican American women crossed paths downtown at the Zenda Ballroom they were on neutral ground and on equal social footing. However, when the two groups met again in the Anglo West Los Angeles restaurants, they were clearly occupying different social positions. On the one hand were the Mexican migrants, less privileged in their spare time, and with a considerably less stable class status. On the other hand were the independent Mexican American women, assimilated and moderately successful enough to navigate the white world with ease, enjoying the fruits of their labor. In these awkward moments, the economic and cultural gap that each side had overlooked while dancing downtown, ultimately kept them separated, despite whatever ethnic similarities they shared.

As we saw in chapter 4, the Mexican Americans who paid to hear honking tenor saxophonists at the Angelus Hall never even thought about dancing to Mexican music at nearby Pontrelli's Ballroom. Nevertheless, Latin music, especially the slow, romantic bolero and the fast, frenetic mambo, along with the steady stream of migrants from Mexico, and the Mexican American generation's own parents and relatives, facilitated a familial relationship, like second cousins connected in a continuing cultural conversation. The bolero and the mambo were originally Cuban musical styles that became part of Mexican life through a process of transculturation, and these styles became an increasingly prominent part of Mexican American life as the Avedon Ballroom, the longtime jitterbug mainstay, started to offer Latin dancing on weeknights, featuring the transitional Mexican American swing/Latin music of the Armenta Brothers and Sal Chico bands. Another Avedon act, the Phil Carreon Orchestra, hired the Mexican vocalist Rudy Macias, who introduced boleros into the band's regular swing songbook. After World War II, Lalo Guerrero mixed corridos, rancheras, danzón, and *guaracha* with pachuco lyrics, while Don Tosti's Pachuco Boogie Boys blended guaracha rumba rhythms with caló lyrics. Eddie Cano's Latin piano playing also sparkled on the Tosti tune, "Montuno # uno," and in 1953 Tosti even wrote a song called "Mambo del pachuco."

Moreover, Don Tosti also wrote best-selling boleros. In 1948, while performing in Berkeley at the University of California as the bassist for Les Brown's Band of Renown, Tosti finally met his biological father, Ramon Martinez, as well as his Irish-Mexican stepbrother, and his Italian-Mexican stepsister, in Oakland. His father, a former U.S. Navy officer, promoted Fiestas Patrias celebrations, as well as wrestling and boxing matches, and hosted a radio program called *South American Way*. Martinez challenged Tosti to write original songs in a Latin idiom, and his son responded by composing "Vine por tí" ("I Came for You"), a bolero about unreturned love, and its B-side, "Ya todo acabó" ("Now Everything Is Over"), arranged by Tosti's fellow swing-era Angeleno Ruben Leon. "Vine por tí" immediately sold one hundred thousand copies on the strength of the lyrics by Tosti, and the vocals by Rubén Reyes, from Cahuila, Mexico. Riding the wave of this success, Tosti worked one-nighters around town as a pianist and arranger for Rubén Reyes, who scored a minor hit with another catchy Tosti bolero called "Búrlate" in 1950.[21] That same year, the Jewish American comedic actor and singer Danny Kaye recorded "Coca Roca," an "up-tempo rumba" based on Don Tosti's "El tírili," originally a guaracha about a pachuco marijuano that featured Eddie Cano's powerful piano riffs. A prominent Hollywood lyricist was brought in to write more suitable English lyrics.[22]

In Los Angeles, pachuco guaracha, society rumba, Mexican tropical, and international bolero styles predominated, but a denser, blacker Latin music also took root. Although many Mexican Americans tried to "go Latin," one needed many years of practice and devoted study to truly master the complex, interlocking Afro-Caribbean rhythms. First and foremost, one needed to play in clave, the two-bar African-derived rhythmic pattern that grounds most "Cuban music, into which every element of arrangement and improvisation should fit."[23] The syncopated clave is "responsible for dictating both rhythmic and harmonic aspects of Cuban music," as well as musicians' concepts "of phrasing and improvising." Although there are several variations, referring to the number of notes in each measure, the "deceptively simple" clave is usually played in "three-two," or, less commonly, "two-three." Striking two small wooden sticks together to produce a sharp, clear sound keeps perfect time for the band, and once begun, the clave pattern is sustained until the end of the song. Even when no one is playing the two claves, every musician internalizes the implied beat, and every dancer moves to it. If an orchestra falls out of clave, the rhythm gets turned around, the instrumentalists' propulsive equilibrium becomes disrupted, and the dancers on the floor will stop dancing in protest.[24]

A typical Cuban popular music arrangement consists of a three-part structure: a "head" section that presents the basic theme; a "montuno" section during which the *coro*, or chorus, begins its unvarying refrain while a singer (*sonero*) or an instrumentalist improvises; and a "mambo" section first developed in 1938 for the danzón by the cellist-pianist Orestes López, then expanded by his brother, the bassist Israel "Cachao" López, and by the Afro-Cuban bandleader Arsenio Rodríguez.[25] Most of these structural and stylistic characteristics were developed from the Cuban *son montuno*, originally an Oriente-province *tres* guitar form that, in its modern reinvention, is "the most important predecessor to what we call salsa today." The son montuno style layers three independent rhythmic figures: the syncopated *tumbao* bass line; an eighth-note pattern played by the guitar, maracas, and bongos; and the clave pattern. Repeating two or three-measure vamps, called montunos, are typically used as opening riffs and maintained ad lib to underscore the instrumental or vocal improvisations.[26] The driving momentum of the music is thus principally achieved by the pianist sustaining a repeated vamp of *guajeos*, or riffs, by the bassist dropping tumbaos, by the congas and bongos working in tandem, and, borrowing from American jazz orchestras, by the brass section riffing on top of, and in contrast with, the melodic lines of the saxophones.

When Afro-Cuban polyrhythms, many of them derived from Yoruba and Bantu religious traditions, first merged with modern jazz harmonies, the resultant music was called Cubop, but it came to be known as Latin jazz. As an improvisational cultural hybrid, Latin jazz found a home in Southern California. In the mid-1940s, when Frank "Machito" Grillo visited Los Angeles, "people from nearby states, from other cities in California came, like it was a pilgrimage to hear the Machito Orchestra and the Afro-Cubans."[27] By 1946, the Havana-born pianist René Touzet, a prodigy who graduated from the Conservatorio Falcón at fourteen, and an award-winning protégé of the composer Ernesto Lecuona, had moved to Miami, New York, and, finally, to Los Angeles, where he quickly established himself as a major Latin jazz proponent downtown at the Avedon Ballroom. His house band included top-notch native Angelenos in the Mexican American bassist Frank Vasquez, the Anglo American saxophonist Art Pepper, and the Jewish American arranger Johnny Mandel.[28] Miguelito

Valdés, the consummate Cuban sonero and skilled conguero, stayed in Los Angeles only briefly, from 1944 to 1945, after performing and recording with Xavier Cugat in New York City and Hollywood. Valdés's father was a white Spaniard, and his mother, América Valdés, a Maya Indian from Yucatán, Mexico, who had raised her seven children on her own in the *Cayo Hueso* barrio of Havana. Valdés adopted the *Santería* faith and its Afro-Cuban music, language, and improvisational singing. He thus fit in perfectly in Los Angeles, where mestizo Mexican Americans were beginning to develop a deep affinity with Caribbean Latino music and culture. Nonetheless, Valdés returned to New York, where he once again became a household name and cemeted his fame.

Valdés had learned the value of showmanship early in his career, and he later witnessed how television "radically changed the function of the musician."[29] As the New York bandleader Manny Oquendo argued, "Miguelito was probably one of the greatest singers to come from Cuba. He was a total performer, he could sing in any style. He was the first Cuban singer that made it internationally, singing with Xavier Cugat in Hollywood. Desi Arnaz was a copy, a total copy of Miguelito Valdés, and a poor one at that. 'Babalu' was Miguelito's hit.[30] At Ciro's on the Sunset Strip, the upper-class Cuban Arnaz's society orchestra act culminated in the Babalú Ayé routine he borrowed from Valdés. In 1946, Arnaz played at Ciro's, recorded in New York, served as the musical director of Bob Hope's radio program, and starred in the film *Cuban Pete*.[31] Gil Bernal, who saw Miguelito Valdés sing at the Orpheum Theater in 1946, argued that "Desi was not a singer, he was a personality."[32] In 1948, Valdés recruited specific Mexican American Angeleno swing veterans like the pianist Eddie Cano, the saxophonist Ruben Leon, and the trumpeter Charlie Mota to play in his new twelve-piece Latin orchestra, which debuted in Lake Tahoe.[33]

In 1948, Valdés took his band to New York City, where they quickly became one of the hottest attractions, playing the Apollo, Strand, La Martinique, and Paramount theaters, and the popular ballrooms. The swing-era Angeleno trumpeter Paul Lopez had just moved to Manhattan, and, like the drummer-*timbalero* Chico Guerrero, who was close friends with Tito Puente, and the bassist Tony Reyes, who played with Puente's first solo band, the Picadilly Boys, as "a Mexican that played jazz," he stood out in New York.[34] After seeing him play a one-nighter at the Palladium Ballroom with the Machito Orchestra, the percussionist Humberto Morales got Lopez a job in the band of his brother, the pianist Noro Morales, one of the major names in downtown Latin music. Soon Lopez became the first trumpet, and he began arranging tunes for the band's book, most notably "110th Street and 5th Avenue"—the address of the Park Plaza—which he cowrote with Noro and recorded for MGM Records. Lopez performed with the Morales orchestra at the grand opening of the Hotel New Yorker in Puerto Rico, and on the recording *Mambo by Morales* (Columbia Records, 1950), soloing on three tracks.[35]

In 1950, Miguelito Valdés hired Lopez to augment the trumpet section of his orchestra, which then inaugurated the grand opening of the Hilton Hotel in Puerto Rico. During this four-month trip to the island, Lopez cowrote one of the band's more popular songs, "Hilton Caribe," with Miguelito and Elayne Valdés. Lopez returned to the Puerto Rico Hilton with Miguelito Valdés in 1951, then played the Ambassador Hotel in Los Angeles with the band as part of a tour that included one-nighters in San Francisco and the Midwest (see figure 33). Of Valdés's band, Lopez said, "we already had the salsa thing going. We had the real rhythm section going. And it was me and Charlie Mota on trumpets." In 1952, Lopez played with Valdés at New York's Strand Theater on Broadway, and with Billy Taylor, Curley Russel, and Max Roach at New York's Birdland club. On the Manhattan jazz scene, Paul worked with the bands of Al Donahue, Woody Herman, and Boyd Raeburn, with whom he had previously played at the Morocco Club in Los Angeles.

From 1948 to 1953 Lopez also played with the Latin bands of Pupi Campo, José Curbelo, Vitín Avilés, Tito Rodríguez, and Tito Puente. Lopez recalled that in those days "a lot of the Puerto Rican and Cuban musicians weren't working with the American bands in New York." Instead, they were "doing their own thing uptown in El Barrio" (East Harlem or "Spanish Harlem").[36] In Los Angeles, Mexican American musicians worked throughout the city with white, black, Mexican American, or mixed-race bands, but in New York City the majority of Latinos were more segregated professionally, playing among, by, and for themselves. To "pick up" bebop gigs, Paul would hang out at Charlie's Tavern, a skating rink with society, bebop, and Latin musicians occupying opposite corners of "union floor." For Latin gigs, "around the corner was the La Salle Cafeteria," where Latin musicians congregated in the afternoons.

In Los Angeles, Paul Lopez had not been impressed by the Latin bandleaders with whom he had worked. For example, in 1946, when he played the Trocadero with Chuy Reyes, who received classical training at Mexico

33. Paul Lopez with Miguelito Valdés, ca. 1951. COURTESY PAUL LOPEZ.

City's Conservatorio de México as a child, Lopez considered it just another society gig.[37] In 1946, when he played Ciro's with Bobby Ramos's band, the bass player plucked out a steady time rather than a tumbao bass line, and the pianist did not know even the most common montuno patterns. In contrast, one time Lopez arrived at a Latin gig in New York to find "four Jewish guys in the rhythm section: a flute player, a bass player, a drummer, and a piano player. I was the only Latin there . . . and there they were all over the place," playing Afro-Cuban riffs, and asking one another, "Do you know this? Let's try this." Because Latin music was so common in New York City by the late 1940s, working musicians had to know the latest Latin tunes, and these particular musicians "played beautifully."

It seemed to Lopez that "the Latin bands in Los Angeles were too laid back," and that, unlike the average New York musicians at the time, the "Latin" musicians in Los Angeles never worked hard enough on their craft, never studied the clave enough to truly understand it.[38] That started to change, Lopez explained, because "from 1948 on was an explosion of new music, and people wanted to hear better things. Prior to that you could lay back and Cugat the thing all the way through. But it took off. Latin music took off right after that."[39] In 1948, the New York Puerto Ricans Tito Puente and Tito Rodríguez recorded their first conjuntos with the small independent label Tico Records, thus spreading the emergent New York mambo style across the country. In 1948, producer Norman Granz ventured into Latin jazz, recording Machito and His Afro-Cubans with Charlie Parker in Los Angeles, after taking Bird to hear the band rehearse at the Hollywood Palladium.[40] At the same time, from Mexico City, a new sound, which merged the assertive tumbaos of Cachao López with the rhythmic saxophone section of the Cuban pianist René Hernández and the brassy, nervous, dramatic jazz arrangements of Stan Kenton, helped popularize Latin music and dancing in mainstream America and around the world.

In 1948, Damaso Pérez Prado and his fellow Afro-Cubano expatriate Beny Moré developed a new kind of mambo when they formed a Mexican big band with a percussion section composed of Cuban musicians and a brass section known for its piercing high notes. In 1948 and 1949, the pianist-arranger-entertainer Prado and the soaring, expressive sonero Moré dominated Mexico's airwaves, recording approximately twenty-four mambo 78 rpm singles for the corporate giant RCA Victor's subsidiary label, Mexicana. In 1949, Pérez Prado signed a recording contract with

RCA, which dubbed him the "Glenn Miller of Mexico" and the "Mambo King." Prado was "mobbed on Mexico City streets by hordes of mambo lovers," his roaring, urban music adored by the common people, the rich elites, and the Mexican motion picture industry. In 1951, Prado's album *Mambo Jambo* was RCA Victor International's top seller.[41] Prado created mambo mania throughout Latin America, but achieved only moderate success in the United States with early singles like "Qué rico el mambo"/ "Mambo #5" (1950). At this point, Prado was only popular on the West Coast, primarily among Mexicanos and Mexican Americans.

By 1950, the latest mambo records from New York City and Mexico City started to catch on in Los Angeles, where a pan-Latino soundscape had already developed. For instance, while the Avedon Ballroom presented swing jam sessions in the afternoon and Latin dancing at night, the Hollywood Palladium hired local Latin bands to play during jazz concert intermissions. Even the city's downtown theaters that catered to Mexicans incorporated jazz and Caribbean elements, particularly the Million Dollar Theater house orchestra, led by Rene Bloch, the Jewish Angeleno swing saxophonist we met in chapter 1. Composed of Mexican, Cuban, and Puerto Rican musicians, the orchestra would open with a Latin jazz set before backing up various visiting musicians from Mexico, Spain, and South America, as well as comedians like Tin Tan.[42]

As the decade began, the Mexican music, Latin jazz, and Hollywood society scenes created the conditions for a new, broader Los Angeles Latin music movement to blossom. The Zenda Ballroom, at Seventh and Figueroa streets in downtown Los Angeles, became a key location during this phase. As we saw in chapter 1, the Zenda impresario Joe Garcia used to put on popular Saturday night swing dances for Mexican Americans. Capitalizing on the rising popularity of Latin music, Garcia began contracting orchestras from New York and Mexico City, for live summer performances.[43] For example, in the fall of 1951, Garcia booked Pérez Prado's California debut, at which an ethnic Mexican crowd of twenty-five hundred "packed the Zenda from wall to wall" at "$1.25 a head." The box office closed at nine o'clock, but soon "a police detail was stationed outside to control the masses of turnaways at the entrance," who had gone "wild in their enthusiasm over Pérez Prado and his band."[44] Prado used his own Cuban percussionists, but, because of union regulations, drew the rest of his sidemen from the professional musicians union local—a standard division of labor in many Latin jazz bands. Like Miguelito Valdés, Prado hired musicians from Local 47 in Hollywood, whose membership included whites and Mexican Americans, but excluded Negroes.[45] The jazz journal *Down Beat* reported that Prado called his hastily assembled unit "the greatest band I've been able to get in the United States."[46]

The bands from Mexico and New York proved so popular that they were hired throughout the year, along with orchestras from Puerto Rico and Cuba. In addition, Joe Garcia began hosting concerts on Saturday nights at the Zenda Ballroom, where Latin music fans flocked to dance the night away.[47] As a result, the Zenda became "the main Latin venue" in Los Angeles in the early 1950s. As Tommy Saito recalled, "You had to walk up one flight of stairs, and there was a long bar to one side of the room. The cover charge was $3.00, and the clientele was 90 percent Mexican American, with the remainder being a few Cubans and Puerto Ricans, a few Anglos, a few Asian Americans, and a few local blacks, as well as visiting blacks from New York."[48] Jaime Corral stated that "the dance place that I used to go to all the time—the real one—was the Zenda. That was the big one. . . . I used to love to dance. I was a dancer, and so that's why I used to like to go there."[49]

East Los Angeles bands like the Armenta Brothers consistently drew large crowds to the Zenda with their mix of swing, rumbas, boleros, and mambos.[50] Most of the Los Angeles Latin music lovers were swing-era Mexican Americans, and Corral remembered that although the Zenda played predominantly Latin styles, the local bands "would play a swing piece every now and then" so the dancers could jitterbug.[51] Ed Frias and Lucie Brac also frequented the Zenda Ballroom, where they danced to the Armenta Brothers.[52] By hiring local Latin bands, providing regular concerts for local Latin dancers, and contracting so many quality Latin artists, especially those, like Pérez Prado, Tito Puente, and Tito Rodríguez, who had not played in Los Angeles before, Joe Garcia facilitated the cultural adoption of Afro-Cuban musical styles by Mexican Americans during the postwar period.

Chico Sesma, the swing-era trombonist from Roosevelt High School, not only helped establish roots for Latin music in Los Angeles, opening up a whole world of rhythms and melodies to local fans, but also added a new twist to the city's tradition of urban civility. In fact, more than any other person, Sesma introduced the general Los Angeles public to Latin music through his pioneering early 1950s radio program. Sesma got his start in radio through George Chavez, an old childhood friend who worked as a

34. Chico Sesma at KOWL, ca. 1955. COURTESY CHICO SESMA.

sales account executive at the Santa Monica AM radio station KOWL. The station executives wanted to repeat the success of Joe Adams's rhythm and blues program, *For Dancers Only*, which had been a debut hit during the previous year, 1948. In short, they wanted a "Mexican Joe Adams" who could tap into the city's large, Mexican American market. George Chavez arranged an audition for Sesma, then coached him on announcing for radio and reading advertisement copy. With the help of his white-collar Mexican American industry contact, Chico Sesma was hired by KOWL in February 1949 (see figure 34).[53]

Immediately following Joe Adams's show, Sesma's half-hour program, *Chico's Swing Time*, began as a mix of pop vocals and jazz, with a couple of society Latin songs. Like most Angelenos, Sesma had little knowledge of Afro-Caribbean music, and he could not tell Tito Puente from Tito Rodríguez. In fact, before he went on the air, the only "Latin" musicians he could name were Xavier Cugat and Carmen Cavallaro. Sesma admitted that, growing up in Los Angeles during the big band era, "Latin music was not a part of me." But he put himself through a crash course, conducting "research" in the listening booths of downtown and East Los Angeles record stores. After the first few months, Sesma gained enough popularity —and control—to convert to an all-Latin play list, including some "romantic music by Mexican groups like Los Diamantes and Trio Los Panchos," and to rename the program *The Chico Sesma Show*. After his unique format was "embraced immediately" by the public, the studio increased his air time to an hour, and, by the end of the first year, to three hours, Monday through Friday, 3:00 P.M. to 6:00 P.M.[54]

With his proper diction, precise enunciation, and expansive vocabulary, Sesma did not confirm traditional stereotypes, and the general public did not think he was Mexican at first. Of course, the city was home to other articulate, bilingual Mexican Americans during this period, most notably Bert Corona, Josefina Fierro, Julian Nava, Edward Roybal, and Anthony Quinn, but they were never heard on the airwaves. Several all-Spanish-language radio stations did play Mexican music programs, but only early in the morning and in the evenings. Consequently, when Sesma switched between English and Spanish, or spoke knowingly about "East Los," his Mexican American listeners were surprised. As Sesma recalled, "My own people didn't believe it, you know? And then I did so many things from the Caribbean, by those artists, like Puerto Ricans and Cubans, they would claim me as one of theirs."[55] A minority in a minority in Los Angeles, Latinos had never heard their music on local radio before, and they were hungry for respectful media representation, as were Mexican Americans.

With his smooth baritone delivery, Sesma was a voice of, and for, the city's Mexican American population, five afternoons a week. By peppering his program with the phrase *con sabor Latino*, by mentioning local Mexican and Cuban restaurants, and by playing music from New York, Cuba, and Mexico, Sesma also promoted a broader pan-Latino expressive culture. In fact, for the first few years of the show, Sesma used Miguelito Valdés's "Harlem Special" as his opening song, but in an example of Mexican American–Cuban creative cooperation, René Touzet wrote an original composition, "Con sabor Latino," as the official theme, with vocal solos by Ray Vasquez. In the context of his generation, Sesma must be seen as a cultural ambassador of Spanish-language Latin music, and of Mexican Americans, in U.S. society. For instance, Sesma read news reports and sports scores, but in a segment called "Social Calendar in Latin," he also announced each upcoming weekend's cultural and musical events across Los Angeles. On Saturdays, a special half-hour segment, "Salute to Youth," "paid tribute to" local Mexican American car clubs and social clubs, the members of which would come on to discuss their neighborhood dances, philanthropic fundraising events, and other activities. Sesma found it "gratifying" to "let the public know some of the positive things our young people were engaged in," while the club members "appreciated . . . being recognized for what they'd been doing."[56]

By 1956, Sesma's eighth year on the air, the trailblazing disc jockey had become a local celebrity. KOWL had just changed its call letters, and throughout Los Angeles, Sesma's face, alongside that of Joe Adams, and those of their white colleagues, Jim Ameche and Frank Evans, appeared on billboards and buses bearing the slogan, "The top D.J.'s on K-Day, KDAY." National and international record companies, and their local distributors, sent him new releases at the station, where he would privately audition the latest Latin tunes, and play his favorites on his program. If Sesma did not necessarily create a demand for Latin music in Los Angeles, as a public radio personality he certainly helped nurture a market for it, particularly among Mexican Americans. Moreover, he piqued the interests, and cultivated the tastes, of a diverse English-speaking audience throughout Southern California. In fact, he received a large amount of non-Spanish-surnamed fan mail at the station, and there were probably more than a few letters from Asian American Angelenos like Tommy Saito, who used to listen to the show as a teenager in the early 1950s.[57]

Yet not everybody in Los Angeles first heard Latin music from Chico Sesma. Take José González, a typical Mexican American Angeleno youth of the postwar period, who joined the Air Force at seventeen in 1953, attending technical school while stationed in Denver, Colorado. Fellow enlistees exposed him to jazz in the military, but in 1954, while he was stationed at Kelley Air Force Base in San Antonio, Texas, some Cuban and Puerto Rican friends introduced him and his half-Italian, half-Mexican friend Frank Canselmo, to Latin dance music. Around this time, González bought his first Latin album, a Tito Rodríguez record with diagrammed instructions for dancing the cha cha chá, and soon the Latin music of Pérez Prado, Tito Puente, Tito Rodríguez, Sonora Matancera, and Celia Cruz got "in [his] blood."[58]

The African American, Mexican American, and Japanese American circle of friends at Polytechnic High School that we met in chapter 3 loved jazz music and rhythm and blues. However, around 1954, these Poly students began listening to Latin music after Kay Nomura and William Roach met an Afro-Cuban New Yorker named Wilfredo "Chongito" Vicente. Vicente had been a conguero with Tito Rodríguez, and he began playing Latin music for Nomura and Roach, both of whom then hipped O'Dell Lomax and Tommy Saito to the exciting new rhythms. After listening to Machito, Tito Puente, and Arsenio Rodríguez, Tommy introduced his friend Bobby Vergara and Bobby's half-Filipino, half-Mexican cousin, Richard.Barrientos, to Latin music. Soon they were all joining in neighborhood *descargas*, or Latin jam sessions with Chongito, who only lived in Los Angeles for about a year before returning to New York.

Afro-Caribbean musical styles and their corresponding dances were performed in Southern California by many Angelenos after World War II, when the number of non-Mexican Latinos in Los Angeles began to increase.[59] For example, the gifted Cuban flautist Rolando Lozano worked in Los Angeles for many years, eventually settling in East Los Angeles with his family. His son, Danilo Lozano, stated that many Puerto Ricans who were stationed in Hawaii during World War II moved to Los Angeles after the war, and that by the early 1950s some white, affluent Cubans arrived and integrated into mainstream society. Barrientos claimed that the first waves of Cuban immigrants settled in Huntington Park, in Orange County, while Saito recalled the presence of Puerto Ricans in inner city Los Angeles in the mid-1950s.[60] In 1963, from Oxnard to Santa Ana lived some 850,000 persons of Mexican descent, an estimated 4,500 Puerto Ricans from New York, Chicago, and industrial Ohio, and 25,000 Cuban refugees for whom Los Angeles had been selected as a "relocation center."[61] As Raúl Fernández notes, Mexican American communities "grew side by side with smaller Puerto Rican and Cuban enclaves that maintained their Afro-Latino traditions."[62]

The presence of Latino Angelenos, Joe Garcia's concerts at the Zenda Ballroom, and Chico Sesma's radio program, combined with the circulation of East Coast and international records, as well as the mainstream mambo and cha cha chá dance crazes, helped spark a Latin music boom that peaked from the early 1950s to the middle 1960s, from Hollywood to South, East, and West Los Angeles. In particular, during the 1950s, the mellow, vibraphone-led Latin jazz sound of Tito Puente, Cal Tjader, and Joe Loco influenced the local quintets of Bobby Montez, Tony Martinez, and Manny Lopez. Producing original compositions, Latin hit covers, and Latin-tinged American standards, these popular bandleaders appealed to young, modern Mexican American, Latino, and Anglo Angelenos.[63] As a Mexican American youth in Arizona, Bobby Montez learned to play the piano, bass, and vibraphone, and his older brothers played pop standards in an orchestra during the 1940s. His quintet, featuring vibraphone, piano, bass, timbales, and congas, performed at the Melody Room and the Latin Quarter, in West Hollywood at the Crescendo and the Interlude, downtown at the Zenda Ballroom, and in East Los Angeles at the M Club, where they were the house band for three years. From the late 1950s to the late 1960s, Montez released five albums on the Jubilee, World Pacific, and Gene Norman Presents (GNP) labels.[64]

The vibraphonist and multi-instrumentalist Tony Martinez studied music in his hometown of San Juan, Puerto Rico, and in New York at Juilliard. He also studied acting and landed small parts in movies from the late 1940s through his role in the 1955 Western *The Naked Dawn*. In Columbia Pictures' 1956 teen film featuring Bill Haley and His Comets, *Rock Around the Clock*, Martinez appeared in three scenes, leading his band, playing the vibraphones, singing in Spanish, dancing the mambo, and even delivering a few lines in English. In the late 1950s, Martinez recorded for RCA Victor, and in 1957, one night as he and his band played at a Hollywood club, he was "discovered" by the television writer-producers Irving and Norman Pincus. They cast the bandleader as a San Fernando Valley Mexican ranch hand named "Pepino Garcia" on the prime-time ABC comedy series, *The Real McCoys*, a ratings hit from 1957 to 1963. In 1959, Martinez released the Del-Fi Records album, *Many Sides of Pepino*, on which he sang and played vibes, bass, piano, and congas, and which included "Real McCoys Cha Cha Cha," "Rum and Coca Cola," "Pepino," and "La Bamba." He also guest starred on 1960s television shows like *F Troop*, *My Favorite Martian*, and *The Lone Wolf*.[65]

The Mexican American vibraphonist Manny Lopez was originally self-taught, but he took his first music lessons from Chico Sesma and eventually, after two years in the Far East with the U.S. Navy, studied three years at the National Conservatory in Mexico City.[66] Lopez recorded for RCA Victor and Imperial Records and also assembled one of the first *charanga* bands in Los Angeles. The charanga is a small, twentieth-century Cuban dance orchestra featuring flute, violins, piano, bass, timbales, maracas, and a vocalist. One of the most famous charanga orchestras, led by the Cuban flautist Antonio Arcaño, is widely credited with creating the first cha cha chá out of the mambo section of the danzón. In 1951, Cuba's innovative dancers devised a step for this new breakaway section, which Arcaño's violinist Enrique Jorrín dubbed "cha cha chá," mimicking the sounds of the dancers' feet scraping on the floor in time with the triple fourth beat conga drum pattern.[67] By 1953, the cha cha chá had swept Cuba, based largely on the success of the Orquesta Aragón. By 1954, the new style had arrived in the United States, where it became immediately popular, due in large part to its simpler rhythms and less demanding dance steps.

René Touzet has been credited with starting the cha cha chá fad in Los Angeles, where he became known as "Mr. Cha Cha Cha." Paul Lopez described Touzet as "a very accomplished piano player" who adapted well "from the old Latin to the new Latin."[68] At the Crescendo, Ciro's, and the Hollywood Palladium, he performed live to promote his albums, many of them on the local label GNP/Crescendo Records. Touzet, who boasted "the most popular Latin band in town," reportedly "blew Manny Lopez and Bobby Montez away."[69] From the 1950s through the 1960s, his band included the soneros Carlos Montiel and Juan Cheda, the percussionists Willie Bobo, Mongo Santamaria, and Carlos Vidal, the saxophonists Jose "Chombo" Silva and Ruben Leon, and the trumpeter Anthony "Tony" Terran. As an arranger and a composer, René Touzet was, in the opinion of Chico Sesma, "the most evolved of [the local bandleaders], musically [and] technically."[70] In the mid-1950s, the Mexican bassist and transplanted Chicago native Johnny Martinez led the second most popular Latin group in the city. Martinez and his swinging band featured Cuban vocalist Juan Cheda and a "solid traditional sound," but rather than creating original songs, they covered current hits.[71]

Another key player was Eddie Cano, born in Los Angeles in 1927 to a Mexicano father from Chihuahua, and a Mexican American mother from Pomona. As we saw in chapter 3, Cano studied classical piano throughout his childhood, and heard both classical and Mexican music growing up in Chavez Ravine. In grammar school, he studied with a Mexican folk-dancing group directed by one of the teachers, an association which he continued while in junior high school, where he learned to play the bass for the school orchestra. During this time, he studied bass with his grandfather and with private teachers. After his family moved to Lincoln Heights, Cano learned to play the trombone for the Lincoln High School orchestra. In high school, his music theory teacher once had the students notate a complex mariachi musical passage, while his uncle, a professional musician, introduced him to the music of Duke Ellington. Lincoln High boasted an impressive jazz dance band, led by a teacher named Mr. Dozier, which Eddie joined in 1942. Within a year, the sixteen-year-old had played his first gig, at the popular Saturday night Royal Palms Hotel dances with local big bandleader Izzy Izar. Managed by the promoter Joe Garcia, the orchestra played a mix of Glenn Miller songs and swing standards, as well as society Latin rumbas and boleros.

After graduation, Eddie attended Los Angeles City College, where he continued his immersion in jazz improvisation. Cano played in U.S. Army bands while stationed in San Pedro from 1945 to 1946, during which time he graduated from the Los Angeles Conservatory of Music after studying music theory and composition. From 1947 through mid-1949, he recorded, performed, and toured with various bands, including Miguelito Valdés's New York City–based unit. In New York, the Latin musicians called him "Norito" as a complementary comparison to the pianist Noro Morales, and he sat in with the bands of Morales, Tito Puente, Machito, and José Curbelo. Of course, beginning in 1948, Eddie Cano also laid down the boogie woogie and Latin piano riffs on Don Tosti's pachuco boogie recordings. In addition, he performed regularly for several years on the Sunset Strip at Ciro's with Bobby Ramos's society orchestra, and in 1952 he played on a recording date with the white exotica bandleader Les Baxter. In 1954, Eddie joined the Cal Tjader Mambo Quintet, and in 1955 he played on Tjader's Fantasy label album, *Ritmo Caliente*. In particular, he wrote and arranged the album's title track, a rapid-fire percussion jam driven by Cano's piano montuno. All the while, he continued leading his own groups, which included the musicians Eddie Aparicio, Tony Reyes, Tommy Tedesco, Carlos Mejia, Freddie Aguirre, and Ruben Leon.[72]

Like Leon and Cano, another contributor, Rene Bloch, was a Latin convert from the swing cohort. Bloch's parents were Jewish, and his mother Caroline, who was born near Sonora, Mexico, spoke Spanish. After receiving a thorough musical training from Samuel Browne at Jefferson High School in the early 1940s, Rene joined Johnny Otis's house band at the Club Alabam on Central Avenue, and he played the solo on Otis's 1945 hit song, "Harlem Nocturne." When the swing era faded, Bloch still "wanted to play with a big band," so after a stint with Harry James, he became a sideman and manager for Pérez Prado's orchestra in 1954. Bloch toured the United States and abroad, but when he returned to Los Angeles in 1958, "the interest in the band was kind of dwindling." Bloch left Prado in 1959, then formed his own Latin orchestra in town.[73]

Throughout the decade, the Los Angeles Latin scene thus supported a diverse group of musicians. For example, by the early 1950s, according to Sesma, the swing bandleader Phil Carreon "made a lot of money copying" songs "that Pérez Prado had already recorded."[74] Carreon had first gone Latin at the Avedon Ballroom in the late 1940s, when he hired Rudy Macias to sing boleros. Macias was born in El Paso, Texas, but raised in Zacatecas, Mexico. He returned to El Paso in 1943 and, after a stint in the U.S. Army, moved to Los Angeles in 1947. Settling first in Echo Park, then, the following year, in Boyle Heights, he joined the white musicians union Local 47. By 1954, Macias fronted his own Latin quintet in East Los Angeles, downtown at the Zenda Ballroom, and in West Hollywood on the Sunset Strip.[75] Al Escobar, one of the decade's finest Latin pianists, accompanied visiting artists at Ciro's, in addition to leading the house band at the Garden of Allah, a Hollywood bungalows hotel at Sunset and Crescent Heights boulevards.[76] The pianist Sammy García performed both society Latin on the Hollywood circuit and mainstream mambos and cha cha chás around town, while the Mexican American conguero Max Garduno segued from East Los Angeles rhythm and blues groups to Latin bands, and even to the Gerald Wilson Orchestra. Other talented Mexican American musicians found work as sidemen, like the pianist Arturo Montez, the bassist Jim Baiz, and the timbalero Mike Gutierrez.[77]

In 1952, Don Tosti scored a regional hit with "Negro corazón" ("Black Heart"), a bolero that he wrote and arranged after his first wife divorced him. In the mid-1950s, the Pachuco Boogie Boys broke up when Eddie Cano left, and Raul Diaz formed his own band.[78] In 1954, Tosti worked as a session musician at Radio Recorders studio in Hollywood, playing bass on three songs from Pérez Prado's RCA Victor album, *Mambo Mania* (1955), and anchoring the four-movement title track of Prado's RCA album, *Voodoo Suite* (1956). Throughout the 1950s, Tosti assembled and led various Latin bands with a mix of musicians, such as the pianists Manny Cerecedes and Armando Loredo, the Anglo pianist/arranger Allen Chaplain, the Italian American timbalero Jack Navarra, and the singers Leticia Cardenas, Margarita Luisa Amos, Chamaco Juárez, and Ray Baxter. Tosti's bands performed during intermission, between the headliners' sets at the

Hollywood Palladium for several years. They also frequently played downtown at the Avedon Ballroom, with Manny Lopez's band at El Sombrero, and with Lalo Guerrero's band on Sunday afternoons at the Italian Village, a "society" nightclub where Tosti had occasionally played jazz during the swing era, as well as at Sardi's restaurant at Hollywood Boulevard and Vine Street.[79]

Unlike Don Tosti, the Mexican American jazz musician Anthony Ortega never tried to switch to Latin styles, but to pay the bills in 1953 he found steady work playing Latin dance music with pianist Armando Loredo's band at La Golondrina restaurant on Olvera Street for seventy-five dollars a week. As Ortega recalled, "It was not jazz, but I had to take whatever I could get." Around 1954, Ortega's old schoolmate, Chuy Ruiz, was working for a finance company during the week, and for Lalo Guerrero's Latin band on the weekends. On Ruiz's recommendation, Guerrero called Ortega to accompany them on different trips to San Joaquin Valley towns like Fresno. Crammed in a station wagon with their instruments, the group would drive north, where they played "strictly Latin music [like] cha chas, cumbias, and boleros." Guerrero's band included straight-ahead jazz musicians like the bassist Manuel Lechuga, who had been a member of the Hep Cats swing band at Jordan High School before Ortega, and the alto saxophonist Bart Caldarell, who had played in one of Stan Kenton's first orchestras. In 1956, Rene Bloch, who had just started contracting musicians for Pérez Prado, called Ortega because the Prado orchestra was about to go on the road and needed a tenor player. After the audition, Rene called Ortega and told him that of all the saxophonists, Prado liked him the best. Ortega told Bloch that he could not go on the road because he wanted to stay in town to be with his wife, Mona, and their newborn infant, and that he had a steady gig on Olvera Street.[80] On another occasion, Stan Kenton was auditioning some alto players for his band. Kenton had heard about Ortega and called him. After the audition, Kenton invited Ortega to join his orchestra on a ten-week engagement in Mexico City, but Ortega declined because he did not want to leave his family alone in Hollywood. "I heard it was a very successful trip," he recalled. "I wished I could have gone, because it was Mexico, and me being of Mexican descent, I would have been heralded as a big . . . hero." In general, Ortega only saw other Mexican American musicians "on Latin gigs," as there were few of them working "in the jazz vein" in Los Angeles by the late 1950s.[81] The black trumpeter Art Farmer remembered running into the white saxophonist Art Pepper on one-nighters with Los Angeles Latin bands, "playing montunos and things."[82]

Anthony Ortega, Don Tosti, and other swing-era musicians, as well as younger local Mexican American players like the trumpeter Marcus Cabuto from Garfield High and the percussionist Mike Pacheco, each played their part.[83] The city's Latin music scene also included the Mexican-born bassist Victor Venegas, who grew up on the South Side of Chicago and served in the U.S. Army during the Korean War. Venegas originally came to Los Angeles around 1959 as the only non-Afro-Cuban member of the Orquesta Nuevo Ritmo de Cuba. Many Latino musicians, such as the Puerto Rican trombonist Juan Tizol, and the Cuban percussionists Carlos Vidal, Francisco Aguabella, Armando Peraza, Mongo Santamaria, and Luis Miranda sojourned in Los Angeles, infusing the city with Afro-Caribbean rhythms and the latest Latin American styles. Tito Rivera's Havana Mambo Orchestra worked at the Mandalay nightclub in Hollywood, as well as the Routland Inn, Club La Bamba, and El Sombrero, playing the arrangements of the Havana-born band member Chico O'Farrill.[84] One major musician, the Puerto Rican vocalist Hector Rivera, never landed recording contracts or high-paying gigs, but his Conjunto Siboney became the house band at the Zenda Ballroom from 1956 through 1960, playing *son cubano*, and occasionally *bomba* and *plena*, the two Afro–Puerto Rican musical styles from his hometown of Ponce (see figure 35).[85]

With all of the different Latin bands performing throughout Los Angeles, loyal Mexican American music fans had plenty of options for dancing to their favorite artists. For instance, Ed Frias remembered seeing Pérez Prado at the Aragon Ballroom in Venice, where Mexican Americans had been going to dance since the early 1940s.[86] El Serape, on Sunset Boulevard at Silver Lake Avenue, offered Mexican, society Latin, and "American music" to an "all Mexican" audience in a nice, spacious setting during the 1940s and 1950s, while a few blocks west, at Ramona's, Mongo Santamaria had a charanga band in the early 1960s.[87] Around that time, Jaime Corral and his sister Gloria would drive from their neighborhood, just south of downtown, to the Riverside Rancho near Griffith Park, and also to the old El Serape, which had now become Club Havana.[88] One of the most popular alternatives to the Zenda Ballroom and the Palladium Ballroom, Club Havana presented many of the same top acts, like Tito Puente, Tito Rodríguez, and Machito, and it attracted a predominantly Mexican

35. Hector Rivera band, with Paul Lopez on trumpet, Richard Barrientos on congas, Rivera on maracas. Broadway Palace, Los Angeles, March 1957. COURTESY PAUL LOPEZ.

American clientele.[89] In the early 1960s, Rene Bloch became half-owner of the Club Havana, where his house band featured Rolando Lozano, a veteran of the Orquesta Aragón and the Orquesta Nuevo Ritmo de Cuba, as well as the Orquesta América, which had introduced the cha cha chá to Mexico City with great success.[90] In addition to drummer Pat Rodriguez, a veteran of Tito Rodríguez's band, Bloch also hired so many former Prado sidemen that his group was often called "the Pérez Prado All-Stars." Bloch's orchestra not only dueled Tito Puente's in dual-stage battles of the bands at Club Havana, but also played several concerts at the Hollywood Palladium, as well as weekend evening shows and Sunday afternoon matinees at the Bolero Inn on East Brooklyn Avenue. The Sunday matinees were broadcast on the Spanish-language radio station KALI.[91]

In Boyle Heights, La Pasadita and Pontrelli's, both on East First Street, offered Latin music, as did the M Club, located between Whittier Boulevard and Seventh Avenue, just west of Soto Street. Throughout the 1960s, at Lalo Guerrero's four-hundred-person-capacity nightclub on Brooklyn Avenue, along the border between City Terrace and East Los Angeles, people "could make requests and dedicate songs to their boyfriends or girlfriends," and Guerrero's band would play "mambo, cha cha cha, polka, swing, or rock and roll."[92] Along Atlantic Boulevard, which bisects East Los Angeles from north to south, stood Club 469, run by Manny Lopez from the middle 1950s to the late 1960s, as well as the Eastside's oldest nightclub, El Club Baion, a "small but nice" place "for listening, not dancing," and Club Boom Boom, a "dive." In West Los Angeles, popular Latin music establishments included the Direct Line, where each table had a large number and a telephone, so that the male patrons could call women at other tables and ask them to dance, Casa Escobar, a restaurant on La Cienega Boulevard, and La Cita, a "nice little Latin hot spot in the late 1950s and early 1960s" on the corner of Lincoln and Pico boulevards in Santa Monica.[93]

While the city's Latin music and dancing were hitting their stride, Paul Lopez had been playing with jazz and Latin bands back east, and with both house and relief bands in Las Vegas. During a "rough" period with "less work," Paul had come back home in 1952, 1954, 1956, and 1957, but in 1958 he returned to Los Angeles for good. Lopez argued that many of the Los Angeles bands "were exploring Latin, but they didn't have too much knowledge about . . . the clave and the rhythms," and that some bandleaders "had no idea how a conjunto should sound." Paul knew that in a Latin conjunto, rather than play double forte, a trumpeter must "play soft, and swing" compactly, and that to play in a Latin band one needed "a different articulation" in order "to phrase it on top of the beat." Applying his knowledge, Lopez immediately began writing arrangements for, and playing trumpet with, most of the local Los Angeles bands. In particular, he worked as an arranger, performer, and soloist on six albums for the former Stan Kenton sideman Jack Constanzo from 1956 through 1960, with two cosongwriting credits, and he worked as a composer, arranger, and performer on four albums for Rene Bloch from 1958 through 1962.[94] In 1960, Lopez arranged the song "Moonlight in Vermont" for the Machito album *The World's Greatest Latin Band* on Crescendo Records.

Paul Lopez had met Richard Barrientos while playing with Hector Rivera's band at the Broadway Palace in 1957. Since 1955, Barrientos and Tommy Saito balanced day jobs with night gigs, especially "casuals" in East Los Angeles ballrooms. Richard Barrientos worked in Los Angeles with Latin musicians like Carlos del Puerto, Joe Torres, and, at the Zenda Ballroom, Hector Rivera.[95] In 1956, Barrientos befriended Willie Bobo and Mongo Santamaria when the two percussionists recorded "Más Ritmo Caliente" with the Cal Tjader Mambo Quintet in Los Angeles, where Mongo was living. In 1959, Santamaria brought Barrientos some congas, *güiros*, bongos, and cowbells from Cuba, and on several occasions, he sent

Tommy Saito to play as his substitute with Tjader. Barrientos and Saito had been honing their skills, and in Paul Lopez they saw a trumpeter well versed in modern harmony who wrote Latin jazz arrangements. The three musicians became friends, and in late 1962 they decided to form a thirteen-piece Latin orchestra.

The core lineup of Paul Lopez's Latin big band included the timbalero Richard Barrientos; the conguero Tommy Saito; the saxophonists Jay Migliori, Pete Gallodoro, Dick "the Bear" Houlgate, and Blas Vasquez; and the trumpeters Ronnie Ossa, Johnny Audino, Jimmy Salko, and Howard "Hotsy" Katz. With Lopez as the "musical director," and Barrientos in charge of the rhythm section, the band also featured the vocalists Papi Torres, from New York, and "Kaskara," billed as "the restless Cuban." Although Barrientos and Saito arranged music, they usually wrote original songs and lyrics—sometimes just the melody to a song—and Lopez would write the arrangements. Barrientos remembered that "Paul wrote more modern tunes than traditional tunes," and Saito agreed that although Lopez wrote a few típica arrangements, his forte was Latin jazz. The band played Latin jazz, mambos, cha cha chás, a few Latin-flavored arrangements of American pop tunes, and a lot of boleros.[96]

According to Barrientos, most of the local bands hired non-Latino, straight-ahead jazz musicians to write arrangements of Latin songs "off the records as they became hits in New York." Likewise, a lot of Los Angeles musicians knew the clave, but few arrangers understood it, with the exception of René Touzet, Eddie Cano, and some of Rudy Macias's arrangers.[97] Paul Lopez's band, in contrast, played half covers, and half originals. Moreover, Lopez wrote a Latin arrangement for the vocalist Papi Torres to sing the ballad "Fools Rush In," as an "English crossover in bolero tempo." Saito pointed out that this big-band style arrangement was not corny, and that New York bands like that of Joe Loco had already been recording American ballads with English lyrics to bolero and mambo tempos with great success. Barrientos wrote one of the band's more popular songs, "Escucha mi guaguanco" ("Listen to My Guaguanco").

Barrientos also wrote the song "Los orientales" after overhearing two Latinos at the Zenda Ballroom say, "Los orientales no saben nada sobre nuestra música." Ironically, Tommy Saito and Barrientos, whose father was a Filipino from the Philippines, and whose mother was a third-generation Mexican American born in Arizona and raised in East Los Angeles, were often called the "Chino rhythm section" by some of their

Latino bandmates. Barrientos thought of his high school friends Tommy Saito and Kay Nomura, then wrote lyrics that described "Orientals" knowing how to dance to Cuban rhythms like the mambo and the cha cha chá, with a chorus of "Los orientales saben los ritmos cubanos."[98] As further proof of a Latin-Asian connection, Peter Chou, who left Cuba when Castro came to power, and who spoke Chinese and Spanish, owned a Chinese Cuban restaurant on the corner of Pico Boulevard and Alvarado Street. Similarly, the Chinese chef who ran the kitchen at the Club Havana also hailed from Cuba.[99] Finally, Saito composed a "novelty" tune, "Guaguanco en Japón," which reflected the popularity that Latin music had enjoyed in Japan since Machito and His Afro-Cubans toured there for three months in the early 1950s.[100] In 1952, Xavier Cugat toured Asia, and the following year, Tito Rodríguez embarked on a twelve-week Asian tour that included stops in Manila and Tokyo.[101] By the time Pérez Prado toured the Philippines, Korea, and Japan in the late 1950s, Latin music had caught on throughout the Far East, as reflected in Saito's Spanish lyrics, which declared, "In the town of Tokyo the people have a good time dancing to the guaguanco rhythm," and the Spanish chorus, which declared, "Even the people of Japan have the guaguanco."[102]

Lopez's band spent the early part of 1963 rehearsing their songbook, then they debuted in April 1963 at the Californian Club, located just west of the Los Angeles Memorial Coliseum on Western Avenue and Santa Barbara Boulevard; owned and ran by Max Millard, a Jewish American businessman nicknamed "Mambo Maxi." The Californian Club offered Latin music on Wednesday nights to an audience composed primarily of African Americans, with a sprinkling of Mexican Americans and other Latinos.[103] After performing at the Californian Club, Lopez's Latin orchestra was invited to play Club Virginia's, a key venue on West Seventh Street, across from MacArthur Park near its western edge. Club Virginia's had formerly featured Dixieland jazz, but in the late 1950s its female Anglo owner, Jackie Thorn, one of the city's premier mambo dancers and married to a Latino, started presenting Latin music. By the early 1960s, new ownership booked Tito Puente, Machito, Tito Rodríguez, and other big-name New York Latin bands, offering live music by "swinging mambo bands" six nights a week.[104] Only established local bandleaders like Johnny Martinez, Bobby Montez, and Rudy Macias performed there, but in April 1963 the owners "took a chance" with Lopez's band, hiring them for a limited engagement (see figure 36).[105]

Paul Lopez

Kaskara

Club Virginia's

2434 West Seventh Street

PROUDLY PRESENTS

THE NEW SENSATION

Paul Lopez (His Trumpet) and

13 PIECE ORCHESTRA

FEATURING VOCALIST *Kaskara*

"THE RESTLESS CUBAN"

Starting June 6th, 1963

Thursdays Thru Sundays

Phone DUnkirk 3-3478

36. Club Virginia's flier for Paul Lopez Orchestra, 1963. COURTESY PAUL LOPEZ.

Billed as "the new sensation," the Paul Lopez Orchestra played to a sold-out house, and from June through August 1963 they appeared at Club Virginia's on Thursday, Friday, Saturday, and Sunday evenings. According to Saito, Club Virginia's audience was 70 percent Mexican American, mixed with other Latinos, Jews, Anglos, and a handful of Asians. Lopez remembered two Japanese American men in particular who "were great Latin dancers."[106] Regular patrons included a few movie stars, especially Cesar Romero, a Cuban American from New York, as well as "the Arthur Murray crowd," those affluent Latin music fans—many of them Jewish—who learned the new steps by taking lessons in expensive dance studios.[107] As Hortencia Garibay recalled, "[Club Virginia's] was really popular . . . everybody [from East Los Angeles] used to go there."[108] The Mexican Americans in the audience would often approach the bandstand and request slow songs so they could be "slick" and whisper sweet nothings in their partners' ears while dancing closely. In contrast, the Cubans and Puerto Ricans preferred the uptempo dance songs, and they would occasionally jump on stage, grab a cowbell and drum stick, and start playing in clave with the band.[109]

In September 1963, the band played at the Hollywood Palladium several times, at Club Havana, and also at the Riverside Rancho for the traditional black and white ball. The group disbanded from 1964 to 1966, when Lopez lived in Puerto Rico, studying at the Pablo Casals Conservatory of Music and writing radio commercial jingles. The band reformed in 1967 and played throughout 1968. Unfortunately, its successful local performances did not lead to greater opportunities. As Lopez noted, "I never made it big, but I did play at Virginia's. All I needed was a hit record, and I couldn't get it out. You've got to produce your own thing here, and the band was too big to record." Actually, Lopez once recorded four of his band's songs, including their original number, "Escucha mi guaguanco," and their bolero version of "Fools Rush In," with some of Tito Puente's visiting musicians, "under the table" in a nonunion studio in Ontario, California.[110]

Lopez attributed his band's fate in Los Angeles to bad luck, since he felt that "Los orientales," with its "cute" lyrics, "would have been a big hit if it had gotten to the right people." With the orchestra seemingly poised for success, not all of the elements were there. Both Saito and Barrientos described the band's main drawback as its size, which was too expensive to maintain. Saito also noted that since club owners often perceived new bands as a risk, the musicians needed a professional promoter, as well as an agent with business moxie. However, Lopez, unable to afford either, assumed both roles. Finally, Barrientos added that because Los Angeles nightclubs were so small, owners could not pay the musicians union-scale wages. In the end, Lopez and his musicians tried to strike a balance between, on the one hand, creative compositions in more "authentic" Afro-Latin styles, and, on the other, commercial attempts at crossover appeal, but this strategy did not lead to recording contracts. Meanwhile, Club Virginia's continued to provide a space for Latin music and dance throughout the 1960s, contracting Joe Cuba, La Playa Sextet, Ray Barretto, and Eddie Palmieri. Blas Vasquez, the brother of Frank Vasquez, the original bassist for René Touzet's Los Angeles Latin jazz group, eventually bought Club Virginia's in the late 1960s.[111]

In South Central Los Angeles, one Latin music night during the week was offered at venues catering to black Angelenos, such as the Broadway Palace, at 52nd Street and Broadway, Billy Berg's 5–4 Ballroom at 54th Street and Broadway, the Mambo Club at 77th Street and South Compton Avenue, the Californian Club, and a few jazz spots in Inglewood.[112] A lot of Barrientos's black "homeboys" from Polytechnic High School danced to Latin music downtown at the Zenda Ballroom, in Silver Lake at the Club

Havana, on the Eastside at the Club Boom Boom, and in Hollywood at the Palladium Ballroom.[113] Finally, many African Americans followed Paul Lopez's Latin big band closely after its debut at the Californian Club, traveling around town to catch its live performances.[114] Since 1951, when Johnny Otis hit number three on the rhythm and blues charts with his song "Mambo Boogie," Latin rhythms had slinked their way into African American R & B. In 1956, the Jefferson High School alumnus and R & B singer Richard Berry, inspired by a René Touzet song, "El Loco Cha Cha," wrote the rock and roll classic "Louie Louie" with a driving 3–2 beat.[115] The 3–2 clave rhythm became a staple of early rock and roll after Bo Diddley's eponymous 1955 hit and can also be heard on Johnny Otis's 1958 song "Willie and the Hand Jive."[116] Not surprisingly, the mambo and other Latin dance styles were very popular among African American Angelenos.

The Latin music scene, perhaps more than the swing, R & B, and rock and roll scenes, facilitated an environment in which Mexican Americans, male and female, tried, sometimes unsuccessfully, to become small business owners. For instance, in August 1956, members of the County License Appeals Board turned down an appeal by Helen Sandoval Jiminez of East Los Angeles for dance and public entertainment licenses for the Congo Inn Café on East Third Street. The board's decision followed a public hearing during which residents of the area testified to alleged noise and other disturbances from the café under a former owner. The County Public Welfare Commission had rejected Jiminez's request for the licenses.[117] By the late 1950s, many different clubs and bars throughout the city offered mambo, cha cha chá, rhythm and blues, and rock and roll, catering to the competing tastes of their neighborhood clientele, which changed over the years due to the ever shifting demographics of Los Angeles. For example, the Cozy Inn, a bar in Florence, operated in 1957 as a one-story stucco building with a dozen tables and barstools, and a small dance floor. On Tuesday, Wednesday, and Thursday nights, the bar's owners, Manuel Olivarria Lopez and Bard Gutierrez Fernandez, shrewdly featured western music, attracting a "white, neighborhood crowd." They made most of their money on weekends, when "Latin music [was] furnished"; "on these three days the clientele [was] normally people of Mexican descent, from other areas." Interestingly, the Los Angeles Sheriff's Department recommended that the owners' 1957 application for a dance license renewal be approved, despite Lopez's 1942 arrest on "suspicion of robbery" and Fernandez's 1942 arrest on "suspicion of kidnap and robbery." The two owners were presumably Mexican Americans, perhaps even ex-pachucos, whose adolescent brushes with the law did not deter them from future entrepreneurship.[118]

In general, casual fans could listen to pleasant Latin pop, discriminating dancers could move to deep Afro-Latin grooves, and bold promoters could turn a profit. Hence, after four years as a radio disc jockey, Chico Sesma tried his hand at concert promotion. He was encouraged by his radio industry mentor, George Chavez, and by the strong track record of Joe Garcia, who consistently attracted capacity crowds to the Zenda Ballroom in downtown Los Angeles, in large part by buying advertising time on Sesma's radio program. Accordingly, in 1953 Sesma staged a successful "Latin Holiday" dance at the Zenda Ballroom.[119] Next, he served as the master of ceremonies for a "Mambo Jumbo" event put on by Irving Granz, the brother of the longtime jazz impresario Norman Granz, at the Shrine Auditorium.[120] The Mambo Jumbo concert featured the orchestras of Tito Rodríguez, Pérez Prado, and Chico O'Farrill, and the quintets of Noro Morales and Tony Martinez.[121] Considering the popularity of the Shrine show, his own first Latin concert, and his own radio program, Sesma decided that he needed a larger location to reach the full potential of Latin music in Los Angeles, so in 1954 he moved his "Latin Holiday" concerts to the Hollywood Palladium.

The former "house of big bands" was no longer the premiere ballroom in Los Angeles, although postwar bandleaders like Harry James, Les Brown, and Gordon "Tex" Beneke would still perform there on the weekends. With the swing era over, the owners of the Palladium had been reduced to renting the space to local industrial and manufacturing companies for "private parties and banquets."[122] Since independent promoters could engage the Palladium, with the option of using whatever band was already booked on a given night, Sesma wisely chose to build his Latin dance lineup around the orchestra of Pérez Prado, a guaranteed draw with marquee name value who was performing there on Sunday evenings. Sesma added the New Yorker Joe Loco, and the Los Angeles bands of Tony Martinez and Manny Lopez, then rented the Hollywood Palladium for eight hundred dollars. More than thirty-six hundred Latin music fans turned out, each paying the $2.50 admission charge.[123] Ironically, Sesma considered Pérez Prado "a bit of a noise-maker" who played "scandalous arrangements." Yet Sesma was an entrepreneur, and his concerts were business ventures. When Sesma's shows made it big, so did he, but when they flopped, he took a heavy personal loss. Luckily for Sesma, and for Los Angeles, his first Latin Holiday dance at the Palladium was a smashing success.

Originally held annually, Sesma's Sunday night Latin Holidays were presented semiannually until 1959, then monthly until 1973, making them the best-attended and longest-lasting of all the live Latin music concerts in Los Angeles. Whereas the Zenda Ballroom could only accommodate twenty-five hundred people, the Palladium could hold six thousand. By promoting his events on his radio program, Sesma consistently averaged three thousand to four thousand patrons.[124] Sesma observed that "the vast majority of those in attendance were . . . Mexican Americans, as opposed to Mexican nationals."[125] The Latin Holiday audience also included "a lot of black people."[126] In addition, Chico Sesma noted, "most of the non-Hispanics that were not blacks were Jewish. The Jews just love Latin music!"[127] Over the years, Sesma's Latin Holidays became a Los Angeles institution. They attracted a legion of Mexican American Latin music fans like David and Hortencia Torres from East Los Angeles and Raul and Dora Rico from Oxnard.[128] By the 1960s, these older couples were joined on the floor by younger Mexican Americans like Romeo Prado, a teenage trombonist and budding arranger from Salesian High School in East Los Angeles.[129] Emma "Emmy" Sánchez and her three sisters used to dance to Sesma's radio program every afternoon in Norwalk. Gracie and Carmen Sánchez had often danced at the Zenda Ballroom, and all four sisters regularly attended the Latin Holiday concerts at the Palladium (see figure 37).[130]

Although most of the artists who performed at the Palladium had previously appeared at the Zenda, several, like Beny Moré, Orquesta Aragón, La Sonora Matancera, and Celia Cruz, made their West Coast debut at one of Sesma's Latin Holiday concerts. Like Joe Garcia, Sesma not only contracted premier performers from New York, Cuba, Puerto Rico, and Mexico, he also hired local Latin orchestras as opening, intermission, and supporting acts. Unlike Garcia, Sesma brought this exciting brand of Latin music—and its core Mexican American fan base—from downtown Los Angeles to Hollywood, long the setting for sugary society bands, while presenting it on a much larger scale. Or, as Sesma maintained, because of his Latin Holiday shows, Mexican Americans crossed the geographic color line, going past Broadway into West Los Angeles.[131] Of course, since the early 1940s, Mexican American dance fans had been crossing town for live

37. Chico Sesma onstage at the Hollywood Palladium, Latin Holiday concert, 1962.
COURTESY CHICO SESMA.

musical performances, from Central Avenue to the Palladium, the Aragon Ballroom in Venice, and the Trianon Ballroom in South Gate. Still, thanks to Sesma, by the mid-1950s, Mexican American and Latino dancers from all over Southern California, and Latin dance bands from all over the hemisphere, converged near the heart of Hollywood to take a Latin holiday (see figure 38).

The Hollywood Palladium had opened in 1940 "to provide a dancing spot with the atmosphere of a 'class' Hollywood supper club, but at prices within the means of the general public."[132] However, even though the average Angeleno could afford to go there during the swing years, as we saw in chapter 2, the Palladium refused entry to Mexican Americans and African Americans sporting zoot suits. Nevertheless, by 1954 its owners were forced by economic circumstance to contract Latin orchestras and accept the patronage of more customers of color. In short, from the mid-1950s throughout the 1960s, Sesma opened up the Palladium to all Angelenos, while retaining its "classy" atmosphere (see figure 39).

Indeed, Sesma considered the people who packed his Latin Holiday shows at the Hollywood Palladium more cultured than the typical Mexican

38. Flier for Làtin Holiday concert at the Hollywood Palladium, October 4, 1959. COURTESY CHICO SESMA.

39. Hollywood Palladium dance floor and stage, October 4, 1959.
COURTESY CHICO SESMA.

American rhythm and blues fans, who had, Sesma argued, lower "vocational levels." According to Sesma, the Mexican Americans who frequented the Angelus Hall in the 1950s were more likely to work as gas station attendants, truck drivers, and mechanic's assistants, while those who frequented the Hollywood Palladium might be accountants or medical assistants.[133] In support of Sesma's hypothesis, Hortencia Garibay remembered that the Palladium patrons had "at least graduated from high school," while Emmy Sánchez recalled that "Kappa Zeta Psi Chicanos," many of them future professionals and city councilmen, used to gather at the left side of the stage.[134] Sesma contended that the people at the Latin Holidays were "not necessarily wealthy, just more sophisticated," that they were "developed" culturally and academically, with an appreciation for the orchestration of the big band era.[135] In other words, "they were on a wholly different social strata. They were assimilated to a far greater degree."[136] Sesma's demographic observations suggest that hitting the town to dance suavely to polyrhythmic Afro-Latin music served as an appealing acculturating option for many upwardly mobile Mexican Americans in the postwar period.

They must have derived a certain social cachet vis-à-vis the white majority by being hip to the Spanish-language lyrics of Latin recording artists. As the Mexican scholar Fernando Muñoz argues, "Listening to the mambos of Pérez Prado or Beny Moré gives you a status of knowledge, and of possessing a culture and an identity."[137] Despite their apparent Americanization and attempted integration, postwar Mexican Americans used the Los Angeles Latin music scene to escape an Anglo-imposed "commodity identity" of Mexicans as merely "cheap labor."[138] Navigating the cultural terrain of a segregated city, whether at the Palladium Ballroom in Hollywood, the Zenda Ballroom downtown, or Club Virginia's by MacArthur Park, they could now entertain a "Latin" identity, refined in manner, but not white. Trading in low-caste connotations for high-class associations, through Latin music fandom they could take part in a pan-Latino cosmopolitanism. Just as the Hollywood Palladium shows provided a "Latin Holiday" at the "World Famous" ballroom, fliers for performances by Latin orchestras at Club Virginia's promised "a Caribbean Party" at the self-described "avant garde social club," much like Mexico City newspaper announcements for the "El Latino" nightclub that advertised a "modern," "elegant" establishment where one could "dance in rhythm to the best orchestras in the world."[139]

The mambo, the cha cha chá, and especially the bolero, enabled Southern California Mexican Americans to evoke a certain *Latinidad*, indulging their social aspirations while participating in an international music industry and ballroom dance culture. The bolero, an urban romantic ballad form with slow, syncopated rhythms and haunting harmonies, became a standard genre throughout the hemisphere, where sinfully risqué boleros "gave Latin Americans a sense of modernity."[140] As Frances Aparicio argues, the bolero is a modern, transnational "musical language" that unites the contradictory "romantic sentimentality" and "macho sensibility" of Latin American masculinity.[141] Mexican composers, foremost among them Agustín Lara, wrote numerous boleros during the 1930s and 1940s, forever linking the style with Mexico. In Mexico, Lara's "most immediate public" was "the urban bohemian nightlife," but "his most faithful listeners" were middle-class housewives, lawyers, and bureaucrats anxious for emotional, poetic romanticism.[142]

The modern bolero thus bridged the gap between traditional Mexican music and society Latin, allowing Mexican Americans to be Latin but still Mexican at heart. For many upwardly mobile Mexican American Angelenos, like their middle-class Tejano counterparts, the bolero captured both their "Mexicanness" and their "sophistication."[143] In Los Angeles, Manuel Peña identified an "acculturationist," "tropical crowd," which he contrasted with a "down-to-earth" ranchero crowd "more strongly tied to [Mexican] ethnic roots and less upwardly mobile."[144] Actually, the correlation between musical taste, class, and cultural identity was much less directly determined in Southern California, where the bolero conveyed both Latino cultural refinement and ethnic Mexican pride, and where working-class East Los Angeles bands played Latin music, Mexican music, and rhythm and blues. As Dora Rico argued, you could not tell who was middle class because a lot of working-class Mexican Americans dressed up and went to the Hollywood Palladium.[145] Indeed, class itself was more open ended, and Mexican Americans with rising expectations and eclectic tastes simply had many more choices for their musical consumption than allowed by binary paradigms like Mexican-versus-Tropical, or R & B–versus-Latin. For example, Ed Frias went dancing at both rhythm and blues and Latin concerts, even as he bought a home in all-white West Covina, while Jaime Corral preferred jazz and Latin, but remained loyal to mariachi music, even as he moved to Whittier and joined a professional white workforce as a Los Angeles County Superior Court judge in Alhambra.[146] While some of the ambitious Mexican American "Latin" bandleaders, like Chico Sesma and Paul Lopez, did not move out of the barrios, many others did. Even Lalo Guerrero, who frequently relied on a ranchero audience, was upwardly mobile himself, as he eventually moved to Palm Springs, following Don Tosti and Manny Lopez.

The fluid class positions and cultural identities of Mexican Americans in Los Angeles come into even sharper focus when compared to Latin music fans in the town of Pomona in eastern Los Angeles County. There, the Mexican American disc jockey Candelario "Cande" Mendoza hosted a Spanish-language, Mexican music morning radio show from 1949 to 1956. Beginning in 1954, he also hosted 5 o'Clock Fiesta, an English-language Latin music afternoon program "with a definite Spanish flavor." On KPMO from 5:00 P.M. to 6:00 P.M. Monday through Friday, Mendoza would say the introduction of the program in English, then repeat it in Spanish. He would also translate words and short sentences and would "throw in ... little sayings" in Spanish. Like Chico Sesma, Mendoza was a radio personality who helped foster a Mexican American audience for Latin music but whose listeners also included whites—in Mendoza's case, Anglo students from Scripps College, the Claremont Colleges, and Pomona College. Mendoza played the mambo, the cha cha chá, and Latin jazz, as well as some romantic bolero trios and singers like Fernando Fernández, and "El Tenor de las Americas," Pedro Vargas. As a result, some of Mendoza's Mexican fans from his morning show listened to the afternoon program, as did the local "avant-garde *raza*." Unlike Sesma, Mendoza played more records by female vocalists, such as María Victoria, Virginia López, Chavalita, and the Castro Sisters, and, as master of ceremonies at the Rainbow Gardens dance hall in Pomona, brought more artists like Carmen y Laura, Abby Chávez, and Julie Reyes and Her Sextet, an all-women ensemble from East Los Angeles, to perform.

In addition, unlike the Palladium in Hollywood, the Rainbow Gardens featured more Tex-Mex style music, from swing-influenced headliners like Beto Villa and His Orchestra to more "raunchy" local intermission conjuntos.[147] While many of the same artists who played at the Zenda and Palladium ballrooms would perform in Pomona, Angeleno entrepreneur Frank Faust would also book Mexicano Latin bands at the Million Dollar Theater in downtown Los Angeles and then send them to the Rainbow Gardens.[148] Indeed, as Carlos Monsiváis noted, while upwardly mobile Mexican Americans may have danced at the Hollywood Palladium, the popular mass of Mexicano Angelenos attended the Million Dollar Theater downtown.[149] In general, the Mexican Americans in Pomona seem to have incorporated rancheras, and a range of Mexican performers, more directly into their Latin music scene. Nonetheless, as in Los Angeles, the Pomona dancers converged on a previously all-white area in their evening suits and dresses, not only as the social equals of Anglos, but in a way as their cultural betters, since ethnic Mexicans were actively participating in a much larger music world. Specifically, they were adept at executing the "difficult" steps of "a strenuous dance" like the fast-paced mambo. Furthermore, as Mendoza argued, "even your bolero can be very sensual and expressive. You can very elegantly do some turns with el bolero as you bend the girl down." According to Mendoza, Latin music is "much more expressive than just plain ballroom dancing. There's the shaking of the hips, the movement of the pelvis, the turns." In short, the Latin dancers "were able to improvise, and they were able to say, 'This is our music.' "[150]

A 1954 *Time* magazine article described a "blonde Boston housewife named Adele Winters and her dark-haired partner" doing "dizzy mambo variations known as chases, double turns, rolls, shine breaks and triples with ripples" while her husband, "Truck Driver Pete Winters," stood sidelined. "I've been trying to learn it," Pete sighed, "but I can't seem to."[151] Dora Rico suggested that Mexican Americans "had looser hips" than the "gabachos," who "had stiffer hips." Dora even compared "Latin music and dancing [to] being addicted—once you start you can't stop."[152] "To me it was wonderful music," said Hortencia Garibay, "and the dancing. . . . I've always liked música tropical. I liked Puerto Ricans and Cubanos. I liked the music very much."[153] The Zenda Ballroom regular Jaime Corral pointed out that "even though it was a completely different kind of music, , you could still relate to it . . . because it was Latino and they spoke Spanish. And you could dance to it. And you know, partying . . . I think that's probably what happened—an identification. . . . It was just a segment of the Mexican community. Not *every* Chicano went out there to dance the mambo and the cha cha chá at those clubs. Not everybody."[154] Nevertheless, Mexican Americans formed a sizable presence in the Latin music scene, as fans, dancers, and promoters.

Sesma reached beyond this bread-and-butter audience from 1954 to 1957, using his position on mainstream English-language radio to promote his Latin Holiday concerts. However, even though he managed to keep his integrity during the disc jockey payola scandals of the 1950s, he lost his autonomy when his original program fell victim to corporate consolidation and the Top-40 pop radio format. In 1958, after a year and a half of local celebrity, Sesma left KDAY for all-Spanish Los Angeles radio station KALI, where he continued to host his Latin music program, now airing from eight o'clock until midnight, and to promote his dances, now held monthly, until 1967. By the late 1960s, Sesma contracted Texas bands like Sunny and the Sunliners and Little Joe y La Familia, as well as the Eastside rockers Thee Midnighters.[155] As Richard Barrientos recalled, "Chico was high on Tito Puente, [Tito] Rodríguez, Joe Loco, and Cal Tjader," but he "held back from playing some of the more traditional, hard-core stuff" by new bands like El Gran Combo, formed by Rafael Cortijo's former band members, or Hector Rivera's band, or Roberto Faz's Conjunto Casino.[156] In 1967, the KALI station was sold, and Sesma began working for the State of California, placing unemployed people in jobs with the Employment Development Department. For the next five years, even when he was no longer a disc jockey, Sesma would still advertise his Hollywood Palladium Latin Holidays by purchasing time slots on Spanish-language KWKW.[157]

During its 1950s "heyday," Latin music crossed over like never before, from major media outlets to the "hinterlands" of the United States. In 1954, *Newsweek* and *Variety* ran articles on "mambomania," Latin band-leaders received unprecedented visibility, and non-Latin novelty tunes like Perry Como's "Papa Loves Mambo" and Rosemary Clooney's "Mambo Italiano" ruled pop radio.[158] In 1955, Pérez Prado's "Cerezo rosa" ("Cherry Pink and Apple Blossom White") stayed on the U.S. pop charts for twenty-six weeks, including ten weeks at number one. Realizing the renewed appeal and higher profile of Latinos, and perhaps wanting to avoid, after June 1954, the anti-Mexican stigma of "Operation Wetback," many Mexican Americans rode the Latin music bandwagon. For example, in the early 1960s, Rudy Macias, who eventually became known as "the Mexican Lawrence Welk," led his ten-piece orchestra, accompanying singers like Vikki Carr, Andy Russell, and Sammy Davis Jr. at luxury hotels like the Westin Bonaventure, Century Plaza, Beverly Hilton, and Regent Beverly Wilshire. In the late 1960s, Macias formed a "Latin pop band" that played weddings in East Los Angeles, and in Montebello, where he had relocated in 1957.[159] Rene Bloch recorded Latin albums like *Mucho Rock with Rene Bloch* (Andex Records, 1958), which included original mambos and Latin jazz arrangements by Paul Lopez, and featured six percussionists, led by Willie Bobo and Mongo Santamaria. On Bloch's 1962 Atco album, *Mr. Latin*, which included the song, "Lamento latino" ("Latin Lament"), Paul Lopez also wrote arrangements and played trumpet in mambo, cha cha chá, *watusi*, and *pachanga* styles. For Capitol Records Bloch recorded *Everybody Likes to Mambo*, with a version of "Cielito lindo," and *Let's Dance the Mambo*, with a Bloch original called "Mambo chicano." He also put out *Everybody Likes to Cha-Cha-Cha* for Hi-Fi Records and *La Pachanga* for Capitol Records.[160]

Bobby Montez reached a mainstream audience with his 1958 album, *Jungle Fantastique!* However, in Paul Lopez's opinion, Montez "had some good musicians here, but his music was not clave-oriented."[161] Jim Baiz, the original bassist for Bobby Montez, had his own take on the bandleader. Baiz, who grew up in the projects in Boyle Heights and attended Hollenbeck Junior High School and Roosevelt High School, argued that the artists and repertoire people at the record labels pressured Bobby Montez to record albums like *Pachanga y Cha-Cha-Cha, Hollywood Themes in Cha*

Cha Cha, and *Gigi and My Fair Lady in Latin* rather than more original, less commercial albums like *Viva Montez*. In the late 1950s, Montez pleased Mexican Americans every weekend at the M Club in East Los Angeles, where, as Baiz noted, the bands "always played a mix of cha chas and Mexican music like boleros."[162]

As Sesma pointed out, René Touzet, the veteran pianist, "wrote a lot of beautiful songs, many of which crossed over and were recorded in English by big American artists" like Peggy Lee, Frank Sinatra, and Bing Crosby. Sesma argued that Touzet "could play more traditional Afro-Cuban music, as could the Afro-Cuban musicians in his bands, but he also went a little commercial."[163] Paul Lopez recalled that Touzet's sound became "very Americanized, with a vocal group," while Richard Barrientos concluded that Touzet "got a little more Hollywood in Los Angeles," a little more "flamboyant." Baiz agreed that the longer Touzet stayed in Hollywood, the more commercial his music became. This pattern can be seen in Touzet's recordings, from his early 78 rpm singles like "Mi música es para tí" and "Por todas mis locuras," and his eponymous Latin jazz album for Capitol Records in 1948, to his later albums of pachangas, show tunes, movie themes, and Hollywood bossa novas. Like many of his West Coast Cubano contemporaries, Touzet eventually left Los Angeles for Miami.[164]

In 1955, Eddie Cano played in Los Angeles and New York City with the Latin quintet of Tony Martinez, who introduced Cano by name for a momentary close-up in a scene from *Rock around the Clock*. In 1956, Cano performed on a Latin flute exotica album by the ballad singer Herb Jeffries, and then he played in Jack Costanzo's Los Angeles Latin band, writing the arrangements for the songbook, along with Paul Lopez, and performing on Costanzo's GNP album, *Mr. Bongo*, where he flexed his Latin jazz muscles on "Just One of Those Things," "Caravan," and "Chopsticks Mambo." In 1956, Cano sent a homemade demo tape to Shorty Rogers, who was then appraising talent for RCA Victor. As a result of Cano's initiative, the label signed him, then recorded his first album, *Cole Porter and Me*, and in 1957, his second, *Duke Ellington and Me*. On these two albums, Cano balanced homage covers, most notably an imaginative Latin arrangement of Ellington's "Prelude to a Kiss," with original compositions like "Algo sabroso" and "Ecstasy" (see figure 40).

In 1957, Cano played on Jack Costanzo's Liberty Records album, *Latin Fever*, which included Latin jazz numbers like "Peanut Vendor," "Malagueña," and "Oye Negra." In 1958, RCA Victor released Cano's third

40. Eddie Cano at the piano, Hollywood Palladium, Latin Holiday concert, ca. 1957. COURTESY CHICO SESMA.

album, *Deep in a Drum*, which, despite the congas on the cover and a few Latin tunes, sported jazz standards like "Night in Tunisia," "Surrey with the Fringe on Top," and "Yesterdays," as well as Cano originals like "Honey Do (Melody in G)." RCA Victor quickly followed with Cano's fourth album, *Time for Cha Cha Cha*, which consisted of slow and mid-tempo Latin-lite, with an emphasis on safe society fare, easy-listening vibraphones, and Paris-café accordions. In 1959, Cano became the first Mexican American musician to record for United Artists with his album, *Cha Cha con Cano*, a collection of ambient Latin versions of melodic standards that showcased his relaxed, confident piano solos. In 1960, Cal Tjader's Fantasy album, *Demasiado Caliente*, featured four Cano big-band compositions that ranged from tame society to snappy swing. That same year, Cano recorded with Costanzo on the GNP album *Dancing on the Sunset Strip* and with Costanzo and Tony Martinez on the album *Mucho Piano*, recorded live at the Crescendo.

In 1961, Cano played on the Eros label recording session for Buddy Collette's album, *Bongo Beat*, and he and his quintet began performing "a little Latin jazz, supper club" music at a small, after-hours West Hollywood nightclub called P. J.'s.[165] In 1961, he also released his first album on

THE BEST OF
EDDIE CANO
HIS PIANO AND HIS RHYTHM

LOVE FOR SALE · HONEY DO · LOVE IS A WONDERFUL THING · CUBAN LOVE SONG · WHAT IS THIS THING CALLED LOVE · LIDA ROSE
I COULD HAVE DANCED ALL NIGHT · COTTON CANDY · THE CONTINENTAL · YESTERDAYS · I CAN GROOVE YOU · TILL THERE WAS YOU

41. *The Best of Eddie Cano* album cover, 1962.

Reprise, *Eddie Cano at P. J.'s*, which produced a Grammy-nominated national hit single, "A Taste of Honey," along with a combination of Cano originals, the jazz standard, film-noir theme "Laura," Judy Garland's "The Trolley Song," and a trendy tune called "Watusi Walk." Cano's 1962 RCA Victor album, *The Best of Eddie Cano: His Piano and His Rhythm* (see figure 41), was a "light amalgam of mood jazz and Latino-style" that signaled his turn to the mainstream.[166] This "best of" recording reflected Cano's steady job at P. J.'s, where he played cocktail lounge Latin music to a white entertainment-industry audience. Celebrities like Sal Mineo, Jackie Cooper, Tony Curtis, Jayne Mansfield, Bobby Darin, Ethel Merman, Frankie Avalon, Elia Kazan, Stanley Kramer, Joey Bishop, and Lenny Bruce were regulars, and some of them would occasionally sit in on bongos. Cano even added the traditional Jewish song "Hava Nagilah" to his repertoire.

The Mexican American singer-guitarist Trini Lopez also performed at P. J.'s at the same time as Cano. Moving from the Dallas barrio to Beverly

Hills and West Hollywood, this transplanted Tejano was discovered at P. J.'s by Frank Sinatra, who signed him to an exclusive eight-year contract with Reprise Records. Trini's 1963 debut album, *At P. J.'s*, became a number one hit and stayed on the U.S. charts for almost two years, producing a rocking version of a Peter, Paul, and Mary song, "If I Had a Hammer," an eventual international hit single. Trini also scored an international hit with his version of "La Bamba," which his father had taught him as an eleven-year-old in 1948, two years after buying him his first guitar. In 1965, the *moreno* Lopez appeared not only as himself in the comedy *Marriage on the Rocks*, starring Sinatra, Dean Martin, and Cesar Romero, but also on the television show *Hullabaloo* in 1965 and 1966, and in the film *The Dirty Dozen* and on TV again on *The London Palladium Show*, both in 1967. As Gil Bernal argued, "Trini Lopez had the appeal of people like Sinatra or Nat Cole. He had many number one sellers all over the world."[167] Lopez recorded numerous successful albums, including *By Popular Demand: More Trini Lopez at P. J.'s*.

After seeing Cano perform at P. J.'s, Jerry Lewis cast the pianist in *The Nutty Professor* in 1963, the same year Cano appeared in the Elvis Presley film *Fun in Acapulco*.[168] Like Lalo Guerrero and Ritchie Valens, Eddie Cano provided an alternative to a slim, blond standard of beauty for men with his heavy-set, mestizo masculine presence in show business. For the next few years, Cano recorded the albums *Here Is the Fabulous Eddie Cano, Cano Plays Mancini, Danke Schoen, The Sound of Music and the Sound of Cano*, and a show tune LP, *Broadway Right Now*, all on Reprise. Cano then shared top billing with the tenor saxophonist Nino Tempo on their 1966 Atco album, *On Broadway*.[169] In short, by the early 1960s Cano definitely tended toward the commercial. Paul Lopez recalled that Cano's band typically used "a conga drummer adapting to a jazz rhythm section" and felt that Cano never got too Latin because he "wanted to reach the American public."[170] Barrientos claimed that when Cano played for the movie-industry folks his music became "real Hollywood," meaning "a lot of flash but no soul."[171]

On the other hand, Jim Baiz argued, "Eddie Cano could swing! With his musicality, even at P. J.'s, which was a place and crowd for listening, rather than dancing, Cano packed 'em in."[172] Cano recorded another Latin-lite LP, *30 Latin American Favorites*, on Pickwick Records, but his spark as a soloist could still be heard on his 1967 Dunhill album, *Brought Back Live from P. J.'s*, which included covers of songs like "La Bamba," "Louie Louie,"

"Guantanamera," and "El Pito." In his career trajectory from improviser to entertainer, in his mastery of modern jazz and Latin jazz, and his incorporation of the latest musical trends, as well as show tunes and Tin Pan Alley ballads, Cano was not unlike other Angelenos of his generational cohort. Like them, he studied, practiced, and worked hard; he served his country and broadened his horizons. Although Cano was arguably coasting on his 1960s albums, he still had his mojo working, representing yet another success story, and a round, brown Mexican face, in mainstream society.

As the contemporary Latin percussionist Raul Rico Jr. argued, "Most musicians went a little Hollywood at some point in their careers," reaching a stage at which they had "to water down the music a little to reach a mass audience, sell records, and make a living."[173] The Hollywood influence led Los Angeles record labels to frown on Spanish lyrics, gearing their artists' material toward an Anglo audience instead, while the commercial bandleaders won the record deals and performed in the affluent Hollywood nightclubs.[174] Even though thirteen Latin record labels had offices on Pico Boulevard, between Vermont and Western avenues, being based in either New York, Puerto Rico, Cuba, or Mexico, they never signed any local artists. Consequently, Barrientos concluded that "Los Angeles was not a town in which to record Latin music."[175] The Los Angeles Latin music industry never matched the local rhythm and blues market of the 1940s and 1950s, when high school music programs cultivated musical talent, contractors produced live concerts, and a glut of independent labels pressed records.

Part of the problem was that society Latin-lite music had been vying for a hedonistic highbrow prominence since the 1930s, thanks to its most popular exponent, the Spanish-born, Havana-raised, former child prodigy classical violinist Xavier Cugat, "Hollywood's most successful Latin."[176] In 1951, Cugat's orchestra was voted the number one "Latin-American Band of the Year."[177] By the early 1950s, the Cocoanut Grove at the Ambassador Hotel still presented society rumba bands and flamenco dancers.[178] In 1952, Xavier Cugat remained one of the top box office draws in the band business, and he exploited his own name value. One jazz writer described the "veteran Xavier Cugat" as "the bandleader cashing in more than any other" on the popularity of Latin rhythms in Los Angeles. In 1954, after ending "a record-breaking run at Ciro's," Cugat and his wife, the singer Abbe Lane, signed a two-picture contract with Columbia Studios, while

Cugat appeared with his band in MGM's *Guys and Dolls* (1955), during the film's Havana nightclub scene.[179] Even as thousands of real-life Mexican Americans and other Latinos descended on Hollywood every month for Latin Holidays, the postwar film industry bombarded Americans with stereotypical depictions of unthreatening Latins. Television, even more than radio and film, helped popularize a tame version of Latin music for a white audience, especially with Desi Arnaz's popular television character Ricky Ricardo, the Cuban singer and bandleader who appeared, from 1951 to 1957, on the number-one-rated situation comedy, *I Love Lucy*. In 1954 on *The Morning Show*, Pupi Campo appeared with host Jack Paar as orchestra leader and comic sidekick, rolling his eyes and delivering one-liners for CBS's national audience, while Xavier Cugat, Abbe Lane, and the dance team of Augie and Margo appeared on *The Ed Sullivan Show* in the mid-1950s.

In Los Angeles, Mexican Americans were particularly well positioned to serve as cultural intermediaries, presenting Latin music to a broader audience. For example, during the early 1950s, the Mexican American society orchestra bandleader Bobby Ramos produced one of the first Latin music television programs, *Latin Cruise*, on Channel 9, an independent English-language station.[180] Broadcasting from the Country Club Hotel in Hollywood, *Latin Cruise* brought viewers aboard the "*S.S. Amigo*," where "Captain" Bobby Ramos, the show's bilingual host, crooned, played maracas, and introduced featured Latina singers and dancers.[181] Beginning in January 1954, a Mexican American former Spanish-language disc jockey, Eddie Rodriguez, produced *Fandango*, the first all-Latin variety show on a major television network. CBS aired the program on prime time through its Los Angeles affiliate station, KNXT Channel 2. Although initially scheduled for only thirteen weeks, the show, hosted by Mauricio Jara, lasted two years, giving exposure to local bandleaders such as Manny Lopez, Eddie Cano, Rudy Macias, Bobby Ramos, Chico Sesma, and Lalo Guerrero, as well as to featured artists, comedians, and other performers. Eddie Rodriguez's efforts in television complemented his efforts in philanthropy, for he would donate his sound equipment, and lend his full support, whenever there was a community event (see figure 42).[182] In the mid-1950s, local independent television stations aired other Latin variety programs, such as *Momentos Alegres*, on which the Pachuco Boogie Boys appeared, and *Latin Time*, hosted by Lupita Beltrán.[183]

Despite such increased media representation, many working Latin jazz

42. Eddie Rodriguez, Chico Sesma, Pete Rodriguez, ca. 1955. COURTESY CHICO SESMA.

bands experienced professional difficulties, and many were short-lived. For instance, the hippest band Richard Barrientos ever played with was the one he formed with Mark Levine, a pianist, arranger, and composer from Boston with degrees from both the Berklee School of Music and Boston University. In 1967, Barrientos was playing timbales and congas at the Kiss Kiss Continental, an obscure jazz club at Pico and Sepulveda boulevards, with Al McKibbon on bass, and Bobby Montez on vibes. Levine had just arrived in town, and since Montez was the only Angeleno Latin musician he had heard of, he checked him out at this West Los Angeles gig. After Levine sat in on piano, he and Barrientos decided to start their own ensemble. In 1968, they recruited Dominican drummer Carmelo García, who had played on most of Mongo Santamaria's pop tunes like "Watermellon Man." They billed themselves under García's name, since his had the most recognition, but the group disbanded after playing throughout 1968 and 1969.

From the latter half of 1967 through the first half of 1969, Barrientos and Tommy Saito were able to quit their day jobs and play music full-time, yet none of the bands they played with broke through to "the big time."[184] The market in Los Angeles was still dominated by either commercial Latin bands or "name" Latin jazz combos, like those of Cal Tjader and George Shearing, who started out in Los Angeles playing at the Zenda Ballroom, but soon began playing in upscale Hollywood venues like the Crescendo and the Interlude. The popular local groups of Manny Lopez and Bobby Montez occasionally opened for the New York, Cuban, and Mexican headliners at the Latin Holidays, but they also played in the traditional Los Angeles Hollywood society mold at the all-Anglo Sunset Strip clubs.

The Latin music urbane civility continued the stylish, classy elegance of the big band period during the eras of barrelhouse rhythm and blues and teeny-bopper rock and roll. Thus, Hortencia Garibay remembered her husband David's tweed, black, and powder blue suits, and "an overcoat that he used to put on with a scarf." As Hortencia recalled, "We used to dress up."[185] Maintaining the swing-era tradition of dancing intricate moves to large orchestras, many of the Hollywood Palladium Latin dancers came from the big band period and were probably jitterbugs in their youth. Earlier, Marshall and Jean Stearns argue, "When the swing era faded in the forties, a blackout of about ten years intervened—from 1945 to 1954—with little or no dancing." By 1955, "with the appearance of rock-and-roll dancing, a revolution in popular taste took place from coast to coast, adding a flexible stance further liberated from European rigidity and accompanied by a more swinging, although rudimentary, music."[186] Given the Stearns' chronology, it seems that the Mexican American Angelenos at the Angelus Hall and the Zenda Ballroom never stopped dancing, even during a decade-long national "blackout."

For the postwar American dancer, the hips have been permanently involved ever since Chubby Checker immortalized the twist in 1960, but Afro-Latin dancing aficionados had been employing this swiveling, swaying motion for years.[187] According to Barrientos, the cha cha chá became especially popular among non-Latinos because it was easier to dance to than the mambo, while Paul Lopez asked, "Isn't it hipper to dance the mambo than the twist?"[188] In 1954, when the mambo attained national popularity, the dance instructor Arthur Murray's wife explained to *Down Beat* readers that the "mambo is performed by dancers according to their individual temperament, and it is quite possible to dance a conventional looking mambo retaining [a] typical, closed, partnership dancing position. But this takes restraint! Most good dancers add break away steps—which means that they break away and separate from each other. They then dance solo facing each other and using various steps and spins. Good mambo dancers are most exciting to watch."[189] As a friend of Tito Puente's re-marked, on watching "the swirling multitude" at the New York Palladium, "the reason the mambo is tremendous is that it's a great exhibition dance —everybody who dances it is a star."[190]

Los Angeles produced many skilled dancers, and just as the Latin music scene provided spaces for Mexican Americans and other Latinos to express a non-Anglo sexuality and sensibility, it also allowed them to claim visi-bility in the public sphere, and to contribute to urban culture. For instance, Club Virginia's hosted mambo contests, with Mambo Maxi as master of ceremonies, which drew ten to twenty couples competing for albums or cash prizes.[191] Jaime Corral also recalled that

> at the Zenda Ballroom and the Club Havana, the couples used to circle the perimeter of the entire dance floor, and the ones that were not dancing were just watching the parade. Some people were dancing [in the middle], but the regulars, the ones who were really good, were the ones that were showing off. And then everybody knew who was a good dancer and who wasn't, so you knew who to pick as a partner. It was great fun.[192]

Displaying their originality and creativity, the Zenda and Club Havana couples were "doing their own stuff."[193] These Latin dancers understood, as Pérez Prado did, "that Americans would enjoy the mambo even more if they were less self-conscious." Prado explained that Americans "could all invent steps of their own . . . so long as they do their steps to the rhythm. That way each dancer is a creative interpreter."[194] Mexican Americans certainly adopted the Afro-Caribbean mambo, just like they had done ear-lier with the African American jitterbug, and they added their own distinct spin to both dances. For example, while the Latin dancers in New York City began on the two, or the second beat of the four-beat measure, in Los Angeles they came in on the one, or the first beat, the downbeat. Likewise, New York dance couples would dip on the four, but in Los Angeles they would dip on the two.[195] For Tommy Saito, transplanted New Yorkers were some of the best dancers at Club Virginia's.[196]

In 1966, New York's Palladium Ballroom closed, and Joe Cuba's Latin boogaloo song, "Bang Bang," reigned at the top of the national *Billboard* charts for ten weeks, thus signaling the definitive end of the mambo's dynasty.[197] A "Latin Soul" movement crystallized in the late 1960s, but the Latin boogaloo, the pachanga, and the shingaling marked a transition in

Latin music from the widespread popularity of the mambo and cha cha chá years to a lull in public interest. Tito Puente argued that these new styles did not last long because they had no corresponding dances.[198] As Puente expounded, with "any rhythm that comes out, if you don't have a dance to it, that rhythm dies. That's why Latin music has always maintained itself, because there's a beautiful dance to it . . . couples get together and they dance."[199] Musician and arranger Ray Santos surmised that after 1965 large orchestras became too expensive, but the new, smaller bands could not achieve "the excitement, volume, and power" of the big mambo bands.[200] The New York disc jockey Dick "Ricardo" Sugar recalled that, as aging Latin dancers began raising families, they stopped going out dancing. The mambo cohort "got older and got away from it," and the new generation preferred rock, which had "infiltrated" Latin music.[201] Tito Puente stated flatly, "Rock and roll came, then Latin music started dying."[202]

A similar shift occurred in Los Angeles, where even the Hollywood society Latin tradition could not sustain itself in the face of rock music. In 1963, the veteran jazz concert impresario Gene Norman sold his Sunset Strip club, the Crescendo, to new owners, who also owned the Whiskey a Go Go. Rene Bloch broke up his Latin band in 1965, not only to spend more time with his Mexican American wife and their baby, but also because he became disillusioned with the music industry in the wake of Beatlemania. Richard Barrientos married his second wife, Elaine, in 1965. Elaine had been born in Kansas to a Spanish father and a Mexican mother, but she was raised in urban central Los Angeles, on Vermont Avenue between Pico and Adams boulevards. By this time, Tommy Saito had married Gloria Chavez, a third-generation Mexican American from an East Los Angeles family. Fittingly, the two met when Gloria saw Tommy playing percussion with Bobby Montez's Latin band. Saito dropped out of the music business in the late 1960s in order to spend more time with his wife and their Mexican American–Japanese American son. On the West Coast, the Latin boogaloo and the pachanga, coupled with increasing competition from rock and roll for the leisure time and spending money of the baby-boom generation, slowed down the popularity of Latin music.[203] By the late 1960s, Chico Sesma could no longer consistently afford to book bands at the Hollywood Palladium, or ensure a large audience turnout, and he finally stopped his Latin Holiday shows in 1973.

Ultimately, Mexican Americans were not immune to the modern Hollywood culture of style over substance, as they negotiated between pandering to Anglo fantasies of carefree "Latins" and introducing Caribbean rhythms to the masses. Because of their unique social location, they could be found from one extreme of this cultural spectrum to the other, wavering between staid Hollywood and saucy Afro-Cuban styles. From the society rumba orchestras of the 1940s to the vibraphone quintets of the 1950s, Latin music in Los Angeles gave certain Mexican American singers and musicians mainstream exposure, modest crossover success, and some upward mobility. At the Zenda Ballroom, Club Havana, Club Virginia's, and the Hollywood Palladium, these performers, along with the many male and female "Latin" dancers, insisted on their own run of the city, in the face of segregation, as part of a more urbane version of the city's multicultural urban civility. Disc jockeys, concert promoters, and television producers like Joe Garcia, Chico Sesma, Candelario Mendoza, Eddie Rodriguez, and Bobby Ramos provided employment, recognition, and positive media representation for Mexican Americans and other Latinos, thereby refuting an Anglo-defined cultural identity as uneducated, expendable Mexican workers, while dispelling demeaning stereotypes and serving as professional role models. In addition, they all ensured that improvisational Afro-*Caribeño* music and dance would remain a permanent part of Mexican American expressive culture. In short, with their considerable cultural contributions, they had their mojo working, from the barrio to Hollywood. As in the swing, rhythm and blues, and rock and roll scenes, Mexican Americans showed once again that, given the opportunity, they would circumvent the limited roles assigned to them by the dominant culture.

alternate takes and
political generations

If a person finds something that they're really good at, and they can utilize it . . . it lifts them up.
—Anthony Ortega, interview by author

When I write music and I've got five instruments, I interlock the harmonies. In order for one of the inner voices not to repeat the same notes, I shoot 'em down to another note, and that instrument shifts up to the other note, so there will be contrary motion . . . So they're complementing, and always fluctuating. . . . Like in harmony it's a weave.
—Paul Lopez, interview by author, June 18, 1999

Musicians aren't born. If you want to be a good one, you have to study. . . . And it's a fine, fine goal to have in life: to surpass your teacher.
—Don Tosti, interview by Rick Mandlebaum and Susan Terrazini,
Palms Springs radio station program, 1997 (tape in author's possession,
courtesy Don Tosti)

But I should have even studied more, because I realized that there were certain teachers there that are dead now. There's no way to study with them.
—Paul Lopez, interview by author, June 18, 1999

This guided tour of Mexican American generation Angelenos, which began in the mid-1930s, has reached its final stop. There are no star maps or Hollywood endings. The book's narrative ends as the young Chicano political generation gained ascendancy. Historical periodization is a useful tool of the historian's craft, although it can be, like the political generation paradigm, imprecise. Still, as Bob Dylan sang in 1964, the times they were a-changin', and by the summer of 1967 rock and roll had become, simply, rock, as in folk rock, or psychedelic rock, within the context of an increasingly commercialized hippie counterculture, and an increasingly radical leftist protest politics. In late 1967, the Young Chicanos for Community Action organization became the Brown Berets. In March 1968, more than one thousand youths boycotted predominantly Mexican American Eastside high schools to protest high dropout rates and dilapidated facilities, and to demand more Chicano counselors, teachers, and history courses in the Chicano student walkouts, or "blowouts."[1] In April 1968, the assassination of Martin Luther King Jr. ignited rioting in over one hundred American cities. Lalo Guerrero documented the political events of the year from a Mexican American point of view, composing "El corrido de Cesar Chávez," about the "great Mexican," and "El homenaje a Roberto Kennedy," about the slain presidential hopeful.[2] In 1969, Thee Midnighters would release their timely recording, "Chicano Power," the Mexican American rock band the V.I.P.'s would change its name to El Chicano, and *Billboard* would change the heading of its "R & B" chart to "Soul."

By the late 1960s, it was obvious that not all members of the greater ethnic Mexican community had achieved social, economic, and educational advancement, and that, as Mario García notes, "poverty continued to coexist with progress. Mexican Americans continued to face discrimination and slower rates of mobility."[3] Nevertheless, the Chicano generation produced not only skilled professionals and college graduates but also activists who participated in social movements that shook American culture to its core. Undoubtedly the young Chicanos of the 1960s learned much from their Mexican American generation parents and elders, who faced life's highs and lows while taking part in America's wars, politics, and pastimes. These experiences forever changed Mexican Americans, and Mexican Americans forever changed the feelings, the flavor, and the face of American culture.

Just as musicians can record alternate takes of the same song to create fresh interpretations, historians can draw different conclusions from the same sources, or offer alternate explanations for the same phenomena. For example, Douglas Monroy charts two "scenarios" or "trajectories" for Mexican Los Angeles and "Mexican America," analyzing "how different strains" like deportation, integration, cultural retention, cultural assimilation, oppositional assertiveness, tradition, and modernity "led to often contradictory, or independent, historical flows."[4] My take on the Mexican American generation rethinks Chicano music history and Chicano historiography by putting this scholarship in dialogue with African American studies, Latino studies, American studies, and, more obliquely, Mexican and Latin American studies. Moreover, neither the language of assimilation nor the language of nationalism can adequately describe an urban civility that incorporated black and pan-Latino music and culture, just as neither histories of Los Angeles that ignore or undervalue ethnic Mexicans nor those that focus solely on East Los Angeles tell the entire story of the city.

Examining the relationship of wartime and postwar Mexican Americans to the culture industries as often critical consumers and producers of popular culture deepens this book's generational portrait of their varied experiences and complex identities. Indeed, the Mexican American Angelenos of this period extended earlier traditions of cultural mixing while forming new survival tactics and creative expressions. José Antonio Robles Cáhero points out that Latin Americans have experienced over four hundred years of religious, political, linguistic, artistic, culinary, and sartorial syncretism. Of course, Mexico has produced a particularly rich history of *música mestiza*, from the blending of baroque Spanish and indigenous American elements to Afro-Mexicano styles like the son jarocho, Cuban imports like the danzón, bolero, and mambo, and *norteamericano* imports like the foxtrot, swing, and rock and roll. As Robles Cáhero posits, there are multiple Mexicos, and thus multiple Mexican identities.[5] Within Chicano history, George Sánchez asks us to consider "the possibility of multiple identities and contradictory positions," arguing that the Mexican custom of cultural blending and creation incorporated adaptations from African Americans and others in multicultural Los Angeles. In Sánchez's estimation, Mexican American culture is neither "a way station on the inevitable path toward assimilation" nor a "U-turn" back to some pure Mexican identity.[6]

Despite the seemingly inherent tension between multiple identities and contradictory positions, on the one hand, and a unique expressive culture, on the other, in reality, musical and stylistic forms were as diverse as "the" Chicano community. Thus, the late 1930s Eastside big bands performed the pop swing hits of the day, as well as a few boleros, rancheras, and congas, while the early 1940s pachuco/pachuca style defied the status quo, declared difference, and asserted a new identity. Yet these features were shared, in varying degrees, by all members of the Mexican American generation, not just by pachucos, pachucas, cholos, and cholas. As Paul Lopez explained, talented arrangers adapt someone else's composition for their particular orchestra, giving it their personal touch and making it their own. Likewise, Mexican American Angelenos borrowed, transformed, and parodied various styles in each era in order to speak to their specific situations. Lopez also noted that "the top orchestras locked into a sustained and deep groove—they swung!"[7] Hence, Mexican Americans had their mojo working throughout the period, and they understood, as Ralph Ellison argues for African Americans, "that the world is ever unexplored, and that while a complete mastery of life is mere illusion, the real secret of the game is to make life swing."[8]

In Don Tosti's opinion, "most musical 'geniuses' borrow from their influences, their peers that they like, then they put it all together. They fuse it in their style."[9] In similar fashion, Mexican Americans created an eclectic style, one which encompassed jazz musicians like Paul Lopez, Eddie Cano, Charlie Mota, and Ruben Leon playing Latin jazz with bandleader Miguelito Valdés in the late 1940s; the Pachuco Boogie Boys effortlessly easing from jazz to Latin to rhythm and blues, with Don Tosti storytelling in Spanish and caló, Raul Diaz scatting, and Eddie Cano pounding out Latin piano montuno vamps; and Lalo Guerrero singing Spanish, English, and caló lyrics with swing, guaracha, and boogie woogie rhythms. The Mexican American style also included the musical versatility of singer, saxophonist, and sex symbol Gil Bernal, and the musical virtuosity of saxophonist, clarinetist, and flautist Anthony Ortega. By the late 1950s, Mexican Americans had assimilated several influences, all of which merged in Southern California, from Anglo cowboy and rockabilly tunes to Mexican folk songs and popular black styles. By the late 1960s, they had absorbed other cultural strands like those of Pérez Prado, René Touzet, Jesse Belvin, the Beatles, Motown, and James Brown, as part of thriving Latin music and brown-eyed soul scenes. Taken as a whole, these Mexican American musicians, singers, songwriters, composers, arrangers, and entertainers created a body of work, a songbook that articulated an emergent expressive culture. Considering the music they danced to and the company they kept, many second- and third-generation Mexican Americans responded as much to African American culture as to their ethnic "parent" culture or the dominant culture, like those who considered the swing played by black bands "their" music, those who gravitated toward black R & B artists, and those who loyally listened to vocal harmony "oldies" across generations. As I have sought to demonstrate in the preceding pages, Mexican Americans' multifaceted cultural productions and affiliations evolved over time in a politicized context of racism and anticommunism; patriotism and propriety; law and order.

The expressive practices and small-business infrastructure associated with the irrepressible swing, R & B, rock and roll, and Latin music scenes complicate pessimistic assessments of postwar Southern California that overemphasize the domination of politicians and the police. These successive popular scenes resisted social segregation and highbrow reification by fostering contact and comprehension, as well as musical and physical expression, in public spaces. Yet tensions between Mexican Americans, blacks, whites, and Asian Americans due to prejudice, and to uneven rates of economic, social, and spatial mobility, complicate optimistic assessments that overemphasize the resistance of subcultures and youth cultures. The simultaneity of fellowship and friction qualifies both pessimistic and optimistic historical interpretations. A pragmatic reading, on the other hand, suggests that urban dance scenes brought people together without completely erasing personal prejudice or the institutional racism that privileged whites and some Mexican Americans over African Americans. Such an interpretation acknowledges internal dissension, but still recognizes that people could be bound together by music, dance, car culture, and clothing styles more than they were separated by race or class.

A pragmatic approach illuminates the full story, warts and all, but still recognizes the power of music to provide not only the soundtrack to a shared expressive culture, but also an impetus to question the patronizing moral values and divisive ethnic notions of the status quo. Nevertheless, although the city's urban civility produced a proliferation of far-flung alternative public spaces, it was continually compromised by internal and external counterveiling forces. Without romanticizing interethnic and interclass cultural sharing, scholars can gauge the transgressive potential of musical dialogues within and across community boundaries. Without overestimating the control of the elites or the opposition of the people, we can better understand the practical possibilities and limitations of popular music and dance, as well as "the ways in which audiences, through their own agency, both challenge and reproduce the dominant ideology."[10]

For a time, postwar liberals retained the Progressive reformers' faith in the ability of social engineering to transform society, as city leaders tried to engage with, and invest in, the life experiences of young Angelenos. Unfortunately, musical uplift went hand in hand with municipal regulation and punitive policing. In response to the legal challenges; the social, economic, and political gains; and the cultural incursions made by racial groups, local authorities attempted to maintain a sense of order by monitoring and disciplining the musicians, dancers, and listeners who navigated the topography of metropolitan Los Angeles. In contrast, social dancing, music education, and grass-roots entrepreneurial activity more successfully brought more music participation to more people, connecting an often fragmented populace in its leisure. Music teachers, record store owners, disc jockeys, concert promoters, nightclub impresarios, and professional performers more fully realized the stated goal of the Los Angeles Music Bureau's programs. Ultimately, the diverse, street-oriented urban culture represented a more populist public sphere than the one envisioned by the city councilmen, county supervisors, and cultural institution apparatchiks who privileged classical symphonies and choral sings when increasing numbers of Angelenos wanted raunchy rockers, romantic ballads, and mellow instrumentals. These competing visions of Los Angeles, from above and below, both hinged on the cultural influence of the region's two largest racial minorities. Yet due to the logical imperatives and racialized rewards of a "possessive investment in whiteness," the dialectic between these two models of civil society developed without reconciliation, without a synthesis between antithetical worldviews.[11]

In sum, from the swing era to the mambo/rock and roll/Motown era, Mexican Americans sustained multicultural democratic spaces and thereby changed the racial geography of a segregated city. The book's five chapters can be read as tales of cross-cultural creativity and interracial improvisation, of cooperation and conflict, dignity and bigotry, success and failure, consent and dissent, mainstream morality and subcultural subversion. They are snapshots from both the cutting edge and the bandwagon of popular culture, from both the barrio and the suburb. They tell of dreams deferred and attained, as Mexican Americans rolled with the punches, but never threw in the towel. These chapters create a cumulative biography of individuals, neighborhoods, and communities, as Mexican Americans indelibly imprinted the city and region with their smooth sensibility and style. From pachuco boogie on 78s through Ritchie Valens on television, film, and the pop charts, the Eastside Sound rockers and soul singers on television and the radio, and the many Latin music variety shows on television, Mexican Americans increased their media visibility and profile. They followed their ambitions and challenged disparaging stereotypes while working in a black-and-white, bottom-line entertainment industry.

In the end, the Mexican American generation musicians learned the hard way that the music industry can be fickle, and fame elusive. For example, Chico Sesma noted, referring to Paul Lopez, that the "masters that come to be recognized in their lifetime are very few."[12] By the same token, Paul Lopez called Anthony Ortega "a real genius. Tony is like a legend, but nobody knows him" in the United States. Lopez also argued that saxophonist Ruben Leon "was a very talented arranger," and that when Leon left music to pursue a PhD, it "was L.A.'s loss because he didn't write anymore." Don Tosti said of Ruben Leon, "He's a greater musician than Eddie Cano, but he didn't make it. Leon's a saxophonist, he's a clarinetist, a flautist, a great pianist, and a great arranger."[13] Finally, Chico Sesma contended that "Ray Vasquez is a very fine singer and he's very typical of so many that are very talented but have never made it. . . . He should have been very successful, but it passed him by. He gained some prominence, but not nearly the level that he deserved" as "a good musician" and "a very professional person."[14]

Like the musicians in this study, the everyday Mexican Americans in wartime and postwar Southern California stuck their feet into closing doors, and pried open windows of opportunity, maximizing any and all advantages. The larger society did not always allow them to do what they wanted, and because of unfair hiring practices and loan considerations, Mexican Americans did not cash in on the postwar economy as much as the working- and middle-class white and white ethnic members of the federally subsidized New Deal–World War II generation. Nonetheless, many Mexican Americans used their family-wage union jobs and instrumental pink-collar salaries to access new ways of life based on home ownership, and, increasingly, suburbanization, as they sought safer neighborhoods with newer public schools for their baby-boom children. Mexican Americans partially or selectively acculturated into the dominant American culture, making their mark and excelling in a variety of different pursuits, yet they did not fit neatly into traditional assimilation models, and they always maintained connections with Mexican—and Latin American—culture, even in dispersed communities.

In the 1930s and 1940s, Mexican American middle-class leaders espoused an ideology of cultural pluralism, insisting that their people could enjoy full acceptance and integration as first-class U.S. citizens while retaining their Mexican cultural heritage and ethnic identity. By 1954, however, the League of United Latin American Citizens, the Mexican American generation's longest-running organization, was less focused on preserving Mexican folklore, history, and national holidays. Instead, seeing themselves as the vanguard of their people, LULAC members "equated Americanism with middle-class success" and their fairly high standard of living fueled their "desire to 'keep up with the Jones' [sic].' "[15] As Neil Foley argues, in order to prove how Americanized they were, LULACers played baseball, ate hot dogs, spoke English, voted and got elected to office, used the court system, actively opposed Mexican immigration, and excluded Mexican citizens from membership in their organization. Foley therefore deduces that some middle-class members of the Mexican American generation were "becoming Hispanic" by making a Faustian pact with whiteness for the promise of privileges and benefits.[16]

Mexican Americans certainly assimilated many aspects of American culture, but they were never granted full admission into the whiteness country club. They still faced racial discrimination and police harassment, they were still perceived as dark, exotic others by both Anglos and white ethnics, and therefore they still ran into, or were reminded of, their Mexicanness, which is to say, their *indio-mestizaje*. Moreover, the culture war that began in the 1930s was also a class war, and by the end of the period many Mexican Americans were still tracked in school toward the bottom rungs of the socioeconomic ladder, and their schools were more segregated than ever. For example, by 1967, of the 544 schools in the Los Angeles Unified School District, 218 were composed of more than 50 percent students of color. Of these racially segregated schools, 95 were predominantly black, and 69 were predominantly ethnic Mexican.[17] The working-class labor activists and political radicals could not eradicate structural inequality, individually or collectively, and this was even less possible for the educationalists, cultural pluralists, and success stories of the Mexican American generation. Since the 1930s, white city councilmen, mayors, downtown businessmen, and urban planners had viewed both the inner city and the eastern city as "blighted" zones where laissez-faire capitalism could construct its freeways, locate its factories, and dump its waste. By 1968, both areas were suffering from a postwar period of not-so-benign neglect. My narrative ends at this moment, in the aftermath of a bloody riot, in the midst of a doomed war, and on the eve of an austere de-industrialization.

In this book, I have tried to plumb the depths and span the breadth of Mexican American expressive culture. Popular music and dance engage the senses and tap into a deep spirituality, even in the commercialized, commodified world of recording studios, radio stations, nightclubs, dance halls, ballrooms, and auditoriums. Notwithstanding some concert-seating and listening-only venues, the glue that kept the multicultural urban civility together over the years was the act of dancing, of bodies moving together, of elbows rubbing. Moreover, as postwar Progressives discovered, social dancing can be a very athletic, positive form of recreation, and not just for at-risk teens. Young and old, Mexican Americans regenerated the mind, body, and spirit in weekly rituals of group dancing. They coped with the stress of urban life through music, dance, and other forms of self-expression. Along this path to relaxation and inner calm in the face of obstacles, they also found a resourceful resolve to push through and succeed, to find a calling beyond, or at least a temporary break from, mere survival laboring at the bottom of a cold-blooded economy.

As Gil Bernal put it, "I'm not Beethoven, or Dizzy Gillespie, or Duke Ellington. I'm just a guy from the neighborhood who got a break and has made a living playing the music that he wanted to play."[18] Anthony Ortega said, of his generation's diverse cultural productions, "If everybody felt the same way, it would be boring. It's good to have all these different kinds of styles . . . as long as it's pretty good music, it all has its place. As long as it's honest, and [the musicians] feel it."[19] Hortencia Garibay simply stated, "[Music] makes me very happy, and I feel alive when I listen to it."[20] Similarly, María Olivas Alvarez succinctly described music and dancing as "something for the soul."[21] Candelario Mendoza, after noting the importance of romantic ballads and dance music in Mexican culture, concluded that "music and dance speak to us."[22]

Just as Mexican American, African American, and Afro-Latin cultures challenged prohibitions against race-mixing and allegedly lascivious dancing, this study questions the supposed superiority of Western industrial society in general, and puritanical white American society in particular.

Although focused on people who created modern urban culture, this book has implicitly argued for an exhilarating, humorous, and emotionally satisfying impulse, which some might label "primitive," but which really stood in opposition to both highbrow preferences and theories of non-white inferiority. Furthermore, despite an academic disciplinary privileging of written sources, the book is enriched by oral history methodology. Likewise, as this conclusion's epigraphs indicate, the Mexican American generation members appreciated the importance of music education. They also valued an oral tradition of informal neighborhood instruction, hands-on music lessons from family members, and the passing on of certain songs to the next generation.

With my research, I have tried to re-create the past, reconnect the present, and inform the future. Telling these stories, from everyday people to avant-garde artists, expands our cumulative knowledge of Chicano expressive culture, Los Angeles history, and the ongoing struggle to forcibly realize America's stated democratic principles of freedom, equality, and justice. There is much to be learned from the Mexican American generation's drive for full enfranchisement and empowerment, and from its expressive cultural production, which symbolized what James Diego Vigil describes as "the Mexican/Chicano mystique."[23]

Regarding this mystique, it could be argued that the members of the Mexican American generation continued an ancient spiritual emphasis on the need for men and women "to develop their full potential in terms of personal character and artistic talent, all with a keen awareness of man's place in the total universe." From this perspective, they improvised variations on "the central theme in Mexican and Native American life, before the European invasion," which "was the desire to gain direct knowledge of" what Jack Forbes calls "the Great Creative Power," "and its manifestations, in every way possible." In its ultimate form, this mysterious foundational source, called *Ometéotl* by the Aztecs, "*Wakan Tanka* by the Sioux and *Ketche Manito* by the Algonkian peoples . . . is a process of creativity, of potentiality, of unfolding."[24] With my alternate take, therefore, I have sought to understand how the city's neighborhoods, music scenes, and culture industries reflected and informed civil society, and how Mexican Americans fought for their rights and found their own great creative power, or mojo.

NOTES

Introduction

1   *Racialization* describes the sociohistorical process by which racial categories are created, inhabited, and—when people of color, along with antiracist
whites, challenge the racial assumptions and theories behind everyday "common sense" ideology—transformed or destroyed. Race is a powerful social
construct, one which signifies supposedly innate differences through cultural
representations and symbolic stereotypes, and which structures institutional
inequality by reorganizing and redistributing resources; Omi and Winant,
Racial Formation.

2   On the Mexican American political generation, see Mario García, *Mexican
Americans*, 3, 5. See also Richard García, "Mexican American Mind"; Richard
García, *Rise of the Mexican-American Middle Class*; and Gutíerrez, *Walls and
Mirrors.*

3   The music and lyrics of "Got My Mojo Working" are credited to composer
Preston Foster, but Muddy Waters appropriated the song after hearing Ann
Cole perform it live while on tour with her. Jim Morrison used the word *mojo*
in the Doors' hit song "L.A. Woman" in 1971. B. B. King and Buddy Guy each
recorded a version of "Got My Mojo Working" in 1977, as did Conway Twitty
in 1987. Mike Myers helped popularize the term *mojo* to the world in his 1997
and 1999 *Austin Powers* films, where it was used to signify the lead character's
libido and sex appeal. The British music magazine *MOJO* has kept the word,
and its historical connection to popular music, in circulation, while "Got My
Mojo Working" has been recorded by new generations of artists throughout
the United States and Europe.

4   *American Heritage Dictionary*, 1132.

5   Major, *From Juba to Jive*, 307. On mojo as "personal magic" that alters "the

fated progression of events to suit one's desires," that is "imbued with . . . the need of indentured peoples to take some control over their lives," see Hopkinson, *Mojo*, vii.

6 The ancient Hawaiians "taught that when the *mana* (personal power) is strong and people accept themselves as the powerful beings that they are—all things are possible"; Willis and Lee, *Tales from the Night Rainbow*, 20.

7 On the arts of hoodoo and the blues, and the parallel roles they play in African American cultural survival and revival, see Schroeder, "Rootwork."

8 *Trickeration* is defined in Calloway, *New Cab Calloway's Hepster's Dictionary*, 261. Also, in African American vernacular, "laying tricks" means casting spells.

9 On black zoot suiters as "modern-day Stagolees," see Kelley, *Race Rebels*, 66. On the pachucos who fought white servicemen during the zoot suit riots as "heroes in a race war," see Moore, *Homeboys*, 55–74. On the comparison between El Pachuco and Stagger Lee, see Daniels, "Los Angeles Zoot," 109.

10 On "range of variation," see Peñalosa, "Toward an Operational Definition," 1.

11 For an overview of pop culture theories, see Tatum, "Definitions and Theoretical Approaches"; and Jenkins, McPherson, and Shattuc, "Defining Popular Culture."

12 On "double consciousness," see DuBois, "Our Spiritual Strivings," 45.

13 On certain cultural expressions that seemed to help African Americans acculturate deeper into the larger society actually containing elements of cultural revitalization, see Levine, *Black Culture and Black Consciousness*, and "Unpredictable Past," 11. On African Americans responding to racism and the appropriation of their music by turning inward to their musical roots, especially the blues, see LeRoi Jones, *Blues People*; Charles Keil, *Urban Blues*; Levine, "Jazz and American Culture," 187. The blues and jazz music emerged from a long history of black cultural production in the United States. See also, e.g., Stuckey, *Slave Culture*; Floyd, *Power of Black Music*; and Roberts, *Black Music*.

14 On cool as "studied indifference," see MacAdams, *Birth of the Cool*, 56.

15 On the history of Los Angeles, see, e.g., Caughey and Caughey, *Los Angeles*; Klein and Schiesl, *Twentieth Century Los Angeles*; Davis, *City of Quartz*, and *Magical Urbanism*; Kurashige, *Shifting Grounds*; Widener, "Something Else"; Avila, *Popular Culture*; Sides, *L.A. City Limits*; Deverell, *Whitewashed Adobe*; and Willard, "Nuestra Los Angeles." On the history of Mexicano-Chicano Los Angeles, see, e.g., Castillo, *Los Angeles Barrio*; Romo, *East Los Angeles*; Acuña, *Community under Siege*; Sánchez, *Becoming Mexican American*; and Acuña, *Anything but Mexican*.

16 On music genres, see Tucker, *Swing Shift*, 17; LeRoi Jones, *Blues People*, 142–65; Frith, *Performing Rites*, 75–95; and Nagus, *Music Genres*, 14–30.

17 Marx, *Eighteenth Brumaire*, 15.

1. The Swing Era

1 Billy Cardenas's mother attended the Bowery Ballroom in the 1930s; Guevara, interview by author.

2 Henry Anton Steig, "Alligators' Idol: Benny Goodman," *New Yorker* 13, April 17, 1937, 30.

3 Simon, *Big Bands*, 207.

4 Steig, "Alligators' Idol," 32.

5 Stowe, *Swing Changes*, 7; George Spink, "King of Swing Reigned from Chicago: Benny Goodman Ascended Throne Here Fifty Years Ago," *Chicago Sun-Times*, November 10, 1985, Sunday Show sec., 6; "Biography," bennygood man.com/about/biography.html (accessed April 12, 2006).

6 As Sherrie Tucker notes, "canonization continues to reproduce careful and strategic decisions made by white-owned recording companies"; Tucker, *Swing Shift*, 15, 14.

7 On the antiblack admission policies at the Palomar Ballroom, see Eastman, "Pitchin' up a Boogie," 80; and "Racial Prejudice and Discrimination," in Bresee Foundation Community Stories, www.bresee.org/biministories/pages/racialdiscrimination.html (accessed April 12, 2006). Information on Mexican Americans being welcome at the Palomar from Sesma interview, August 23, 2004. On Goodman and Krupa's ethnic backgrounds, see "American Jazz Artists," *Common Ground* 7 (Autumn 1946): 59, 56.

8 Vince Ramírez, interview by author.

9 Sesma, interview by author, September 4, 1998; Sesma, interview by author, September 1, 2004.

10 Stowe, *Swing Changes*, 245, 143, 142.

11 Erenberg, *Swingin' the Dream*, 56, 41; Erenberg, "Things to Come," 277. Ralph Ellison calls African American music and culture an agent of racial democracy. See Ellison, *Shadow and Act*, 256.

12 On Duke Ellington's elegance and dignity, see Erenberg, *Swingin' the Dream*, 113. As Ingrid Monson argues, "Dignity can function as a strategy of self-respect and assertion"; Monson, "Problem," 419.

13 Porter, *What Is This Thing Called Jazz?*, 31.

14 On Ellington vis-à-vis the more rhythmically adventurous bands, see Erenberg, *Swingin' the Dream*, 110–11. Fletcher Henderson's New York big bands were also rhythmically driving.

15 Stearns and Stearns, *Jazz Dance*, 323, 329, 325, 330.

16 On the phrase "framework in time," see Evans, liner notes, *Kind of Blue*. In musicians' slang, "cutting" typically refers to the back-and-forth riffs of instrumentalists dueling in one-on-one contests, but I also use it to refer to the inspired steps of dancers, and to the interplay between soloists on the bandstand and dancers on the floor.

17 The basic jitterbug step had existed in Harlem, and was called the hop, long before Charles Lindbergh "hopped" from New York to Paris in 1927; Stearns and Stearns, *Jazz Dance*, 328, 323. The myth that the Lindy Hop was named after Lindbergh's transatlantic flight has been commonly accepted as fact.

18 Stearns and Stearns, *Jazz Dance*, 324, 320.

19 Malone, "Jazz Music," 286, 288.

20 Lunceford, *Lunceford Special*.

21 Stearns and Stearns, *Jazz Dance*, 330, 329.

22 Quoted in Burns, *Jazz*, episode 5, *Swing*.

23 Erenberg, *Swingin' the Dream*, 112–13.

24 As scholarly studies of African American expressive culture contend, African Americans' urge to shine, or show off, is always enacted in a communal context where observers become participants, and where individual accomplishments elevate the entire group. In particular, Caponi makes a compelling case for the significance on American culture of an African American aesthetic that makes life swing and jump, from black music and dance to verbal virtuosity and public displays of bodily style, especially strutting one's stuff in nonconformist hairstyles and clothes. The continuum of African American cultural expressions, from the shuffling ring shout to the present, reflects an artistic aesthetic, "a set of techniques and practices," and an articulation of unifying, dignifying values, ethics, and beliefs that subvert the dominant culture. See Caponi, *Signifyin(g)*, 1, 4–8, 12, 30. See also Gay and Baber, *Expressively Black*; Wallace, *Black Popular Culture*; and White and White, *Stylin'*.

25 Malone, "Keep to the Rhythm," 223, 227, 229.

26 In April 1940, the swing big bandleader Jimmie Lunceford held a concert at the Shrine Auditorium, where, according to one sensationalistic story, "a rival promoter had hired several dozen Mexicans to break up the afternoon date," resulting in a disturbance that called for 25 police officers and left seven people injured. See Jack Hirshberg, "Six Thousand Jitterbugs Riot at Lunceford Date: Negroes, Filipinos and Mexicans Hammer at Each Other and Smash L.A. Auditorium after Imbibing Free Liquor," *Metronome*, April 1940, 10; also quoted in Stowe, *Swing Changes*, 31. Trumpeter Gerald Wilson, who performed that night in the Lunceford Orchestra, simply recalled that "they had so many people they had to stop the dance." See Bryant et al., *Central Avenue Sounds*, 325–26. It is doubtful that one of the greatest acts of the swing era, the Jimmie Lunceford Orchestra, a "jazzy dance band" known for "light, bouncy blues swing" tunes in intricate arrangements, tight, imaginative ensemble interplay, "precision in performance, excellence in dress, and a sophisticated, though humorous, stage show," incited any violent outburst. See Wynn, *All Music Guide*, 430–31.

27 "Leaders Protest Dance Hall Ban," *California Eagle*, May 30, 1940. Yet in 1940

the LAPD let 20 robed Ku Klux Klansmen march through the streets of downtown to the steps of city hall, passing out propaganda leaflets along the way. See "Charges Mayor Thinks More of Klan Rights Than Curbing Hate," *California Eagle*, May 16, 1940. Also quoted in Eastman, "Pitchin' up a Boogie," 80.

28 Bryant et al., *Central Avenue Sounds*, 199; "No More Swing Street," *California Eagle*, May 16, 1940.

29 My use of the term *civility* is inspired by Roger Keil, who writes about the "contradictory civility" of Los Angeles, where workers of color began "to claim spaces of alternative civility" after the 1992 uprising, building "a civil society from below" through "a network of democratic self-organization"; Keil, *Los Angeles*, 34–35.

30 Pitt and Pitt, *Los Angeles A to Z*, 56.

31 Records of the Federal Home Loan Bank Board of the Home Owners Loan Corporation, City Survey File, Los Angeles, 1939, Neighborhood D-53, box 74, RG 195. National Archives, Washington, D.C.; as quoted in Lipsitz, "Land of a Thousand Dances," 270; Lipsitz, "Cruising," 137; Lipsitz, *Possessive Investment*, 6; and George Sánchez, "What's Good for Boyle Heights," 138–39.

32 U.S. Bureau of the Census, as quoted in Fisher, *Problem*, 6–7.

33 George Sánchez, "What's Good for Boyle Heights," 137.

34 Sesma, interview by author, September 4, 1998. Brooklyn Avenue is now César Chávez Avenue.

35 Tosti, interview by author, August 20, 1998.

36 Fisher, *Problem*, 6–7.

37 "Juvenile Delinquency and Poor Housing in the Los Angeles Metropolitan Area," prepared under the direction of Executive Board, Los Angeles County Coordinating Councils, December 1937, John Anson Ford Papers, box 33, folder B III, 7b (5), Huntington Library.

38 Fisher, *Problem*, 6.

39 Sesma, interview by author, September 4, 1998.

40 Information on Filipinos in Boyle Heights from Tosti, interview by author, August 20, 1998. Information on Chinese and Italians in Boyle Heights from Lee-Sung, "Boyle Heights." On Italians in Boyle Heights, see also George Sánchez, "What's Good for Boyle Heights," 137.

41 Sesma, interview by author, September 4, 1998.

42 Ibid.; Sesma, interview by author, September 1, 2004; Sesma, interview by author, April 7, 2005; Lopez, interview by author, September 2, 1998.

43 The Hollenbeck Junior High School figures only add up to 89 percent, the Stevenson Junior High figures to 81 percent, the 1936 Roosevelt High figures to 96 percent, and the 1938 Roosevelt High figures to 86 percent; Gustafson, "Ecological Analysis," 67, 58, 122.

44 Lee-Sung, "Boyle Heights," 2.

45 Sesma, interview by author, September 4, 1998.

46 Tosti, interview by author, August 20, 1998.

47 John Tumpak, "Chico Sesma: L.A.'s Latin Jazz Pioneer," *L.A. Jazz Scene* 210 (March 2005): 3; Sesma, interview by author, September 4, 1998; Lopez, interview by author, September 2, 1998; Sesma, interview by author, April 7, 2005.

48 Lopez, interview by author, September 2, 1998.

49 Tosti, interview by author, August 20, 1998.

50 Sesma, interview by author, September 4, 1998.

51 "Los Angeles Neighborhood Music School Fills Need in Community," *Southwestern Musician* 15 no. 10 (June 1949): 7; Sesma, interview by author, September 4, 1998; Lopez, interview by author, September 2, 1998.

52 In the 1940s the board of directors hired Anina Mueller, a member of the Mu Phi Epsilon national music sorority educated at the Julliard School of Music and the University of Southern California, to run the school. Renamed the Los Angeles School of Music, it eventually moved to the corner of Fourth Street and Boyle Avenue; "Los Angeles Neighborhood Music School." See also Marcus, *Musical Metropolis.*

53 Morton H. Levine, chairman, Screening Committee of the Los Angeles County Music Commission to the Honorable Los Angeles County Board of Supervisors, January 11, 1949, John Anson Ford Papers, box 40, folder B III, 9e, dd (5), Huntington Library.

54 Sesma, interview by author, September 4, 1998; Lopez, interview by author, September 2, 1998; Tosti, interview by author, August 20, 1998.

55 Sesma, interview by author, September 4, 1998.

56 Tumpak, "Chico Sesma," 3.

57 See "Last Japs in County Going to Camp Today," *Los Angeles Examiner*, May 29, 1942; quoted in Pagán, "Sleepy Lagoon," 200n441. President Roosevelt's executive order no. 9066 authorized the secretary of war to establish isolated domestic "military areas." The War Relocation Authority chose ten remote sites, the majority of which were on Indian reservations in Western states. Whether or not one argues that the "internment camps," with their barbed wire and guard towers, were more like prisons or concentration camps, without a doubt the detainees were held against their will without legal representation, with no charges levied against them other than suspicion that they might commit some future act of aggression, sabotage, or espionage against the United States, and with no prospect of a judge, jury, or military tribunal ever hearing their cases.

58 Nash, *American West*, 94.

59 At the time of its construction, the 802-unit Aliso Village–Pico Gardens site was the largest public housing development west of the Mississippi River, a distinction eventually held by the 1,066-unit Nickerson Gardens housing

project in Watts. Due to the inadequate operating budgets of the City of Los Angeles Housing Authority, the Aliso Village–Pico Gardens housing soon became dilapidated, and remained so. This deteriorated infrastructure, as well as problems with street gangs, drugs, and lack of security led to the demolition of the complex in 1997—and its replacement with a new project, Pueblo del Sol, a mixed-income housing development. See Cuff, "Figure of the Neighbor."

60 Ortega, interview by Isoardi.

61 Shevky and Levine, *Your Neighborhood*, 10.

62 Pitt and Pitt, *Los Angeles A to Z*, 537. By 1920, 40% of the black population of Los Angeles lived within a few blocks on either side of Central Avenue between 11th and 42nd streets. See Gioia, *West Coast Jazz*, 4. The number of African Americans in Los Angeles increased from 55,114 in 1940 to 118,888 in 1944, and between 1942 and 1945 alone, 200,000 black migrants poured into the city. See Verge, "Impact," 303; and Bunch, "Past," 117. See also Graaf, "City."

63 Robinson, interview by Isoardi.

64 Genaro Ortega's father, Félix Ortega, was a general during the Mexican Revolution; Anthony Ortega, interview by Isoardi; Ortega, interview by author; Ortega, telephone conversation with author, July 31, 2005.

65 Ortega, interview by Isoardi. The La Colonia barrio ran east along 103rd Street toward Alameda Street.

66 Robinson, interview by Isoardi.

67 Ortega, interview by author.

68 For the 1940 census data on Watts, see Fisher, *Problem*, 6.

69 Robinson, interview by Isoardi.

70 Ibid.

71 Ibid.; Ortega, interview by Isoardi.

72 Robinson, interview by Isoardi.

73 Ibid.

74 Ortega, interview by Isoardi; Ortega, interview by author.

75 Ortega, interview by Isoardi.

76 Ortega, interview by author. The African American Angeleno saxophonist Jackie Kelso mentioned "a Mexican piano player" at Lafayette Junior High School named Jesús "Chuey" Reyes, describing him as "a great bandleader." See Bryant et al., *Central Avenue Sounds*, 208.

77 Ortega, interview by Isoardi.

78 Ortega, interview by author.

79 Curtis, "Music in the Los Angeles Public Schools," 194, 190.

80 Ibid., 194.

81 Tosti, interview by author, August 20, 1998; Sesma, interview by author, September 4, 1998.

82 Ortega, interview by author.

83 Lopez, interview by author, June 18, 1999.

84 When Ortega's mother took him to Lockie's Music Store on Broadway in downtown Los Angeles to buy his first horn on credit, they brought along Seymour Simon, a Jewish American friend of Ray Vasquez's and an experienced saxophonist, to judge the alto saxophone's worth. Ortega, interview by Isoardi; Ortega, interview by author.

85 Ortega, interview by Isoardi; Robinson, interview by Isoardi.

86 Ortega, interview by author; Ortega, telephone conversation with author, July 31, 2005.

87 Visser, liner notes, *Dexter Gordon*, 8; Porter, *What Is This Thing Called Jazz?* 62–63; Robinson, interview by Isoardi. Reese also taught Dexter Gordon, Buddy Collette, Hampton Hawes, Charles Mingus, Eric Dolphy, and William Douglass, among others. See Bryant et al., *Central Avenue Sounds*, 236.

88 Ortega, interview by Isoardi.

89 Bryant et al., *Central Avenue Sounds*, 25, 198, 209, 235, 265, 295, 325, 327. Other Samuel Browne students included Dexter Gordon, Chico Hamilton, Melba Liston, Vi Redd, Frank Morgan, and Jackie Kelso. Visser, liner notes, *Dexter Gordon*, 8.

90 In Detroit during the 1940s, the student body at Miller High School was predominantly black, but the musical theory and composition instructor was a Mexican American named Louis Cabrera. The African American jazz guitarist Kenny Burrell recalled that Cabrera represented "more than just 'another music appreciation teacher.' He went further with us than most instructors would. Not only did he furnish us with a thorough grounding in the academic aspects of music, but he also provided us with the philosophy that our music should be a paying thing." Cabrera encouraged his students to get the practical experience of performing in clubs, ensuring that "those of his students who worked professionally got credits which were applied towards their classwork." In addition, Cabrera would explain to his students "the financial aspects of their craft, warning them against . . . exploitation by clubowners" and telling them how he had personally overcome such obstacles. See Lewis K. McMillan, "Kenny Burrell: Man with a Mission," *Down Beat* 38 no. 12 (June 1971): 12.

91 Lopez, interview by author, September 2, 1998; Sesma, interview by author, September 4, 1998; Lopez, conversation with author, September 10, 2004.

92 William Phillips's father was a Russian Jew and his mother an Austrian Jew raised in Scotland. Phillips, interview by Zwick.

93 Lopez, interview by author, December 20, 2004; Tommy Saito, telephone conversation with author, July 2, 2004; Sesma, conversation with author, September 3, 2007. Before they joined the musicians union, both Paul Lopez

and Chico Sesma considered five dollars "a good wage for a Saturday night gig"; Sesma, interview by author, September 4, 1998.

94 Early in his career, Phil Carreon worked for a Mexican American jukebox industry entrepreneur named Navarro, driving around town replacing older albums with recent hit records. Carreon also eventually married an Anglo woman. Tosti, interview by author, August 20, 1998. Lennie Niehaus, who came from a family of musicians, was writing arrangements by the time he was a teenager. Ortega, interview by Isoardi.

95 Sesma, interview by author, September 4, 1998; Sesma, interview by author, September 1, 2004.

96 Lopez, interview by author, September 2, 1998.

97 Lupe Leyvas, "Interview," *Lowrider* 2, no. 4 (1979): 22–23, as quoted in Pagán, *Murder at the Sleepy Lagoon*, 51; "Mexican Boy Gangs," Sleepy Lagoon Defense Committee Papers, box 7, file 8, Department of Special Collections, Young Research Library, University of California, Los Angeles, as quoted in Pagán, *Murder at the Sleepy Lagoon*, 185.

98 Arthur Arenas quotation, PBS American Experience, Zoot Suit Riots: Zoot Suit Culture, Music and Dance, "Downtown L.A.," www.pbs.org/wgbh/amex/zoot/eng_sfeature/pop_zoot.html (accessed April 16, 2003).

99 Gloria Rios Berlin quotation, PBS American Experience, Zoot Suit Riots: Zoot Suit Culture, Music and Dance, "Dance Halls," www.pbs.org/wgbh/amex/zoot/eng_sfeature/pop_zoot.html (accessed October 18, 2004).

100 Stowe, *Swing Changes*, 44. Mexican Americans also helped establish a countercultural urban tradition that would carry an even more inclusive New Deal politics into the postwar period.

101 Peña, *Mexican American Orquesta*, 171; Sesma, conversation with author, September 3, 2007.

102 Sesma, interview by author, September 1, 2004.

103 Sesma, interview by author, August 23, 2004; Tosti, interview by author, August 20, 1998; Ray, interview by author; Loza, *Barrio Rhythm*, 153; Peña, *Mexican American Orquesta*, 171.

104 Lopez, interview by author, September 2, 1998.

105 McWilliams, *North from Mexico*, 218.

106 Vince Ramírez, interview by author. On Duke Ellington's *Jump for Joy* at the Mayan Theater, see Porter, *What Is This Thing Called Jazz?*, 85.

107 Hernandez, interview by author. "Chole" Camarena Ray recalled that Duke Ellington always appeared in theaters, and the tickets always cost more than for other performances; Ray, interview by author.

108 Edward Rodriguez, interview by González.

109 Erenberg, *Swingin' the Dream*, 40.

110 Arthur Arenas quotation, PBS American Experience, Zoot Suit Riots: Zoot

Suit Culture, Music and Dance, "The Big Band Scene," www.pbs.org/wgbh/amex/zoot/eng_sfeature/pop_zoot.html (accessed April 16, 2003).

111 Emge, "How Palladium," 6.
112 Withers, "Problems," 83.
113 Sesma, interview by author, September 4, 1998.
114 Vince Ramírez, interview by author.
115 Tosti, interview by author, August 20, 1998.
116 Esquivel, interview by author.
117 Ray, interview by author.
118 Hernandez, interview by author.
119 On Central Avenue, see Cox, *Central Avenue*; and Marmorstein, "Central Avenue Jazz."
120 Vigil, interview by author.
121 Pagán, *Murder at the Sleepy Lagoon*, 52; Vince Ramírez, interview by author.
122 In the spring of 1942 Joe Morris opened the Plantation Club, which had formerly been known as Jazzland, and before that, as Baron Long's Tavern. See Bryant et al., *Central Avenue Sounds*, 81, 109, 184, 201, 359.
123 Lucie Brac Frias, interview by author.
124 Ray, interview by author.
125 The Elks Hall also hosted various community functions, from church meetings to high school proms and formals. See Bryant et al., *Central Avenue Sounds*, 125, 142, 205, 240. The Elks Hall originally opened in December 1930 at the corner of Washington Boulevard and Central Avenue, near downtown Los Angeles. See Eastman, "Pitchin' up a Boogie," 81.
126 Ray, interview by author.
127 Alvarez, "Zoot Violence," 148. Jack's Basket Room, a down-home dive on 33rd Street and Central Avenue, has been remembered as "the Chicken Basket," "Chicken in the Basket," or "Bird in the Basket," as one could order fried chicken, which would be served in a basket.
128 More research is needed to confirm whether the four ethnic Mexican barrios in West Los Angeles can be traced back to nineteenth-century Alta California: to the Rancho La Ballona, in present-day Culver City, Venice, and Ocean Park, the Rancho Boca de Santa Monica, or the Rancho San Vicente y Santa Monica, in present-day Santa Monica and Brentwood.
129 Esquivel, interview by author.
130 Vince Ramírez, interview by author.
131 Wilson, interview by Isoardi; Eastman, "Pitchin' up a Boogie," 80.
132 Dora Rico, interview by author.
133 Lopez, interview by author, September 2, 1998.
134 Tosti, interview by author, August 20, 1998.
135 Farmer, interview by Isoardi. In addition to Billy Berg's Hollywood clubs, other spots where, as Marshall Royal put it, a black musician could "be ac-

cepted as a person," included the Finale Club in Little Tokyo, and Billy Berg's
5-4 Ballroom near Central Avenue; Royal, interview by Isoardi.

136 Wallace, "Musicians' Union," 72; Professional Musicians Local 47 Web site, "Local 47 History," www.afm47.org/history.htm (accessed February 12, 2006).

137 Wallace, "Musicians' Union," 76, 73–74.

138 Ibid., 72–74, 76–77.

139 In 1943, the only American Federation of Musicians unions that were fully integrated were Detroit's Local 5 and New York's Local 802; Eastman, "Pitchin' up a Boogie," 81; Stowe, *Swing Changes*, 127.

140 Callendar and Cohen, *Unfinished Dream*, 106.

141 Bloch, interview by Isoardi.

142 Ibid.

143 Tosti, interview by author, August 20, 1998.

144 Callendar and Cohen, *Unfinished Dream*, 107.

145 Robinson, interview by Isoardi.

146 Bryant et al., *Central Avenue Sounds*, 57.

147 Hampton and Haskins, *Hamp*, 28–29.

148 Bloch, interview by Isoardi; Farmer, interview by Isoardi. Some light-skinned African American musicians may have "passed" as Creole to get work, but others actually identified as Creoles of color—perhaps with the simultaneous, strategic understanding that they would get paid more if they were perceived as "not black"—especially those connected with the New Orleans migrants who had fled Louisiana during the Americanization racial reclassification. See Hirsch and Logsdon, *Creole New Orleans*.

149 Ortega, interview by Isoardi.

150 Ortega, interview by author.

151 Sesma, interview by author, September 4, 1998.

152 Tucker, *Swing Shift*, 12.

153 Ortega, interview by author.

154 On the concept of "wages of whiteness," see DuBois, *Black Reconstruction*, 700–701; and Roediger, *Wages of Whiteness*, 12–14.

155 Lopez, interview by author, June 18, 1999.

156 Born in 1906 in Michoacán, Mexico, Rafael Mendez played trumpet in the bullrings of Mexico and Spain, then, after immigrating to the United States in 1926, in the Detroit Fox Theater orchestra and the Russ Morgan band, with which he toured the country during the Great Depression. See "Rafael Mendez," in Meier, *Mexican American Biographies*, 139.

157 Tosti, interview by author, August 20, 1998; Bruce Fessier, "Secret Star," *Desert Sun*, July 15, 1994. In another account, a dance promoter changed Tostado's name in order to fit it onto a poster; Varela, liner notes, *Pachuco Boogie*, 8.

158 Guerrero and Mentes, *Lalo*, 14–15, 42, 38–39; Guerrero interview, June 1986.

159 Guerrero and Mentes, *Lalo*, 53–54, 89, 43–44.

160 Ibid., 51–52, 55, 62–64; Guerrero, interview by Heisley and Pill.

161 Guerrero and Mentes, *Lalo*, 66, 70; Sonnichsen, "Lalo Guerrero," 13.

162 Guerrero and Mentes, *Lalo*, 66. Serapes are long, hand-loomed, woolen blanket–like shawls, brightly colored with Indian patterns and fringed ends, worn by men in northern Mexico, and by the Navajo, Apache, and Comanche of the U.S. Southwest. *Huaraches* are traditional Mexican Indian, hand-woven leather sandals, which range from light to dark leather, and from the typical open-toe style to nearly closed, with, in the twentieth century, automobile tire tread rubber soles. The regalia of the charro, or northern Mexican horseman, featured short, snug jackets with decorative inlaying along the borders, and tight pants with embroidery or silver buttons along the side of each leg.

163 Ibid., 91–93, 95; Sonnichsen, "Lalo Guerrero," 13; Guerrero, interview by Heisley and Pill.

164 Sesma, interview by author, September 4, 1998.

165 Tosti, interview by author, August 20, 1998; Varela, liner notes, *Pachuco Boogie*, 8–9.

166 Sesma, interview by author, September 4, 1998.

167 Tumpak, "Chico Sesma," 2.

168 Sesma, interview by author, September 4, 1998; Tumpak, "Chico Sesma," 3.

169 Figueroa, interview by author; Tosti, interview by author, June 29, 2004.

170 Emilio Caceres's grandson, David Caceres, became a contemporary jazz vocalist and saxophonist schooled at the Berklee School of Music in Boston, seasoned in New York City, and successfully performing, recording, and teaching in Houston, Texas.

171 Ortega, interview by author.

172 Vince Ramírez, interview by author.

173 On Mexicans "walking the color line," see Foley, *White Scourge*, 13.

174 Verge, *Paradise Transformed*, 47, 51. President Franklin D. Roosevelt issued Executive Order 8802, which outlawed racial discrimination by private defense contracting companies and created the FEPC, in October 1941, but only after Harlem union activist A. Philip Randolph and other African American civil rights leaders threatened to march on Washington with over 200,000 African Americans that July.

175 Starr, *Embattled Dreams*, 97.

176 Martinez, "Unusual Mexican," 44, 55.

177 Ibid., 24. On other wartime restraints on ethnic Mexicans' socioeconomic mobility, see Escobar, *Race, Police*, 166–71.

178 Verge, *Paradise Transformed*, 50.

179 Quoted in Nash, *American West*, 91.

180 Esquivel, interview by author.

181 Leonard, " 'Brothers under the Skin'?," 191.

182 Scott Greer, "The Participation of Ethnic Minorities in the Labor Unions of Los Angeles County" (PhD diss., University of California, Los Angeles, 1952), 117–18, quoted in Monroy, "Mexicanos in Los Angeles, 1930–1941," 91.

183 Leonard, " 'Brothers under the Skin'?," 203.

184 Mario García, "Americans All," 202. See Quiñonez, "Rosita the Riveter."

185 Sesma, interview by author, September 4, 1998.

186 Garibay, interview by author.

187 Vince Ramírez, interview by author.

188 Esquivel, interview by author.

189 Wartime Pacoima church bazaars have been described as often flirtatious social functions; Mary Helen Ponce, *Hoyt Street: An Autobiography* (Albuquerque: University of New Mexico Press, 1993), 28, as quoted in Pagán, *Murder at the Sleepy Lagoon*, 50. The Pomona disc jockey and club promoter Candelario Mendoza also mentions jamaicas; Mendoza, interview by author.

190 Vince Ramírez, interview by author.

191 Alvarez, interview by author.

192 Ortega, interview by Isoardi.

193 Esquivel, interview by author.

194 Lopez, interview by author, September 2, 1998.

195 Vince Ramírez, interview by author.

196 Lucie Brac Frias, interview by author.

197 Another strong early influence on Paul Lopez was swing trumpeter Bunny Berigan, "early jazz's [second] quintessential tragic White jazz figure," after Bix Beiderbecke, according to jazz critic Ron Wynn. See Wynn, *All Music Guide*, 82.

198 Ortega, interview by Isoardi.

199 Tosti, interview by author, August 20, 1998.

200 Peña, *Mexican American Orquesta*, 169.

201 Sesma's father, who was from Arizona, loved American country and western music, especially the western swing of Bob Wills and His Texas Playboys; Sesma, interview by author, September 4, 1998.

202 Lopez, interview by author, September 2, 1998.

203 Peña, *Mexican American Orquesta*, 169, 192.

204 Sesma, interview by author, September 4, 1998.

205 Lopez, interview by author, September 2, 1998.

206 Peña, *Mexican American Orquesta*, 199.

207 Guerrero, interview by Heisley and Pill.

208 Ortega, interview by Isoardi; Ortega, interview by author.

209 The Frantic Five members would get paid $5 each for these early gigs. Ortega

was first exposed to bebop at a record store on 103rd Street in Watts owned by Pete Kynard, a former tenor saxophonist, and his wife, Ruth; Ortega, interview by Isoardi.

210 Mario García, "Americans All," 204–5.

211 Ruth Martinez "taught the Mexicans in the Chafey district for over twelve years." For the purpose of her study, an "unusual Mexican" was defined as one who graduated from Chafey High School or Chafey Junior College; Martinez, "Unusual Mexican," ix.

212 Ibid., 28.

213 Ibid., 17–19, 33, 34.

214 Ibid., 7, 20, 21, 39–43, 45, 55. Regarding education and mentorship, "the young people interviewed commented on the splendid treatment accorded them by the teachers and pupils," while "other informants mentioned particular teachers who had had a tremendous influence on their lives, aiding them in crises beyond their duties, and extending their friendship outside of school hours as well as in school." Also profiled was "an outstanding art student" with a topical weekly cartoon in his school paper, and a promising writer with a column in his school paper. Finally, this group also produced a barber college graduate, Manuel Guerrero, who ran his own barbershop in Azusa until he began retraining for defense work.

215 Ibid., 45, 46, 55. On Mexican Americans using employment at the Padua Hills Theater in Claremont to expand their options and to pay for higher education, see Matt Garcia, *World of Its Own*, 144, 150, 153.

216 Martinez, "Unusual Mexican," 47, 48, 52, 55. Another Mexican American woman, who "had always intended to become a dressmaker," "married an American boy and was living in West Riverside," while Cruz Huerta Hodges married "an American" and became office manager, bookkeeper, and telephone operator of a lumber company in Albuquerque, New Mexico, where she co-owned a "better than average home," after her graduation from junior college six years earlier.

217 Ibid., 46, 47, 55.

218 In the town of San Bernardino, all of the popular big bandleaders would perform at Hickory Park to a predominantly Mexican American crowd drawn from the surrounding areas; Hernandez, interview by author.

2. Intercultural Style Politics

1 Himes, *If He Hollers*, 203.

2 "Ban on Freak Suits Studied by Councilmen," *Los Angeles Times*, June 10, 1943, 2.

3 Escobar, *Race, Police*, 173–75, 191–92, 194–95. In earlier decades the LAPD had used vagrancy laws to control Mexican adults. On police harassment,

mistreatment, and brutality, see also McWilliams, *North from Mexico*; Tovares, *Zoot Suit Riots* (videocassette); and Pagán, *Murder at the Sleepy Lagoon*.

4 Escobar, *Race, Police*, 182–83.

5 On the "pleasure pier" of Venice, see Pitt and Pitt, *Los Angeles A to Z*, 526. On the Venice Amusement Pier and Venice of America, see Jeffrey Stanton, *Venice, California*. See also Avila, *Popular Culture*, 111.

6 Griffith, *American Me*, 18–19. This story is also quoted in Pagán, *Murder at the Sleepy Lagoon*, 163.

7 Acuña, *Occupied America*, 251.

8 Tovares, *Zoot Suit Riots* (videocassette).

9 On "taxi-cab brigades" during the zoot suit riots, see McWilliams, *North from Mexico*, 221.

10 Quoted in Griffith, *American Me*, 22–23.

11 Escobar, *Race, Police*, 166.

12 On wartime antiblack hate strikes and housing projects confrontations, see Lipsitz, *Rainbow at Midnight*, 50, 69–70, 76–78.

13 Billy Berg, whose friends were all "Jewish comics—old vaudeville guys," brought Dizzy Gillespie and Charlie Parker to the West Coast first when he hired their integrated band, which included the pianist Al Haig and the drummer Stan Levy, to play his club in December 1945. See Gioia, *West Coast Jazz*, 10, 17–18.

14 "The California Cats: Sonny Criss Talks to Bob Porter and Mark Gardner," *Jazz Monthly* (April 1968): 8.

15 Eastman, "Pitchin' up a Boogie," 95.

16 Granz's Jazz at the Philharmonic concerts were the first completely unsegregated musical performance in many southern cities, and the largest-scale mixed audience performance in many northern cities. Granz later held concerts for the Anti-lynching Legislation Committee, and for many intercultural institutions. See Mike Nevard, "He Carries a Torch for Jazz and Racial Freedoms," *Melody Maker* 26 no. 873 (April 29, 1950): 3; Nat Hentoff, "JATP Sells Democracy," *Down Beat* 19 no. 9 (May 7, 1952): 9; and Wynn, *All Music Guide*, 708.

17 Mazón, *Zoot Suit Riots*, 67–68; George Sánchez, quoted in Tovares, *Zoot Suit Riots* (videocassette).

18 Stowe, *Swing Changes*, 161–62.

19 Tucker, "They Got Corns"; Gioia, *West Coast Jazz*, 17. On Hollywood culture vis-à-vis the greater Los Angeles area, see Davis, *City of Quartz*; and Starr, *Dream Endures*.

20 Hampton and Haskins, *Hamp*, 28–29.

21 Gioa, *West Coast Jazz*, 17; Eastman, "Pitchin' up a Boogie," 80.

22 Porter and Keller, *There and Back*, 67.

23 Gioa, *West Coast Jazz*, 18. In New York City, police officers on foot patrol

would canvas the sidewalks of 52nd Street in threes, harassing any black men accompanying young white women. See Gillespie, *To BE*, 285. In June 1943, just before the Harlem riots, civilian and military police shut down the legendary Savoy Ballroom in Harlem, allegedly to stop drugs and prostitution, but really to stop black men from dancing with white women. See Stowe, *Swing Changes*, 163; Erenberg, *Swingin' the Dream*, 207–8; and White and White, *Stylin'*, 260.

24 "Only Superiority of Consequence Is One of Intellect," *Down Beat* 10 no. 19 (October 1, 1943): 10; "An Ugly Story," *Metronome* 59 (November 1943): 6.

25 "Niteries Facing Race Problem: L.A. Columnist Takes Slam at Discrimination," *Down Beat* 10 no. 5 (March 1, 1943): 6.

26 "Charge Prejudice behind Club Drive," *Down Beat* 12 no. 5 (March 1, 1945): 6.

27 Gitler, *Swing to Bop*, 231; Gitler, liner notes, *Babs Gonzales*.

28 Himes, *If He Hollers*, 60.

29 Pitt and Pitt, *Los Angeles A to Z*, 373–74.

30 Kelley, *Race Rebels*, 56–59.

31 Gioia, *West Coast Jazz*, 17.

32 Almaguer, *Racial Fault Lines*, 210. See also Saxton, *Rise and Fall*.

33 For mention of a Mexican American zoot suiter in Detroit, and his Irish and Polish American associates, see Norman Daymond Humphrey, "The Stereotype and the Social Types of Mexican American Youths," *Journal of Social Psychology* 22 (1945): 72–73.

34 Cosgrove, "Zoot Suit," 78.

35 McWilliams, *North from Mexico*, 242–43.

36 Carlos Espinoza quotation, PBS American Experience, Zoot Suit Riots: Zoot Suit Culture, Fashion, "Cuffs, Shoes and Hats," www.pbs.org/wgbh/amex/zoot/eng_sfeature/pop_zoot.html (accessed October 18, 2004); Arthur Arenas quotation, PBS American Experience, Zoot Suit Riots: Zoot Suit Culture, Fashion, "The Fashion," www.pbs.org/wgbh/amex/zoot/eng_sfeature/pop_zoot.html (accessed October 18, 2004); Ed Frias, interview by author.

37 Withers, "Problems," 73.

38 Bogardus, "Gangs," 55; Griffith, *American Me*, 7. Griffith, a 1933 graduate of Pomona College, also worked with several hundred Mexican American boys and girls as an art project supervisor for the National Youth Administration.

39 Malcolm X and Haley, *Autobiography*, 52.

40 Guerrero, interview by Heisley and Pill. For those who wanted to buy on installment, it is unclear whether shops extended lines of credit.

41 Mendoza, interview by author.

42 Ed Frias, interview by author.

43 Ray, interview by author.

44 Sesma, interview by author, September 4, 1998. One of the few remaining

Jewish stores in the neighborhood, Zalman's Clothiers, is still owned by the same family.

45 Vince Ramírez, interview by author.

46 Cosgrove, "Zoot Suit," 80; Mazón, *Zoot Suit Riots*, 5–8; Sánchez, *Becoming Mexican American*, 265; Pagán, *Murder at the Sleepy Lagoon*, 109.

47 "Ban on Freak Suits," 2; McWilliams, *North from Mexico*, 225; William Overend, " '43 Zoot Suit Riots Reexamined," *Los Angeles Times*, May 9, 1978, sec. IV, 5 (thanks to Catherine Ramírez for this article); Mazón, *Zoot Suit Riots*, 75; Tovares, *Zoot Suit Riots* (videocassette); Alvarez, "Zoot Violence," 163.

48 On zoot suiters portrayed as unpatriotic, see Kelley, *Race Rebels*, 172.

49 Tovares, *Zoot Suit Riots* (videocassette).

50 McWilliams, *North from Mexico*, 231; Tovares, *Zoot Suit Riots* (videocassette).

51 Overend, " '43 Zoot Suit Riots," 5.

52 McWilliams, *North from Mexico*, 231.

53 "Explains Zoot Suit Problem," *Pittsburgh Courier*, June 26, 1943, 3.

54 "Mrs. Roosevelt Blindly Stirs Race Discord," *Los Angeles Times*, June 18, 1943, editorial, 4.

55 Quoted in McWilliams, *North from Mexico*, 230.

56 "Explains Zoot Suit Problem."

57 Acuña, *Occupied America*, 243; Robert Jones, "Integration of the Mexican Minority," 177n8.

58 Raul Morin, *Among the Valiant: Mexican-Americans in WW II and Korea* (Alhambra, Calif.: Borden, 1963), 89, 256, quoted in Scott, "Mexican-American," 259–61.

59 Scott, "Mexican-American," 256, 259.

60 Ibid., 261–62; Acuña, *Occupied America*, 243; Griffith, *American Me*, 264.

61 Bogardus, "Gangs," 55.

62 Carey McWilliams, "Los Angeles' Pachuco Gangs," *New Republic*, January 18, 1943, 76.

63 Himes, *If He Hollers*, 43. In the late 1930s and early 1940s, *conk* referred to the chemical process used to straighten curly hair. See Kelley, *Race Rebels*, 167–68.

64 Mazón, *Zoot Suit Riots*, 17. The servicemen and the zoot suiters, were, Mazón argues, like two "gangs" with respective initiation rites, speech, walk, and uniforms; ibid., 65–66. Some African American soldiers at Fort Huachua in Arizona reportedly "had their uniforms tailor-made in 'drapes' and long coats resembling the 'zoot suit' "; White and White, *Stylin'*, 257–58.

65 Pagán, *Murder at the Sleepy Lagoon*, 38, 104, 129–30; Braddy, "Pachucos," 257–58.

66 Alvarez, interview by author.

67 In a 1943 *Negro Digest* article, Ellison also urged black leaders to recognize the

"great potential power" concealed in "the symmetrical frenzy of the Lindy Hop"; quoted in Kelley, *Race Rebels*, 161.

68 On pachucas, particularly the Sleepy Lagoon trial "38th Street girls," including their court testimony, see Escobedo, "Mexican American Home Front"; Ramírez, "Sayin' Nothin' "; and Ramírez, *Lady Zoot Suiter*.

69 Bogardus, "Gangs," 56.

70 Griffith, *American Me*, 47.

71 Esquivel, interview by author.

72 "Clashes Few as Zoot War Dies Down: Girls Knife Woman; Sailors and Gangs in Sporadic Battles," *Los Angeles Times*, June 11, 1943, sec. A, 1.

73 Quoted in Alvarez, "Zoot Violence," 151.

74 McWilliams, *North from Mexico*, 219.

75 On the significance of the pachuca hair and clothing styles, see Ramírez, "Crimes of Fashion," 7, 14; and Pagán, *Murder at the Sleepy Lagoon*, 102, 104.

76 Lupe Leyvas quotation, PBS American Experience, Zoot Suit Riots: Zoot Suit Culture, Fashion, "Girls' Style," www.pbs.org/wgbh/amex/zoot/eng_sfea ture/pop_zoot.html (accessed October 18, 2004).

77 Garibay, interview by author. Vince Ramírez also remembers pachucas wearing white athletic socks; Ramírez, interview by author.

78 Carlos Espinoza quotation, PBS American Experience, Zoot Suit Riots: Zoot Suit Culture, Fashion, "Looking Good," www.pbs.org/wgbh/amex/zoot/ eng_sfeature/pop_zoot.html (accessed October 18, 2004).

79 Ray, interview by author.

80 Mendoza, interview by author. Used as a pejorative, *marijuano* connotes a strung-out young pot user, or a shaky, disoriented bum.

81 Tovares, *Zoot Suit Riots* (videocassette).

82 Garibay, interview by author.

83 Carlos Espinoza quotation, PBS American Experience, Zoot Suit Riots: Zoot Suit Culture, Fashion, "Wearing the Zoot Suit," www.pbs.org/wgbh/amex/ zoot/eng_sfeature/pop_zoot.html (accessed April 16, 2004).

84 Ybarra-Frausto, "*Rasquachismo*," 156, 160.

85 Lucie Brac Frias, interview by author.

86 Ray, interview by author.

87 Tosti, interview by author, August 20, 1998.

88 Gloria Rios Berlin quotation, PBS American Experience, Zoot Suit Riots: Zoot Suit Culture, Music and Dance, "Dance Halls," www.pbs.org/wgbh/amex/ zoot/eng_sfeature/pop_zoot.html (accessed October 18, 2004).

89 Vince Ramírez, interview by author.

90 Ed Frias, interview by author.

91 Esquivel, interview by author.

92 Arthur Arenas quotation, PBS American Experience, Zoot Suit Riots: Zoot Suit Culture, Music and Dance, "Pachuco Attitude," www.pbs.org/wgbh/

amex/zoot/eng_sfeature/pop_zoot.html (accessed October 18, 2004); Tovares, *Zoot Suit Riots* (videocassette).

93 Sesma, interview by author, August 23, 2004.

94 Ed Frias, interview by author; Lucie Brac Frias, interview by author.

95 Mendoza, interview by author.

96 Vince Ramírez, interview by author.

97 Withers, "Problems," 47–48.

98 Griffith, *American Me*, 8, 20.

99 For photographs of Mexican American youths wearing leather jackets, see
Tovares, *Zoot Suit Riots*.

100 Ortega, interview by Isoardi.

101 Arthur Arenas quotation, PBS American Experience, Zoot Suit Riots: Zoot
Suit Culture, Fashion, "The Fashion," www.pbs.org/wgbh/amex/zoot/eng_
sfeature/pop_zoot.html (accessed October 18, 2004).

102 Chibnall, "Whistle and Zoot," 58.

103 Rosaura Sánchez, *Chicano Discourse*, 132.

104 Ibid., 133. Sánchez argues that the distinctive caló slang was used primarily by,
for, and between young Chicano males, and was probably not used around
adults or women, although pachucas also used caló.

105 Hebdige, *Subculture*, 91.

106 Ibid., 113–17. Dick Hebdige calls this unifying aspect of subcultural structures
"homology."

107 Kelley, *Race Rebels*, 166. See also LeRoi Jones, *Blues People*, 202; Cosgrove,
"Zoot Suit," 78–80; and Lott, "Double V—Double Time," 598, 600.

108 Berman, *All That Is Solid*, 23, 16, 5.

109 Barker, "Pachuco," 14, 15. Beatrice Griffith claimed that the first El Paso
pachucos came to Los Angeles in the 1920s; Griffith, "Pachuco Patois," 79.

110 Griffith, "Pachuco Patois," 82.

111 Some words, like *tacuche* or *chante*, may have Nahuatl etymologies. This
book's definitions of caló words are derived, in part, from Fuentes and López, *Barrio Language Dictionary*; Galván and Teschner, *Diccionario*; Hinojos,
"Notes," 58–59; Polkinhorn, Velasco, and Lambert, *Libro de Caló*; Ortega,
Caló Orbis; and Rosaura Sánchez, "The Spanish of Chicanos," in *Chicano Discourse*. See also Vasquez, *Regional Dictionary*; and Ramírez, "Sayin' Nothin'."

112 González, "Pachuco," 81–85; Barker, "Pachuco," 32–35.

113 On the drawl effect, see Griffith, "Pachuco Patois," 81; and Barker, "Pachuco,"
8, 13.

114 On the black Angeleno "Calabama" drawl, see Kelley, *Race Rebels*, 300.

115 Galindo, "Dispelling the Male-Only Myth," 6.

116 Malcolm X and Haley, *Autobiography*, 49.

117 Pepper and Pepper, *Straight Life*, 41–44.

118 Alvarez, interview by author.

119 Ramírez, "Crimes of Fashion," 25, 12.

120 Tucker, *Swing Shift*, 19.

121 Ramírez, "Crimes of Fashion," 16–18, 14, 12.

122 "Mexican-American Girls Meet in Protest," *Eastside Journal*, June 16, 1943; Ramírez, "Crimes of Fashion," 21–22; Pagán, *Murder at the Sleepy Lagoon*, 123–24.

123 McWilliams, *North from Mexico*, 231.

124 Griffith, *American Me*, 322n6.

125 See Carby, *Reconstructing Womanhood*; and Higginbotham, *Righteous Discontent*. See also Monson, "Problem," 418.

126 Ramírez, "Crimes of Fashion," 16. See also Fregoso, "Homegirls, Cholas, and Pachucas"; Miranda, *Homegirls*. On the zoot style's "body politics," and its opposition to white middle-class norms, see Alvarez, *Power of the Zoot*. On working-class sexual challenges to middle-class respectability in the early twentieth century, see D'Emilio and Freedman, "Civilized Morality." 127. On Latina stereotypes see, e.g., Ramírez Berg, *Latino Images*; and Bender, *Greasers and Gringos*.

128 Griffith, *American Me*, 47.

129 Himes, "Zoot Riots," 200–201.

130 An earlier cohort of adolescent Mexican American Angelenas employed similar acculturation strategies, responding to a barrage of conflicting gender norms by subverting stereotypes of passive, subservient Mexicanas. As Vicki Ruiz argues, they were inspired to adopt flapper clothing, makeup, and hair styles by Hollywood movie stars, including the Mexicanas Dolores Del Rio and Lupe Vèléz, by East Los Angeles beauty pageants and "future star" discovery contests, and by Spanish-language newspaper movie reviews, nationally syndicated gossip columns, and fashion and cosmetics advertisements. They behaved boldly toward men, ignored parental authority, and evaded chaperone supervision, but larger mitigating factors like unequal educational opportunities, labor exploitation, and the threat of repatriation continually limited the transgressive power of their bobs, makeup, and slinky dresses. Ruiz notes that since "dressing up . . . could be interpreted as an affirmation of individual integrity . . . they did not surrender their self esteem." See Ruiz, "Star Struck," 123, 117. Ruiz's article, with its emphasis on single Mexican American women, including working mothers and daughters, makes a compelling case against a strictly patriarchal view of Mexican families. Through their supplemental earnings, working-class Mexican American women engaged Anglo popular culture as consumers, grappling with new forms of sexual and financial independence. See Fregoso, *Bronze Screen*, 97.

131 Monroy, *Rebirth*, 189, 181–82.

132 Withers, "Problems," 47–48.

133 Ironically, the American values promulgated by Hollywood films were cre-

ated largely by Jewish immigrant business moguls who were in the process of reinventing themselves as they produced their own vision of the American dream. See Gabler, *Empire.*

134 Monroy, "Our Children," 91, 93.

135 Stuart Cosgrove concedes that wearers of the zoot suit "refused to concede to the manners of subservience," but he claims that the drape shape represents only a "natural and unconscious expression," an intangible, "inarticulate rejection of the straight world"; Cosgrove, "Zoot Suit," 78, 89. Bruce Tyler calls "Black zoot suiters, dandies, hustlers and nightlifers . . . cultural rebels who threatened White supremacy by violating racial taboos in music and in entertainment"; Tyler, "Black Jive," 61. To Robin Kelley, zoot-suited African American hipsters and hustlers challenged "middle-class ethics and expectations, carving out a distinct generational and ethnic identity, and refusing to be good proletarians"; Kelley, *Race Rebels,* 163. George Sánchez, meanwhile, concludes that the zoot suit was emblematic of working-class Mexican American Angelenos' increasing estrangement "from a society unable to provide adequate jobs or education"; Sánchez, *Becoming Mexican American,* 264–65. Finally, according to Carey McWilliams, the zoot suit is "often used as a badge of defiance by the rejected against the outside world and, at the same time, as a symbol of belonging to the inner group. It is at once a sign of rebellion and a mark of belonging. It carries prestige"; McWilliams, *North from Mexico,* 219. On the cultural meanings of the zoot suit, see also Green, "Zoot Suiters."

136 Withers, "Problems," 15.

137 Sánchez-Tranquilino and Tagg, "Pachuco's Flayed Hide," 562–63.

138 Lucie Brac Frias, interview by author.

139 Mendoza, interview by author.

140 Escobar, *Race, Police,* 156.

141 Lopez, interview by author, September 2, 1998.

142 Ed Frias, interview by author.

143 Guerrero, interview by Heisley and Pill.

144 Mendoza, interview by author.

145 Pitt and Pitt, *Los Angeles A to Z,* 559.

146 Kelley, *Race Rebels,* 50, 163, 166.

147 Himes, *If He Hollers,* 153.

148 Ibid., 31.

149 George Lipsitz argues that "ownership of Cadillacs and other commodities" by African Americans is "symbolic terrain" because they face many "obstacles to asset accumulation" in "a structure of racialized power and unequal opportunity"; Lipsitz, *Possessive Investment,* 164. In 1938, youth worker Henry Marin was pulled over by a Los Angeles Police Department squad car while driving his new Plymouth through downtown. The officer ordered him out of

the car, punched him in the stomach, and then demanded to know where he got the car. Marin replied that it belonged to him, and that he had bought it with his own money. The officer asked if he had obtained the money by "pushing dope," but when Marin explained that he had a full-time job, he was allowed to move on. See Escobar, *Race, Police*, 173.

150 Gioa, *West Coast Jazz*, 18.

151 Monroy, "Our Children," 12.

152 Quoted in Tyler, "Black Jive," 60.

153 Monroy, *Rebirth*, 179; Boorstein, *Americans*, 92.

154 Leach, *Land of Desire*, 3.

155 Kelley, *Race Rebels*, 50, 169. Black and brown zoot suiters' personal resistance tactics created autonomous survival spaces, yet their very participation in the liberating swing era nightlife may have implicated them in the maintenance of the larger power structure, for only a few of the clubs and dance halls they attended were owned by members of their own ethnic groups. By spending their time and "precious little money" at commercialized venues, African American workers were, "in many cases, reinforcing black working-class ties to consumer culture"; Kelley, *Race Rebels*, 48.

156 Withers, "Problems," 83, 80.

157 Griffith, *American Me*, 205; Escobar, *Race, Police*, 173.

158 Withers, "Problems," 83–84.

159 Wilson, interview by Isoardi. Snooky Young and Harry "Sweets" Edison were also barred from seeing Jimmie Lunceford's orchestra at the Trianon Ballroom in South Gate; Bryant et al., *Central Avenue Sounds*, 201.

160 Arthur Arenas quotation, PBS American Experience, Zoot Suit Riots: Zoot Suit Culture, Music and Dance, "The Big Band Scene," www.pbs.org/wgbh/amex/zoot/eng_sfeature/pop_zoot.html (accessed October 18, 2004).

161 McWilliams, *North from Mexico*, 217.

162 Arthur Arenas quotation, PBS American Experience, Zoot Suit Riots: Zoot Suit Culture, Music and Dance, "The Big Band Scene," www.pbs.org/wgbh/amex/zoot/eng_sfeature/pop_zoot.html (accessed October 18, 2004).

163 Pagán, *Murder at the Sleepy Lagoon*, 49, 55.

164 The Harlem minister Adam Clayton Powell preached a gospel of integration on blacks' own terms, and the *Pittsburgh Courier* and *Chicago Defender* spread the news. On the "Double V" campaigns, see Bunch, "Past," 117; Verge, "Impact," 299; and Kelley, *Race Rebels*, 154, 163–64.

165 On El Congreso, see Mario García, *Mexican Americans*; and Mario García, *Memories of Chicano History*.

166 Escobar, *Race, Police*, 153.

167 Griffith, *American Me*, 242.

168 On "cultural pluralism" and the Mexican American generation, see Mario García, *Mexican Americans*.

169 Chibnall, "Whistle and Zoot," 58.

170 Barker, "Pachuco," 24, 25. Barker conducted fieldwork in Tucson during the late 1940s, but the attitudes and lifestyles he describes were forged in the El Paso–Ciudad Juárez borderlands of the 1930s, and in the Los Angeles ethnoscapes of the 1940s.

171 By accepting the dominant view of criminal behavior as social deviance, latter-day commentators often duplicate earlier criminalizations of zoot suiters. Instead, Kelley argues, hustling, marijuana dealing, and similar illegal activities should be regarded as "economic strategies" to escape the "industrial discipline" of alienating, unfulfilling low-wage labor, while petty theft actually "implied a refusal to recognize the sanctity of private property"; Kelley, *Race Rebels*, 174, 178.

172 Ibid., 175–76.

173 Barker, "Pachuco," 25.

174 Griffith, *American Me*, 79. In Los Angeles, marijuana, which was legal and even grew wild in back alleys, became popular among African Americans by at least the late 1920s and early 1930s. See Bryant et al., *Central Avenue Sounds*, 32. Cab Calloway recorded "Reefer Man" in 1932. On Harlem hipsters buying Mexican marijuana from "some Spanish boys," see Mezz Mezzrow and Bernard Wolfe, *Really the Blues* (New York: Random House, 1946), 214–15, as quoted in Pagán, *Murder at the Sleepy Lagoon*, 39. The use of drugs, particularly marijuana, amphetamines, and heroin, was extensive among hipsters and jazz musicians, who took a more permissive, often satirical view, as evidenced by Harry "the Hipster" Gibson's 1946 tune, "Who Put the Benzadrine in Mrs. Murphy's Ovaltine?" Dizzy Gillespie, who condemned heroin use, stated that "almost all of [the jazz musicians] that I knew smoked pot, but I wouldn't call that drug abuse"; Gillespie, *To BE*, 279, 283.

175 Moore, *Homeboys*, 56–59.

176 Escobar, *Race, Police*, 183–84.

177 Griffith, *American Me*, 51. The corrido is the traditional ballad of the Mexican people wherein the acoustic guitarist sings four-line stanzas, or quatrains, with the second and fourth lines rhyming. Often tragic folk songs which became standardized by the mid-nineteenth century, corridos flourished in Mexico and the American Southwest before and after the turn of the twentieth century and continue to the present. They typically describe a historical event, specifying names, dates, and locations, although styles range from amorous to humorous to heroic. Like classical epic poets and twelve-bar blues guitarists, *corridistas* improvise new lines to their sung stories every time they perform them.

178 On unjustified police beatings in the street as well as in the station house, and on police shooting unarmed Mexican American youths in the back, see Griffith, *American Me*, 202–12.

179 González, interview by author, June 8, 1999; González, interview by author, June 11, 1999.
180 Ybarra-Frausto, "*Rasquachismo*," 160.
181 Griffith, *American Me*, 50–51.
182 Quoted in Escobar, *Race, Police*, 184–85.
183 Barker, "Pachuco," 25.
184 Griffith, *American Me*, 52.
185 Ray, interview by author.
186 Griffith, *American Me*, 52.
187 Lucie Brac Frias, interview by author. Dick Hebdige makes a similar distinction between the "authentic," core members of subcultures, and those engaged only on the fringes, or only superficially. See Hebdige, *Subculture*, 122.
188 Barker, "Pachuco," 14, 22.
189 Griffith, *American Me*, 53–54.
190 Martinez, "Unusual Mexican," 52.
191 See Nava, *My Mexican-American Journey*.
192 Overend, "Zoot Suit Riots Reexamined," 5.
193 George Sánchez, *Becoming Mexican American*, 256–60.
194 Mario García, "Americans All," 210.
195 Ibid., 202–3.
196 Martinez, "Unusual Mexican," 53, 54, 62.
197 Ed Frias, interview by author.
198 George Sánchez, *Becoming Mexican American*, 255; Mario García, "Americans All," 210.
199 Alvarez, interview by author.
200 Vince Ramírez, interview by author.
201 Ortega, interview by author.
202 Ed Frias, interview by author.
203 Griffith, "Pachuco Patois," 78.
204 Garibay, interview by author.
205 Esquivel, interview by author.
206 Alvarez, interview by author.
207 Guerrero and Mentes, *Lalo*, 178.
208 Ortega, interview by author.
209 On Central Avenue zoot suiters, see Pepper and Pepper, *Straight Life*, 41–44. On Anglo interpretations of pachuco effeminacy and homoeroticism, see Walter Davenport, "Swing It, Swing Shift!" *Collier's* 110 no. 8 (August 22, 1942): 24, 26; Braddy, "Pachucos," 259–60. On pachucos' masculinity as ambiguous, see Sánchez-Tranquilino and Tagg, "Pachuco's Flayed Hide," 569; and Ramírez, "Crimes of Fashion," 10–11, 23.
210 Pagán, *Murder at the Sleepy Lagoon*, 115, 108.
211 Bogardus, "Gangs," 56.

212 Ramírez, "Crimes of Fashion," 21–23.
213 Chicano Forums, "Pachuco and Zoot-Suiters," blog essay by "raider-gonzo," posted May 7, 2005, www.chicanoforums.com/forums/lofiversion/index.php/t690.html (accessed August 30, 2006), 7.
214 Sánchez-Tranquilino and Tagg, "Pachuco's Flayed Hide," 559.
215 Meisel, *Cowboy*, 9.
216 Davenport, "Swing It, Swing Shift!," 24.
217 Ed Frias, interview by author.
218 Niedorf, conversation with author.
219 Griffith, *American Me*, 54. Some Mexican Americans used the term *paddy*, a racial slur historically used against the Irish, to denote Anglo Americans in general.
220 Sesma, interview by author, September 4, 1998.
221 Tosti, interview by author, August 20, 1998.
222 Ortega, interview by Isoardi. East Los Angeles musician Manuel Armenta said that because "one of the toughest guys" in his high school wanted to carry his saxophone, "no one would touch [him]"; Reyes and Waldman, *Land of a Thousand Dances*, 20.
223 Lopez, interview by author, September 2, 1998.
224 Sesma, interview by author, September 4, 1998.
225 Himes, "Zoot Riots," 221.
226 Ortega, interview by Isoardi.
227 Ed Frias, interview by author.
228 Jessie Rodriguez, interview by González; Edward Rodriguez, interview by González.
229 Sesma, interview by author, September 4, 1998.
230 Lucie Brac Frias, interview by author.
231 Hernandez, interview by author.
232 Ray, interview by author.
233 Overend, "'43 Zoot Suit Riots," 6.
234 Ibid., 5.
235 Griffith, *American Me*, 51.
236 Horace R. Cayton, "'Bigger Thomas' Mentality Grips Zoot-Suiters," *Pittsburgh Courier*, June 26, 1943, 13.
237 Himes, *If He Hollers*, 79.
238 Cosgrove, "Zoot Suit," 81, 83, 84.
239 McWilliams, *North from Mexico*, 225; Turner and Surace, "Zoot-Suiters and Mexicans," 21.
240 Overend, "'43 Zoot Suit Riots," 6.
241 Tovares, *Zoot Suit Riots* (videocassette).
242 Hank Leyvas had African American friends, according to his brother Rudy; Overend, "'43 Zoot Suit Riots," 6; Tovares, *Zoot Suit Riots*.

243 Pagán, *Murder at the Sleepy Lagoon*, 180.

244 Bogardus, "Gangs," 58. On some of the Sleepy Lagoon defendants from Jefferson High School being influenced by their black classmates to "talk back" to and challenge unjust and unfair authority figures, see Acuña, *Occupied America*, 249.

245 This African American young man was, by 1949, a university student in Los Angeles; McDonagh, "Status Levels," 452.

246 Himes, *If He Hollers*, 181.

247 Rios-Bustamante and Castillo, *Illustrated History*, 147.

248 Monroy, "Mexicanos," 77. See also Monroy, *Rebirth*, 259.

249 Camarillo, "Chicano Urban History," 91.

250 Alfred Barela, Letter to the Honorable Arthur S. Guerin, May 21, 1943, quoted in George Sánchez, *Becoming Mexican American*, 253; Escobar, *Race, Police*, 231–32.

251 Paz, *Labyrinth of Solitude*, 16, 14.

252 Ibid., 15–16. For refutations of Octavio Paz's conclusions, see Madrid-Barela, "In Search of the Authentic Pachuco," 35–38; Monsiváis, "Este es el pachuco," 85–86; Sánchez-Tranquilino, "Mano a Mano"; and George Sánchez, *Becoming Mexican American*, 268.

253 Tosti, interview by author, August 20, 1998.

254 Muñoz Castillo, *Musas de "Tin Tan,"* 27–28.

255 Monsiváis, *Mexican Postcards*, 109, 111–12. *Pocho* is a pejorative word for a "gringoized" Mexican who has been "bleached" of his or her Mexican ways due to overexposure to U.S. culture. The Anglicized or Spanglish pachucoisms the pochos brought back to Mexico, called *pochismos*, were blamed for corrupting the language of Mexico's young people; "Authentic Pachuco," *Time*, July 10, 1944, 72.

256 Monsiváis, *Mexican Postcards*, 110, 106.

257 Paz, *Labyrinth of Solitude*, 15.

258 Esquivel, interview by author.

259 McWilliams, *North from Mexico*, 208–9.

260 Griffith, *American Me*, 51.

261 Barker, "Pachuco," 14.

262 España Maram, "Brown 'Hordes.' " See also España Maram, *Creating Masculinity*.

263 Matsumoto, *Farming the Home Place*, 129. *Nisei* is the term used to refer to American-born, second-generation Japanese Americans.

264 Griffith, *American Me*, 321.

265 Chibnall, "Whistle and Zoot," 61.

266 Barker, "Pachuco," 20–22. There is no connection between joining the Army and abandoning caló, for many Mexican Americans actually learned the slang while in the service. Regarding fluid cultural identities, Barker's article offers

intriguing glimpses of Freddy and Joe, two mixed-race pachucos who had Mexican mothers and "American" fathers.

267 Griffith, *American Me*, 77.

3. The Rhythm and Blues Era

Robert C. Jones, quoted in this chapter's first epigraph, was the acting chief of the Pan-American Union's Division of Labor and Social Information, in Washington, D.C. The Pan-American Union was originally established in 1890 for the purpose of promoting peace, friendship, and commerce among North and South American member republics. In 1948 the Pan-American Union became the central organ and general secretariat of the Organization of American States.

1 Max Roach, quoted in Malone, "Jazz Music," 293.

2 Stowe, *Swing Changes*, 181–82.

3 Gioa, *West Coast Jazz*, 18.

4 "Carter Wins Right to Live in Home," *Down Beat* 12 no. 17 (September 1, 1945): 6; "Color Edict Hits Bandmen Again," *Down Beat* 12 no. 23 (December 1, 1945): 6.

5 Gioa, *West Coast Jazz*, 17; Hoskyns, *Waiting for the Sun*, 8.

6 Tosti, interview by author, August 20, 1998.

7 Max Salazar, "Paul Lopez: 'Both Sides of the Fence,'" *Impacto: A Latino Arts and Entertainment Magazine* 3 no. 8 (May 1998): 4.

8 Sesma, interview by author, September 4, 1998. Sesma earned as much with Russ Morgan as his highest-paying gig with his biggest-name band, yet Tosti compared Morgan's music to that of Guy Lombardo, calling them both "watered-down and corny"; Tosti, interview by author, August 20, 1998.

9 Pitt and Pitt, *Los Angeles A to Z*, 144.

10 Philips, interview by Zwick.

11 Tosti, interview by author, August 20, 1998; Phillips, interview by Zwick.

12 On the Okie subculture, including its music, see Gregory, *American Exodus*.

13 "Empire, Berg's, Be-Bop's Hollywood Homes, Close," *Down Beat* 16 no. 8 (May 6, 1949): 9; Charles Emge, "Hillbilly Boom Can Spread Like Plague," *Down Beat* 16 no. 8 (May 6, 1949): 2.

14 Esquivel, interview by author.

15 Tosti, interview by author, August 20, 1998. The Casa Mañana had replaced the whites-only Cotton Club in 1945, and, under new management, permitted mixed-race dancing. However, the new liberalized policies were apparently not always followed; Bryant et al., *Central Avenue Sounds*, 199; Eastman, "Pitchin' up a Boogie," 84.

16 Ortega, interview by Isoardi.

17 Lucie Brac Frias, interview by author. During the late 1940s, in addition

to Sarah Vaughan, the Billy Eckstine Orchestra included Dizzy Gillespie, Charlie Parker, Gene Ammons, Art Blakey, Miles Davis, Kenny Dorham, Dexter Gordon, Fats Navarro, Lucky Thompson, and Lena Horne; Wynn, *All Music Guide*, 220.

18 Lucie Brac Frias, interview by author; Saito, interview by author, July 21, 2004.

19 Ed Frias, interview by author.

20 The brainchild of Christine Sterling, Olvera Street opened in 1930 as a colorful alley of Mexican merchants selling traditional wares and crafts in which the old Spanish and Mexican traditions and culture were being preserved for posterity, and for tourist consumption. Opposite Olvera Street across Alameda Street, Union Station would be built in 1939 over the razed remains of Old Chinatown, as the urban renewal schemes of city planners and real estate developers forced the Plaza area's Chinese population to relocate directly north to New Chinatown, and its Mexican population to relocate directly east to the flats of Boyle Heights.

21 Guerrero, interview by Heisley and Pill; Guerrero and Mentes, *Lalo*, 96.

22 Barker, "Pachuco," 16; Guerrero and Mentes, *Lalo*, 99, 191; Sonnichsen, "Lalo Guerrero," 13; Guerrero interview, June 1986.

23 Barker, "Pachuco," 16; Guerrero, interview by Heisley and Pill.

24 Guerrero and Mentes, *Lalo*, 99.

25 Reyes and Waldman, *Land of a Thousand Dances*, 7; Guerrero and Mentes, *Lalo*, 92; Loza, *Barrio Rhythm*, 162.

26 Reyes and Waldman, *Land of a Thousand Dances*, 7.

27 Guerrero, interview by Heisley and Pill.

28 Tosti, interview by author, August 20, 1998; Varela, liner notes, *Pachuco Boogie*, 5, 6; Stuart Goldman, "New Wave Rides High on a Latin Beat," *Los Angeles Times*, October 12, 1980, Calendar sec., 6.

29 Tosti, interview by author, August 20, 1998; Wynn, *All Music Guide*, 10. The boogie woogie style likely originated in Western mining and lumber camps; LeRoi Jones, *Blues People*, 114. An ostinato is a clearly defined phrase that continually repeats throughout a composition or a section of it.

30 Tosti, interview by the author, August 20, 1998; Varela, liner notes, *Pachuco Boogie*, 5, 6; Goldman, "New Wave Rides High On a Latin Beat," 7; "Don Tosti, 81; Inspired Latin Music Craze," *Los Angeles Times*, August 4, 2004, Obituary, sec. B, 12.

31 Roberts, *Latin Tinge*, 262.

32 Goldman, "New Wave," 7.

33 The slang expression *chicas patas* literally means "little feet." Lalo Guerrero translates *chicas patas* as "Pachucos" or "Chicanos." See Guerrero and Mentes, *Lalo*, 101. It is used similarly in Valdez, *Zoot Suit*.

34 Varela, liner notes, *Pachuco Boogie*, 9. See also Loza, *Barrio Rhythm*, 156. For the definition of *montuno*, see chap. 5.

35 Guerrero, interview by Heisley and Pill.

36 Varela, liner notes, *Pachuco Boogie*, 5, 6.

37 In what Dick Hebdige calls "style as homology," songs evoke a "symbolic fit between the values and lifestyles of a group, its subjective experience and the musical forms it uses to express or reinforce its focal concerns"; Hebdige, *Subculture*, 113, 114, 122.

38 On the political relationship between marijuana and Mexican immigrant deportation in the early 1930s, and on the federal criminalization of cannabis in 1937, see Yaroschuk, *Hooked*.

39 On the wartime Hollywood vice crackdown, see Stowe, *Swing Changes*, 39.

40 Tosti, interview by author, August 20, 1998.

41 The "poesía del tírili" lyric, from the corrido "El bracero y la pachuca," by Dueto Taxco con Mariachi Caporales del Norte, quoted in Varela, liner notes, *Pachuco Boogie*, 21.

42 Tosti, interview by author, June 29, 2004.

43 Guerrero and Mentes, *Lalo*, 190–92.

44 Lyrics to "Marihuana Boogie" quoted and translated in Vera, liner notes, *Jumpin' Like Mad*, 16.

45 Peña, *Mexican American Orquesta*, 188, 176.

46 Guerrero, interview by Heisley and Pill.

47 Guerrero and Mentes, *Lalo*, 101.

48 Guerrero interview, June 1986.

49 Sesma, interview by author, September 4, 1998.

50 Tosti, liner notes, *Don Tosti, a.k.a. "El Tostado."*

51 Guerrero, interview by Heisley and Pill; Loza, *Barrio Rhythm*, 77–78.

52 Tosti, interview by author, August 20, 1998. Frank Sinatra brought jazz phrasing, and what John Gennari calls "stylish virility," to the dominant American culture; Gennari, "Crooners and Gangsters." Sinatra paved the way for Italian American singing sensations like Frankie Laine, Perry Como, and Dean Martin. While Como and Martin were Hollywood crooners, Laine, like Louis Prima before him, was mistaken as black by both black and white listeners when he first became popular; "Whites Who Sing Like Negroes: Influence of Colored Singing Styles Heard in Voices of Top White Vocalists of Country," *Ebony* 6 no. 14 (February 1951): 49, 52.

53 Mario García, "Americans All," 211.

54 Mario García, *Mexican Americans*. The first successful desegregation case, the May 1931 decision in *Roberto Alvarez v. the Board of Trustees of the Lemon Grove School District*, which involved Mexican American students in San Diego, predated the May 1954 Supreme Court decision in *Brown v. Board of Education*, which involved African American students in Topeka.

55 Rose, "Gender and Civic Activism," 180–81; Mario García, *Memories of Chi-*

cano History, 156, 168; Burt, "Latino Empowerment," 10–15; Burt, "Los Angeles Council," 460.

56 Griffith, *American Me*, 288, 299.

57 The Servicemen's Readjustment Act of June 1944, commonly known as the G.I. Bill, along with the Veterans' Readjustment Assistance Act of 1952, which covered veterans of the Korean War, spent $13.5 billion in federal funds between 1945 and 1955 for veterans' education.

58 Lucie Brac Frias, interview by author.

59 McWilliams, *North from Mexico*, 228–29.

60 Law Enforcement, Crime Control and Prevention, Courts, 1934–57, John Anson Ford Papers, box 33, folder B III, 7a (16), Huntington Library. On Sheriff Biscailuz in the August 1947 La Fiesta parade in Santa Barbara, and as "a descendant of 'an early California family,'" see McWilliams, *North from Mexico*, 45, 229.

61 Scott, "Mexican American," 316.

62 Acuña, *Occupied America*, 291–92.

63 American Council on Race Relations, 1945–46, John Anson Ford Papers, box 72, aa, Huntington Library. The American Council on Race Relations was also known as the National Association of Intergroup Relations Officials.

64 Fisher, *Problem*, 10.

65 Ibid., 11–12, 14.

66 Ibid., 8.

67 Ibid., 14–15.

68 Joseph P. Hill, "The Church and the Zoot-Suiter," Conference Report: Catholic Council for the Spanish Speaking, 1946, 16; quoted in Scott, "Mexican American," 250.

69 Fisher, *Problem*, 18–19.

70 Rios-Bustamante and Castillo, *Illustrated History*, 173.

71 In March 1943 Alex Bernal, a 32-year-old California-born Mexican American man, his Mexican-born wife, and their two daughters moved into a racially restricted area in Fullerton, just south of the border between Los Angeles and Orange counties. Although three Anglo residents sued Bernal, producing witnesses to prove that Mexicans were dirty, noisy, and lawless, a Superior Court judge eventually declared Fullerton's 1923 deed restriction unconstitutional. See "California: Across the Tracks," *Time* 42 no. 10 (September 6, 1943): 25. Also quoted in Scott, "Mexican American," 197.

72 Letter from the Los Angeles County Committee on Human Relations (formerly the Committee for Interracial Progress), January 8, 1947, John Anson Ford Papers, box 72, folder B IV, 5a, cc (2), Huntington Library.

73 Quoted in Ruiz, *From out of the Shadows*, 68.

74 Semiannual Summary, Los Angeles County Committee on Human Rela-

tions, July 1951 to December 1951, John Anson Ford Papers, box 72, folder B IV, 5a, cc (6), Huntington Library.

75 Rios-Bustamante and Castillo, *Illustrated History*, 173, 156, 158, 198.

76 George Sánchez, "Reading Reginald Denny," 390.

77 C. Sharpless Hickman, "Civic Music Administration in Los Angeles," *Music Journal* 10 no. 4 (April 1952): 21.

78 City of Los Angeles brochure, undated, John Anson Ford Papers, box 41, folder 9, Huntington Library.

79 Hickman, "Civic Music Administration," 34; C. Sharpless Hickman, "Community Sings in Los Angeles," *Music Journal* 10 no. 1 (January 1952): 28–29.

80 City of Los Angeles brochure.

81 Author unknown, article in *Note* magazine, February 13, 1948, John Anson Ford Papers, box 75, folder B IV, 5 i, dd, "Mexican, 1933–1958" (14), Huntington Library.

82 City of Los Angeles brochure.

83 Goldberg, *Multiculturalism*, 6.

84 Hickman, "Civic Music Administration," 34, 33.

85 Sesma, interview by author, September 4, 1998.

86 Eddie Cano's father played the guitar and enjoyed classical music and opera; Loza, *Barrio Rhythm*, 150, 151, 157, 262, 156; Lopez, interview by author, September 2, 1998; Child, "Eddie Cano," 206; Green, liner notes, *Cha Cha con Cano*; Fessier, "Secret Star," D 3; Reyes and Waldman, *Land of a Thousand Dances*, 23. Founded in 1919 by the millionaire William Andrews Clark Jr. as a highbrow cultural institution, the Los Angeles Philharmonic was well-endowed by private donors and, through the Southern California Symphony Association, by the city. In 1951 the Los Angeles Philharmonic's president began negotiating a new contract with the musicians union to increase musicians' income by $20,000 a year; Southern California Symphony Association, 1937–1955, Letter from Henry Duque, June 25, 1951, John Anson Ford Papers, box 41, hh, folder 8 (10), Huntington Library.

87 City of Los Angeles brochure.

88 Loza, *Barrio Rhythm*, 262.

89 Corral, interview by author.

90 Hickman, "Civic Music Administration," 32; City of Los Angeles brochure; "Outline of Tentative Program for the Belvedere Park Lake Dedication," John Anson Ford Papers, box 41, folder B III, 10a (7), Huntington Library. The Spanish word *típica* means traditional, or typically characteristic, with rural, "roots," or folkloric connotations.

91 City of Los Angeles brochure.

92 In the early 1950s, Samuel Browne would tell his Jefferson High School music students, some of whom were failing other classes, "I don't care how

good you are, because of the racist society you live in, you're going to have to be much better than the student over at . . . Palisades and Hollywood High, they're going to be the ones that took care of business. And you're going to be hip. All you're going to be is be a hipster. . . . But if you want more, you'll try to do more. You'll try to study and learn more"; Tapscott, interview by Isoardi.

93 City of Los Angeles brochure.

94 Hickman, "Civic Music Administration," 21.

95 Hickman, "Community Sings," 28, 46.s

96 C. Sharpless Hickman, "Municipal Music and Money," *Music Journal* 10 no. 5 (May 1952): 32; Hickman, "Community Sings," 29.

97 Hickman, "Municipal Music and Money," 23.

98 Letter dated February 14, 1948, John Anson Ford Papers, box 41, folder 10, Huntington Library.

99 "1951–52 Statement of Program," John Anson Ford Papers, box 40, folder 5, Huntington Library.

100 Villa, *Barrio-Logos*, 71.

101 Charles Emge, "L.A. Council Votes down Anti-discrimination Law," *Down Beat* 16 no. 21 (November 4, 1949): 3.

102 On the term *musical miscegenation*, see George, *Death of Rhythm and Blues*, 86; Rogin, "Black Face," 440.

103 Hickman, "Community Sings," 21.

104 "Peace and Brotherhood and Citizenship" pamphlet, John Anson Ford Papers, box 60, folder 14, Huntington Library.

105 "Over-All Outline Plan of Recreational Services Which Should Be Offered in the Los Angeles Area," May 20, 1952, John Anson Ford Papers, box 61, folder 2, Huntington Library.

106 Kelley, *Race Rebels*, 46–50, 171. Similarly, Katrina Hazzard-Gordon argues that within African Americans' urban leisure spaces flourished not only "change and innovation," but also "cultural resilience and recuperative creativity." See Hazzard-Gordon, *Jookin'*, 173.

107 Fregoso, *Bronze Screen*, 26. On the ritual West African roots and continuing spiritual significance of black vernacular dancing, see Malone, "Keep to the Rhythm."

108 Pagán, *Murder at the Sleepy Lagoon*, 49.

109 "Twilight 'til Dawn Dance to Benefit Boy Scout Jamboree," *California Eagle*, May 18, 1950, 10. Thanks to Michael Willard for this article.

110 Reyes and Waldman, *Land of a Thousand Dances*, 20, 30; Saito, interview by author, December 29, 1999. Laguna Park has been renamed Ruben Salazar Park, in honor of the Mexican American journalist, born in Ciudad Juárez but raised in El Paso. A U.S. Army veteran, University of Texas, El Paso, alumnus, war correspondent, and *Los Angeles Times* and KMEX-TV reporter, Salazar was

assassinated by the Los Angeles County Sheriffs Department after it violently dispersed the peaceful crowd at the anti–Vietnam War National Chicano Moratorium March, in August 1970.

111 George, *Death of Rhythm and Blues*, 26–28; Maultsby, "Rhythm and Blues," 251.

112 Dawson, "Boogie Down," 65.

113 Ibid., 64–65; Molina, *Old Barrio Guide*, 5; Guevara, "View," 116. Joe Adams had been airing live remote broadcasts since 1939 from the Club Alabam on Central Avenue, and, in the 1940s, for NBC Radio. Adams was a jazz lover at heart, as seen in his television program, *Joe Adams Presents*, which premiered in 1951 on KTTV Channel 11, and which featured Gerald Wilson as its music director and a series of guest jazz artists. Adams also acted on Broadway and in film, and eventually became Ray Charles's manager.

114 The Barrelhouse co-owners were Johnny Miller, and Bardu and Tila Ali; Dawson, *Nervous Man Nervous*, 25; "Johnny Otis Biography," www.johnnyotis world.com/biography/index.html (accessed July 26, 2006).

115 Guevara, "View," 117; Lipsitz, "Cruising," 141; Ed Frias, interview by author.

116 Reyes and Waldman, *Land of a Thousand Dances*, 20–21; "Johnny Otis Biography," www.johnnyotisworld.com/biography/index.html (accessed July 26, 2006).

117 Ed Frias, interview by author.

118 Ray, interview by author.

119 As illustrated by whiteness studies, especially work that addresses minstrelsy and its present-day manifestations, love of and loyalty to black popular culture often go hand in hand with profound antiblack attitudes.

120 Ray, interview by author.

121 Lucie Brac Frias, interview by author; emphasis in original.

122 Ed Frias, interview by author.

123 "Lincoln Heights," 9.

124 Camarena and Ray also went dancing at La Golondrina in the mid-1950s; Ray, interview by author.

125 George, liner notes, *Rites of Rhythm and Blues*, vol. 2.

126 Ed Frias, interview by author.

127 Maultsby, "Rhythm and Blues," 250–51.

128 Collins, "California Rhythm and Blues," 215, 236.

129 Reed, *Black Music History*, 12.

130 "Chuck Higgins Biography," www.oldies.com/artist-biography/Chuck-Hig gins.html (accessed August 29, 2006); Dawson, liner notes, *Honk! Honk! Honk!*, 5. See also Lipsitz, "Cruising," 140.

131 Dawson, *Nervous Man Nervous*, 96.

132 Reyes and Waldman, *Land of a Thousand Dances*, 12–14.

133 Dawson, liner notes, *Honk! Honk! Honk!*, 5; "Chuck Higgins: Singles," compiled by Pete Hoppula, koti.mbnet.fi/wdd/chuckhiggins.htm (accessed August 30, 2006).

134 Dawson, liner notes, *Honk! Honk! Honk!* 6. See also Reyes and Waldman, *Land of a Thousand Dances*, 12.

135 Dawson, liner notes, *Honk! Honk! Honk!*, 9–10.

136 Dawson, *Nervous Man Nervous*, 97.

137 Plascencia, "Low Riding"; Gradante, "Art among the Low Riders"; Stone, "*Bajito y suavecito*"; Sandoval, "Cruising"; and David "iowahawk" Burge, "Bajito y suavecito," blog essay posted May 9, 2006, at http://iowahawk.typepad.com/iowahawk/2006/05/bajito_y_suavec.html, 1 (accessed February 23, 2008).

138 Ranker, "Study of Juvenile Gangs," 89.

139 Vigil, "Car Charros," 72.

140 Dawson, *Nervous Man Nervous*, 70.

141 Ibid., 76.

142 Reyes and Waldman, *Land of a Thousand Dances*, 49.

143 Dawson, *Nervous Man Nervous*, 71–72; Bryant et al., *Central Avenue Sounds*, 115. On "Billy Goat Acres," see Pitt and Pitt, *Los Angeles A to Z*, 44–45.

144 Dawson, *Nervous Man Nervous*, 71.

145 Reyes and Waldman, *Land of a Thousand Dances*, 49; Dawson, "Boogie Down," 83; Dawson, *Nervous Man Nervous*, 60–61, 79, 68.

146 Waldie, *Holy Land*, 51, 56, 58, 73–74, 103, 160–63, 173.

147 Piersen, "African American Festive Style," 429, 418.

148 On how Big Jay McNeely used his formal music training, and on the primal tension and religious fever produced and released by the best honkers, see Dawson, *Nervous Man Nervous*, 73, 75, 41.

149 Ramsey, *Race Music*, 177.

150 Dawson, *Nervous Man Nervous*, 88–92, 98; Fein, *L.A. Musical History Tour*, 43–44; Molina, *Old Barrio Guide*, 6; Reyes and Waldman, *Land of a Thousand Dances*, 49.

151 Terry McDermott, "Behind the Bunker Mentality," *Los Angeles Times*, June 11, 2000, sec. A, 28.

152 Davis, *City of Quartz*, 294.

153 Dawson, *Nervous Man Nervous*, 92, 93, 98.

154 "White Fans Hyping R & B Platter Sales," *Billboard*, May 1952; quoted in Dawson, *Nervous Man Nervous*, 75–76.

155 Bertrand, *Race, Rock, and Elvis*, 70.

156 Ed Frias, interview by author.

157 González, interview by author, June 8, 1999; González, interview by author, June 11, 1999.

158 Romo, interview by González.

159 Alvarez, interview by author.

160 Corral, interview by author.

161 Vigil, interview by author.

162 Corral, interview by author.

163 Ibid. In the summer of 1955 Polytechnic was shut down, renamed Los Angeles Trade Technical, and reopened as a general vocational school.

164 Saito, interview by author, December 29, 1999. At the age of eight, Tommy Saito was forcibly relocated to the Amache internment camp, where he lived in barracks under the shadow of barbed-wire fences and gun towers; Tommy Saito, telephone conversation with author, July 2, 2004.

165 Vigil, interview by author; Corral, interview by author.

166 Vigil, interview by author.

167 Wilson, interview by Isoardi. Perhaps Wilson knew Mexicans or Mexican Americans in Detroit.

168 Dawson, *Nervous Man Nervous*, 119. Anthony Ortega claims that Gil originally went by the surname of Rodriguez, but that he later adopted his mother's maiden name, Bernal; Ortega, interview by Isoardi.

169 Bernal, interview by Isoardi; Bernal, interview by author.

170 Ortega, interview by Isoardi.

171 Reyes and Waldman, *Land of a Thousand Dances*, 27.

172 Bernal, interview by author. Hampton's Apollo Theater performances, with Bernal and the Japanese American trombonist Paul Lee Higaki the only non-blacks in the band, were recorded as "telescriptions" and used by local television stations with few sponsors as "filler" programming; *Showtime at the Apollo/Harlem Variety Review*, Snader Telescription, 12–25B, MacDonald and Associates. In 1950, Bernal played at a club called the Oasis on Western Avenue, where jazz attractions like George Shearing, Stan Kenton, Sarah Vaughn, and Lionel Hampton drew "a lot of Hollywood people." One evening, the owner, Jerry Fine, informed him that Rita Hayworth and Charles Feldman, an influential Hollywood producer/agent, after seeing his performance the previous night, had left a phone number for Gil to call. This led to meetings in Feldman's Beverly Hills office and his Coldwater Canyon house. Feldman and his associates told Bernal that they wanted to send him to acting classes and develop him into a combination of Tony Curtis and John Derrick, but they lost interest and failed to follow up; Bernal, interview by Isoardi; Bernal, interview by author.

173 When Anthony Ortega joined the segregated armed forces in 1948, he was stationed at Fort Sam Houston, Texas, where he played in the 4th Army Band until 1951. The other musicians were "all white guys," plus "a couple of Italians," an older Mexican piccolo player, Sergeant Rodolfo Cedillo, and "a bass player and arranger from Texas, Private Jorge Valadez"; Ortega, interview by author.

174 Anthony Ortega's childhood nickname was "Naff," and his graffiti tag was "Naff del Watts" ("Naff from Watts"); Ortega, interview by Isoardi.

175 Ortega, interview by author; Ortega, interview by Isoardi. On similar incidents of Mexican American musicians causing confusion and mistaken identity while touring the South and Midwest, see Reyes and Waldman, *Land of a Thousand Dances*, xiii; and Lipsitz, "Land of a Thousand Dances," 146.

176 Reyes and Waldman, *Land of a Thousand Dances*, 28.

177 Bernal, interview by author.

178 Smith and Fink, *Off the Record*, 120.

179 Palmer, *Baby, That Was Rock and Roll*, 19; Patrick, liner notes, *The Lieber and Stoller Story*, vol. 1.

180 Palmer, *Baby, That Was Rock and Roll*, 19. See also George, *Death of Rhythm and Blues*, 65; Lipsitz, "Cruising," 140.

181 Smith and Fink, *Off the Record*, 122.

182 Palmer, *Baby, That Was Rock and Roll*, 16.

183 On Lieber and Stoller being influenced by the stop-time riffs of Muddy Waters's 1954 hit songs, see Palmer, *Deep Blues*, 167.

184 Ortega, interview by Isoardi; Ortega, interview by author.

185 Garibay, interview by author. The word *güero* refers to someone with light-colored hair, eyes, and especially, skin.

186 McDonagh, "Status Levels," 450.

187 Ortega, interview by author; Ed Frias, interview by author.

188 Lucie Brac Frias, interview by author.

189 Professional Musicians Local 47 official Web site, "Local 47 History," www.afm47.org/history.htm (accessed February 12, 2006). On the merging of the two unions, see Bryant et al., *Central Avenue Sounds*; and Dickerson, "Central Avenue Meets Hollywood." San Francisco was one of the last major U.S. cities to perpetuate segregated musicians unions, as its Local 6 and Local 669 did not merge until April 1960. See Gioia, *West Coast Jazz*, 62.

190 Vince Ramírez, interview by author. Lalo Guerrero recalled that "in the late forties, the pachucos just disappeared along with their music." See Guerrero and Mentes, *Lalo*, 101.

191 Vigil, "Car Charros," 71.

192 On the etymology of the word *cholo*, see Monroy, *Thrown among Strangers*, 158–59; Rosaura Sánchez, *Telling Identities*, 59; and Vigil, *Indians to Chicanos*, 133. In the 1940s, pachucas were also called *cholitas*, the diminutive for *chola*.

193 Vigil, "Car Charros," 71.

194 Luckenbill, "Pachuco Era," 10.

195 Barker, "Pachuco," 18. Tellingly, *veterano* (veteran) describes not only a combat-tested serviceman, but also a battle-hardened gang member.

196 Luckenbill, "Pachuco Era," 10; Braddy, "Pachucos," 257; Lucie Brac Frias,

interview by author. Beginning in the 1960s and 1970s, as agricultural work clothes influenced urban Chicano style, "cotton bandanas were worn in wide folds as headbands," often with classic 1940s-style hats over them, or with one end tucked into the belted waist and the other dangling down the pant leg. See Luckenbill, "Pachuco Era," 10. Of course, folded bandanas had long been worn as headbands by southwestern Native Americans like the Apache.

197 On placas as "barrio calligraphy," see Marcos Sánchez-Tranquilino, "Mi Casa No Es Su Casa: Chicano Murals and Barrio Calligraphy as Systems of Signification at Estrada Courts, 1972–1978" (Master's thesis, University of California, Los Angeles, 1991), quoted in Villa, *Barrio-Logos*, 64. See also Villa, *Barrio-Logos*, 153.

198 On servicemen in 1954 with cholo tattoos on their hands, forearms, shoulders, and faces, see Braddy, "Pachucos," 257.

199 MacAdams, *Birth of the Cool*, 23.

200 Malcolm X and Haley, *Autobiography*, 52.

201 Ramírez, "Pachucos and Pachucas," 315–16.

202 Arroyo, "La Raza Influence in Jazz," 80–81.

203 Chibnall, "Whistle and Zoot," 62.

204 Ranker, "Study of Juvenile Gangs," 9.

205 Corral, interview by author.

4. The Rock and Roll Era

1 Gillett, *Sound of the City*, 167, 421–27.

2 Garofalo, *Rockin' Out*, 6, 7, 27.

3 Palmer, *Rock and Roll*, 33.

4 Chapple and Garofalo, *Rock 'n' Roll Is Here to Pay*, 46.

5 Ibid., 30; Guevara, "View," 117; Lipsitz, "Land of a Thousand Dances," 276.

6 Metropolitan Recreation and Youth Services Council, Lettergram listing teenage clubs in East Los Angeles, December 19, 1956, John Anson Ford Papers, box 61, Los Angeles County Government, III, Services, folder 14, bbb (5), Huntington Library.

7 Norman S. Johnson, Director, Los Angeles County Department of Parks and Recreation, "Dedication Program, Belvedere Lake," October 13, 1956, John Anson Ford Papers, box 41, folder B III, 10a (7), Huntington Library.

8 Rock and Roll Fan Club, Jordan High School, Watts, black-and-white photograph in Otis, *Upside Your Head!*, 63.

9 Molina, *Old Barrio Guide*, 6.

10 Reyes and Waldman, *Land of a Thousand Dances*, 45–46; Ben Quiñones, "Do You Remember Rock and Roll Radio? Then You Must Know Art Laboe," posted September 8, 2005, www.laweekly.com/music/music/do-you-remember-

rock-roll-radio/300/ (accessed August 31, 2006); "Killer Oldies Sunday Special with Art Laboe," www.killeroldies.com/artlaboe.htm (accessed August 31, 2006); Molina, *Old Barrio Guide*, 5.

11 "Johnny Otis Biography," www.johnnyotisworld.com/biography/index.html (accessed July 26, 2006); "The Greatest Johnny Otis Show," www.johnnyotis world.com/cds/greatest.htm (accessed August 28, 2006); Bill Dahl, "Johnny Otis," *All Music Guide*, music.yahoo.com/ar-260227-bio_Johnny-Otis (accessed August 28, 2006); Otis, *Upside Your Head!*, 61.

12 Lipsitz, "Cruising," 142.

13 Otis, *Upside Your Head!*, 60–61. Chief Parker used similar tactics when he invoked a long-dormant statute, the Criminal Syndicalist Law, to arrest John Harris, a black Angeleno labor and civil rights activist, in 1966. Thanks to Ralph Shaffer for this point.

14 Metropolitan Recreation and Youth Services Council, Program Study Report, May 17, 1956, John Anson Ford Papers, box 61, Los Angeles County Government, III, Services, folder 14, bbb (5), Huntington Library.

15 "Shelve Proposal for Out-of-Doors Dancing in Parks," news clipping, June 1956, John Anson Ford Papers, box 33, folder B III, 7b (4), Huntington Library.

16 Letter from Los Angeles County Probation Officer, August 1936, Parks and Recreation Correspondence, 1936–1958, John Anson Ford Papers, box 41, folder B III, 10a (1), Huntington Library.

17 Reyes and Waldman, *Land of a Thousand Dances*, 45; Molina, *Old Barrio Guide*, 5; Otis, *Upside Your Head!*, xxvi, 61; Matt Garcia, *World of Its Own*, 199; Ben Quiñones, "Do You Remember Rock and Roll Radio? Then You Must Know Art Laboe," posted September 8, 2005, www.laweekly.com/music/ music/do-you-remember-rock-roll-radio/300/ (accessed August 31, 2006).

18 Otis, *Upside Your Head!*, 61–62.

19 Matt Garcia, *World of Its Own*, 208.

20 Matt Garcia, "Colonies, *Colonias*, and Culture," 255–56.

21 Matt Garcia, *World of Its Own*, 206.

22 Otis, *Upside Your Head!*, xxvii, 61.

23 Levine, "Jazz and American Culture," 181. From the blues to jazz to rock and roll, William Barlow identifies a "proclivity to break down cultural barriers and to refashion race and social relations along more egalitarian lines" that has historically presented "a radical alternative to the color-coded, hierarchical dominant culture." See Barlow, *Looking up at Down*, 345–46.

24 Norris Poulson, "Music Is the Heart of a City," *Music Journal*, March 1958, 7, 8, 121.

25 The "Los Reyes" singers and guitarists were: "Chief" Hernandez, Al "Bomber" Ortiz, Robert "Pato" Renteria, Art "Tudy" Brambilla, Freddie Russi, Pete Ruiz, and Hector Vizcarra; "Lincoln Heights," 2.

26 Matt Garcia, *World of Its Own*, 206.

27 Loza, *Barrio Rhythm*, 82; Guevara, "View," 118; Reyes and Waldman, *Land of a Thousand Dances*, 23–24; Garofalo, *Rockin' Out*, 91.

28 Molina, *Old Barrio Guide*, 5.

29 By 1957, the Scrivner Drive-In fans had been requesting so many songs from the early-to-mid-1950s, that Laboe started calling these vocal R & B hits "oldies but goodies." In early 1959, Laboe released the first album to assemble hit songs by various artists from different labels, the compilation *Oldies but Goodies*, vol. 1, which stayed on *Billboard* magazine's top 100 LPs chart for over three years; Ben Quiñones, "Do You Remember Rock and Roll Radio?: Then You Must Know Art Laboe," posted September 8, 2005, www.laweekly .com/music/music/do-you-remember-rock-roll-radio/300/ (accessed August 31, 2006); "Killer Oldies Sunday Special with Art Laboe," www.killer oldies.com/artlaboe.htm (accessed August 31, 2006); Molina, *Old Barrio Guide*, 5.

30 Late 1940s vocal harmony groups, such as the Ink Spots and the Mills Brothers, reflected the intricate harmonies, melodic progressions, and complicated arrangements of big band jazz, while the early-to-mid-1950s groups maintained the sexual lyrics of blues and R & B; Gribin and Schiff, *Doo-Wop*, 24–32, 46.

31 Hoskyns, *Waiting for the Sun*, 32. See also Propes and Gart, *L.A. R & B Vocal Groups*.

32 Reed, *Black Music History*, 382–83; Molina, *Old Barrio Guide*, 63; Warner, *American Singing Groups*, 229–30.

33 Warner, *American Singing Groups*, 272–73.

34 Gribin and Schiff, *Doo-Wop*, 120–21; Molina, *Old Barrio Guide*, 5, 68.

35 "Rock 'n' Roll Helping Race Relations, Platters Contend," *Down Beat* 23 (May 30, 1956): 14.

36 Don Snowden, "The Sound of East L.A.," *Los Angeles Times*, October 28, 1984, Calendar sec., 6.

37 Loza, *Barrio Rhythm*, 134.

38 Reed, *Black Music History*, 383. In the Midwest and on the East Coast, the main nonblack support for doo wop came from Puerto Ricans and Italian Americans; in Southern California, it came from Mexican Americans.

39 Thanks to Merry Ovnick for this telephone-pole flier anecdote.

40 Reyes and Waldman, *Land of a Thousand Dances*, 33.

41 Lipsitz, "Cruising," 142.

42 Reyes and Waldman, *Land of a Thousand Dances*, 17.

43 Lipsitz, "Cruising," 142–43; George Lipsitz., introduction to Otis, *Upside Your Head!*, xxvii.

44 Mendheim, *Ritchie Valens*, 16–22; Keane, narrative track, *Ritchie Valens Story*; Lehmer, *Day the Music Died*, 48–49.

45 Mendheim, *Ritchie Valens*, 23.

46 Ibid., 27–28, 31–35; Lehmer, *Day the Music Died*, 49–50; Reyes and Waldman, *Land of a Thousand Dances*, 40.

47 Mendheim, *Ritchie Valens*, 34, 36.

48 Reyes and Waldman, *Land of a Thousand Dances*, 39; Lehmer, *Day the Music Died*, 52.

49 Vera, "Introduction," liner notes, *Come On, Let's Go*, 6.

50 Mendheim, *Ritchie Valens*, 94–102; Lehmer, *Day the Music Died*, 51–56; Bryan Thomas, "The Real Story of Ritchie Valens," liner notes, *Come On, Let's Go*, 17, 30, 33–36, 41–43, 47–49, 52; Tanenbaum, "Reissue Producer's Notes," liner notes, *Come On, Let's Go*.

51 Mendheim, *Ritchie Valens*; Jim Dawson, "Valens: The Forgotten Story," *Los Angeles Times*, February 3, 1980, Calendar sec., 100.

52 Mendheim, *Ritchie Valens*, 18–19. Mexican "ranch music" shares some similarities with country and western music, including a highly emotional message and vocalization, and the use of 3/4 time or brisk 2/4 polka time. In the 1940s, country and western bands occasionally recorded Americanized versions of Mexican songs like "Allá en mi rancho grande." According to George Lewis, the two traditionally working-class genres "are tinged with sadness," glorify rural life, and "can evoke a vague sort of nationalistic feel." Lewis argues that the passion of the ranchera singers is seldom matched in U.S. country and western singing. See Lewis, "Pistola y el Corazón," 58–59.

53 Rock and roll, of course, drew from western swing and early country music. See, e.g., Lipsitz, "Ain't Nobody Here but Us Chickens."

54 Mendheim, *Ritchie Valens*, 99; Lehmer, *Day the Music Died*, 55.

55 Loza, "Veracruz to Los Angeles," 179–81; Lewis, "Pistola y el Corazón," 54.

56 *Clave* describes the traditional rhythm that is the basis for much of Cuban music, and claves are the small wooden sticks used to tap it out. For a full definition, see chap. 5.

57 Apparently Ritchie understood enough Spanish to communicate with his grandmother, who spoke no English; Keane, narrative track, *Ritchie Valens Story*; Lehmer, *Day the Music Died*, 53; Benz, *Ritchie Valens Story*; Mendheim, *Ritchie Valens*, 22.

58 On "Malagueña," see Mendheim, *Ritchie Valens*, 88–89.

59 Dick Dale claimed that he absorbed the tremolo picking style from the Lebanese music of his father's family heritage. In particular, he was influenced by an uncle who played belly dance music on an oud, as heard in Dale's early use of exotic scales and Middle Eastern melodies; Charles McGovern, correspondence with author, July 26, 1998. Dale's roaring ocean-inspired sound employed extreme volume, powerful amplifiers, heavy reverb, and rapid-fire licks. On Dick Dale, Ritchie Valens, and Bob Keene, see Mendheim, *Ritchie Valens*, 90; Lehmer, *Day the Music Died*, 51.

60 Bob Keane has maintained that rather than full compositions, Valens would usually only play the first lines, opening chords, and a catchy riff or rhythm, which would then be repeated and ad-libbed. Keane asserted that he had to fix lyrics that rambled or made no sense, and he claimed cowriting credits on five Valens recordings, yet as Rene Hall countered, "They were [Ritchie's] tunes. He was making them up." Keane has given himself ample credit for editing, overdubbing, remixing, correcting, and completing many of Valens's songs, yet Rene Hall insisted that "the music was very well planned in Ritchie's mind." See Mendheim, *Ritchie Valens*, 48, 46, 50; Keane, narrative track, *Ritchie Valens Story*; and Lehmer, *Day the Music Died*, 52–53. As Hall noted, Valens was "a creative artist. He couldn't read or write music, but he knew what he wanted and what every instrument was to play. He couldn't set it down, so he'd play riffs on his guitar or hum them to show me what he wanted." See Dawson, "Valens." Hall explained how Valens "communicated ideas" to his session bandmates in a process of professional collaboration, and how Valens, who never played the same song the same way twice, intuitively overcame his instrument's technical limitations to create the sounds he imagined in his mind. Hall said of him, "He wasn't a technical guitarist, but a creative guitarist." See Mendheim, *Ritchie Valens*, 48, 50–51, 47.

61 Peña, *Mexican American Orquesta*, 71, 88. Valens is mentioned along with other "co-opted" commercial acts Vicki Carr, Andy Russell, Thee Midnighters, and Los Lobos.

62 Mendheim, *Ritchie Valens*, 63; Thomas, "The Real Story of Ritchie Valens," liner notes, *Come On, Let's Go*, 6.

63 Scherman, *Backbeat*, 114.

64 Benz, *Ritchie Valens Story*.

65 Reyes and Waldman, *Land of a Thousand Dances*, 40; Dawson, "Valens," 101.

66 In addition to many published accounts and CD liner notes on the subject, three documentaries will be forthcoming: *The West Coast Eastside Sound Story*, financed by Hector González and directed by Emmy Award–winner Jimmy Velarde; *Chicano Rock*, a PBS film based on the Reyes and Waldman book, directed by Jon Wilkman; and an independent video by Max Uballez and Ruben Molina. Mexican Americans also made up the Dallas, Texas, band, Sam the Sham and the Pharoahs ("Wooly Bully," 1965), and the Saginaw, Michigan, band, Question Mark and the Mysterions ("96 Tears," 1965). See Garofalo, *Rockin' Out*, 168; and Reyes and Waldman, *Land of a Thousand Dances*, ix, 55.

67 Snowden, "Sound of East L.A." 6.

68 Reyes and Waldman, *Land of a Thousand Dances*, xix.

69 Iggy Pop, when asked about the influences on the protopunk rock music and aesthetic of his late 1960s Ann Arbor–Detroit area band, the Stooges, replied, "I was aware of 'Naa Na Na Na Naa' by Cannibal and the Headhunters"; Iggy

Pop, interview by Terry Gross, *Fresh Air*, National Public Radio, original air date, July 14, 2005.

70 Davis, interview by Joseph, liner notes, *East Side Sound*.

71 Reflecting a general ethnic Mexican and Latin influence, several years earlier The Lighthouse All-Stars had recorded songs like "Mexican Passport," "Viva Zapata! No. 1," and "Mambo Los Feliz"; Ortega, interview by Isoardi.

72 Ibid.

73 Ibid. Red Norvo also hired a talented young Tejano saxophone, clarinet, and flute player named Modesto Briseño, who then moved to Los Angeles, but Briseño died in an automobile accident before he could make his name. There was also a gifted young Mexican American trumpeter named Alex Rodriguez who, according to Paul Lopez, "should have gone to New York." Unable to find enough work in Los Angeles, Rodriguez eventually fell on hard times; Lopez, interview by author, August 5, 1999.

74 Sesma, interview by author, April 7, 2005.

75 Ortega, interview by Isoardi; Ortega, interview by author; Bernal, interview by author. Ray Victor eventually worked his solo act in Las Vegas and abroad. In 1937, John Harrah and his son Bill Harrah used the money they made as the most successful bingo parlor operators on the Venice Pier to build a casino first in Reno, and then in Lake Tahoe, Nevada.

76 Ortega, interview by Isoardi.

77 Ibid. In the 1950s, Mexican trumpeter Rafael Mendez appeared as a guest artist on several popular early television programs, and performed concerts at high schools, colleges, and concert halls throughout the United States. Between 1954 and 1969, Mendez undertook several European concert tours, and in 1964 he became the first trumpeter to play a solo performance at Carnegie Hall. See "Rafael Mendez" obituary, *Variety* 304 no. 9 (September 30, 1981): 130; "Rafael Mendez," in Meier, *Mexican American Biographies*, 139; "Featured TV Guests: Rafael Mendez and His Olds," *Down Beat* 20 no. 8 (April 22, 1953): 22; Rafael Mendez, "Trumpeter on a Teaching Tour," *Music Journal* 10 no. 6 (September 1952): 25, 50–51; and "Mendez Makes a Classic Return," *Melody Maker* 29 no. 1018 (March 21, 1953): 6.

78 Tapscott, interview by Isoardi.

79 Ortega, interview by Isoardi. On Jews opening doors for black musicians, see Farmer, interview by Isoardi; Bryant et al., *Central Avenue Sounds*, 68.

80 Ortega, interview by author.

81 Ortega, interview by Isoardi; Ortega, interview by author.

82 Ortega, interview by author; Ortega, telephone conversation with author, April 19, 2007; Hardy, "Anthony Ortega, New Dance!," original liner notes, Ortega, *New Dance!*; Hardy, "Anthony Ortega, Permutations," original liner notes, Ortega, *New Dance!*; Lange, liner notes, Ortega, *New Dance!*

83 Ortega, interview by author.

84 Tosti, interview by author, June 29, 2004; Tosti, interview by author, August 20, 1998; Lopez, interview by author, June 18, 1999; Sesma, interview by author, September 1, 2004.

85 Ortega, interview by Isoardi; Tapscott, interview by Isoardi.

86 Lopez, interview by author, September 2, 1998; Lopez, interview by author, June 18, 1999.

87 Tosti, interview by author, August 20, 1998.

88 Ortega, interview by Isoardi.

89 Bernal, interview by Isoardi; Bernal, interview by author.

90 Ed Frias, interview by author.

91 Bernal, interview by Isoardi.

92 "Jones Spikes Rumors about His Not Playing Dance Music," *Down Beat*, April 22, 1953, 44.

93 Dawson, *Nervous Man Nervous*, 120; Bernal, interview by author.

94 Bernal, interview by Isoardi; Bernal, interview by author.

95 Bernal, interview by author.

96 Guerrero and Mentes, *Lalo*, 120–24.

97 Ibid., 112–13, 127–28, 130–34, 198–205, 212; Lalo Guerrero, musical recordings, CA108, CA109, Braun Research Library, Southwest Museum of the American Indian, Mt. Washington, Calif.; *Lalo Guerrero's Greatest Parodies* (Sounds of Sancho Records, 1998). Thanks to Richard Barron for this compact disc.

98 Guerrero, interview by Pill, fall 1983.

99 Villarino, *Mexican and Chicano Music*, vi.

100 Agustin Gurza, "Lalo Guerrero, 88; Pioneering Barrio Singer," *Los Angeles Times*, March 18, 2005, Obituary, sec. B, 10.

101 On the appeal of black music, and of "hoods and greasers," for middle-class "Beat and bohemian subcultures," whose members engaged in "a rejection of bourgeois respectability" that included smoking marijuana, using black slang, and wearing either black clothes or "Levi's and work shirts," see Breines, "'Other' Fifties," 383, 385, 392–94, 399. On white beatniks' self-consciously sporting dark, somber colors to suggest mystery and outsider alienation, see Mercer, "Black Hair/Style Politics," 255. See also Carr, Case, and Dellar, *Hip*.

102 David Reyes and Tom Waldman, "That Barrio Sound," *Pulse*, June 1992, 49–50, quoted in Lipsitz, *Dangerous Crossroads*, 86, 93.

103 "Lincoln Heights," 9.

104 Vigil, *Barrio Gangs*, 121–24. On the other hand, contrary to the image of Marlon Brando's biker gang in *The Wild One* (1953), Mexican Americans and California Indians may also have participated in the state's motorcycle subculture, drawn by its freedom on the outskirts of the mainstream. On teens, class, hot rods, and drag racing, see Moorehouse, "'Work' Ethic."

105 Lipsitz, "Land of a Thousand Dances," 272.
106 In a manifest destiny culture clash between civilized, racially superior white order and primitive, mongrel Mexican civil chaos, the term *greaser* did hegemonic ideological work. By portraying Tejanos as lazy, lewd, un-American, morally defective, and subhuman, Anglos justified the use of violence to keep Mexicans in their place. See Leon, *They Called Them Greasers*. On the 1855 California "Vagrancy Act," or, as it was commonly known, the "Greaser Act," and on Hollywood silent movies like *The Greaser's Gauntlet* (1908), *Tony the Greaser* (1911), *The Girl and the Greaser* (1913), *The Greaser's Revenge* (1914), and *Bronco Billy and the Greaser* (1914), see Bender, *Greasers and Gringos*, xviii–xiv.
107 By the 1970s, the British rockers' successors were called "greasers." See Hebdige, *Subculture*, 52, 44, 130.
108 "Lincoln Heights," 9.
109 Lucie Brac Frias, interview by author.
110 Ranker, "Study of Juvenile Gangs," 40.
111 Matt Garcia, *World of Its Own*, 201.
112 Guevara, "View," 118; Matt Garcia, *World of Its Own*, 201–2.
113 Ray, interview by author; Reyes and Waldman, *Land of a Thousand Dances*, 11.
114 Matt Garcia, "Memories of El Monte," 160–61.
115 Reyes and Waldman, *Land of a Thousand Dances*, 88–89.
116 Pagán, *Murder at the Sleepy Lagoon*, 54.
117 Barrientos, interview by author, January 7, 2000.
118 Guevara, "View," 118; Pagán, *Murder at the Sleepy Lagoon*, 54.
119 Guevara, "View," 118.
120 Burge, "Bajito y suavecito," 2–3; Matt Garcia, *World of Its Own*, 201.
121 Guevara, "View," 118.
122 Davis, interview by Joseph, liner notes, *East Side Sound*.
123 Espinoza, *"Tanto tiempo disfrutamos,"* 95, 92–93.
124 Miranda, "East Side Revue," 23.
125 Miranda, "Dancing."
126 Hebdige, *Subculture*, 52, 54.
127 Reyes and Waldman, *Land of a Thousand Dances*, 88.
128 Metropolitan Recreation and Youth Services Council, Report on Second Phase of the Recreation and Group Program Study of Future Needs for Recreation Facilities and Services in Eight Communities within Los Angeles County, June 30, 1956, John Anson Ford Papers, box 61, Los Angeles County Government, III, Services, folder 14, bbb (5), Huntington Library.
129 Metropolitan Recreation and Youth Services Council, Program Study Report, May 17, 1956, John Anson Ford Papers, box 61, Los Angeles County Government, III, Services, folder 14, bbb (5), Huntington Library.
130 González, "Factors Relating to Property Ownership of Chicanos in Lincoln Heights, Los Angeles," 111–14, 118, 123, 127–28. The Dogtown barrio was

crisscrossed by the construction of the Pasadena Freeway (1940–53), and the Golden State Freeway (1956–75), near the present-day Metro Gold Line's "Lincoln Heights/Cypress Park" stop.

131 "Lincoln Heights," 9.

132 McNamara, "Mexican Americans," 69, 71–72.

133 Ibid., 74–77.

134 Ibid., 85–93.

135 Ibid., 93–94, 122, 108, 81, 96.

136 Ibid., 98, 105, 102.

137 Edward Roybal, interview by Robin Fitzgerald Scott; quoted in Scott, "Mexican American," 298.

138 McNamara, "Mexican Americans," 102–7, 99–101, 59–60.

139 Alvarez, interview by author.

140 McEntire, *Residence and Race*, 241.

141 Moore and Mittlebach, "Residential Segregation," 21, 13, 33.

142 *Negroes and Mexican Americans*, 23.

143 Born Richard Anthony Marin in 1946, "Cheech" earned his nickname from his childhood love of *chicharrón* (Mexican fried pork rinds). As a suburban youth, Marin sang jazz, R & B, and rock in neighborhood bands, eventually majoring in English at California State University, Northridge. In addition to the successful "Cheech and Chong" comedy albums and movies, and his many television, film, and animation voice credits, Marin also wrote and directed *Born in East L.A.* (Universal Pictures, 1987), and, as one of the foremost collectors of Chicano art, organized the traveling museum exhibit, "Chicano Visions." www.cheechandchong.com/biography.html (accessed March 2, 2006); www.chicano-art-life.com/cheech.html (accessed May 11, 2007).

144 Alvarez, interview by author.

145 Bryant et al., *Central Avenue Sounds*, 109.

146 Nicolaides, *My Blue Heaven*, 194, 211–12, 288.

147 Vince Ramírez, interview by author; Edna Ramírez, interview by author.

148 Moore and Mittelbach, *Residential Segregation*, as quoted in Mittelbach, Moore, and McDaniel, *Intermarriage*, 6.

149 *Negroes and Mexican Americans*, 30.

150 Reyes and Waldman, *Land of a Thousand Dances*, 115; Ben Quiñones, "Naa Na Na Na Naa: How the West Coast Eastside Sound Changed Rock and Roll," *LA Weekly*, December 30–January 5, 2006, 31.

151 *Californians of Spanish Surname*, 5, 6, 9.

152 Ortiz, "Mexican American," 1–4, 10, 9.

153 Ibid., 6, 7, 9.

154 Ibid., 6, 11.

155 *Special Employment Problems*, 21–31.

156 Ibid., 42–44.

157 Ibid., 48, 51–56.

158 Ibid., 59, 60, 68–72.

159 Snowden, "Sound of East L.A.," 7.

160 Ibid.

161 Guevara, "View," 120.

162 Snowden, "Sound of East L.A.," 7. The El Monte Legion Stadium building was closed to live musical performances in 1974 and eventually torn down.

163 On the cold war period bringing "the end of twenty years of New Deal progressivism in Southern California," see Avila, *Popular Culture*, 156.

5. Latin Jazz, the Mambo

1 George Sánchez, "The Familiar Sounds of Change: Music and the Growth of Mass Culture," in *Becoming Mexican American*.

2 Barrientos, interview by author, January 7, 2000; Loza, *Barrio Rhythm*.

3 Lopez, interview by author, September 2, 1998.

4 Lopez, interview by author, June 18, 1999; Barrientos, interview by author, January 7, 2000.

5 Before the establishment of casinos in Las Vegas, rich Hollywood Anglos gambled and took in musical revues across the border in Tijuana. See Ramírez Berg, "Colonialism and Movies." On "lite colonial" as "colonial subordination . . . impelled by markets and oriented toward consumers," see Flores, *Bomba to Hip-Hop*, 38. In the 1940s, "racism in Cuba was such . . . that black Cubanos and white Cubanos could not mix in the front of the clubs; black musicians had to come in the back door"; Barrientos, interview by author, January 7, 2000. Both Miami and Las Vegas remained segregated until the 1960s, when African American and Afro-Latin bandleaders finally forced the end of Jim Crow policies. On earlier desegregation efforts, see "Battle Jim Crow in Miami Locals," *Down Beat* 16 no. 18 (September 23, 1949): 1.

6 Paul Lopez, guest lecture, Chicano Studies 182, University of California, Los Angeles, May 24, 2000.

7 Pitt and Pitt, *Los Angeles A to Z*, 489.

8 Lopez, interview by author, June 18, 1999.

9 Mario García, *Mexican Americans*, 156.

10 "Trocadero Gets Carter, Cole Trio," *Down Beat* (March 1, 1945), 6.

11 Loza, *Barrio Rhythm*, 69.

12 Tosti, interview by author, August 20, 1998; Hernandez, interview by author.

13 Lopez, interview by author, June 18, 1999.

14 Lopez, interview by author, September 2, 1998; Lopez, interview by author, June 18, 1999; Tosti, interview by author, August 20, 1998.

15 Guerrero, interview by Heisley and Pill; Guerrero and Mentes, *Lalo*, 66. See also Loza, *Barrio Rhythm*, 68–69. During the war years, Bobby Ramos sang and waited tables at Club La Bamba, but his band eventually played the Latin clubs on the Sunset Strip, the Cocoanut Grove at the Ambassador Hotel in Los Angeles, the Saint Francis Hotel in San Francisco, and the Stevens Hotel in Chicago; Guerrero and Mentes, *Lalo*, 66; Mario García, *Memories of Chicano History*, 120.

16 Lopez, interview by author, September 2, 1999; Lopez, interview by author, June 18, 1999; Tosti, interview by author, August 20, 1998.

17 Hernandez, interview by author.

18 Tosti, interview by author, August 20, 1998.

19 Lucie Brac Frias, interview by author; Ray, interview by author. As part of the Bracero Program, the wartime agreement between the U.S. and Mexico that was renewed in the postwar period, Mexican contract laborers, or "guest workers," filled positions in agriculture and industry, and on the railroads.

20 Lucie Brac Frias, interview by author.

21 Tosti, interview by author, August 20, 1998; Varela, liner notes, *Pachuco Boogie*, 9; Fessier, "Secret Star."

22 Tosti, interview by author, April 23, 1999.

23 Roberts, *Latin Tinge*, 259.

24 Mauleón, "Heart of Salsa," 33–34; Roberts, *Latin Tinge*, 259; Leymarie, *Cuban Fire*, 37–38.

25 Roberts, *Latin Tinge*, 102.

26 Mauleón, "Heart of Salsa," 33–34; Roberts, *Latin Tinge*, 265. See also Mauleón, *Salsa Guidebook*; Salazar, *Mambo Kingdom*.

27 Max Salazar, quoted in *Notes from the Mambo Inn*.

28 Roberts, *Latin Tinge*, 114.

29 Fernández, *Latin Jazz*, 39–40; Salazar, *Mambo Kingdom*, 37–39, 43–45; Ralph J. Gleason, "Miguelito Valdes Makes a Mighty Pitch for Progress," *Down Beat* 19 no. 16 (August 13, 1952): 2.

30 González and Oquendo, liner notes, *More than Mambo*.

31 On Arnaz at Ciro's, see Roberts, *Latin Tinge*, 112. The original "Cuban Pete" was a New York Puerto Rican dancer named Pedro Aquilar. See Stearns and Stearns, *Jazz Dance*, 360.

32 Bernal, interview by author.

33 Lozano, interview by author; Saito, interview by author, December 29, 1999; Lopez, interview by author, September 2, 1998; Salazar, *Mambo Kingdom*, 47.

34 Salazar, *Mambo Kingdom*, 47; Lopez, interview by author, June 18, 1999. Tony Reyes came back to Los Angeles in the 1950s and opened a tortilla factory, although he still played occasionally. Little is known about Reyes's later years, but he allegedly met a tragic death under very mysterious circumstances.

35 Lopez, interview by author, September 2, 1998; Salazar, "Paul Lopez," 5.

36 Lopez, interview by author, September 2, 1998; Lopez, interview by author, June 18, 1999.

37 Ibid. On Chuy Reyes's classical music background, see Loza, *Barrio Rhythm*, 61.

38 Lopez, interview by author, September 2, 1998; Lopez, interview by author, June 18, 1999.

39 Lopez, interview by author, September 2, 1998.

40 Roberts, *Latin Tinge*, 117.

41 Sublette, *Cuba and Its Music*, 508–9, 512, 554; Morales, *The Latin Beat*, 44–45; "Mambo King: Cuban Negro Pianist Creates New Beat That Becomes a Colorful Dance Craze," *Ebony* 6 (September 1951): 45. See also Ralph Gleason, "Latin Leaders Explain Origin of the Mambo," *Down Beat* 19 no. 2 (January 25, 1952): 2.

42 Lozano, interview by author.

43 Barrientos, interview by author, January 7, 2000.

44 "Prado One-Niter Sets L.A. on Ear," *Down Beat* 18 no. 19 (September 21, 1951): 1.

45 Charles Emge, "Move Grows to Scrap L.A.'s Jim Crow Union," *Down Beat* 18 no. 12 (June 15, 1951): 1.

46 "Prado One-Niter," 1.

47 Barrientos, interview by author, January 7, 2000.

48 Saito, interview by author, July 12, 1999.

49 Corral, interview by author.

50 Reyes and Waldman, *Land of a Thousand Dances*, 19–21.

51 Corral, interview by author.

52 Ed Frias, interview by author. Richard Barrientos also saw the Armenta Brothers at the Zenda; Barrientos, interview by author, January 7, 2000.

53 From his beginnings as a sales account executive, George Chavez had become executive vice president and part owner of the Santa Monica radio station by 1957; Sesma, interview by author, September 4, 1998. On Sesma's start in radio, see also Loza, *Barrio Rhythm*, 84; Reyes and Waldman, *Land of a Thousand Dances*, 4–5; and Loza, *Tito Puente*, 94–95.

54 Sesma, interview by author, August 23, 2004.

55 Sesma, interview by author, September 4, 1998.

56 Ibid.; Sesma, interview by author, September 1, 2004; Sesma, interview by author, August 23, 2004. On the "Aesthetics of *Sabor*," see Fernández, *From Afro-Cuban Rhythms to Latin Jazz*, chap. 3.

57 Sesma, interview by author, September 4, 1998; Saito, interview by author, July 12, 1999.

58 González, interview by author, June 8, 1999; González, interview by author, June 11, 1999. González was arrested as an accessory to grand theft auto after

an accident in his friend's uncle's car. Since he already had a juvenile police record, the judge gave him the choice between reform school or the armed forces.

59 Loza, *Barrio Rhythm*, 75.

60 Lozano, interview by author; Barrientos, interview by author, June 30, 1999; Saito, interview by author, December 29, 1999.

61 Ortiz, "Mexican American," 3, 4.

62 Fernández, "Notes from East L.A.," 444.

63 Saito, interview by author, December 29, 1999.

64 Nelson Rodríguez, "Bobby Montez: Unearthing a Gem," *Latin Beat Magazine*, August 2001. By the mid-1950s, after Ed Frias married Lucie Brac, they remember dancing to Bobby Montez at the Zenda; Ed Frias, interview by author.

65 Dennis McLellan, "Tony Martinez, 'Pepino' on 'Real McCoys,' Dies at 82," www.latinamericanstudies.org/cine/tony-martinez.htm (accessed February 4, 2006).

66 Sesma, interview by author, August 23, 2004; Broderick, liner notes to Lopez, *Cha-Cha-Cha If You Please*.

67 Mauleón, "Heart of Salsa," 152; Roberts, *Latin Tinge*, 131–32; Leymarie, *Cuban Fire*, 69.

68 Lopez, interview by author, June 18, 1999.

69 Saito, interview by author, December 29, 1999.

70 Sesma, interview by author, August 23, 2004.

71 Sesma, interview by author, September 4, 1998; Barrientos, interview by author, January 7, 2000.

72 Loza, *Barrio Rhythm*, 150, 152–55, 157, 262; Child, "Eddie Cano," 206–7; Green, liner notes, *Cha Cha con Cano*; Fernández, *Latin Jazz*, 67; "Eddie Cano," www.spaceagepop.com/cano.htm (accessed March 20, 2006); Eugene Chadbourne, "Eddie Cano," *All Music Guide*, www.answers.com/topic/eddie-cano (accessed September 2, 2006); Bob Caro, "Eddie Cano: A Great and Versatile Musician," *L.A. Jazz Scene* (June 1999): 25–26.

73 Bloch, interview by Isoardi.

74 Sesma, interview by author, August 23, 2004.

75 Macias, interview by author.

76 Baiz, interview by author.

77 Saito, interview by author, July 12, 1999; Saito, interview by author, December 29, 1999.

78 Tosti, interview by author, April 23, 1999.

79 Tosti, interview by author, August 20, 1998; Sesma, interview by author, September 4, 1998; Tosti, interview by author, April 23, 1999.

80 Ortega, interview by Isoardi.

81 Ortega, interview by author.

82 Ortega, interview by Isoardi; Farmer, interview by Isoardi.

83 Saito, interview by author, December 29, 1999.

84 Saito, interview by author, July 21, 2004; Loza, *Tito Puente*, 96.

85 Barrientos, interview by author, June 30, 1999; Barrientos, interview by author, January 7, 2000; Saito, interview by author, January 7, 2000; Saito, interview by author, July 21, 2004; Baiz, interview by author.

86 Ed Frias, interview by author.

87 Tosti, interview by author, August 20, 1998; Alvarez; interview by author; Dora Rico, interview by author.

88 Corral, interview by author; Barrientos, interview by author, January 7, 2000.

89 After shows at Club Virginia's and Club Havana, some of the musicians and dancers would eat at the Nayarit, a late-night Mexican restaurant on Sunset Boulevard just past Echo Park Avenue, and also at Toñita's, a hole-in-the-wall restaurant on Sunset Boulevard and Alvarado Street owned by a Cuban husband and Puerto Rican wife; Saito, interview by author, January 7, 2000.

90 Lozano, interview by author; Ramón Inclán, "Hecho aquí, con sabor de allá: Danilo Lozano es el director musical de 'Cuba L.A.,' un disco que reúne a músicos cubanos del área en versiones instrumentales de temas clásicos de la isla," *La opinión*, July 27, 1998, sec. D, 1.

91 Bloch's orchestra also included "Little" Joe Terranova, an Italian American musician who eventually became a hair stylist to the stars on Sunset Boulevard; Bloch, interview by Isoardi.

92 Guerrero and Mentes, *Lalo*, 137. Lalo Guerrero owned and operated his nightclub, Lalo's, until 1972.

93 Saito, interview by author, July 12, 1999; Dora Rico, interview by author.

94 Paul Lopez considered Don Tosti "a good bass player." As Paul said, "When I came back from New York [Don] asked me to write something. I did, I wrote him a very difficult thing. And he practiced it and practiced it, and played it . . . [a Latin arrangement] of 'Wouldn't You?' "; Lopez, interview by author, June 18, 1999.

95 Hector Rivera eventually became a business agent in the musicians union. He moved back to Miami and ultimately retired to Montebello. Joe Torres moved to Las Vegas, where he continued to play; Barrientos, interview by author, January 7, 2000.

96 Barrientos, interview by author, January 7, 2000; Saito, interview by author, December 29, 1999.

97 Barrientos, interview by author, January 7, 2000.

98 Barrientos, interview by author, August 20, 2004; Barrientos, interview by author, June 30, 1999.

99 Barrientos, interview by author, January 7, 2000. Richard Barrientos, who

never identified exclusively with either his Filipino or his Mexican heritage, blended in with other Filipinos, but when he played Latin music with Latino musicians, people thought he was Latino. He even picked up a little Spanish, as spoken by Cubans and Puerto Ricans, from playing so many Latin gigs; Barrientos, interview by author, August 20, 2004; Barrientos, interview by author, June 30, 1999.

100 *Notes from the Mambo Inn.*

101 "New Vistas Open for Latino Bands; Hinterland Yens Mambo, Rumba Beat," *Variety* 192 no. 3 (September 23, 1953): 47.

102 Barrientos gave the copywritten arrangements of "Los orientales" and "Guaguanco en Japón" to Nora Suzuki, one of the founders of the Japanese salsa band Orquesta de la Luz, for her first solo album; Barrientos, interview by author, June 30, 1999; Barrientos, interview by author, January 7, 2000.

103 Lopez, interview by author, June 18, 1999; Saito, interview by author, December 29, 1999. Santa Barbara Boulevard is now Martin Luther King Jr. Boulevard.

104 Lopez, interview by author, July 6, 1999; Saito, interview by author, December 29, 1999; Barrientos, interview by author, January 7, 2000.

105 Lopez, interview by author, June 18, 1999.

106 Saito, interview by author, December 29, 1999; Lopez, interview by author, July 6, 1999.

107 Saito, interview by author, July 21, 2004; Lopez, interview by author, July 6, 1999.

108 Garibay, interview by author, September 15, 2004.

109 Paul Lopez, guest lecture, Chicano Studies 197G, University of California, Los Angeles, February 26, 2001.

110 Lopez, interview by author, August 5, 1999.

111 Barrientos, interview by author, January 7, 2000.

112 Lopez, interview by author, June 18, 1999.

113 Barrientos, interview by author, June 30, 1999.

114 Saito, interview by author, December 29, 1999.

115 Reyes and Waldman, *Land of a Thousand Dances*, 15. See also Marsh, *Louie Louie.*

116 Bo Diddley's original band consisted of Diddley on guitar, supported by a drummer and a maraca player. Maracas are small gourds filled with pebbles or seeds, and are similar to other indigenous rattles found throughout the Americas. On Bo Diddley, see Roberts, *Latin Tinge*, 137.

117 John Anson Ford, news release regarding Los Angeles County License Appeals Board, August 24, 1956, John Anson Ford Papers, box 33, folder B III, 7b (4), Huntington Library.

118 Los Angeles County Sheriff's Department Office Correspondence from J. A.

Eddington, Captain, License Detail, to Public Welfare Commission, July 19, 1957, John Anson Ford Papers, box 33, folder B III, 7b (5), Huntington Library.

119 Sesma, interview by author, September 4, 1998. See also Loza, *Barrio Rhythm*, 84; Loza, *Tito Puente*, 95–96.

120 Charles Emge, "Boom in Latin Rhythms Bigger than Ever in L.A.," *Down Beat* 21 no. 15 (July 28, 1954): 5; Saito, interview by author, July 12, 1999.

121 "Mambo Jumbo" concert program. The front cover sports jazzy pen-and-ink sketches of silhouetted African dancers and drummers against a yellow backdrop; the back, a publicity still of Chico Sesma, courtesy Tommy Saito.

122 Sesma, interview by author, September 4, 1998; Charles Emge, "How Palladium Became One of Nation's Top Ballrooms," *Down Beat* 23 no. 8 (April 18, 1956): 16.

123 Sesma, interview by author, September 4, 1998. See also Loza, *Barrio Rhythm*, 84; Loza, *Tito Puente*, 95; Reyes and Waldman, *Land of a Thousand Dances*, 5.

124 Sesma, interview by author, September 4, 1998.

125 Sesma, interview by author, August 23, 2004.

126 Garibay, interview by author.

127 Sesma, interview by author, September 4, 1998.

128 Ibid.; Dora Rico, interview by author.

129 Romeo Prado became the trombonist and horn arranger for Thee Midnighters; Reyes and Waldman, *Land of a Thousand Dances*, 6.

130 Loza, *Barrio Rhythm*, 196; Emmy Sánchez, interview by author. The Sánchez sisters' little brother, Poncho, became a Grammy award–winning conguero and Latin bandleader.

131 Sesma, interview by author, September 4, 1998.

132 Emge, "How Palladium," 6.

133 Sesma, interview by author, September 4, 1998.

134 Garibay, interview by author; Emmy Sánchez, interview by author.

135 Sesma, interview by author, September 4, 1998.

136 Sesma, interview by author, August 23, 2004.

137 Muñoz Castillo, interview by author.

138 On Mexicans and a "commodity identity," see Vélez-Ibañez, *Border Visions*, 7.

139 Club Virginia's flier courtesy Tommy Saito. On the Mexico City "El Latino" advertisement, see Jiménez, *Cabarets*, 146. El Latino was the first jazz club in Mexico City. See Don Freeman, "Mexico City Jazz Concerts Started by Record Dealer," *Down Beat* 23 no. 7 (April 4, 1956): 10.

140 Quiroga, *Tropics of Desire*, 157.

141 Aparicio, *Listening to Salsa*, 127, 139.

142 Monsiváis, *Mexican Postcards*, 181. Other Mexican bolero composers include Rafael Hernández, Maria Grever, Gonzálo Curiel, Gabriel Ruiz, Consuelo Velázquez, Guty Cárdenas, Armando Manzanero, and Trio Los Panchos.

143 Peña, *Texas-Mexican Conjunto*, 13.

144 Peña, *Mexican American Orquesta*, 187, 188.

145 Garibay, interview by author.

146 Ed Frias, interview by author; Corral, interview by author.

147 For three years in the mid-1950s, Candelario Mendoza owned a record store that sold both African American and Mexican music, then he co-owned a record label, "Conde," with his business partner, Bob Rios, for another three years; Mendoza, interview by author. *La raza* literally translates as "the race," but it is used by Chicanos to refer to themselves, as in "the people" or "the folk." In the mid- to late 1950s, Mendoza also hosted an afternoon rock and roll radio program for teens, as well as Friday night rock and roll dances at Rainbow Gardens; Matt Garcia, *World of Its Own*, 195. See also Matt Garcia, " 'Memories of El Monte,' " 157–61, 167–69.

148 Mendoza, interview by author.

149 Monsiváis, interview by author.

150 Mendoza, interview by author.

151 "Darwin and the Mambo," *Time* 64 no. 10 (September 6, 1954): 34.

152 Dora Rico, interview by author.

153 Garibay, interview by author.

154 Corral, interview by author; emphasis in the original.

155 Sesma, interview by author, September 4, 1998; Sesma, interview by author, September 7, 2004; Reyes and Waldman, *Land of a Thousand Dances*, 87, 98, 99.

156 Barrientos, interview by author, January 7, 2000. The Afro-Puerto Rican bandleader Rafael Cortijo is considered by many to be the "father" of the plena. See Flores, "Cortijo's Revenge."

157 Sesma, interview by author, September 4, 1998.

158 "New Vistas," 47; "Mambomania," *Newsweek* 44 no. 7 (August 16, 1954): 54; "Carnegie Hall Just a Top-Hatted Palladium as Mambo Takes Over," *Variety* 196 no. 8 (October 27, 1954): 53; "Mambo Fever Hits Peak in Music Biz, with More to Come," *Variety* 196 no. 7 (October 20, 1954): 121.

159 Macias, interview by author; Barrientos, interview by author, January 7, 2000.

160 Bloch, interview by Isoardi.

161 Lopez, interview by author, June 18, 1999.

162 Baiz, interview by author.

163 Sesma, interview by author, August 23, 2004; Sesma, interview by author, September 7, 2004.

164 Lopez, interview by author, June 18, 1999; Barrientos, interview by author, January 7, 2000; Baiz, interview by author.

165 Sesma, interview by author, August 23, 2004; Caro, "Eddie Cano," 25–26; Loza, *Barrio Rhythm*, 155.

166 Liner notes, *Best of Eddie Cano*.

167 "Trini Lopez, Biography," www.trinilopez.com/bio.htm (accessed October 14, 2005); Bernal, interview by author.

168 Dora Rico, interview by author; "Eddie Cano," www.spaceagepop.com/cano .htm (accessed March 20, 2006).

169 Child, "Eddie Cano," 207.

170 Lopez, interview by author, June 18, 1999; Loza, *Barrio Rhythm*, 156; Child, "Eddie Cano," 207.

171 Barrientos, interview by author, January 7, 2000.

172 Baiz, interview by author.

173 Raul Rico Jr., interview by author. Raul Rico Jr. began playing timbales and bongos with the Estrada Brothers Latin Jazz Sextet in 1976, and began hosting a Latin music radio program as a disc jockey in 1984.

174 Paul Lopez, guest lecture, Chicano Studies 197G, University of California, Los Angeles, February 26, 2001.

175 The major labels, like Columbia, Capitol, RCA, and Decca, were not located on Pico Boulevard, nor were the Descuba and Maype labels, which had come from Cuba to Los Angeles in the late 1950s; Barrientos, interview by author, January 7, 2000.

176 Roberts, *Latin Tinge*, 106.

177 "Latin-American Band of the Year," *Billboard* 63 (September 15, 1951): 42.

178 Emge, "Boom in Latin Rhythms," 5.

179 "Hampton, Cugat Rank among Top Box Office Draws in Band Biz," *Variety* 188 no. 8 (October 29, 1952): 45. The exotic Cuban interlude in *Guys and Dolls* featured a Latin dance routine by Marlon Brando's character, Sky Masterson.

180 Loza, *Barrio Rhythm*, 154, 162; Guerrero and Mentes, *Lalo*, 66.

181 *Latin Cruise* television episode, n.d. Videocassette copy in author's possession, courtesy J. Fred MacDonald.

182 Loza, *Barrio Rhythm*, 66; Sesma, interview by author, September 1, 2004.

183 Loza, *Barrio Rhythm*, 67; Rios-Bustamante and Castillo, *Illustrated History*, 173; Fessier, "Secret Star."

184 Barrientos, interview by author, June 30, 1999.

185 Garibay, interview by author.

186 Stearns and Stearns, *Jazz Dance*, 1, 358.

187 Ibid., 361.

188 Barrientos, interview by author, June 30, 1999; Lopez, interview by author, September 2, 1998.

189 Mrs. Arthur Murray, "What the Heck Is the Mambo?" *Down Beat* 21 no. 24 (December 1, 1954): 2.

190 Nat Hentoff, "The Mambo!! They Shake A-Plenty with Tito Puente," *Down Beat* 21 no. 20 (October 6, 1954): 29.

191 Lopez, interview by author, July 6, 1999.

192 Corral, interview by author.

193 Ibid.

194 Nat Hentoff, "Prado Tells How Mambo Made It, but Not How He Makes It Tick," *Down Beat* 21 no. 24 (December 1, 1954): 3.

195 Lopez, interview by author, July 6, 1999; Dora Rico, interview by author.

196 Saito, interview by author, December 29, 1999.

197 In addition to Joe Cuba's "Bang Bang," the other best-known boogaloo songs were Johnny Colón's "Boogaloo Blues," Pete Rodríguez's "I Like It Like That," and Hector Rivera's "At the Party," all of which came out in 1966 and 1967; Flores, *Bomba to Hip Hop*, 79–83.

198 Paraphrase of Tito Puente, quoted in *Mambo Memories*.

199 Loza, *Tito Puente*, 38.

200 Ray Santos, quoted in *Mambo Memories*.

201 Dick "Ricardo" Sugar, quoted in *Mambo Memories*.

202 Loza, *Tito Puente*, 39.

203 Saito, interview by author, December 29, 1999.

Conclusion

1 On the Brown Berets, see Chávez, *"¡Mi Raza Primero!"* On the high school walkouts, see Rosales, *Chicano!*; and Agustin Gurza, "Reborn in East L.A.," *Los Angeles Times*, December 25, 2005, Calendar sec., E 1, 34.

2 Lalo Guerrero, musical recordings, CA108, Braun Research Library, Southwest Museum of the American Indian, Mt. Washington, Calif.; Guerrero and Mentes, *Lalo*, 200, 202.

3 Mario García, "Americans All," 211.

4 Monroy, *Rebirth*, 257–58, 267–69.

5 Robles Cahero, "Occidentalización," 57–58; Robles Cahero, "Mexican Resonances in American Soundscapes." On rock and roll in Mexico, see Zolov, *Refried Elvis*.

6 George Sánchez, *Becoming Mexican American*, 8, 9, 6.

7 Lopez, interview by author, December 20, 2004.

8 Ralph Ellison, "What America Would Be Like without Blacks," *Time* 95 no. 14 (April 6, 1970): 54. Also quoted in Stowe, "Uncolored People," 71.

9 Tosti, interview by author, June 28, 2004.

10 Kelley, "Notes on Deconstructing 'the Folk,' " 1408.

11 Lipsitz, *Possessive Investment*.

12 Sesma, interview by author, September 4, 1998.

13 Lopez, interview by author, June 18, 1999; Tosti, interview by author, August 20, 1998; Sesma, interview by author, September 1, 2004.

14 Sesma, interview by author, August 23, 2004.

15 Mario García, *Mexican Americans*, 37.

16 Foley, "Becoming Hispanic," 62–64.

17 Nicolaides, *My Blue Heaven*, 288.

18 Bernal, interview by author.

19 Ortega, interview by author.

20 Garibay, interview by author.

21 Alvarez, interview by author.

22 Mendoza, interview by author.

23 Vigil, "Car Charros," 78.

24 Forbes, *Aztecas del Norte*, 68, 57, 53. On the importance of sacred places and people's interconnectedness not only with each other but also with the spirit world, and for a compelling critique of white Christian American culture and the Western/European linear conception of History, see Deloria, *God Is Red*.

BIBLIOGRAPHY

Primary Sources

Archives and Collections

Braun Research Library, Southwest Museum of the American Indian, Mt. Washington, Calif.

Central Avenue Sounds Collection, Center for Oral History Research, Department of Special Collections, Young Research Library, University of California, Los Angeles.

John Anson Ford Papers, Huntington Library, San Marino, Calif.

Lalo Guerrero Collection and Don Tosti Collection, California Ethnic and Multicultural Archives, Department of Special Collections, Donald Davidson Library, University of California, Santa Barbara.

Interviews and Oral Histories

Alvarez, María Olivas. Interview by author. San Gabriel, Calif. September 9, 2004.

Baiz, Jim. Telephone interview by author. October 22, 2004.

Barrientos, Richard. Telephone interview by author. June 30, 1999.

——. Telephone interview by author. January 7, 2000.

——. Telephone interview by author. August 20, 2004.

Bernal, Gil. Interview by Steven Isoardi. Transcript, Central Avenue Sounds Collection, Center for Oral History Research, Department of Special Collections, Young Research Library, University of California, Los Angeles. 1998.

——. Interview by author, Highland Park, Calif. August 3, 2004.

Bloch, Rene. Interview by Steven Isoardi. Transcript, Central Avenue Sounds Collection, Center for Oral History Research, Department of Special Collections, Young Research Library, University of California, Los Angeles. 1995.

Corral, Jaime. Interview by author. Alhambra, Calif. July 19, 1999.

Esquivel, Hortencia. Interview by author. Culver City, Calif. September 2, 2004.

Farmer, Art. Interview by Steven Isoardi. Transcript, Central Avenue Sounds Collection, Center for Oral History Research, Department of Special Collections, Young Research Library, University of California, Los Angeles. 1991.

Figueroa, Ernie. Telephone interview by author. July 2, 2004.

Frias, Ed. Interview by author. Pasadena, Calif. August 17, 1998.

Frias, Lucie Brac. Interview by author. Pasadena, Calif. August 17, 1998.

Garibay, Hortencia Rodarte Torres. Interview by author. Montebello, Calif. September 15, 2004.

González, José. Telephone interview by author. June 8, 1999.

———. Telephone interview by author. June 11, 1999.

Guerrero, Lalo. Interview by Albert S. Pill, fall 1983. Untranscribed audio recording, CA102. Braun Research Library, Southwest Museum of the American Indian, Mt. Washington, Calif.

———. Interview by M. Heisley and Albert S. Pill. Cathedral City, Calif., February 21, 1986. Untranscribed audio recording, CA102. Braun Research Library, Southwest Museum of the American Indian, Mt. Washington, Calif.

———. Interview, June 1986. Transcript, Lalo Guerrero Collection, box 1, folder 5. California Ethnic and Multicultural Archives, Department of Special Collections, Donald Davidson Library, University of California, Santa Barbara.

Guevara, Rubén. Interview by author. University of California, Los Angeles. June 10, 2004.

Hernandez, Mary Gonzalez. Interview by author. Redlands, Calif. August 8, 1998.

Lopez, Paul. Interview by author. El Sereno, Calif. September 2, 1998.

———. Interview by author. El Sereno, Calif. June 18, 1999.

———. Telephone interview by author. July 6, 1999.

———. Interview by author. El Sereno, Calif. August 5, 1999.

———. Conversation with author. Altadena, Calif. September 10, 2004.

———. Interview by author. Altadena, Calif. December 20, 2004.

Lozano, Danilo. Interview by author. Whittier College. Whittier, Calif. September 4, 1998.

Macias, Rudy. Interview by author. Whittier, Calif. August 27, 1998.

Mendoza, Candelario. Interview by author. Pomona, Calif. December 10, 2003.

Monsiváis, Carlos. Interview by author. Mexico City, Mexico. August 4, 2003.

Muñoz Castillo, Fernando. Interview by author. Mexico City, Mexico. August 1, 2003.

Niedorf, Saul. Conversation with author. Echo Park, Calif. October 2, 1999.

Ortega, Anthony. Interview by Steven Isoardi. Transcript, Central Avenue Sounds

Collection, Center for Oral History Research, Department of Special Collections, Young Research Library, University of California, Los Angeles. 1994.

———. Interview by author. Encinitas, Calif. September 24, 2004.

———. Telephone conversations with author. July 31, 2005, and April 17, 2007.

Phillips, William. Interview by Tamara Zwick. Boyle Heights, Calif. February 22, 1990.

Ramírez, Edna. Interview by author. Monterey Park, Calif. July 19, 2004.

Ramírez, Vince. Interview by author. Monterey Park, Calif. July 19, 2004.

Ray, Chole Camarena. Interview by author. Colton, Calif. August 19, 1999.

Rico, Dora. Interview by author. Oxnard, Calif. July 25, 2004.

Rico, Raul, Jr. Telephone interview by author. July 16, 2004.

Robinson, Minor. Interview by Steven Isoardi. Transcript, Central Avenue Sounds Collection, Center for Oral History Research, Department of Special Collections, Young Research Library, University of California, Los Angeles. 1995.

Rodriguez, Edward Martinez. Interview by Manuel I. González. East Los Angeles, Calif. June 2, 2000.

Rodriguez, Jessie. Interview by Manuel I. González. East Los Angeles, Calif. June 2, 2000.

Romo, Virginia Vital. Interview by Manuel I. González. East Los Angeles, Calif. June 2, 2000.

Royal, Marshall. Interview by Steven Isoardi. Transcript, Central Avenue Sounds Collection, Center for Oral History Research, Department of Special Collections, Young Research Library, University of California, Los Angeles. 1991.

Saito, Tommy. Telephone interview by author. July 12, 1999.

———. Telephone interview by author. December 29, 1999.

———. Telephone interview by author. January 7, 2000.

———. Telephone conversation with author. July 2, 2004.

———. Telephone interview by author. July 21, 2004.

Sánchez, Emmy. Telephone interview by author. September 4, 2004.

Sesma, Chico. Interview by author. Boyle Heights, Calif. September 4, 1998.

———. Interview by author. Boyle Heights, Calif. August 23, 2004.

———. Interview by author. Boyle Heights, Calif. September 7, 2004.

———. Interview by author. Boyle Heights, Calif. April 7, 2005.

———. Conversation with author. Boyle Heights, Calif. September 3, 2007.

Tapscott, Horace. Interview by Steven Isoardi. Transcript, Central Avenue Sounds Collection, Center for Oral History Research, Department of Special Collections, Young Research Library, University of California, Los Angeles. 1993.

Tosti, Don. Interview by author. Palm Springs, Calif. August 20, 1998.

———. Telephone interview by author. April 23, 1999.

———. Telephone interview by author. June 28, 2004.

———. Telephone interview by author. June 29, 2004.

Vigil, James Diego. Telephone interview by author. August 15, 1998.

Wilson, Gerald. Interview by Steven Isoardi. Transcript, Central Avenue Sounds Collection, Center for Oral History Research, Department of Special Collections, Young Research Library, University of California, Los Angeles. 1991.

Reports, Government Documents, and Published Primary Sources

Californians of Spanish Surname: Population, Employment, Income, Education. San Francisco: California Department of Industrial Relations, Fair Employment Practices Committee, 1964.

Curtis, Louis Woodson. "Music in the Los Angeles Public Schools." In Rodríguez, *Music and Dance in California*, 1940.

Fisher, Lloyd H. *The Problem of Violence: Observations on Race Conflict in Los Angeles.* San Francisco: American Council on Race Relations, 1947.

McEntire, Davis. *Residence and Race: Final and Comprehensive Report to the Commission on Race and Housing.* Berkeley: University of California Press, 1960.

Mittelbach, Frank G., Joan W. Moore, and Ronald McDaniel. *Intermarriage of Mexican-Americans.* Division of Research, Graduate School of Business Administration, University of California, Los Angeles, 1966.

Moore, Joan W., and Frank G. Mittlebach, with the assistance of Ronald McDaniel. *Residential Segregation in the Urban Southwest: A Comparative Study.* Division of Research, Graduate School of Business Administration, University of California, Los Angeles, 1966.

Negroes and Mexican Americans in South and East Los Angeles: Changes between 1960 and 1965 in Population, Employment, Income, and Family Status. San Francisco: California Department of Industrial Relations, Fair Employment Practices Committee, 1966.

Ortiz, Martin. "The Mexican American in the Los Angeles Community." In *Community Intelligence Bulletin*, no. 3. Los Angeles: Community Relations Educational Foundation, 1963.

Rodríguez, José, ed. Compiled by William J. Perlman. *Music and Dance in California.* Hollywood, Calif.: Bureau of Musical Research, 1940.

Shevky, Eshref, and Molly Levine. *Your Neighborhood: A Social Profile of Los Angeles.* Los Angeles: Haynes Foundation, 1949.

Special Employment Problems of the Mexican-American. Transcript of Proceedings, California State Assembly, Committee on Industrial Relations Hearing. Los Angeles, January 10, 1964.

Wallace, J. K. "The Musicians' Union." In Rodríguez, *Music and Dance in California*, 1940.

Secondary Sources

Acuña, Rodolfo. *A Community under Siege: A Chronicle of Chicanos East of the Los Angeles River, 1945–1975.* Los Angeles: Chicano Studies Research Center Publications, 1984.

——. *Anything but Mexican: Chicanos in Contemporary Los Angeles.* London: Verso, 1996.

——. *Occupied America: A History of Chicanos,* 5th ed. New York: Pearson Longman, 2004.

Almaguer, Tomás. *Racial Fault Lines: The Historical Origins of White Supremacy in California.* Berkeley: University of California Press, 1994.

Alvarez, Luis. "Zoot Violence on the Home Front: Race, Riots, and Youth Culture during World War II." In *Mexican Americans and World War II,* ed. Maggie Rivas-Rodriguez. Austin: University of Texas Press, 2005.

——. *The Power of the Zoot: Youth Culture and Resistance during World War II.* Berkeley: University of California Press, 2008.

The American Heritage Dictionary of the English Language, 4th ed. Boston: Houghton Mifflin, 2000.

Aparicio, Frances R. *Listening to Salsa: Gender, Latin Popular Music, and Puerto Rican Cultures.* Hanover, N.H.: Wesleyan University Press / University Press of New England, 1998.

Arroyo, Ronald. "La Raza Influence in Jazz." *El Grito* 5, no. 4 (Summer 1972): 80–84.

Avila, Eric. *Popular Culture in the Age of White Flight: Fear and Fantasy in Suburban Los Angeles.* Berkeley: University of California Press, 2004.

Barker, George C. "Pachuco: An American-Spanish Argot and Its Social Functions in Tucson, Arizona." *University of Arizona Bulletin* 21, no. 1 / *Social Science Bulletin,* no. 18 (January 1950): 5–38.

Barlow, William. *Looking up at Down: The Emergence of Blues Culture.* Philadelphia: Temple University Press, 1989.

Bender, Steven W. *Greasers and Gringos: Latinos, Law, and the American Imagination.* New York: New York University Press, 2003.

Berman, Marshall. *All That Is Solid Melts into Air: The Experience of Modernity.* New York: Penguin, 1988.

Bertrand, Michael T. *Race, Rock, and Elvis.* Urbana: University of Illinois Press, 2000.

Bogardus, Emory. "Gangs of Mexican American Youth." *Sociology and Social Research* 28, no. 1 (September–October 1943): 55–66.

Boorstin, Daniel J. *The Americans: The Democratic Experience.* New York: Vintage, 1974 [1973].

Braddy, Hadleen. "The Pachucos and Their Argot." *Southern Folklore Quarterly* 24, no. 4 (December 1960): 255–71.

Breines, Wini. "The 'Other' Fifties: Beats and Bad Girls." In *Not June Cleaver: Women and Gender in Postwar America, 1945–1960*, ed. Joanne Meyerowitz. Philadelphia: Temple University Press, 1994.

Brown, Elsa Barkley. "Polyrhythms and Improvization: Lessons for Women's History." *History Workshop* 31 (Spring 1991): 85–90.

Bryant, Clora, et al., eds. *Central Avenue Sounds: Jazz in Los Angeles*. Berkeley: University of California Press, 1998.

Bunch, Lonnie G. "A Past Not Necessarily Prologue: The Afro-American in Los Angeles since 1900." In Klein and Schiesl, *Twentieth Century Los Angeles*, 1990.

Burt, Kenneth C. "Latino Empowerment in Los Angeles: Postwar Dreams and Cold War Fears, 1948–1952." *Labor's Heritage* 8, no. 1 (Summer 1996): 4–25.

——. "Los Angeles Council, Congress of Industrial Organizations." In *Encyclopedia of the American Left*. 2nd ed. Edited by Mari Jo Buhle, Paul Buhle, and Dan Georgakas. New York: Oxford University Press, 1998.

Callendar, Red, and Elaine Cohen. *Unfinished Dream: The Musical World of Red Callendar*. New York: Quartet, 1985.

Calloway, Cab. *The New Cab Calloway's Hepster's Dictionary: The Language of Jive*. New York: Cab Calloway, 1944.

Camarillo, Alberto M. "Chicano Urban History: A Study of Compton's Barrio, 1936–1970." *Aztlán* 2, no. 2 (Fall 1971): 79–106.

Caponi, Gena Dagel, ed. *Signifyin(g), Sanctifyin' and Slam Dunking: A Reader in African American Expressive Culture*. Amherst: University of Massachusetts Press, 1999.

Carby, Hazel V. *Reconstructing Womanhood: The Emergence of the Afro-American Woman Novelist*. New York: Oxford University Press, 1987.

Carr, Roy, Brian Case, and Fred Dellar. *The Hip: Hipsters, Jazz, and the Beat Generation*. London: Faber and Faber, 1986.

Castillo, Richard del. *The Los Angeles Barrio, 1850–1890: A Social History*. Berkeley: University of California Press, 1979.

Caughey, John, and LaRee Caughey. *Los Angeles: Biography of a City*. Berkeley: University of California Press, 1976.

Chapple, Steve, and Reebee Garofalo. *Rock 'n' Roll Is Here to Pay: The History and Politics of the Music Industry*. Chicago: Nelson-Hall, 1978 [1977].

Chávez, Ernesto. *"¡Mi Raza Primero!" (My People First!): Nationalism, Identity, and Insurgency in the Chicano Movement in Los Angeles, 1966–1978*. Berkeley: University of California Press, 2002.

Chibnall, Steve. "Whistle and Zoot: The Changing Meaning of a Suit of Clothes." *History Workshop* 20 (Autumn 1985): 56–81.

Child, John. "Eddie Cano." In *The Penguin Encyclopedia of Popular Music*. 2nd ed. Edited by Donald Clarke. New York: Penguin, 1998.

Collins, Willie R. "California Rhythm and Blues Recordings, 1942–1972: A Diversity of Styles." In *California Soul: Music of African Americans in the West*, ed.

Jacqueline Cogdell Djedje and Eddie S. Meadows. Berkeley: University of California Press, 1998.

Cosgrove, Stuart. "The Zoot Suit and Style Warfare." *History Workshop* 18 (Autumn 1984): 77–91.

Cox, Bette Yarbrough. *Central Avenue—Its Rise and Fall (1890–c. 1955): Including the Musical Renaissance of Black Los Angeles*. Los Angeles: BEEM, 1996.

Cuff, Dana. "The Figure of the Neighbor: Los Angeles Past and Future." *American Quarterly* 56, no. 3 (September 2004): 66–68.

Daniels, Douglas Henry. "Los Angeles Zoot: 'Riot,' the Pachuco, and Black Music Culture." *Journal of African American History* 87, no. 1 (Winter 2002): 98–118.

Davis, Mike. *City of Quartz: Excavating the Future in Los Angeles*. London: Verso, 1992.

——. *Magical Urbanism: Latinos Reinvent the U.S. Big City*. London: Verso, 2000.

Dawson, Jim. *Nervous Man Nervous: Big Jay McNeely and the Rise of the Honking Tenor Sax*. Milford, N.H.: Big Nickel, 1994.

Deloria, Vine, Jr. *God Is Red: A Native View of Religion*. 30th anniv. ed. Golden, Colo.: Fulcrum, 2003 [1973].

D'Emilio, John, and Estelle B. Freedman. "'Civilized Morality' under Stress." In *Intimate Matters: A History of Sexuality in America*. New York: Harper and Row, 1988.

Deverell, William. *Whitewashed Adobe: The Rise of Los Angeles and the Remaking of Its Mexican Past*. Berkeley: University of Californai Press, 2004.

Dickerson, Lowell. "Central Avenue Meets Hollywood: The Amalgamation of the Black and White Musicians' Unions in Los Angeles." PhD diss., University of California, Los Angeles, 1998.

DuBois, W. E. B. "Of Our Spiritual Strivings." In *The Souls of Black Folk*. New York: Signet Classic, 1969 [1903].

——. *Black Reconstruction in America, 1860–1880*. New York: Free Press, 1998.

Eastman, Ralph. "'Pitchin' up a Boogie': African-American Musicians, Nightlife, and Music Venues in Los Angeles, 1930–1945." In *California Soul: Music of African Americans in the West*, ed. Jacqueline Cogdell Djedje and Eddie S. Meadows. Berkeley: University of California Press, 1998.

Ellison, Ralph. *Shadow and Act*. New York: Vintage, 1964.

Erenberg, Lewis. *Swingin' the Dream: Big Band Jazz and the Rebirth of American Culture*. Chicago: University of Chicago Press, 1998.

——. "Things to Come: Swing Bands, Bebop, and the Rise of a Postwar Jazz Scene." In *Recasting America: Culture and Politics in the Age of Cold War*, ed. Lary May. Chicago: University of Chicago Press, 1989.

Escobar, Edward J. *Race, Police, and the Making of a Political Identity: Mexican Americans and the Los Angeles Police Department, 1900–1945*. Berkeley: University of California Press, 1999.

Escobedo, Elizabeth. "Mexican American Home Front: Gender, Culture, and Community in World War II Los Angeles." PhD diss., University of Washington, 2004.

España Maram, Linda N. "Brown 'Hordes' in McIntosh Suits: Filipinos, Taxi Dance Halls, and Performing the Immigrant Body in Los Angeles, 1930s–1940s." In *Generations of Youth: Youth Cultures and History in Twentieth-Century America*, ed. Joe Austin and Michael N. Willard. New York: New York University Press, 1998.

——. *Creating Masculinity in Los Angeles's Little Manila: Working-Class Filipinos and Popular Culture, 1920s–1950s*. New York: Columbia University Press, 2006.

Espinoza, Dionne. " 'Tanto tiempo disfrutamos . . . ': Revisiting the Gender and Sexual Politics of Chicana/o Youth Culture in East Los Angeles in the 1960s." In *Velvet Barrios: Popular Culture and Chicana/o Sexualities*, ed. Alicia Gaspar de Alba. New York: Palgrave MacMillan, 2002.

Fein, Art. *The L.A. Musical History Tour: A Guide to the Rock and Roll Landmarks of Los Angeles*. Winchester, Mass.: Faber and Faber, 1990.

Fernández, Raúl. "Notes from East L.A." Review of *Barrio Rhythm*, by Steven Loza. *American Quarterly* 46, no. 3 (September 1994): 441–47.

——. *Latin Jazz: The Perfect Combination/La Combinación Perfecta*. San Francisco: Chronicle Books/Smithsonian Institution, 2002.

——. *From Afro-Cuban Rhythms to Latin Jazz*. Berkeley: University of California Press, 2006.

Flores, Juan. "Cortijo's Revenge." In *Divided Borders: Essays on Puerto Rican Identity*. Houston: Arte Público, 1993.

——. *From Bomba to Hip-Hop: Puerto Rican Culture and Latino Identity*. New York: Columbia University Press, 2000.

Floyd, Samuel A., Jr. *The Power of Black Music: Interpreting Its History from Africa to the United States*. New York: Oxford University Press, 1995.

Foley, Neil. *The White Scourge: Mexicans, Blacks, and Poor Whites in Texas Cotton Culture*. Berkeley: University of California Press, 1997.

——. "Becoming Hispanic: Mexican Americans and the Faustian Pact with Whiteness." *Reflexiones 1997: New Directions in Mexican American Studies* (Austin, Texas: Center for Mexican American Studies, 1998): 53–70.

Forbes, Jack D. *Aztecas del Norte: The Chicanos of Aztlán*. Greenwich, Conn.: Fawcett, 1973.

Fregoso, Rosa Linda. *The Bronze Screen: Chicana and Chicano Film Culture*. Minneapolis: University of Minnesota Press, 1993.

——. "Homegirls, Cholas, and Pachucas in Cinema: Taking over the Public Sphere." *California History* 74, no. 3 (1995): 316–27.

Frith, Simon. *Performing Rites: On the Value of Popular Music*. Cambridge: Harvard University Press, 1996.

Fuentes, Dagoberto, and José A. López. *Barrio Language Dictionary: First Dictionary of Caló*. La Puente, Calif.: El Barrio, 1974.

Gabler, Neil. *An Empire of Their Own: How the Jews Invented Hollywood*. New York: Crown, 1988.

Galindo, D. Letticia. "Dispelling the Male-Only Myth: Chicanas and Calo." *Bilingual Review* 17, no. 1 (January–April 1992): 3–35.

Galván, Roberto A., and Richard V. Teschner. *The Dictionary of Chicano Spanish / El Diccionario del Español Chicano* [1977]. 2nd ed. Lincolnwood, Ill.: National Textbook, 1995.

García, Mario T. "Americans All: The Mexican American Generation and the Politics of Wartime Los Angeles, 1941–45." In *The Mexican American Experience: An Interdisciplinary Anthology*, ed. Rodolfo de la Garza et al. Austin: University of Texas Press, 1985 [1984].

——. *Mexican Americans: Leadership, Ideology, and Identity, 1930–1960*. New Haven, Conn.: Yale University Press, 1989.

——. *Memories of Chicano History: The Life and Narrative of Bert Corona*. Berkeley: University of California Press, 1994.

Garcia, Matt. "Colonies, *Colonias*, and Culture: Intercultural Relations in the Citrus Belt of Southern California, 1900–1960." PhD diss., Claremont Colleges, 1997.

——. " 'Memories of El Monte': Intercultural Dance Halls in Post–World War II Greater Los Angeles." In *Generations of Youth: Youth Cultures and History in Twentieth-Century America*, ed. Joe Austin and Michael N. Willard. New York: New York University Press, 1998.

——. *A World of Its Own: Race, Labor, and Citrus in the Making of Greater Los Angeles, 1900–1970*. Chapel Hill: University of North Carolina Press, 2001.

García, Richard A. "The Mexican American Mind: A Product of the 1930s." In *History, Culture, and Society: Chicano Studies in the 1980s*, ed. Mario T. García et al. Ypsilanti, Mich.: Bilingual Press/Editorial Bilingüe, 1983.

——. *Rise of the Mexican-American Middle Class: San Antonio, 1929–1941*. College Station: Texas A&M University Press, 1991.

Garofalo, Reebee. *Rockin' Out: Popular Music in the USA*. 2nd ed. Upper Saddle River, N.J.: Prentice Hall, 2002.

Gay, Geneva, and Willie L. Baber, eds. *Expressively Black: The Cultural Basis of Ethnic Identity*. New York: Praeger, 1987.

Gennari, John. "Crooners and Gangsters: Love and Violence in Black/Italian Crossover." Paper presented at the Annual Conference of the American Studies Association, Kansas City, Mo. November 2, 1996.

George, Nelson. *The Death of Rhythm and Blues*. New York: E. P. Dutton, 1989.

Gillespie, Dizzy. *To BE, or not . . . to BOP: Memoirs*. Garden City, N.Y.: Doubleday, 1979.

Gillett, Charlie. *The Sound of the City: The Rise of Rock and Roll*. New York: Da Capo, 1996.

Gioia, Ted. *West Coast Jazz: Modern Jazz in California, 1945–1960*. New York: Oxford University Press, 1992.

Gitler, Ira. *From Swing to Bop: An Oral History of the Transition in Jazz in the 1940s*. New York: Oxford University Press, 1985.

Goldberg, David Theo, ed. *Multiculturalism: A Critical Reader*. Oxford: Blackwell, 1994.

González, Gilbert G. "Factors Relating to Property Ownership of Chicanos in Lincoln Heights, Los Angeles." *Aztlán* 2, no. 2 (Fall 1971): 107–43.

González, Rafael Jesús. "Pachuco: The Birth of a Creole Language." *Perspectives in Mexican American Studies* 1 (1988): 75–87.

Graaf, Lawrence de. "The City of Black Angels: Emergence of a Los Angles Ghetto, 1890–1930." *Pacific Historical Review* 39, no. 3 (August 1970): 323–52.

Gradante, William. "Art among the Low Riders." In *Folk Art in Texas*, ed. F. E. Abernethy. Dallas: Southern Methodist University Press, 1985.

Grebler, Leo, Joan W. Moore, and Ralph C. Guzman. *The Mexican-American People: The Nation's Second Largest Minority*. New York: Free Press, 1970.

Green, Susan. "Zoot Suiters: Past and Present." PhD diss., University of Minnesota, 1997.

Gregory, James N. *American Exodus: The Dust Bowl Migration and Okie Culture in California*. New York: Oxford University Press, 1989.

Gribin, Anthony J., and Matthew M. Schiff. *Doo-Wop: The Forgotten Third of Rock 'n Roll*. Iola, Wisc.: Krause, 1992.

Griffith, Beatrice. "The Pachuco Patois." *Common Ground* 7 (Summer 1947): 77–84.

———. *American Me*. Westport, Conn.: Greenwood, 1948.

Guerrero, Lalo, and Sherilyn Meece Mentes. *Lalo: My Life and Music*. Tucson: University of Arizona Press, 2002.

Guevara, Rubén. "The View from the Sixth Street Bridge: The History of Chicano Rock." In *The First Rock and Roll Confidential Report: Inside the Real World of Rock and Roll*, ed. Dave Marsh et al. New York: Pantheon, 1985.

Gustafson, Cloyd V. "An Ecological Analysis of the Hollenbeck Area of Los Angeles." Master's thesis, University of Southern California, 1940.

Gutíerrez, David G. *Walls and Mirrors: Mexican-Americans, Mexican Immigrants, and the Politics of Ethnicity*. Berkeley: University of California Press, 1995.

Hampton, Lionel, and James Haskins. *Hamp: An Autobiography*. New York: Warner, 1989.

Hazzard-Gordon, Katrina. *Jookin': The Rise of Social Dance Formations in African-American Culture*. Philadelphia: Temple University Press, 1990.

Hebdige, Dick. *Subculture: The Meaning of Style*. London: Routledge, 1979.

Higginbotham, Evelyn Brooks. *Righteous Discontent: The Women's Movement in the Black Baptist Church, 1880–1920*. Cambridge: Harvard University Press, 1993.

Himes, Chester. "Zoot Riots Are Race Riots." In *Black on Black: Baby Sister and Selected Writings*. Garden City, N.Y.: Doubleday, 1973 [1943].

———. *If He Hollers Let Him Go*. New York: Thunder's Mouth, 1989 [1945].

Hinojos, Francisco. "Notes on the Pachuco: Stereotypes, History and Dialect." *Atisbos: Journal of Chicano Research* (Summer 1975): 53–65.

Hirsch, Arnold R., and Joseph Logsdon. *Creole New Orleans: Race and Americanization*. Baton Rouge: Louisiana State University Press, 1992.

Hopkinson, Nalo, ed. *Mojo: Conjure Stories*. New York: Aspect/Warner, 2003.

Hoskyns, Barney. *Waiting for the Sun: Strange Days, Weird Scenes, and the Sound of Los Angeles*. New York: St. Martin's, 1996.

Jenkins, Henry, Tara McPherson, and Jane Shattuc. "Defining Popular Culture." In *Hop on Pop: The Politics and Pleasures of Popular Culture*, ed. Jenkins, McPherson, and Shattuc. Durham, N.C.: Duke University Press, 2002.

Jiménez, Armando. *Cabarets de antes y de ahora en la Ciudad de México*. Mexico City: Narra, 1997.

Jones, LeRoi (Amiri Imamu Baraka). *Blues People: The Negro Experience in White America and the Music That Developed from It*. New York: Morrow Quill, 1963.

Jones, Robert C. "Integration of the Mexican Minority in the United States into American Democracy." *Events and Trends in Race Relations: A Monthly Summary* 4 (January 1947): 175–77.

——. "Mexican American Youth." *Sociology and Social Research* 32, no. 4 (March–April 1948): 793–97.

Keil, Charles. *Urban Blues*. Chicago: University of Chicago Press, 1966.

Keil, Roger. *Los Angeles: Globalization, Urbanization and Social Struggles*. Chichester: John Wiley and Sons, 1998.

Kelley, Robin D. G. "Notes on Deconstructing 'the Folk.'" *American Historical Review* 97, no. 5 (December 1992): 1400–1408.

——. *Race Rebels: Culture, Politics, and the Black Working Class*. New York: Free Press, 1996.

Klein, Norman, and Martin Schiesl, eds. *Twentieth Century Los Angeles: Power, Promotion, and Social Conflict*. Claremont, Calif.: Regina, 1990.

Kurashige, Scott. *The Shifting Grounds of Race: Black and Japanese Americans in the Making of Multiethnic Los Angeles*. Princeton: Princeton University Press, 2007.

Leach, William. *Land of Desire: Merchants, Power, and the Rise of a New American Culture*. New York: Pantheon, 1993.

Lee-Sung, Audrey. "Boyle Heights: Neighborhood Sites and Insights, a Multicultural Community Partnership Initiative of the Japanese American National Museum." *First Monday* 6, no. 4 (April 2001), firstmonday.org/issues/issue6_4/lee-sung/index.html (accessed July 11, 2005).

Lehmer, Larry. *The Day the Music Died: The Last Tour of Buddy Holly, the "Big Bopper," and Ritchie Valens*. New York: Schirmer, 1997.

Leon, Arnoldo de. *They Called Them Greasers: Anglo Attitudes towards Mexicans in Texas, 1821–1900*. Austin: University of Texas Press, 1983.

Leonard, Kevin Allen. "'Brothers under the Skin'? African Americans, Mexican

Americans, and World War II California." In *The Way We Really Were: The Golden State in the Second Great War*, ed. Roger W. Lotchin. Urbana: University of Illinois Press, 2000.

Levine, Lawrence W. *Black Culture and Black Consciousness: Afro-American Folk Thought from Slavery to Freedom*. Oxford: Oxford University Press, 1977.

——. "Jazz and American Culture." In *The Unpredictable Past: Explorations in American Cultural History*. New York: Oxford University Press, 1993.

——. "The Unpredictable Past: Reflections on Recent American Historiography." In *The Unpredictable Past: Explorations in American Cultural History*. New York: Oxford University Press, 1993.

Lewis, George H. "La Pistola y el Corazón: Protest and Passion in Mexican-American Popular Music." *Journal of Popular Culture* 26, no. 1 (1992): 51–67.

Leymarie, Isabelle. *Cuban Fire: The Story of Salsa and Latin Jazz*. London: Continuum, 2002 [1997].

Lipsitz, George. "Land of a Thousand Dances: Youth, Minorities, and the Rise of Rock and Roll." In *Recasting America: Culture and Politics in the Age of Cold War*, ed. Lary May. Chicago: University of Chicago Press, 1989.

——. "Cruising around the Historical Bloc: Postmodernism and Popular Music in East Los Angeles." In *Time Passages: Collective Memory and American Popular Culture*. Minneapolis: University of Minnesota Press, 1990.

——. *Rainbow at Midnight: Labor and Culture in the 1940s*. Urbana: University of Illinois Press, 1994.

——. " 'Ain't Nobody Here but Us Chickens': The Class Origins of Rock and Roll." In *Rainbow at Midnight*, 1994.

——. *Dangerous Crossroads: Popular Music, Postmodernism and the Poetics of Place*. New York: Verso, 1994.

——. *The Possessive Investment in Whiteness: How White People Profit from Identity Politics*. Philadelphia: Temple University Press, 1998.

Lott, Eric. "Double V, Double-Time: Bebop's Politics of Style." *Callaloo* 36 (Summer 1988): 597–605.

Loza, Steven. "From Veracruz to Los Angeles: The Reinterpretation of the Son Jarocho." *Latin American Music Review* 13, no. 2 (Fall/Winter 1992): 179–94.

——. *Barrio Rhythm: Mexican American Music in Los Angeles*. Urbana: University of Illinois Press, 1993.

——. *Tito Puente and the Making of Latin Music*. Urbana: University of Illinois Press, 1999.

MacAdams, Lewis. *Birth of the Cool: Beat, Bebop, and the American Avant-Garde*. New York: Free Press, 2001.

Madrid-Barela, Arturo. "In Search of the Authentic Pachuco: An Interpretive Essay." *Aztlán* 4, no. 1 (Spring 1973): 31–60.

Major, Clarence, ed. *From Juba to Jive: The Dictionary of African-American Slang*. New York: Penguin, 1994.

Malcolm X, with Alex Haley. *The Autobiography of Malcolm X*. New York: Ballantine, 1964.

Malone, Jacqui. "Jazz Music in Motion: Dancers and Big Bands." In *The Jazz Cadence of American Culture*, ed. Robert G. O'Meally. New York: Columbia University Press, 1998.

———. " 'Keep to the Rhythm and You'll Keep to Life': Meaning and Life in African American Dance." In Caponi, *Signifyin(g)*, 1999.

Marcus, Kenneth. *Musical Metropolis: Los Angeles and the Creation of a Music Culture, 1880–1940*. New York: Palgrave Macmillan, 2004.

Marmorstein, Gary. "Central Avenue Jazz: Los Angeles Black Music of the Forties." *Southern California Quarterly* 70, no. 4 (Winter 1988): 415–26.

Marsh, Dave. *Louie Louie: The History and Mythology of the World's Most Famous Rock 'n' Roll Song*. New York: Hyperion, 1993.

Martinez, Ruth L. "The Unusual Mexican: A Study in Acculturation." Master's thesis, Claremont Colleges, 1942.

Marx, Karl. *The Eighteenth Brumaire of Louis Bonaparte*. New York: International, 1984 [1852].

Matsumoto, Valerie. *Farming the Home Place: A Japanese American Community in California, 1919–1982*. Ithaca, N.Y.: Cornell University Press, 1993.

Mauleón, Rebecca. *Salsa Guidebook: For Piano and Ensemble*. Petaluma, Calif.: Sher Music Company, 1993.

———. "The Heart of Salsa: Exploring Afro-Caribbean Piano Styles." *Keyboard* 22, no. 1 (January 1996): 28–44.

Maultsby, Portia K. "Rhythm and Blues." In *African American Music: An Introduction*, ed. Mellonee V. Burnim and Portia K. Maultsby. New York: Routledge, 2006.

Mazón, Mauricio. *The Zoot Suit Riots: The Psychology of Symbolic Annihilation*. Austin: University of Texas Press, 1984.

McDonagh, Edward C. "Status Levels of Mexicans." *Sociology and Social Research* 33, no. 6 (July–August 1949): 449–59.

McNamara, Patrick Hayes. "Mexican Americans in Los Angeles County: A Study in Acculturation." Master's thesis, Saint Louis University, 1957.

McWilliams, Carey. *North from Mexico: The Spanish-Speaking People of the United States*. New York: Praeger, 1990 [1948].

Meier, Matt S., ed. *Mexican American Biographies: A Historical Dictionary, 1836–1987*. New York: Greenwood, 1988.

Meisel, Perry. *The Cowboy and the Dandy: Crossing over from Romanticism to Rock and Roll*. New York: Oxford University Press, 1999.

Mendheim, Beverly. *Ritchie Valens: The First Latino Rocker*. Tempe, Ariz.: Bilingual Press/Editorial Bilingüe, 1987.

Mercer, Kobena. "Black Hair/Style Politics." In *Out There: Marginalization and Contemporary Cultures*, ed. Russell Ferguson et al. Cambridge: MIT Press, 1990.

Miranda, Marie "Keta." *Homegirls in the Public Sphere*. Austin: University of Texas Press, 2003.

——. " 'The East Side Revue, 40 Hits by East Los Angeles' Most Popular Groups!': The Boys in the Band and the Girls Who Were Their Fans." In *Beyond the Frame: Women of Color and Visual Representation*, ed. Angela Davis and Neferti X. M. Tadiar. New York: Palgrave Macmillan, 2005.

——. "Dancing to 'Whittier Boulevard': Choreographing Social Identity." In *Dancing across Borders: Danzas y Bailes Mexicanos*, ed. Norma Cantú, Olga Nájera-Ramírez, and Brenda Romero. Urbana: University of Illinois Press, forthcoming.

Molina, Ruben. *The Old Barrio Guide to Low Rider Music, 1950–1975*. La Puente, Calif.: Mictlan, 2002.

Monroy, Douglas. "Mexicanos in Los Angeles, 1930–1941: An Ethnic Group in Relation to Class Forces." PhD diss., University of California, Los Angeles, 1978.

——. " 'Our Children Get So Different Here': Film, Fashion, Popular Culture and the Process of Cultural Syncretism in Mexican Los Angeles, 1900–1935." *Aztlán* 19, no. 1 (Spring 1988–90): 79–108.

——. *Thrown among Strangers: The Making of Mexican Culture in Frontier California*. Berkeley: University of California Press, 1990.

——. *Rebirth: Mexican Los Angeles from the Great Migration to the Great Depression*. Berkeley: University of California Press, 1999.

Monsiváis, Carlos. "Este es el pachucho: Un sujeto singular." In *A través de la frontera*. Mexico City: Centro de Estudios Económicos y Sociales del Tercer Mundo, 1983.

——. *Mexican Postcards*. London: Verso, 1997.

Monson, Ingrid. "The Problem with White Hipness: Race, Gender, and Cultural Conceptions in Jazz Historical Discourse." *Journal of the American Musicological Society* 48 (Fall 1995): 396–422.

Moore, Joan. *Homeboys: Gangs, Drugs and Prison in the Barrios of Los Angeles*. Philadelphia: Temple University Press, 1978.

Moorehouse, H. F. "The 'Work' Ethic and 'Leisure' Activity: The Hot Rod in Postwar America." In *Consumer Society in American History: A Reader*, ed. Lawrence B. Glickman. Ithaca: Cornell University Press, 1999.

Morales, Ed. *The Latin Beat: The Rhythms and Roots of Latin Music from Bossa Nova to Salsa and Beyond*. Cambridge, Mass.: De Capo Press, 2003.

Muñoz Castillo, Fernando. *Las musas de "Tin Tan": Crónicas y recuerdos*. Mexico City: Cuadernos de la Cineteca Nacional, n.s., no. 12, 1999.

Nagus, Keith. *Music Genres and Corporate Cultures*. London: Routledge, 1999.

Nash, Gerald D. *The American West Transformed: The Impact of the Second World War*. Bloomington: Indiana University Press, 1985.

Nava, Julian. *My Mexican-American Journey*. Houston: Arte Público, 2002.

Nicolaides, Becky M. *My Blue Heaven: Life and Politics in the Working-Class Suburbs of Los Angeles, 1920–1965*. Chicago: University of Chicago Press, 2002.

Omi, Michael, and Howard Winant. *Racial Formation in the United States: From the 1960s to the 1990s*. New York: Routledge, 1994.

Ortega, Adolfo. *Caló Orbis: Semiotic Aspects of a Chicano Language Variety*. New York: P. Lang, 1991.

Otis, Johnny. *Upside Your Head! Rhythm and Blues on Central Avenue*. Hanover, N.H.: Wesleyan University Press/University Press of New England, 1993.

Pagán, Eduardo Obregón. "Sleepy Lagoon: The Politics of Youth and Race in Wartime Los Angeles, 1940–1945." PhD diss., Princeton University, 1996.

——. *Murder at the Sleepy Lagoon: Zoot Suits, Race, and Riot in Wartime L.A.* Chapel Hill: University of North Carolina Press, 2003.

Palmer, Robert. *Baby, That Was Rock and Roll: The Legendary Lieber and Stoller*. New York: Harcourt Brace Jovanovich, 1978.

——. *Deep Blues: A Musical and Cultural History of the Mississippi Delta*. New York: Penguin Books, 1982.

——. *Rock and Roll: An Unruly History*. New York: Harmony, 1995.

Paz, Octavio. *The Labyrinth of Solitude: Life and Thought in Mexico*. New York: Grove, 1961.

Peña, Manuel. *The Texas-Mexican Conjunto: History of a Working-Class Music*. Austin: University of Texas Press, 1985.

——. *The Mexican American Orquesta*. Austin: University of Texas Press, 1999.

Peñalosa, Fernando. "Toward an Operational Definition of the Mexican American." *Aztlán* 1, no. 1 (Spring 1970): 1–12.

Pepper, Art, and Laurie Pepper. *Straight Life: The Story of Art Pepper*. New York: Da Capo, 1979.

Piersen, William D. "African American Festive Style." In Caponi, *Signifyin(g)*, 1999.

Pitt, Leonard, and Dale Pitt, eds. *Los Angeles A to Z: An Encyclopedia of the City and County*. Berkeley: University of California Press, 1997.

Plascencia, Luis. "Low Riding in the Southwest: Cultural Symbols in the Mexican Community." In *History, Culture, and Society: Chicano Studies in the 1980s*, ed. Mario T. García et al. Ypsilanti, Mich.: Bilingual Press/Editorial Bilingüe, 1983.

Polkinhorn, Harry, Alfredo Velasco, and Malcolm Lambert. *El Libro de Caló*. Rev. ed. Oakland, Calif.: Floricanto, 1986.

Porter, Eric. *What Is This Thing Called Jazz? African American Musicians as Artists, Critics, and Activists*. Berkeley: University of California Press, 2002.

Porter, Roy, with David Keller. *There and Back: The Roy Porter Story*. Baton Rouge: Louisiana State University Press, 1991.

Propes, Steve, and Galen Gart. *L.A. R & B Vocal Groups, 1945–1965*. Milford, N.H.: Big Nickel, 2001.

Quiñonez, Naomi. "Rosita the Riveter: Welding Tradition with Wartime Transfor-
mations." In *Mexican Americans and World War II*, ed. Maggie Rivas-Rodriguez.
Austin: University of Texas Press, 2005.

Quiroga, José. *Tropics of Desire: Interventions from Queer Latino America*. New York:
New York University Press, 2000.

Ramírez, Catherine S. "Crimes of Fashion: The Pachuca and Chicana Style Politics."
Meridians: Feminism, Race, Transnationalism 2, no. 2 (March 2002): 1–35.

——. "Pachucos and Pachucas." In *Encyclopedia of Latinos and Latinas in the United
States*, ed. Suzanne Obeler and Deena González. New York: Oxford University
Press, 2005.

——. " 'Sayin' Nothin' ": Pachucas and the Languages of Resistance." *Frontiers* 27,
no. 2 (Winter 2007): 1–33.

——. *The Lady Zoot Suiter: The Pachuca and the Rearticulation of Race, Class, Gender,
and Nation*. Durham, N.C.: Duke University Press, forthcoming.

Ramírez Berg, Charles. *Latino Images in Film: Stereotypes, Subversion, and Resistance*.
Austin: University of Texas Press, 2002.

——. "Colonialism and Movies in Southern California, 1910–1954." *Aztlán* 28, no. 1
(2003): 75–96.

Ramsey, Guthrie P., Jr. *Race Music: Black Cultures from Bebop to Hip-Hop*. Berkeley:
University of California Press, 2003.

Ranker, Jr., Jess Elwood. "A Study of Juvenile Gangs in the Hollenbeck Area of East
Los Angeles." Master's thesis, University of Southern California, 1957.

Reed, Tom. *The Black Music History of Los Angeles: Its Roots—A Classical Pictorial
History of Black Music in Los Angeles from 1920–1970*. Los Angeles: Black Accent
on L.A., 1992.

Reyes, David, and Tom Waldman. *Land of a Thousand Dances: Chicano Rock 'n'
Roll from Southern California*. Albuquerque: University of New Mexico Press,
1998.

Rios-Bustamante, Antonio, and Pedro Castillo. *An Illustrated History of Mexican Los
Angeles, 1781–1985*. University of California, Los Angeles: Chicano Studies Research Center Publications, monograph no. 12, 1986.

Roberts, John Storm. *Black Music of Two Worlds: African, Caribbean, Latin, and
African-American Traditions*. New York: Schirmer, 1998.

——. *The Latin Tinge: The Impact of Latin American Music on the United States*. 2nd
ed. New York: Oxford University Press, 1999 [1979].

Robles Cahero, José Antonio. "Mexican Resonances in American Soundscapes: Old
and New Musical Exchanges on Both Sides of the Border." Paper presented for
the Department of Ethnomusicology and the Chicano Studies Research Center,
University of California, Los Angeles. November 12, 2003.

——. "Occidentalización, mestizaje y 'Guerra de los sonidos': Hacia una historia de
las músicas mestizas de México." In *Musical Cultures of Latin America: Global*

Effects, Past and Present, ed. Steven Loza. University of California, Los Angeles: Selected Reports in Ethnomusicology, vol. 11, 2003.

Rodríguez, Luis J. *Always Running: La Vida Loca, Gang Days in L.A.* Willimantic, Conn.: Curbstone, 1983.

Roediger, David R. *The Wages of Whiteness: Race and the Making of the American Working Class.* London: Verso, 1991.

Rogin, Michael. "Blackface, White Noise: The Jewish Jazz Singer Finds His Voice." *Critical Inquiry* 18, no. 3 (Spring 1992): 417–53.

Romo, Ricardo. *East Los Angeles: History of a Barrio.* Austin: University of Texas Press, 1983.

Rosales, Francisco A. *Chicano! The History of the Mexican American Civil Rights Movement.* Houston: Arte Público, 1996.

Rose, Margaret. "Gender and Civic Activism in Mexican American Barrios in California: The Community Service Organization, 1947–1962." In *Not June Cleaver: Women and Gender in Postwar America, 1945–1960,* ed. Joanne Meyerowitz. Philadelphia: Temple University Press, 1994.

Ruiz, Vicki L. " 'Star Struck': Acculturation, Adolescence, and the Mexican American Woman, 1920–1950." In *Building with Our Hands: New Directions in Chicana Studies,* ed. Adela de La Torre and Beatriz Pesquera. Berkeley: University of California Press, 1993.

——. *From Out of the Shadows: Mexican Women in Twentieth-Century America.* New York: Oxford University Press, 1998.

Salazar, Max. *Mambo Kingdom: Latin Music in New York.* New York: Schirmer Trade, 2002.

Sánchez, George J. *Becoming Mexican American: Ethnicity, Culture and Identity in Chicano Los Angeles, 1900–1945.* New York: Oxford University Press, 1993.

——. "Reading Reginald Denny: The Politics of Whiteness in Late Twentieth Century America." *American Quarterly* 47, no. 3 (September 1995): 388–94.

——. " 'What's Good for Boyle Heights Is Good for the Jews': Creating Multiracialism on the Eastside during the 1950s." *American Quarterly* 56, no. 3 (September 2004): 135–63.

Sánchez, Rosaura. *Chicano Discourse: Socio-historic Perspectives.* Houston: Arte Público, 1994.

——. *Telling Identities: The Californio Testimonios.* Minneapolis: University of Minnesota, 1995.

Sánchez-Tranquilino, Marcos. "Mano a Mano: An Essay on the Representation of the Zoot Suit and Its Misrepresentation by Octavio Paz." *Journal: Los Angeles Institute of Contemporary Art,* Winter 1987, 34–42.

Sánchez-Tranquilino, Marcos, and John Tagg. "The Pachuco's Flayed Hide: Mobility, Identity, and Buenas Garras." In *Cultural Studies,* ed. Lawrence Grossberg et al. New York: Routledge, 1992.

Sandoval, Denise M. "Cruising through Low Rider Culture: Chicana/o Identity in the Marketing of *Low Rider Magazine*." In *Velvet Barrios: Popular Culture and Chicana/o Sexualities*, ed. Alicia Gaspar de Alba. New York: Palgrave Macmillan, 2002.

Saxton, Alexander. *The Rise and Fall of the White Republic: Class, Politics, and Mass Culture in Nineteenth-Century America*. New York: Verso, 1990.

Scherman, Tony. *Backbeat: Earl Palmer's Story*. Washington, D.C.: Smithsonian Institution, 1999.

Schroeder, Patricia R. "Rootwork: Arthur Flowers, Zora Neal Hurston, and the 'Literary Hoodoo' Tradition." *African American Review* 36, no. 2 (Summer 2002): 263–73.

Scott, Robin Fitzgerald. "The Mexican American in the Los Angeles Area, 1920–1950: From Acquiescence to Activity." PhD diss., University of Southern California, 1971.

Sides, Josh. *L.A. City Limits: African American Los Angeles from the Great Depression to the Present*. Berkeley: University of California Press, 2004.

Simon, George T. *The Big Bands*. New York: Schirmer, 1981.

Smith, Joe, and Mitchell Fink, eds. *Off the Record: An Oral History of Popular Music*. New York: Warner, 1988.

Sonnichsen, Philip. "Lalo Guerrero: Pioneer in Mexican-American Music." *La Luz* 6, no. 5 (May 1977): 11–14.

Stanton, Jeffrey. *Venice, California: Coney Island of the Pacific*. 3rd ed. Los Angeles: Donahue, 1993.

Starr, Kevin. *The Dream Endures: California Enters the 1940s*. New York: Oxford University Press, 1997.

——. *Embattled Dreams: California in War and Peace, 1940–1950*. New York: Oxford University Press, 2002.

Stearns, Marshall, and Jean Stearns. *Jazz Dance: The Story of American Vernacular Dance*. New York: Da Capo, 1994.

Stone, Michael Cutler. "*Bajito y suavecito*: Low Riding and the 'Class' of Class." *Studies in Latin American Popular Culture* 9 (1991): 85–126.

Stowe, David. "Jazz in the West: Cultural Frontier and Region during the Swing Era." *Western Historical Quarterly* 23 (February 1992): 53–73.

——. *Swing Changes: Big-Band Jazz in New Deal America*. Cambridge, Mass.: Harvard University Press, 1994.

——. "Uncolored People: The Rise of Whiteness Studies." *Lingua Franca* 6, no. 6 (September–October 1996): 68–77.

Stuckey, Sterling. *Slave Culture: Nationalist Theory and the Foundations of Black America*. New York: Oxford University Press, 1987.

Sublette, Ned. *Cuba and Its Music: From the First Drums to the Mambo*. Chicago: Chicago Review Press, 2004.

Tatum, Charles M. "Definitions and Theoretical Approaches to Popular Culture." In *Chicano Popular Culture: Que Hable el Pueblo.* Tucson: University of Arizona Press, 2001.

Tucker, Sherrie. *Swing Shift: "All-Girl" Bands of the 1940s.* Durham, N.C.: Duke University Press, 2000.

———. " 'They Got Corns for My Country': Hollywood Canteen Hostesses as Subjects and Objects of Freedom." Paper presented at the Annual Conference of the American Studies Association, Atlanta. November 13, 2004.

Turner, Ralph H., and Samuel J. Surace. "Zoot-Suiters and Mexicans: Symbols in Crowd Behavior." *American Journal of Sociology* 62 (July 1956–May 1957): 14–20.

Tyler, Bruce. "Black Jive and White Repression." *Journal of Ethnic Studies* 16, no. 4 (1989): 31–66.

Vasquez, Librado K. *Regional Dictionary of Chicano Slang.* Austin, Texas: Jenkins, 1975.

Vélez-Ibañez, Carlos G. *Border Visions: Mexican Cultures of the Southwest United States.* Tucson: University of Arizona Press, 1996.

Verge, Arthur C. *Paradise Transformed: Los Angeles during the Second World War.* Dubuque, Iowa: Kendall/Hunt, 1993.

———. "The Impact of the Second World War on Los Angeles." *Pacific Historical Review* 63, no. 3 (August 1994): 289–314.

Vigil, James Diego. *Barrio Gangs: Street Life and Identity in Southern California.* Austin: University of Texas Press, 1988.

———. "Car Charros: Cruising and Low-Riding in the Barrios of East L.A." *Latino Studies Journal* 2, no. 2 (May 1991): 71–79.

———. *From Indians to Chicanos: The Dynamics of Mexican-American Culture.* Prospect Heights, Ill.: Waveland, 1998.

Villa, Raúl Homero, *Barrio-Logos: Space and Place in Urban Chicano Literature and Culture.* Austin: University of Texas Press, 2000.

Villarino, José "Pepe." *Mexican and Chicano Music.* New York: McGraw-Hill, 1996.

Waldie, D. J. *Holy Land: A Suburban Memoir.* New York: St. Martin's, 1997.

Wallace, Michelle, ed. *Black Popular Culture.* Seattle: Bay, 1992.

Warner, Jay. *American Singing Groups: A History from 1940 to Today.* Milwaukee: Hal Leonard, 2006.

White, Shane, and Graham White. *Stylin': African American Expressive Culture from Its Beginnings to the Zoot Suit.* Ithaca, N.Y.: Cornell University Press, 1998.

Widener, Daniel. "Something Else: Creative Community and Black Liberation in Postwar Los Angeles." Ph.D. diss., New York University, 2003.

Willard, Michael Nevin. "Nuestra Los Angeles." *American Quarterly* 56, no. 3 (September 2004): 309–37.

Willis, Koko, and Pali Jae Lee. *Tales from the Night Rainbow: The Story of a Woman, a People, and an Island.* Honolulu: Night Rainbow, 1990.

Withers, Charles Dinnijes. "Problems of Mexican Boys." Master's thesis, University of Southern California, 1942.

Wynn, Ron, ed. *All Music Guide to Jazz: The Best CDs, Albums, and Tapes*. San Francisco: Miller Freeman, 1994.

Ybarra-Frausto, Tomás. "*Rasquachismo*: A Chicano Sensibility." In *Chicano Art: Resistance and Affirmation, 1965–1985*, ed. Richard Griswold del Castillo, Teresa McKenna, and Yvonne Yarbro-Bejarano. Tucson: University of Arizona Press, 1991.

Zolov, Eric. *Refried Elvis: The Rise of the Mexican Counterculture*. Berkeley: University of California Press, 1999.

Miscellaneous

Newspapers, Journals, and Magazines

Billboard
California Eagle
Chicago Sun-Times
Collier's
Common Ground
Down Beat
Eastside Journal
Ebony
Impacto: A Latino Arts and Entertainment Magazine
Jazz Monthly
Journal of Social Psychology
L.A. Jazz Scene
La opinión
Latin Beat Magazine
LA Weekly
Los Angeles Times
Melody Maker
Metronome
Music Journal
New Republic
Newsweek
New Yorker
Pittsburgh Courier
Southwestern Musician
Time
Variety

Other

Benz, Jim, dir. *The Ritchie Valens Story: Viva Ritchie!* In *The Complete Ritchie Valens.* DVD. Whirlwind Media, 2000.

Broderick, Richard. Liner notes, Manny Lopez, *Cha-Cha-Cha If You Please.* RCA Victor, 1957.

Burns, Ken, dir. *Jazz,* episode 5, *Swing: Pure Pleasure.* DVD. Florentine Films/PBS, 2000.

Davis, Eddie. Interview by Lee Joseph. Liner notes, *The East Side Sound, 1959–1968.* Bacchus Archives, 1996.

Dawson, Jim. "Boogie Down on Central: Los Angeles' Rhythm and Blues Revolution." Liner notes, *Central Avenue Sounds: Jazz in Los Angeles (1921–1956).* Rhino Records, 1999.

———. Liner notes, *Honk! Honk! Honk!* Ace Records, 2000.

Duncan, Donald. Liner notes, Eddie Cano, His Piano and Orchestra, *Time for Cha Cha Cha.* RCA Victor, 1958.

Evans, Bill. Liner notes, Miles Davis, *Kind of Blue.* Columbia Records, 1959.

George, Nelson. Liner notes, *Rites of Rhythm and Blues,* vol. 2. Motown Records, 1994.

Gitler, Ira. Liner notes, *Babs Gonzales: Weird Lullaby.* Blue Note Records, 1992.

González, Andy, and Manny Oquendo. Liner notes, *More than Mambo: The Introduction to Afro-Cuban Jazz.* Verve Records, 1995.

Green, Stanley. Liner notes, Eddie Cano Quintet, *Cha Cha con Cano.* United Artists, 1959.

Hardy, John William. "Anthony Ortega, New Dance!" Original liner notes, Revelation Records, June 9, 1967. On Anthony Ortega, *New Dance!* Hat Hut Records, 1990.

———. "Anthony Ortega, Permutations." Original liner notes, Revelation Records, November 23, 1968. On Anthony Ortega, *New Dance!* Hat Hut Records, 1990.

Keane, Bob. Narrative track, *The Ritchie Valens Story.* Del-Fi Records, 1993.

Lange, Art. Liner notes, Anthony Ortega, *New Dance!* Hat Hut Records, 1990.

"Lincoln Heights Will Shine Tonight." Souvenir Program, Eastside Clover Club Sixth Annual Reunion Dance. International Hall, Pico Rivera. October 8, 1988. Courtesy Lucie Frias.

Liner notes, *The Best of Eddie Cano: His Piano and His Rhythm.* RCA Victor, 1962.

Luckenbill, Dan. "The Pachuco Era." Exhibit catalog. Department of Special Collections, Young Research Library, University of California, Los Angeles. September–December 1990.

Lunceford, Jimmie. *Lunceford Special: 1939–1940, Columbia Records.* Sony, 2001.

"Mambo Jumbo" Concert Program. Shrine Auditorium, Los Angeles, Calif. 1954. Courtesy Tommy Saito.

Mambo Memories: The Palladium Years, part 2. Visiones documentary series. WNBC-TV, 1990.

Notes from the Mambo Inn: The Story of Mario Bauzá. Videocassette. Boston: WGBH Television Educational Foundation, 1992.

Patrick, Mick. Liner notes, *The Lieber and Stoller Story*. Vol. 1: *Hard Times, The Los Angeles Years, 1951–56*. Ace Records, 2004.

Tanenbaum, Gary. "Reissue Producer's Notes." Liner notes, *Ritchie Valens: Come On, Let's Go*. Del-Fi Records, 1998.

Thomas, Bryan. "The Real Story of Ritchie Valens." Liner notes, *Ritchie Valens: Come On, Let's Go*. Del-Fi Records, 1998.

Tosti, Don. Liner notes, *Don Tosti, a.k.a. "El Tostado."* Don Tosti/Broadway Productions, 2003.

Tovares, Joseph, dir. *Zoot Suit Riots*. Videocassette. PBS: American Experience, 2002.

Valdez, Luis, dir. *Zoot Suit* [1981]. DVD. Universal Studios, 2003.

Varela, Chuy. Liner notes, *Pachuco Boogie*. Arhoolie Records, 2002.

Vera, Billy. Liner notes, *Jumpin' Like Mad: Cool Cats and Hip Chicks Non-Stop Dancin'*. Capitol Records, 1996.

——. "Introduction." Liner notes, *Ritchie Valens: Come On, Let's Go*. Del-Fi Records, 1998.

Visser, Joop. Liner notes, *Dexter Gordon: Settin' the Pace*. Proper Records, 2001.

Yaroschuk, Tom, dir. *Hooked: Illegal Drugs and How They Got That Way—Marijuana, Assassin of Youth.* Television documentary. Tera Media, 2000.

INDEX

Aragon Ballroom, 39, 40, 65, 66, 252
Arenas, Arthur, 35, 37, 83, 84, 96
Armenta Brothers, 33, 123, 148, 234, 242; Manuel, 315n222
Army, U.S. *See* military service
Arnaz, Desi, 237, 275
assimilation: bicultural, 97; class and, 264; meaning of, 9; Mexican culture and, 54; middle-class organizations and, 102–5; pachucos and pachucas and, 92; squares and, 102
athletics, 104, 108, 137
Atlantic Boulevard, 253–54
automobiles, 77, 94, 152, 177, 210, 311n149
Avedon Ballroom, 158, 234, 241

"Babalu," 161, 237
Baiz, Jim, 250, 269, 270, 273
Barker, George, 97–98, 102, 115, 313n170, 316n266
Barrientos, Richard, 253; on Cano, 273; descargas and, 246; ethnicity and, 340n99; Latin music and, 159, 254–58, 274, 276–77; marriages of, 279; on Sesma, 268; on Touzet, 270
barrios, 5, 128, 138; freeways and, 11, 213, 219, 334n130; study of (1957), 213–16; Westside, 39, 300n128
Basie, Count, 15, 16
"battle of the bands," 35, 56, 147, 192, 253; as "saxophone battles," 161, *161*, 181
Beatles, 192, 211
Beats, 207, 333n101
Belmont High School, 158, 164
Benny Goodman Orchestra. *See* Goodman, Benny
Berg, Billy, 67, 68, 258, 305n13
Bernal, Gil, 1, *161*, *165*, *203*; background, 160, 325n168; career of, 161–65, 201–4; on Desi Arnaz, 237; Hollywood and, 325n172; on musicianship, 289; on Trini Lopez, 273

big band. *See* swing
Birdland, 193, 201
black and white balls, 35–36
blacks. *See* African Americans, blacks
Bloch, Rene, 42, 159, 241, 249–53, 279
blues, urban, 174–75. *See also* R & B
Board of Education, City of Los Angeles, 224–25
Bobo, Willie, 248, 254, 269
bolero, 234, 265–66, 267
boogie woogie, 119, 318n29
Bowron, Fletcher, 17, 72–73, 139–45
Boyle Heights: car customizing in, 152; demographic changes in, 121–22, 212, 221; Latin music in, 253; Mexican music in, 51, 156; music education in, 19–24; 1930s bands in, 33; overview of, 18–19; pachucos and squares in, 102; race conflict in, 136; Watts vs., 25
Brac, Lucie. *See* Frias, Lucie Brac
bracero workers, 221, 233–34, 337n19
Brambila, Tudy, 150, 207, 213, 328n25
Brando, Marlon, 202, 207
Broadway Palace, 253, 254, 258
Browne, Samuel, 27, 31–32, 249, 298n87, 321n92
Buckner, Milt, 161, 166

Caceres, Ernie, 49
Californian Club, 256, 258–59
California State Assembly Industrial Relations Committee hearing, 222–26
Calloway, Cab, 71, 114, 175
caló: etymologies of, 309n111; in military, 316n266; in pachuco boogie, 126–28, 131–32; pachucos and, 84–89, 114, 116; use of, 309n104
Cal Tjader Mambo Quintet, 249, 254–55
Cano, Eddie, *271*; *The Best of Eddie Cano*, 272, *272*; boogie woogie style and, 126; classical music and, 141; Latin

consumerism, 93–94, 211, 312n155

cool, 171; Mexican Americans' cultural capital of, 207

Coordinating Council for Latin-American Youth, 57, 103–4, 105

Corona, Bert, 133, 244

Corral, Jaime, 142–43, 157–59, 242, 252, 266, 268, 278

corridos, 98, 124–25, 313n177

Costanzo, Jack, 254, 270

Cotton Club, 45, 317n15

Crescendo, 231, 279

crime, and pachuco hustlers, 97–98

cruising, 151–52

Cuba, Joe, 258, 278, 345n197

Cuban music, 235–37

Cubans in Los Angeles, 246

Cugat, Xavier, 237, 256, 274–75

culture, Mexican. *See* Mexican music and culture, traditional

Dale, Dick, 189–90, 330n59

dance: balboa, 83; ballroom, 120, 267; black dance and worldview, 17; "breakaway" improvisation, 15–16, 277, 293n16; cholos' "closed style," 209; contests, 37, 210, 278; as emotional release, 145–46; hully gully, 209; to Latin music, 252–54, 262, 267–68, 277–78; Mexican American culture and, 17, 146; pachucos and, 82–83; pachuco swing and pachuco hop, 83, 209; Puente on, 279; regulation of public dances, 178–79, 193; rock and roll era styles, 209–10; "stoic moves," 83; television programs, 177, 181–82, 186–87; twist, 277; urban civility kept together by, 289. *See also* jitterbug

Davis, Eddie, 191, 210

Dean, James, 207

delinquency. *See* juvenile delinquency

demographic shifts and trends: in R & B era, 121–22; in rock and roll era, 212; of southern black migrants, 217; suburbanization and, 138, 153, 214–20; after World War II, 24

Detroit, 32, 42, 298n90

Diaz, Raul, 126–27, *128*, 250

Digger, 159

Dig Records, 183

disc jockeys, 176–77, 186, 192

Discos Real, 204

Discos Taxco, 126

discrimination: automobile insurance and, 135; Browne on, 321n92; Executive Order 8802 on, 302n174; homeowners and, 120–21, 215–16, 320n71; in R & B era, 120–21, 135–38; skin color and, 58; in swing era, 105–6; in wage differentials, 43; on Westside, 123. *See also* police harassment, intimidation, and brutality; segregation

Disney, Walt, 204–5

diversity, 14–15, 20, 26. *See also* integration

Dolphin's of Hollywood, 154–55

Dolphy, Eric, 30, 31

"Donna," 186–87

doo wop, 175, 182–84, 329n30, 329n38

Dorsey, Jimmy, 37, 39, 47

Dorsey, Tommy, 37, 39, 49, 53, 56, 95

draft, military, 63, 74

drapes. *See* zoot suiters; zoot suits

drape shape, 71

drugs: amphetamines and heroin, 313n174; dealers, pushers, druggies and, 101; narcotics, 213, 221; police crackdown on, 155, 306n23. *See also* marijuana

East Los Angeles: Atlantic Boulevard, 253–54; barrios in, 214; black presence in, 25, 171–72; definition of, 10; demographics of, 217, 227; departure from, 219; Mexican music in, 51; overemphasis on, 283; police harassment in, 96, 135, 162; Reform Council projects in, 104; as rock and roll "factory," 192; teenage clubs in, 176; unemployment in, 224; Youth Training and Employment Project in, 222–24

East Los Angeles College, 102, 169, 209, 214, 219

Eastside: definition of, 10; sound, 191–93

Eckstine, Billy, 94, 171

education, 221, 223, 282; Compensatory Program and, 225; in Detroit, 32, 298n90; dropouts and, 223, 224–25; educationists and, 103–5; Extended Day Program and, 225; musical, 20–23, 26–32, 281; parochial schools, 215; in rock and roll era, 214, 215, 304n214; segregation patterns in, 57–58

El Babalu, 232

El Club Baion, 254

El Congreso del Pueblos que Hablan Español (Congress of Spanish-Speaking Peoples), 96–97

El Hollo, 130

El Hoyo Maravilla barrio, 78, 98

El Janitzio, 233

Elks Hall, 38, 300n125

Ellington, Duke, 15, 36, 232, 299n107

Ellis, Don, 199, 201

Ellison, Ralph, 78, 284, 293n11, 307n67

El Monte American Legion Stadium, 179–83, 192, 208–10, 336n162

El Paso, Texas, 21–22, 87, 309n109

El Serape, 252

El Sombrero, 146, 232

"El tírili" ("The Marijuana Smoker"), 127, 130

"Elvis Perez," 205

"El Viti," 199

employment and unemployment, 221–26. See also work and jobs

entrepreneurship, 134, 154, 214, 231, 259–61, 267, 299n94

Equal Opportunity Foundation, 225–26

Erenberg, Lewis, 15, 16–17

Espinoza, Carlos, 81, 82

Esquivel, Hortencia, 37, 39, 50–52, 78, 83, 122–23

Fair Employment Practices Committee (FEPC), 50, 93, 220, 226, 302n174

Fairfax district, 121–22, 163, 165

Farmer, Art, 41, 166, 252

"Fast Freight," 189

femininity, 89–91, 107. See also women

Fierro, Josefina, 231, 244

Filipinos, 115, 341n99

film, films: Cugat in, 275; Eddie Cano and Trini Lopez in, 273; Go Johnny Go!, 187; Jewish moguls and, 311n133; Latin music, dance, and stereotypes in, 274–75; popularity of, among Mexican Americans, 91–92; Rebel without a Cause, 207; Rock Around the Clock, 175, 247, 270; Spanish-language, 157; Tarzan, 114

5 o'Clock Fiesta, 266–67

Flats (Russian Flats), 19, 24

Ford, John Anson, 143, 145, 178–79

For Dancers Only, 147, 243

"Framed," 164, 185

Freed, Alan "Moondog," 164, 176, 187

Fremont High School, 26, 182

Frias, Ed: on barrio rivalries, 109; on basketball, 108; Central Avenue and, 149; on education, 104, 106; on jitterbug, 83; in LAPD, 169; Latin music and, 252; on Little Richard, 150; musical taste and, 266; on pachucos, 62, 93; in postwar era, 123; on R & B era, 118; in U.S. Army, 169; on venues, 148, 156; Zenda Ballroom and, 242, 339n64

Frias, Lucie Brac: on assimilation, 92; MAYF and, 134; on music and dance, 82, 83; in postwar era, 123; on racial mixing, 149; tardeadas and, 233–34; Zenda Ballroom and, 242, 339n64; on zoot suit style, 101–2, 109–10

gangs, 75, 108–9, 170, 213–14, 227, 296n59

Garcia, Frank, 215–16

Garcia, Frankie "Cannibal," 192, 220

Garcia, Joe, 35–36, 241–42, 249, 261

García, Mario, 57–58, 105, 133, 282

Garcia, Willie, 192

Garfield High School, 167, 192

Garibay, Hortencia Torres: on Club Virginia's, 257; as "Hortencia Torres," 261; on Latin dance, 268; at Latin Holidays, 261; on Latin music, 229; on Latin style, 277; as "Mexican American," 106; on music, 289; music at home of, 51; on pachuca style, 62, 81, 82, 308n77; on Palladium patrons, 264

gender, 8, 90–91, 107–8, 310n130. See also pachucas; women

General Artists Corporation, 186–87

George Brown Orchestra, 35; as "George Brown Band," 12

G.I. Bill, 134, 214, 320n57

Gillespie, Dizzy, 171, 305n13, 313n174

Gold Star Studios, 190, 191

Gonzales, Babs (né Lee Brown), 69

González, José, 98, 156, 245, 338n58

Gonzalez, Mary. See Hernandez, Mary Gonzalez

Goodman, Benny, 13–15, 17

Gordon, Dexter, 27, 53, 56, 162

graffiti, 75; as "barrio calligraphy" or "placas," 170, 326n174

Granz, Norman, 67–68, 240, 305n16

"greasers," 207, 334n106

Green, Bill, 31, 198

Griffith, Beatrice, 71, 84, 89, 91, 98–102, 106–10, 306n38, 309n109

guaracha, 127

Guerrero, Chico, 43, 132, 197, 237

Guerrero, Lalo, 125; biculturalism of, 53, 55; on "Chicana," 106; childhood and school years, 44–46; corridos by 124–25, 206, 282; as "Don Edwards," 125; Latin music and, 232, 234, 251; nightclub of, 253; original songs by, 44, 204–5; pachuco boogie woogie and, 124–33; on pachucos, 93, 326n190; in rock and roll era, 203–6; upward mobility and, 266

Guevara, Rubén, 192, 227

"Güisa gacha" ("Stuck-Up Chick"), 126, 129

"Güisa guaina" ("Wino Chick"), 127, 130

hairstyle: beehives, 211; bleached hair, 211; conk, 75, 307n63; ducktail, 75, 76, 207–8, 213; of pachucos, 75; pompadours on pachucas, 78, 80; in rock and roll era, 207–9; shaven heads, 75

Hall, Rene, 190, 331n60

Hampton, Lionel, 15, 43, 68, 160–63

Hancock, Hunter, 147–53, 165, 182

Hancock Park, 121, 163

Harlem Matinee, 147, 151

"Harlem Special," 244

Harris, Wynonie, 119, 150, 153

Havana Mambo Orchestra, 252

Hebdige, Dick, 86, 207, 309n106, 314n187, 319n37

hep cats: flamboyance of, 109–10; hairstyle of, 75; language of, 86–87; meaning of, 27; slick chicks and, 89; women, living off, 97; zoot suit and, 70–71

Hermosa Beach Lighthouse Café, 194, 199

Hernandez, Gene, 36, 232

Hernandez, George, 196, *197*
Hernandez, Mary Gonzalez, 36–37, 38, 109–10
Herrera, Little Julian (né Ron Gregory), 183–84
Higgins, Chuck, 151, 181
Himes, Chester, 62–63, 75, 91, 94, 109, 113
Holiday in Harlem, 147
Hollenbeck district, 18–19, 212
Hollywood: "going Hollywood," 270–74; jazz nightclubs in, 67–69; police harassment in, 95; postwar changes to music scene in, 122
Hollywood Bowl, 139, 144, 180, 182, 193
Hollywood Palladium, 37–38, 68; African Americans at, 259; capacity of, 262; exclusion and, 95–96; integration at, 262; Latin dancing at, 241; Latin Holiday dances at, 261–64, *262–64*, 279; numbers at, 180–81; in postwar era, 123–24
Hollywood studio orchestras, 30, 53; Mexican American musicians and, 43–44, 196–98
homeownership, 134, 212, 214–17
"honking" tenor saxophone, 151
housing, 24, 221, 296n59; Mexican American Committee for Justice in, 133
Houston, Joe, 154, 181, 208
Huggy Boy, 152–55, 176–77

identity, identities: "generational and ethnic," 311n135; "hybrid formation" of, 115; "Latin," 265–66; Mexican American, 4, 5, 96–97, 191; multiple, 283
Imperial Records, 124, 131, 132, 206
Indians, California, 9, 169, 333n104
influences, musical, 52–53
integration: Hollywood efforts, 69; at Hollywood Palladium, 262; integra-

tionism and, 140–41; in 1940s, 67; mixed dating and dancing and, 68, 148–49, 159, 179; suburbanization and, 215; swing and, 15

Jack's Basket Room, 57, 149, 300n127
Jaguars, 182
jamaicas, 52, 303n189
jam sessions, 56–57; as "descargas," 246
Japanese Americans: in Boyle Heights and City Terrace, 122; internment of, 24, 115, 296n57, 325n164; in zoot suits, 115
Jarvis, Al, 56, 126, 147, 153, 186
jazz: Black and Brown Brotherhood Band and Pan-Afrikan Peoples Arkestra, 201; Bernal's career in, 201–4; "Chicano jazz," 127; decline of, in late '50s, 194; free, 199–200; hard bop, 194; Lopez's career in, 201; Ortega's career in, 193–200; race and, 197–200; "West Coast," 163. *See also* swing
Jazz at the Philharmonic (JATP), 67–68, 158, 305n16
Jazz for Young Moderns, 193–94
Jefferson High School, 27, 31–32, 143, 158, 164, 321n92
Jesters, 176, 210
Jews: in Boyle Heights, 19–20, 136; as cultural middlemen, 165; Mexican Affairs Committee and, 136–37; Phillips Music Store and, 32–33; postwar movement of, 121–22; Sesma on, 262; Zalman's Clothiers, 307n44
jitterbug: legacy of, 120; origins of, 16, 294n17; pachuca style and, 79; pachucos and, 82–83; swing and, 15–17; at Zenda Ballroom, 35; zoot suits and, 71
jive, 84, 87; Mexican Americans speaking, 88, 159, 160, 174

nightclubs, 232; on fame, 287; gigs of, in South Central Los Angeles, 40; on harmony, 281; influences on, 53, 303n197; jazz work of, 201; Latin music and, 237–40, 254–58, 269; on Leon, 287; on mambo, 277; on music education, 281; on music in childhood, 12; on Ortega, 287; on pachucos, 93, 108; in postwar era, 121; on Mexican music vs. jazz, 54; school years of, 20–23, 30; on "society rumba," 231; on Tosti, 340n94; on Touzet, 248, 270; traditional Mexican music and, 54; union membership of, 41; World War II and, 46–47

Lopez, Trini, 272–73

Los Angeles Bureau of Music, 120, 139–44, 147, 180–81

Los Angeles City College (LACC), 47, 164, 249

Los Angeles County Commission on Human Relations, 224

Los Angeles County Committee on Human Relations, 138, 320n72

Los Angeles County Music Commission, 143

Los Angeles Metropolitan Recreation and Youth Services Council, 145, 178

Los Angeles Philharmonic, 67, 141, 143, 180, 321n86

Los Angeles Police Department (LAPD). See police; police harassment, intimidation, and brutality

Los Carlistas, 45–46

"Los chucos suaves," 127–29

"Los orientales," 255–58, 341n102

low riders, 12, 151–52, 177

Lozano, Rolando, 246, 253

Lunceford, Jimmie, 16, 153, 175, 294n26

Machito and His Afro-Cubans, 240, 256; Frank "Machito" Grillo, 236

Macias, Rudy, 234, 250, 269

"Malagueña," 189

Malcolm X, 89, 115

mambo, 229, 234, 240–41, 265, 267–68, 277–78. See also Latin music

Mambo Club, 258

"Mambo Jumbo" concert, 260, 342n121

Mambo Maxi, 256, 278

Man and His Horns, A, 195, 195–96

"Marihuana Boogie," 127, 129–31

marijuana, 88, 90, 129–31, 313n174

marijuanos, 82, 308n80

Marin, Cheech, 207, 217, 335n143

Martinez, Johnny, 248

Martinez, Tony, 246–47, 261, 270, 271

Marty's, 198

masculinity, 86, 107–8, 204, 265, 314n209

McKibbon, Al, 276

M Club, 253, 270

McNeely, Big Jay, 148, 152–53, 181

McWilliams, Carey, 36, 78, 90, 311n135

media, 72–73, 90. See also radio; television

Mendez, Rafael, 43, 197, 301n156, 332n77

Mendoza, Candelario, 266–67, 289, 343n147

mestizos, 169–70

Mexican Affairs Committee, 136–37

Mexican American Movement (MAM), 102–3

Mexican Americans: biculturalism and, 6, 55–56, 82, 205–6; cosmopolitanism and, 265; cultural pluralism and, 97, 288; expressive culture, 3–4, 17, 54–55, 82, 128, 165, 174, 193, 210–12, 280, 289–90; Latinos and, 230, 244; in Los Angeles, Philharmonic, 141, 181; neighborhood association dances and, 146; on-air radio dedications and, 176–77, 227; style and, 3, 284; as term, 9, 106; whiteness and, 2, 11, 43, 200, 209, 211, 232, 288

Mexican American Teachers' Association, 103

Mexican American Youth Foundation (MAYF), 134

Mexican music and culture, traditional: corridos, 98, 124–25, 313n177; Guerrero and, 44, 206; maracas, 341n116; Music Bureau and, 142–43; Ramírez and, 218; in R & B era, 156–59; rock and roll and, 181, 189, 210; social clubs, 99, 100; society Latin and, 265–66; swing vs., 51–56

Mexican Teachers Organization, 104

Mexican Típica Orchestra, 143

Mexico, pachuco influence on, 114

Mexico City, 45, 114, 240–41

middle class, 102–5, 113, 138–39, 175, 266, 288. See also class

Midnighters, Thee, 192–93, 211–12, 282, 342n129

military service: caló slang in, 316n266; draft and zoot suiters, 63; Frias in, 169; by José González, 245; Mexican-Americans in, 73–74, 167–69; Ortega in 4th Army Band, 325n173; servicemen on leave in Los Angeles, 68; uniforms tailored like zoot suits, 307n64

Miller, Glenn, 49, 127

Million Dollar Theater, 36, 157, 160–61, 241, 267

Mocambo, 231

modernity, modernization, 87, 265; movies and, 91–92

mojo, 2–4, 291n3, 291n5, 292n6

Monroy, Douglas, 91–92, 283

Montebello, 192, 214, 215, 219

Monterey Park, 218–19

Montez, Bobby, 246–47, 269–70, 276, 277

Morales, Noro, 237–38, 249

morality: censorship and, 155, 177; El Monte City Council and, 179–80; pachucas and, 90–91

Moré, Beny, 240, 261

Mota, Charlie, 237, 238

Motown Records, 174, 192

movies. See film, films

municipal and metropolitan music programs, 139–46

Murray's clothing store, 72, 81

Nava, Julian, 102, 244

Neighborhood Music School (later Los Angeles School of Music), 22–23, 296n52

New York City, 238–40

Niehaus, Lennie, 33, 299n94

Nomura, Kay, 159, 246, 256

Norman, Gene, 153, 231, 279

Norwalk, 214

oldies, 183, 193, 285, 329n29

Olivas, María. See Alvarez, María Olivas

Olvera Street, 124, 318n20

Ørbeck, Mona, 166–67, 198

Orquesta América, 253

Orquesta Aragón, 248, 261

Orquesta Neuvo Ritmo de Cuba, 252, 253

Ortega, Anthony, 29, 168, 197; bebop, early exposure to, 304n209; Bernal and, 160, 325n168; on Caceres, 49; on Chicano as term, 106–7; on denim blue jeans, 84; on discrimination, 105–6; first horn, 298n84; Frantic Five and, 56, 303n209; on improvisation, 173; on jazz and race, 200; jazz career of, 193–200; Latin music and, 251–52; with Lionel Hampton Orchestra, 162, 165–66, 166; Lopez on, 287; A Man and His Horns, 195, 195–96; marriage of, 166–67; on musicianship, 281; on music styles, 289; New Dance, 199–200; nickname of, 326n174; on pachucos, 108; Permutations, 199–

200; in postwar era, 123; school years of, 25–31; union membership of, 41, 43; U.S. Army and, 167–69, 325n173; on Watts vs. Eastside, 109

Otis, Johnny, 147–48, 164, 177–79, 183–84, 208, 249, 259

Our Lady of Lourdes Catholic Church, 52, 123

P. J.'s, 272–73

pachucas: aging of, 116; "Black Widow" image, 4; defiance and, 92, 96–101; gender ambiguity and, 107–8; *La opinión* on, 90; style of, 78–81, *79, 80,* 308n77; wartime norms challenged by, 89–91. *See also* zoot suits

"Pachuco Boogie," 126, 129–32

pachuco boogie woogie, 124–33, 165

pachucos: aging of, 116; alliance of, with blacks, 110–13; Anglo, 114–15; dance and, 82–83, 209; defiance and, 92, 96–101; disappearance of, 326n190; "El Pachuco" image and, 4; El Paso origins of, 87, 309n109; gangs and violence surrounding, 75, 108–9; gender ambiguity and, 107–8; hairstyle of, 75; hep cat style vs., 109–10; hustler lifestyle and, 97–98; musicians and, 108; Octavio Paz on, 113–14; poses of, 171; postwar influence of, 116; pride of, 93; squares and, 102, 116; style of, *76, 77, 78; tarzanes,* 114, 124. *See also* zoot suits

Pacoima, 102, 184, 302n189

Palladium. *See* Hollywood Palladium

Palmer, Earl, 190, 191

Palomar Ballroom, 13–14

Pan American Optimist Club (PAOC), 136

"Pancho Lopez," 204, 206

Paramount Ballroom, 130, 183

Paramount Theater, 49, 157

Parker, Charlie "Bird," 121, 199, 240, 305n13

Parker, William, 155, 328n13

Pasadena Civic Auditorium, 83, 122

Peña, Manuel, 54, 131, 266

Penguins, 182

Pepper, Art, 163, 236

Pérez Prado, Damaso, 229, 240–42, 249–51, 256, 261, 269, 278

Phillips, William, 32–33, 122, 298n92

Pico Rivera, 216

Plantation Club, 38, 300n122

Platters, 183

pochos, pochismos, 114, 316n255

police: La Ley (Mexican Police Association), 218; Mexican Americans in LAPD, 169; retaliation against, 98; zoot suiters and, 63, *64;* zoot suit riots and, 65–66, 73

police harassment, intimidation, and brutality: "Bloody Christmas" incident, 135; cars and, 214, 311n149; in Deep South, 162; at Dolphin's of Hollywood, 155; in El Monte, 152; in New York, 305n23; in R & B era, 134–35; rock and roll and, 177–78; vagrancy laws and, 304n3; zoot suit riots and pachucos and, 68–69, 95–97, 120

"politics of rising expectations," 133

Polytechnic High School, 157–58, 245–46, 325n163

Pomona, 266–67

Poulson, Norris, 180

Prado, Romeo, 211–12, 261, 342n129

Premiers, 192–93, 210

public dances, regulation of, 178–79, 193

public health services, 221

Puente, Tito: at Club Havana, 253; Garcia and, 242; Guerrero and, 237; Latin jazz sound and, 246; on Latin Soul, 279; mambo and, 240

Puerto Ricans in Los Angeles, 246

Puerto Rico, 238

race riots of 1943 (nationwide), 67
racialization, 2, 291n1
racial labels, hip, 158
racial uplift politics, 103–5
racism: in Cuba, 336n5; institutional, 134, 169, 285; internalization of, 149, 211. *See also* discrimination; police harassment, intimidation, and brutality; segregation
radio: Bloch orchestra on, 253; Chico Sesma's shows, 242–45; Latin Music on, 266–69; R & B and, 147; rock and roll and, 176–77; Spanish-language, 231, 244; Top-40 format, 268
Radio Recorders studio, 126, 250
Rainbow Gardens, 267, 343n147
Ramírez, Catherine, 89–91, 107
Ramírez, Edna, 218
Ramírez, Vince, 14, 36–40, 49–52, 83, 105, 169, 218–19
Ramos, Bobby, 232, 240, 275, 337n15
ranchera music, 53–54, 143, 330n52
R & B (rhythm and blues): African Americans and, 147–51; Bernal and Ortega in, 160–67; broader audience for, 153; definition of, 119–20; interculturalism in, 159–60, 167–69; Latin rhythms in, 259; low riders and Big Jay McNeely, 151–53; traditional Mexican music in era of, 156–59; "West Coast," 150–51; white youths and, 153–55
Ray, Chole Camarena: black music and, 38–39; on Hollywood Palladium, 37–38; Leslie Ray and, 149–50; at Lincoln Heights venues, 150; mixed dancing and, 148–49; pachuca style and, 81, 101, 110; on rock and roll style, 208; swing and, 82; tardeadas and, 233
recreation programs, 145, 178
Reese, Lloyd, 30–31, 121, 298n87

respectability, 15, 89–90, 94, 107, 310n126
restrictive housing covenants, 26, 138
Reyes, Chuy, 232, 238–40
Reyes, Tony, 43, 197, 237, 249, 337n34
rhythm and blues. *See* R & B
Rico, Dora, 40, 261, 266, 268
Rico, Raul, Jr., 274, 344n173
"Riot in Cell Block #9," 164
Rivera, Hector, 252, 253, 340n95, 345n197
Rivera, Luis (né Louis Washington), 167, 198
Robins, 148, 164, *165*
Robinson, Minor, 25–27, 31, 42
rockabilly, 174, 175
rock and roll: "the big beat" and, 175; careers of swing and R & B cohorts in era of, 193–206; clothing and style of, 206–12; doo wop, 182–84; Eastside sound, 191–93; Latin music and, 279; origins of term, 175–76; public dances and crack down on, 177–81; Ritchie Valens and, 184–91; venues, 192; Vietnam War and Eastside scene and, 227
Rodriguez, Eddie, 126, 275, *276*
Rodríguez, Tito, 240, 242, 256
Rogers, Shorty, 163, 270
Roosevelt High School, 20–22, 143, 158
Ross Snyder Recreation Center, 31
Royal Palms Hotel, *34*, 35–36, 249
Roybal, Edward, 101, 133, 135, 215, 221, 244
Ruiz, Chuy, 27, 30, 56, 251
Russell, Andy (né, Andrés Rábago Pérez), 33, 125, 269

sabor, 230, 338n56
Sacred Heart High School, 52, 102
Saito, Tommy, 159, 242–46, 254–58, 276–79, 325n164
Sal Cervantes Orchestra. *See* Cervantes, Sal

Salesian High School, 192
San Bernadino County, 58–61, 304n218
Sánchez, Emmy, 261, 264
Sánchez, George, 102–5, 283, 311n135
San Fernando Valley, 135, 184
Santamaria, Mongo, 248, 252, 254–55, 269
Savoy Ballroom, 15, 16, 306n23
Scrivner's Drive-In Restaurants, 177, 329n29
Second World War. *See* World War II
segregation: in Cuba, Miami, and Las Vegas, 336n5; in dance venues vs. other spaces, 38; desegregation cases and, 319n54; in East Los Angeles, 41; in Fullerton, 320n71; at music venues, 39–40; in 1940s, 68–69; Palladium and, 37; pessimistic, optimistic, and pragmatic readings of, 285; in public schools, 57–58, 288; in R & B era, 120–21; restrictive housing covenants and, 26, 138; in rock and roll era, 217; school hiring practices and, 26; Shrine Auditorium and, 17; social dynamic of, 18; in South, 162; uneven breakdown of, 40
self-determination and zoot suiters, 101
self-esteem, 28, 55, 310n130; lack of, 106
Sesma, Lionel "Chico," 24, 197, 276; barrios and, 266; classical music and, 141; on fame and success, 287; influences on, 53; at LACC, 47; Latin Holiday dances and, 260–64, 262–64, 279; Latin music and, 242–45; Manny Lopez and, 247; on pachucos, 108–9; in postwar era, 121; on radio, 243–45, 268–69; Russ Morgan and, 121, 317n8; school years of, 19–24, 32–33, 37; in swing bands, 47; on Touzet, 248, 270; traditional Mexican music and, 53–54; union membership of, 41, 43; on Vasquez, 287;

World War II and, 46–47; on zoot suits, 72
"Sex on a Sax," 202
sexuality, 90–91, 107, 130–31, 171, 314n209. *See also* gender
Shrine Auditorium, 17, 192, 294n26
Silhouettes, 185
Sleepy Lagoon Defense Fund, 67
Sleepy Lagoon trial, 115
social clubs, 99, *100*, 137, 176, 210–11; Club Juvenil, 35; La Fiesta Club, 17
society bands, 231, 279
son jarocho style, 189
son montuno style, 236
South Central Los Angeles, 40, 68–69, 157, 219
South Gate, 40, 217
South Gate High School, 217–18
Spanish language: bilingual parents raising English-speaking children, 214, 215–16; *gabacho* vs., 98; Latin music lyrics and, 265; Mexican Americans and maintenance of, 58; in military, 74; pachuco slang vs. proper, 124, 316n255; radio and, 55, 126, 160, 231, 253, 266, 269; as spoken in Mexico, 3–4. *See also* caló
Spark Records, 163, 164, 201
squares, 90, 102–5, 116
stereotypes, 91, 93, 291n1
Stoller, Mike, 163–65, 185, 205
streetcars, 70, 151
style politics, 63, 91, 105
suburbanization, 138, 153, 214–20. *See also* homeownership; upward mobility
Sunset Strip, 231–32
"Surfin' U.S.A.," 189–90
swing: big band Mexican American musicians and, 33–35, 47, 49; black, 82; decline of, 122–24; diversity and, 14–15; Eastside bands, 33–35; jam sessions, 56–57; jitterbug and, 15–17;

swing (*continued*)

Jordan Hep Cats, 27; meaning of, 15; origins of, 13–14; postwar transitional years of, 121; in R & B era, 122–24; traditional Mexican music and culture vs., 51–56; venues of, 35–41. *See also under names of specific orchestras*

Tapscott, Horace, 197, 201

tardeadas (afternoon socials), 233

tattoos, 75, 98, 170

television: Bernal and, 203; Guerrero and, 204; *Joe Adams Presents,* 323n113; Latin music in, 275; Ortega and, 198; Otis and, 177; telescriptions, 325n172; Tony Martinez on, 247; Trini Lopez on, 273

"Tequila," 181

"Tequila Hop," 151

Tex-Mex music, 267

Thee Midnighters, 192–93, 211–12, 282, 342n129

Tin Tan (né Germán Valdés), 114, 132

Tizol, Juan, 120–21, 252

Tjader, Cal, 246, 249, 254–55, 271, 277

Tosti, Don (né Edmundo Martínez Tostado), 47, 48; boleros by, 235, 250; in Cervantes Orchestra, 35; classical music and, 141; on downtown clubs, 232–33; on fame, 287; at Flamingo Club, 40–41; influences on, 52–53; at LACC, 47; in Las Vegas and Palm Springs, 201; Latin music and, 234–35, 250–51; on Leon, 287; Leon and, 200; Lopez on, 340n94; on musical style, 284; on music education, 281; Orchestra and, 32; pachuco boogie woogie and, 124, 126–33; on pachucos, 108; on pachuco swing, 83; on Palladium, 37; in postwar era, 123; on Reese, 121; school years of, 20–24, 30, 32; stage name of, 44, 301n157; in

swing bands, 47; traditional Mexican music and, 53; union membership of, 41–44; World War II and, 46–47

Touzet, René, 236, 244, 248, 255, 259, 270

traditional Mexican music. *See* Mexican music and culture, traditional

Trianon Ballroom, 40, 69, 312n159

Trocadero, 45, 121, 231–32

Tucker, Sherrie, 13–14, 68, 89, 293n6

tumbao bass line, 236, 240

"Twilight 'til Dawn" benefit dance, 146–47

unions. *See* Local 47 union; Local 767 union

United Service Organization (USO), 46, 56

upward mobility: Chicano generation and, 282; musical taste and cultural identity and, 266; in R & B era, 138–39, 167, 169; in rock and roll era, 211–20; in swing era, 58–61, 113. *See also* homeownership; suburbanization

Valdés, Miguelito, 236–38, *239,* 244

Valens, Ritchie (né Richard Steve Valenzuela), 184–91, *188,* 331n60

"Vamos a bailar," 127–28

Vasquez, Blas, 164, 255, 258

Vasquez, Ray (Ray Victor), *197;* on "Con sabor Latino," 244; in Don Tosti Orchestra, 32; in Frantic Five, 56; influences on, 53; Ortega and, 30, 196; Sesma and, 23, 287; solo act of, 332n75

Venice Pier, 65, 332n75

Vernon Avenue, 154

veterans, 134

Veterans Center Posts, 123

Vigil, James Diego, 157–58, 290

Watson, Johnny "Guitar," 150, 183

Watts: Barrelhouse nightclub in, 147–48; Boyle Heights vs., 25; Catholic

Church in, 137; demographic shifts in, 212, 217; La Colonia district in, 52; Nickerson Gardens housing project in, 296n59; pachucos in, 108–9; race conflict in, 136; racial heterogeneity in, 26

Watts riots, 227

West Covina, 214, 266

Westside, defined, 10

"The Whip," 164

whiteness, 73, 169; minstrelsy and, 323n119; "possessive investment in," 286, 311n149; as "the racial order," 40; wages of, 43, 70, 301n154; "white male entitlement" and, 70

whites: African American culture and, 164–65; Anglo and white, meaning of terms, 9; Chicano culture and, 114–15, 208; as "gabachos," 98, 209; jitterbug and, 83; Latin music radio programs and, 245, 267; marijuana and, 98; Midwestern migrants, 9, 70, 213; "Okies," 122, 153; vigilantism and, 66, 94; western swing and, 122; white ethnics, 9, 139, 287

Whittier, 214, 266

Whittier Boulevard, 150, 152, 192, 210, 211

Wilson, Gerald, 95, 159–60, 294n26, 323n113

"Wine-O Boogie" 126–27

women: in car clubs and social clubs, 210–11; college and work among, 59–61; hep cats preying on, 97; norms and stereotypes of, 89–91, 310n130; in rock and roll era, 208–9; slick chicks, 89, 90, 110. *See also* pachucas

work and jobs: in rock and roll era, 215, 219–26; success stories of, 59–61; union membership and, 41–44; during World War II, 50–51, 93

World War II, 24, 46, 50, 60–61, 73–74, 89–90, 93. *See also* military service

XEW, 114

Ybarra-Frausto, Tomás, 82, 98

Youth Opportunities Board of Greater Los Angeles, 221, 225

Youth Training and Employment Project, 222–24

Zeiger, Hal, 177, 179, 181

Zenda Ballroom: African Americans at, 258; capacity, 262; Conjunto Siboney at, 252; jitterbug and, 35; Latin Holiday dances and, 261; Latin music movement and, 241–42; mambo contests and, 278; tardeadas at, 233

zoot suiters: on Central Avenue, 39; different types of, 101–2; in Himes's *If He Hollers Let Him Go*, 62–63; interethnic connections among, 110–13; media and, 72–73; Mexican, 114; middle-class Mexican Americans and Mexicans, opinions of, 113–14; personal resistance tactics of, 312n155; poses, 171; public opinion on, 66–67; self-determination and, 101; squares vs., 90, 102–5. *See also* pachucos

zoot suit riots, 65–66, 70, 72–73, 112

zoot suits: appropriation of, by fashion industry, 116; colors of, 109–10, *111*; cost of, 71–72; criminalization of, 72, 313n171; cross-cultural borrowing of, 114–15; decline of, 171; defiance symbolized by, 92; description of, 71; "equality of appearances" and, 94; evolution of, 70–71; meaning of, 311n135; Mexican American expression of, 84; military uniforms tailored like, 307n64; non-pachucos wearing, 101–2, 109; on pachucas, 81; parental reactions to, 81–82; as subversive icon, 107–8

Anthony Macías is assistant professor of ethnic studies
at the University of California, Riverside.

Library of Congress Cataloging-in-Publication Data
Macias, Anthony F.
Mexican American mojo : popular music, dance, and
urban culture in Los Angeles, 1935–1968 /
Anthony Macías.
p. cm. — (Refiguring American music)
Includes bibliographical references and index.
ISBN 978-0-8223-4339-4 (cloth : alk. paper)
ISBN 978-0-8223-4322-6 (pbk. : alk. paper)
1. Popular music—California—Los Angeles—History
and criticism. 2. Mexican Americans—California—Los
Angeles—Music—History and criticism. 3. Mexican
Americans—California—Los Angeles—Social life and
customs. I. Title.
ML3477.8.L67M33 2008
781.6408968'72079494—dc22   2008026450